The Florida experience
Land and water policy in a growth state

THE FLORIDA EXPERIENCE

Land and water policy in a growth state

Luther J. Carter

PUBLISHED FOR RESOURCES FOR THE FUTURE, INC.
BY THE JOHNS HOPKINS UNIVERSITY PRESS,
BALTIMORE AND LONDON

Copyright © 1974 by The Johns Hopkins University Press
All rights reserved
Manufactured in the United States of America
Library of Congress Catalog Card Number 74-6816
ISBN 0-8018-1646-7

Library of Congress Cataloging in Publication data will be found on the last printed page of this book.

Preface

The genesis of this book cannot be too precisely placed, but it goes back to my need about five years ago for a respite from the journalist's task of tracking fleeting events. I wanted a chance to take a more reflective look at the increasingly frequent conflicts between conservation and economic growth or development. Since 1965, the year I had joined the staff of *Science* magazine (having given up my job as a Washington correspondent for a Southern newspaper), I had followed the emergence of the environmental movement as a substantial force in the nation's intellectual and political life. My articles had dealt with a wide range of conflicts between conservation and development—for instance, over proposed dams in the Grand Canyon, pollution and dredging for oyster shells in Galveston Bay, clear-cutting in national forests, nuclear testing on Amchitka Island, and oil development on the Alaskan north slope. I also had followed closely some important attempts at establishing a framework of law and government for coping with environmental controversies in a more coherent and orderly fashion. Most notably, there had been the efforts, led by Senator Edmund Muskie of Maine, to establish a federal-state system for the abatement of air and water pollution and those by Senator Henry Jackson of Washington to have Congress pass the National Environmental Policy Act of 1969 and begin work on legislation to establish a national land use policy.

I now wanted somehow to sort out my impressions of the environmental movement and its reverberations in both Washington and one or more of the major state capitals. Joseph L. Fisher, then president of Resources for the Future, Inc., was receptive to my suggestion that RFF support me in a book project. Initially, he suggested that I investigate a number of widely separated conservation and development conflicts around the United States and seek to draw some useful generalizations. For a book meant to be relevant to a national readership, this approach would offer obvious advantages. But after reflection it seemed to me that it would be more useful to focus on a single fast-growing state where a variety of problems could be discussed against a common background. Florida was an obvious choice because, besides being the fastest growing major state in the country, it was the scene of several celebrated conservation and development conflicts such as those over the Cross Florida Barge Canal, the south Florida jetport, and the Florida Power and Light Company's nuclear power station on Biscayne Bay. Fisher readily agreed to this approach, and, in January 1971, I took leave from *Science* with the ambitious aim of producing—within the coming year and a half—a book on conservation and development conflicts in Florida.

Somehow this broad subject had to be made manageable, and I decided early to make land use issues (and closely related questions of water management) the focus of the book. Several things lay behind this decision. First, the intensive and potentially destructive land sales campaigns I had observed in scenic areas such as Virginia's Shenandoah Valley and Massanutten Mountains had made me sensitive to the land use issue and sympathetic to Aldo Leopold's call for a "land ethic." Also, I had been much impressed by writings such as William H. Whyte's *The Last Landscape* and Ian McHarg's *Design with Nature*. Furthermore, the particular conservation and development conflicts that I wanted to use as case histories all posed important and unavoidable questions of land use policy.

Although I was now making progress in defining the scope of my work, I was to discover that a book project can take on a life and direction of its own, quite independently of what the author had in mind at the outset. A broad look at land use in a state such as Florida takes one beyond the problems of maintaining essential or desirable natural ecosystems and into the endlessly complex subject of growth policy and urban development. Conscious of my mid-1972 deadline, I was determined not to become mired in so difficult a subject. I expected to confine myself largely to the problem of conservation and development as it involved Florida's rural and natural environment, as in the Everglades, the Big Cypress Swamp, and perhaps the citrus grove region of the Central Highlands. And this, after all, would be consistent with the major orientation of the land use legislation that was then taking shape in Washington, legislation which was clearly not addressed to the overall issue of growth policy and the quality of life in the urban environment.

But I could find no sensible way of avoiding the larger issue of growth policy. I ultimately reoriented the whole plan of the book to address that issue in part at least, and did not try to confine myself merely to some selective questions of land use. As a consequence, my project became so large an undertaking that it was not to be completed until the late spring of 1974, a year and a half after I had left RFF and returned to *Science*. In a way, my dilemma illustrated the unavoidable interdependence of the growth and land use policy issues.

During the three-and-a-half years devoted in whole or part to the book, five months were spent in Florida, mostly during 1971 but including one extremely useful swing through the state in early 1974. Altogether my travels in Florida took me some 20,000 miles by car and into every part of the state except the western half of the panhandle. By courtesy of the Central and Southern Florida Flood Control District, the U.S. Forest Service, and the National Park Service, I was flown over most of central and southern Florida at low altitude. I have partaken of many outdoor experiences only Florida offers: I have caught snook in the Ten Thousand Islands, drifted for kingfish on the edge of the Gulf Stream, canoed down some 65 miles of wild semitropical rivers and spring runs, waded in the cypress ponds of the Big Cypress' Fahkahatchee Strand, gone deep into the Everglades by airboat, and snorkeled on the coral reef of Biscayne National Monument.

Records of my hundreds of interviews with environmentalists, developers, state and local officials, and other Floridians fill seventeen notebooks and more than sixty reels of cassette tape. In reconstructing the events related to the Cross Florida Barge Canal and the south Florida jetport, I interviewed nearly all of the principals involved.

The persons to whom I owe acknowledgment make up a far longer list than could be included here. I mention only those to whom the debt is especially heavy. Anyone who writes today about the environmental problems of south Florida owes much to Marjory Stoneman Douglas and her book, *The Everglades: River of Grass*, which ever since its publication in 1947 has stood as a remarkably vivid and insightful account of man's relation to south Florida's unique and in some ways awesome environment. In addition, the writings of Charlton W. Tebeau, Alfred and Kathryn Hanna, Samuel Proctor, Manning Dauer, Polly Redford, and Edward Sofen helped me to put my work in a perspective that otherwise would be lacking. I have been influenced to some degree in the recommendations contained in this book by the proposed guidelines for development prepared in 1972 by the staff of the Florida Coastal Coordinating Council. Another influence on my thinking has been the California Tomorrow Plan, an excellent and imaginative document published in 1972 by California Tomorrow in San Francisco.

No book of this kind, much of it dealing with events of the hour, could be written without the information made available through Florida newspapers. Several writers on whom I relied repeatedly were Mike Toner and Juanita Greene of the *Miami Herald* and Pat Cullen of the *Palm Beach Post*.

A number of persons went beyond any professional obligation in helping me to experience and understand Florida. They include Captain Ted Smallwood of Everglades, Bernard T. Yokel of the Rookery Bay biological station, Gary Schmelz of the Big Cypress Nature Center, Dennis Holcomb and Bucky Wegener of the Florida Game and Fresh Water Fish Commission, and George Sites of the Biscayne National Monument staff. A special word of appreciation is due Noble Enge of the Jacksonville District, U.S. Army Corps of Engineers, who as a connoisseur of Florida's wild rivers, joined me on an overnight canoe trip down the Oklawaha. Two who served me well as patient and astute guides to the political ecology of Tallahassee were James Etheridge of the attorney general's staff and my old friend Arthur Canaday, formerly an assistant attorney general and now general counsel to Governor Reubin Askew. The governor himself graciously found time in his schedule for a lengthy interview.

As a research organization that supports the work of scholars, RFF was venturing upon an experiment when it undertook to support the work of a mere journalist. For me, certainly, it was a happy experiment. Parts of my manuscript were read and commented upon, much to my benefit, by the following people at RFF: Joe Fisher, Allen V. Kneese (who read virtually the entire first draft of the manuscript), Clifford S. Russell, Blair T. Bower, Edwin T. Haefele, Marion Clawson, and Robert G. Healy. Mark Reinsberg, RFF's director of publications, and Brigitte Weeks, who edited the manuscript, provided strong technical assistance, moral support, and—at times —necessary goading.

Others to whom I am indebted for reviewing parts of the manuscript are Assistant Secretary of the Interior Nathaniel P. Reed (formerly adviser to the Governor of Florida), and his special assistant, George Gardner; John DeGrove of Florida Atlantic University, a key adviser to Governor Reubin Askew on land and water management matters and a member of the governing board of the Central and Southern Florida Flood Control District (FCD); G. E. Dail, Jr., executive director of the FCD; Eugene Brown, public information officer of the Jacksonville District, Corps of Engineers; Aileen Lotz, former assistant to the Dade County manager and now a planning consultant; Darrey Davis, former Dade County Attorney and more recently attorney for the Saga Development Corporation; Richard Judy of the Dade County Port Authority and Norman Arnold, a DCPA consultant; Martin Convisser and Robert Bacon of the U.S. Department of Transportation; several environmentalists, namely Arthur Marshall, Jim and Polly Redford, Charles Lee, Hal Scott, Edward T. LaRoe, Gary Soucie, Joe Browder, William M. Partington, Jr., and Marjorie Carr. Helpful comments and criticism were also given by William K. Reilly, director of the Rockefeller Brothers task force on land use and now president of the Conservation Foundation; Wendell Fletcher, formerly of the Conservation Foundation staff; John Walsh and Robert Gillette of *Science*; and Fred Bosselman, coauthor of the *Quiet Revolution in Land Use Control* and an influential consultant to both the Council on Environmental Quality and the state of Florida. To all the foregoing I give thanks and offer the usual waiver of responsibility for any errors of fact or judgment, for which I alone am to be held to account.

Special thanks are also due to my wife, Marsha, who saved me untold hours by clipping Florida newspapers and, at the last, taking on a numbing job of typing. Finally, I want to express my appreciation for the sympathetic interest of my two daughters, Amy and Marsha—it is to them and their generation that a book of this kind is best dedicated.

Washington, D.C.
July 1974

Contents

PREFACE   v

PART I
INTRODUCTION

1. THE LAND AND THE CRISIS   1
Growth and a Threatened Environment   A Continuing Boom; Red
Flagging the Danger; Seeking Means of Control   4
Defining the Growth Issue   Not "No Growth" but "Controlled
Growth"; Preserving a Sense of Place   10
A Unique and Delicate Environment   Areas of Slight Tolerance (or
None); Tolerant Areas   15
The Impact of Development   Agriculture; The Retiree-Oriented Real
Estate Boom; Tourism; Manufacturing, Mining, and Oil   24
Some Conclusions   39

2. THE FIGHT AGAINST PORK CHOP RULE   **41**
Pork Chop Rule   **43**
The Pork Choppers Overthrown   **47**
A New Set of Actors   Environmentalists and the Conservation
Groups; The Governor's Advisers; Conservation '70s   **49**
Fruits of Reform   **53**

PART II
SOUTH FLORIDA I: AN EVOLVING LAND POLICY

3. LAND DISPOSAL AND DRAINAGE   **57**
The Challenge of a Swampy Domain   Surveyors' Errors; The
Swamp Lands Act of 1850; An Early Dream: "Reclaiming"
the Everglades   **58**
Land Disposal   The "I.I. Board" in Receivership; The Disston Sale;
The Bourbon Era; Railroad Barons: Plant and Flagler   **63**
Draining the Everglades   Napoleon Bonaparte Broward; The
Everglades Drainage District   **66**
Florida for Sale   Richard Bolles: The First Swamp Salesman; A
National Scandal   **69**
Settlement Follows the Canal Builders   Drainage Advances, Slowly;
Combating "The Common Enemy"; The Everglades Agricultural
Area   **71**
The Creators of Miami Beach and Collier County   Carl Fisher and
Miami Beach; Barron Collier Creates a County   **74**
The Miccosukis: A Commentary on Property Rights   **80**

4. THE PARK AND THE FLOOD CONTROL DISTRICT   **82**
Hurricanes, Drought, and Flood   Years of Great Hurricanes—1926
and 1928; An Environment Under Stress; Muck Fires; Soil
Subsidence; The Drying Up of the 'Gator Holes; Saltwater
Intrusion; Eight and a Half Feet of Rainfall   **83**
The Flood Control District   Seeds of an Idea; Mapping the Glades;
Bulletin 442; The Hurricane Levee; An Intractable Problem   **89**
The Project Plan   Some Successes; Some Failures   **92**
A Tragic Blunder: The Kissimmee Channelization   **103**
The Everglades National Park   Ernest Coe, A Man Obsessed;
The Wilbur Report; "A Snake Swamp Park"; Unsettled Boundaries;
Speculation in Oil Leases; Florida Meets its Commitment; The
Big Cypress Excluded; Poker at Horseshoe Lake; Boundaries
Meeting the Park's "Most Vital Needs"   **107**

PART II
SOUTH FLORIDA II: THE PROBLEMS OF GROWTH

5. THE YEARS OF DROUGHT AND THE LAND AND WATER
LAWS OF 1972   117
The Park Suffers, Congress Responds   The FCD Fails to Deliver;
The 1968 Water Resources Report; A Water Guarantee for the Park 118
More Drought and the Governor's Water Conference   125
New Laws Are Prepared and Enacted   A Comprehensive or a
Selective Approach?; What the Legislation Provided; Necessary
Compromises; Hard Lobbying by Both Sides; A Model for the
Nation?   126

6. DADE COUNTY: THE MINI-STATE   138
Rich Amenities and a Gateway   140
Three Waves of Growth   141
Declining Quality of Life   146
The Politics of Growth   151
The Beginnings of Dade Metro   Metro's Concessions to the
Municipalities   152
Land Use Decisions in South Dade   The City of Islandia; The Land
Use Master Plan; Mix Up on South Bay; Turkey Point; The Saga
New Town Project; The Bulkhead Line; The South Bay Area Study   155
The Growth Issue and Metro's New Leadership   Enter John B.
Orr, Jr.   172
Development of a New Master Plan   175
The Development Policies   176
New Directions for Growth   Rejuvenation of Urban Dade; More
Industrial Growth in Northwest Dade; A Strategy for South Dade;
The Municipalities Remain Important   177
Metro's Commitment Is Being Tested   Task Force Proposals under
Attack; Where Metro Shows Its Resolve; Where the Commitment
Wavers   183
Dade As a Potential Model   186

7. THE JETPORT: MISPLACED RESPONSIBILITY   187
The First Search for a Site   The Port Authority and Aviation in
Dade County; The Search Ends in the Big Cypress   188
The Jetport Controversy Unfolds   An FCD Official Raises
Questions; The Everglades Coalition; Secretary Hickel against
the Project; Luna Leopold and the Impact Study; The White
House Forces the Issue   194

The Jetport Pact   **207**
The Search for a New Site   Focusing on Dade County; Palm Beach
County Site Is Eliminated; Pros and Cons of the North Dade Site;
Metro Initially Rejects the Site; A Conditional Acceptance   **210**
The Case for Reopening the Search   **225**

8. SAVING THE BIG CYPRESS   **228**
Collier County: Past Development Trends and Local Government
The County's Split Personality—The Developers and the Snow Birds;
Gulf American and the Rape of the Land; Conflicting Interests and
Governmental Incompetence   **231**
The Big Cypress National Preserve   Compensable Regulation; The
Demands for Public Purchase; Action at the White House and in
Congress; The State Contributes $40 Million   **242**
The Big Cypress Critical Area   The Basic Policy Questions; "How
Would You Like to Live in a Police State?"; Retreat from the First
Plan; The Cabinet Acts   **246**
End of the Collier Fiefdom   The Developers Lose Their Political
Dominance; The Modernization of County Government   **255**
The Search for New Land Management Mechanisms   Water
Management District 6   **257**
A Comprehensive Policy for the Big Cypress   The State as a
Senior Partner   **260**

PART III
THE VAGARIES OF POWER

9. THE BARGE CANAL: THE USES OF POWER   **265**
The Oklawaha River and Its Region   **267**
The Abortive Ship Canal, 1826–1936   Selecting a Route; The Canal
as a Nostrum of the New Deal; Unbearable Shortcomings   **270**
Beginnings of the Barge Canal   An Answer to the Submarine
Menace; Languishing in the Corps' Unfunded Backlog; JFK Delivers
on a Campaign Promise   **273**
The Campaign to Save the Oklawaha   Up against a Formidable
Apparatus; The Cabinet Won't Listen; Part of the Oklawaha Is Lost   **278**
The Project Is in Trouble   The Florida Defenders of the
Environment; EDF Sues, FDE Writes an Impact Statement;
Washington: The Bureaucratic Interplay; The Corps Proposes an
Alternate Route; The CEQ Says "Terminate the Project"; The
President's Decision and the Court Order   **284**
Reaction to the President's Order   The Cabinet Witholds Support;
The Project Is in "Limbo"; Judge Holds Termination Is Unlawful   **302**
An Overlooked Opportunity   **308**

PART IV
CONCLUSION

10. FINDING THE WAY   313
A Proposed Solution   317
Policy   First Policy: Directing Growth; Second Policy: The Florida
Standards; Third Policy: Zoning; Fourth Policy: Infrastructure   317
Structure   Reform of Local Government; Reform in Tallahassee;
Some Executive Rearrangement; The Role of Regional Planning
Councils   326
Politics   Citizen Participation in Planning; Tax Reform; Private
Attorneys General   333
A Major Testing Ground   336
Respect for the Land   337

EPILOGUE   340
INDEX   345

LIST OF FIGURES

1–1   Topography of Florida   2
1–2   Climatic conditions in north, central, and south Florida   3
1–3   Population distribution in 1970   6
1–4   Comparative electricity use in Florida and total United States   7
1–5   Major regional ecosystems remaining, in relation to population
      centers   9
1–6   Areas of differing development tolerance   15
1–7   Ecologic zones of south Florida prior to development   17
1–8   Land use in Florida   25
1–9   Inventory of large-scale developments   32
3–1   Everglades drainage canals built between 1907 and 1929   72
3–2   North Biscayne Bay and Miami Beach   77
3–3   Tamiami Trail across the Big Cypress and the Everglades   78
4–1   Central and Southern Flood Control District system in south
      Florida   93
4–2   1934 maximum boundaries of the Everglades National Park and
      more restrictive actual boundaries of 1958   111
5–1   Three major natural drainage systems of the Everglades-Big
      Cypress region   119
5–2   Decision-making structure for regulation of critical areas under
      1972 Land and Water Management Act   134
5–3   Structure for regulation of developments of regional impact   134
5–4   Decision-making structure established under the Water
      Resources Act of 1972   136

6–1   Dade County   **139**

6–2   Flooding from hurricane tides   **142**

6–3   Proposed development projects—Biscayne Bay area and Biscayne National Monument   **157**

6–4   Coastal ridge and lowlands of south Dade   **180**

7–1   Original site for south Florida jetport   **192**

7–2   Sites considered for south Florida jetport   **211**

7–3   Alternative ground-access routes to jetport site   **215**

7–4   Final three jetport sites considered   **218**

8–1   The proposed Big Cypress National Preserve   **230**

8–2   Land in Collier County acquired by Gulf American Corporation   **234**

8–3   The Big Cypress critical area as first proposed and subsequent reduced boundaries   **250**

9–1   The Cross Florida Barge Canal   **266**

9–2   The Oklawaha River and its region   **268**

9–3   Ecologic changes to result from flooding the Oklawaha River   **289**

9–4   Alternate route for canal proposed by Corps of Engineers   **294**

The Florida experience
Land and water policy in a growth state

The land and the crisis

The early 1970s will be recorded as the years when Florida's environmental crisis, or, more specifically, its land crisis, was proclaimed. Ever since intensive settlement of Florida began a century ago, people have been trying to remake, with increasingly troubling results, a delicate, low-lying peninsula wrought by natural forces over the geological ages. Florida is for the most part a long, relatively narrow subtropical appendage of the main landmass of the continental United States. It embraces an area as large as England and Wales (or 58,560 square miles, to be precise), extending 400 miles from north to south and (at the peninsula's widest point) reaching some 130 miles from east to west (see figures 1–1 and 1–2). There is a coastal lowlands province extending well inland all along Florida's 1,300 miles of general shoreline, and a "highlands" province going three-quarters of the way down the peninsula like an irregular backbone. The whole state rests on a deep bed of water-bearing limestone and even the highest point is not more than a few hundred feet above sea level. In a time of good rains, the peninsula is a long, nearly unbroken mat of green, beginning with the

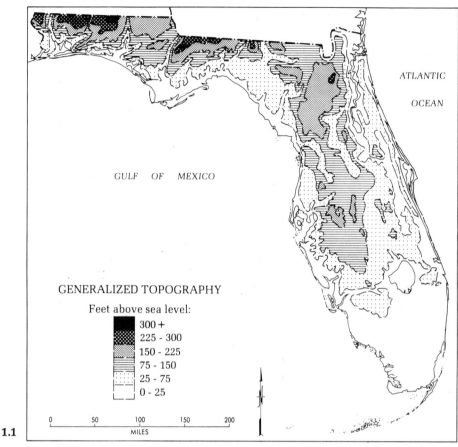

1.1

Topography of Florida

pine and hardwood forests of north Florida, down through the citrus-clad hills and lakes of the Central Highlands, the pine flatwoods, cypress heads, and prairies and marshes of the Kissimmee and Saint Johns river basins, the sugarcane fields south of Lake Okeechobee, the vast wetlands complex of the Everglades and the Big Cypress Swamp, and finally, the crescent of mangroves around Florida's southern tip. On the peninsula's Atlantic side, a long series of barrier islands with appealing sandy beaches lie between the salt marshes and the open ocean; on the Gulf of Mexico side, a similar series of barrier islands exists, but is less complete, there being long stretches where labyrinths of mangrove islands or of salt marsh laced by tidal channels face directly on the open Gulf. Of all Florida's natural features, the most remarkable and distinctive is the Everglades, that wilderness of saw grass where alligators in incredible number once dominated the ecology as completely as the buffalo once dominated the ecology of the Great Plains.

    Descriptions of Florida as an earthly, somewhat awesome paradise go back at least as far as the eighteenth century. In writing of his travels in the Florida of the 1770s, William Bartram, the Philadelphia naturalist, gave his impressions of the Saint Johns River, Lake George, and the surrounding countryside in terms of extravagant beauty, variety, and abundance—"enchanting forests" of live oaks (12 to 18 feet in girth, with huge branching limbs), wild orange trees, towering magnolias and royal palms; waters teeming with "trout" (largemouth bass) of as much as 15, 20, even 30 pounds and enormous alligators of up to 20 feet long; and a profusion of other animals and birds, including deer, bear, wolves, panther, sandhill cranes, anhingas, and wild turkeys.[1] Later, in the 1840s, Stephen R. Mallory

1. William Bartram, *Travels of William Bartram*, ed. Mark Van Doren (New York: Dover Publications, Inc., 1955), pp. 100–211.

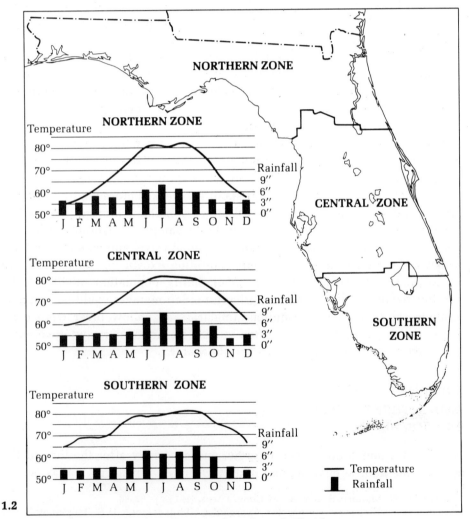

1.2

Climatic conditions in north, central, and south Florida

THE LAND AND THE CRISIS

of Key West (later to become the Confederacy's Secretary of the Navy), described the pineland ridge in south Florida between the Atlantic and the Everglades: "This...is a fine country for a man...who wishes to be independent. The woods and streams abound with game and fish, frost is rarely seen, the coomty [or coontie, a tropical vegetable with an edible root] grows profusely.... The most indolent man I ever knew prospered [here]."[2] Promotional literature for railroads ordinarily does not offer work by celebrated poets, but the Atlantic Coastline Railway commissioned Sidney Lanier to write a Florida guidebook; Florida was prominent in nineteenth century travel literature as an exotic frontier.

Most travelers of the late 1800s ventured no farther than the end of the railroad or steamboat line, but a few visited places seldom seen by white men since the Seminole Wars. For instance, in the winter of 1897, a naval reserve officer from Rhode Island named Lieutenant Hugh L. Willoughby made his way by canoe through the mangrove jungle at the southern tip of Florida to the lower rim of the Everglades basin, then poled his slender craft across this "sea of grass" to Miami, which he finally reached by running the rapids of the Miami River where this stream flowed through a break in the coastal ridge.[3] Willoughby was one of the last whites to experience the pristine Everglades, for an era of pell-mell drainage and land reclamation was almost at hand.

However great its beauty and diversity, the pristine Florida environment was one in many ways troublesome for settlers. Torrential summer and autumn rains sometimes left a surfeit of water which, given the flat terrain in many parts of Florida, might stand for weeks before finally evaporating or draining away. Indeed, as will later be explained, more than half of Florida had been officially declared to be "swamp and overflowed lands." The vast interior swamps and marshes impeded travel and communications, and were generally unfit for human habitation except on the larger hammocks and pine islands where a small, hardy population might live by hunting, fishing, and subsistence agriculture. Salt marshes could be breeding grounds for swarms of mosquitoes (malaria and yellow fever were common), and the mangroves were often viewed by landowners and developers as barriers standing between them and the water.

GROWTH
AND A THREATENED
ENVIRONMENT

As Florida's population began to grow, and especially after the turn of the century, the natural environment underwent rapid transformation as people

2. Stephen R. Mallory, S. Doc. 89, 62 Cong. 1 sess. (1911), p. 62–63.
3. Hugh L. Willoughby, *Across the Everglades* (Philadelphia: J. B. Lippincott Company, 1898).

sought to make more of it amenable for settlement. Mangrove flats and salt marshes were often filled and enclosed within seawalls. Interior wetlands, including the upper Everglades, were drained—indeed, water was regarded in the courts of law as the "common enemy"—then cultivated and criss-crossed with roads. Sinuous rivers were straightened and "channelized" for better navigation and disposal of flood waters. Then, there were all the other changes that often accompany development—waters were polluted, forests were cut, and numerous species of wildlife were pushed into a few places of precarious refuge.

A CONTINUING BOOM. Degradation of the Florida environment was to become particularly evident and widespread after World War II, as growth of the state's population came in a great, unchecked surge. In 1950 Florida had 2.7 million people and ranked only twentieth among the states in popu-lation; by 1970, it had 6.7 million [see figure 1–3] and ranked ninth and was growing faster than any other large state. The population's rapid growth has since continued. By mid-1973, the total had reached 7.8 million and the influx of retirees and other migrants was now a flood, with an average of more than 6,000 newcomers arriving each week. Tourism also had shown extraordinary growth. An estimated 25 million tourists and other visitors came in 1972, a number fivefold the total of a generation earlier. Along with the growth of population and tourism there had, of course, been an enormous increase in residential and commercial development—new hotels, motels, condominiums, mobile home parks, apartment buildings, and huge new subdivisions had proliferated. The total valuation placed on Florida real estate was only $2.1 billion in 1941; in 1970, the valuation had reached $51.2 billion, an immense growth even allowing for inflation and changes in methods of assessment. Each new year for the developers seemed bigger and better than the last. By the 1970s, the upward and onward trend of development had become even more pronounced. Construction of 282,279 new housing units was authorized by permit during the year 1972 alone.[4] This was slightly more than the number authorized in California and three times more than that in the state of New York; Florida accounted for about an eighth of the total number of new housing units authorized in the entire nation. In central Florida, within the sphere of influence of Disney World, the state's most important new tourist attraction, small towns such as Kissimmee and St. Cloud as well as metropolitan Orlando were ex-periencing tremendous growth—the $36 million of new construction ap-proved by Kissimmee in 1972 would be almost enough to remake that once insignificant cattle town.

An especially compelling manifestation of growth was the increase in demand for electricity (see figure 1–4). The Florida Power and Light Com-

4. U.S. Bureau of the Census, *Housing Authorized by Building Permits and Public Contracts, States and Metropolitan Statistical Areas* (March 1973).

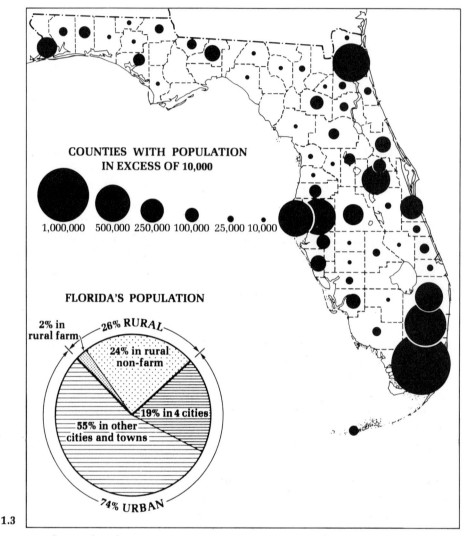

COUNTIES WITH POPULATION IN EXCESS OF 10,000

1,000,000   500,000   250,000   100,000   25,000   10,000

FLORIDA'S POPULATION

2% in rural farm

26% RURAL

24% in rural non-farm

19% in 4 cities

55% in other cities and towns

74% URBAN

1.3

Population distribution in 1970

pany (FP&L), serving all of south Florida and part of the remainder of the state, was experiencing the largest growth in demand—both in percentage and absolute terms—of any electric utility in the United States. In south Florida, new power plants, several of them nuclear, were already being built or planned along Biscayne Bay, Lake Okeechobee, and the Atlantic Ocean, yet FP&L could foresee a need for more and more.

In many places, Florida was becoming dominated by the artifacts of an urban civilization in which nature was too often only grudgingly admitted. No longer the natural paradise described by William Bartram, Florida by the early 1970s was becoming what has been called—with as much truth as exaggeration—"the man-made state."[5] In October 1973, Governor Reubin Askew, addressing a conference he had called on "growth and the environment," described the situation in rueful terms:

> Let's look around and see what unchecked, unplanned growth has done to Florida. It [threatens] to create megalopolis along the entire length of the east coast and from Jacksonville across central Florida to Tampa Bay and down the south Suncoast. Its waste products have polluted our waterways from one end of the state to the other. . . . It has transformed vast estuarine areas and wetlands into waterfront home sites and canals. It has destroyed beautiful and valuable sand dunes and lined our beaches with hotels and high-rise condominiums . . . resulted in severe water shortages . . . intolerable traffic congestion in many urban areas . . . and threatened [public access to] recreational areas. . . . True, we have enjoyed economic prosperity. But

5. Neal R. Pearce, *The Megastates of America* (New York: W. W. Norton, 1972), pp. 450–94.

Index: 1955 = 1

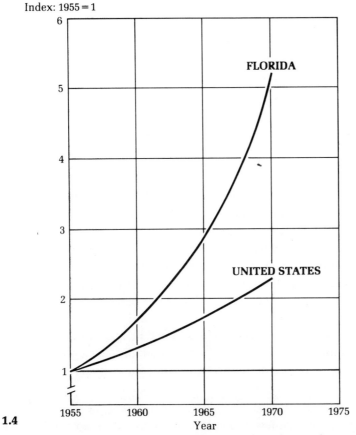

1.4

Comparative electricity use in Florida and total United States

[all can see] the warning signals and what they portend if we don't grab the reins of this galloping giant.

RED FLAGGING THE DANGER. The consequences of poorly controlled growth and development had been cataloged at a three-day "Red Flag Charrette" or conference sponsored in March of 1972 by the Florida Chapter of the American Institute of Architects and a university-based group called the Florida Defenders of the Environment (of which I shall have much to say later). A map of Florida was prepared in which each threat to a local or regional environment was designated by a red flag.

When finished, the map bristled with more than 150 flags, some signifying that entire regional ecosystems were endangered. Warm, shallow, and closely confined estuaries and sluggish coastal rivers had been subjected to a variety of insults—to industrial pollutants or excessive heat from badly situated chemical plants, pulp mills, and electric power stations; to untreated or insufficiently treated sewage from communities allowed to outgrow their waste management facilities; and to landfill operations by developers of deluxe waterfront homes and apartments. More than 60,000 acres of prime estuarine habitat for fish and shellfish had been lost to dredging and filling alone. More than a fourth of Florida's 700 miles of sandy beaches had suffered erosion in part because of activities such as the bulldozing of protective dunes, the building of seawalls, and the cutting of inlets. Almost every large lake in Florida was rapidly becoming highly eutrophic—if it was not already in that condition—because of overenrichment from sewage, citrus wastes, and storm flood runoff from farm lands and city streets. Algae blooms were appearing each spring and summer in Lake Okeechobee, giving substance to fears that soon even this immense lake (covering 720 square miles, it is the largest lake in the United States except for the Great Lakes) would soon be "pea soup." In central Florida thousands of acres had been stripped of phosphate, with large areas left as unreclaimed wasteland; four times since 1960, the beautiful Peace River had flowed yellow and lifeless after clay slimes produced in phosphate recovery had burst through retaining dams. Also, investigation by the U.S. Geological Survey had documented that, between 1949 and 1969, water levels in an important part of the Floridan Aquifer in the heart of the phosphate mining region had declined by 40 to 60 feet.[6] Prime farm lands, including some planted in citrus and noted for their beauty and compatibility with water conservation, were becoming increasingly subject to speculation for subdivision and development. Further, the loss of marshes, wet prairies, and river swamps—from drainage, dredging and filling, and stream channeliza-

6. *Potentiometric Surface and Areas of Artesian Flow, May 1969, and Change of Potentiometric Surface 1964 to 1969, Floridan Aquifer, Southwest Florida Water Management District, Florida.* Hydrologic Investigations Atlas HA-440, U.S. Geological Survey (Washington, D.C., 1971).

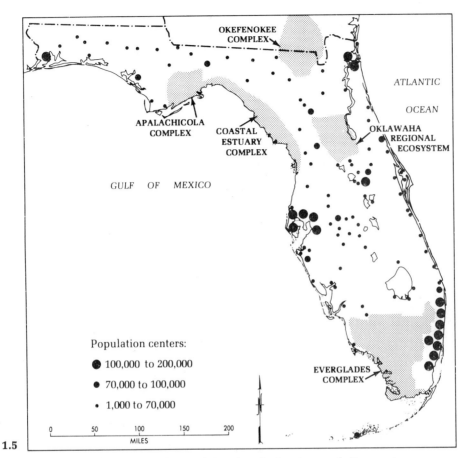

<figure>

1.5

Major regional ecosystems remaining, in relation to population centers
</figure>

tion—had gone so far that it appeared possible that, within a few decades, not a single large, relatively undisturbed natural regional ecosystem would be left anywhere in Florida. Even in the early 1970s only three or four remained (see figure 1–5).

SEEKING MEANS OF CONTROL. As early as March of 1971, the then president of the Florida Senate, Senator Jerry Thomas, had issued a statement declaring that if past growth trends continued the state's resources would be placed under a "catastrophic burden." Shortly thereafter, at Thomas's urging, the legislature reduced the funds available to the state Department of Commerce for the promotion of Florida outside the state. But this was of small consequence in light of the millions spent by land developers and other interests for such promotion. At best, it amounted to but a minor departure from the unrestrained boosterism of the past. The essential question remained unanswered: By what means was the state to gain enough control over the growth process to protect and enhance the

9 THE LAND AND THE CRISIS

quality of life? This was no simple matter of controlling waste discharges. Rather, it was one of having public officials influence every major aspect of Florida's physical development, even though such development is largely within the province of private enterprise.

Many have concluded that the surest and most direct way for state and local officials to influence growth is through their authority to control the use of land and related water resources. In fact, a water conference that Governor Askew convened in September 1971, after one of the most severe droughts in Florida history, led to important legislative initiatives to regulate the growth process through land and water management. Of that seminal conference and its consequences, I shall have more to say in a subsequent chapter. Here, it is enough to point out that a major initial thrust looked to the regulation of certain "critical" areas and critical uses of land, with the responsibility for this to be entrusted chiefly to local government acting under state guidance and oversight. Later, the state would move toward a policy under which the local governments—67 counties and some 390 cities, varying widely in their political maturity and governmental competence—would undertake programs of comprehensive planning and land management.

This challenge undertaken by the state was formidable in its complexity and political difficulty. To establish a workable policy and implementation process statewide would take years. On the other hand, Floridians were taking more than a passing interest in the problem and clearly wanted to see it through to a solution. In March of 1974, three years after the "growth issue" had first come to the fore, Cambridge Research Survey found that 72 percent of the 600 Florida voters it had polled felt that strong land use controls were needed to control growth. Moreover, this poll (which, though sponsored by environmentalists, included few members of conservation groups in the sample) indicated that Floridians regard growth and related environmental concerns as the state's most important problem.

DEFINING THE GROWTH ISSUE

NOT "NO GROWTH" BUT "CONTROLLED GROWTH." In defining Florida's growth problem one must recognize that, considered overall, Florida is not now a densely populated state. Its average population density in 1970 of 116 inhabitants per square mile was less than that of fourteen other states and was certainly light by comparison with that of a country such as the Netherlands where densities exceed 800 inhabitants per square mile. Only in Greater Miami, the Tampa Bay region, and a few other metropolitan areas were densities reaching high levels. Furthermore, as I will make clearer later in describing various Florida regions, much of the land in the state that is naturally suitable for development is found in regions still only lightly populated. I refer principally to the panhandle and to north Florida generally, Jacksonville and Pensacola excepted. The climate map (see figure 1–2) shows that there is no part of Florida where most winter days are not sunny and conducive to golf, fishing, and other outdoor sports.

The growth problem, therefore, does not arise from lack of space for new people in regions that could be highly appealing. It arises from the fact that newcomers tend to settle in the same areas chosen by the migrants who preceded them, and it is greatly aggravated by the fast pace at which the population increases and related developments have been occurring.

Immigration accounted for nearly three-fourths of the state's population growth during the 1950s and 1960s: two-thirds of all Florida residents in 1973 had been born out of state.[7] A study prepared by Jerome Pickard for the Federal Commission on Population Growth and the American Future predicts that over the next twenty-five years, peninsular Florida will become one of the United States' great urban regions, with 13.5 million people to be living there by the year 2000.[8] Pickard's projections support Governor Askew's vision of much of the peninsula becoming a megalopolis. On the Atlantic coast he foresees an urban belt extending for 350 miles from the Georgia border to below Miami. On the Gulf Coast there would be a 200-mile-long urban belt beginning at a point well to the north of St. Petersburg and reaching south to Naples and Marco Island. Then, reaching diagonally across the peninsula, another belt would extend from Tampa Bay to Jacksonville and Daytona on the Atlantic, taking in the Orlando area along the way. The Tampa Bay, Orlando, and Gold Coast areas would number among the nation's fastest growing, and the Gold Coast—its population to increase by almost a third every decade—would be the fastest. If Pickard's projections are borne out, continued environmental degradation on the peninsula seems inevitable, with conditions growing far worse than anything seen to date. Possibly the peninsula could be made to accommodate comfortably the twofold population increase projected, but, given the primitive stage of development of land use policy and regulation in many jurisdictions, that would be unlikely.

Just to meet the burgeoning population's needs for electric power

7. The 1970 Census document, *Detailed Characteristics, Florida*, shows (table 140) that of the 6.7 million Floridians, 2.3 million were born in Florida; 1 million in the northeastern United States; .8 million in the north central states; 1.4 million in other southern states; .1 million in the West. In addition, there were some 361,000 for whom the state of birth was not reported, and 540,000 foreign born.

8. According to the Pickard projections, the population of southeast Florida will increase from 2.2 million in 1970 to 5.6 million in the year 2000; this would be more than a third of Florida's entire population. A more conservative projection, made by Stanford Research Institute in connection with a regional jetport study, put the year 2000 total for this southeast region at 4.4 million; but even this represents a doubling of the 1970 population.

11 THE LAND AND THE CRISIS

Photos by Patricia Caulfield

Above, spike rush and lilies on a wet prairie in the Big Cypress; *below*, pond cypress in the Big Cypress and prop roots of mangroves; *at right*, perphyton and saw grass in the Everglades.

12 INTRODUCTION

could put the peninsular environment under heavy stress. In its report of March 1974 to the governor and legislature, the Florida Energy Committee set forth three different projections of power demand through the year 2000.[9] There were high-growth, low-growth, and slowed-growth cases. In the high-growth case, which rested on the assumption that past trends for energy consumption and population growth would continue, the demand projected was simply mind-boggling and obviously unrealistic. Especially disconcerting, however, was the fact that one could take little comfort even in the slowed-growth case, wherein it was assumed that past population growth trends would continue but that per capita consumption of energy would be reduced to half that projected in the high-growth case. The demand for power could be such as to require 50 new 1,000-megawatt generating plants and 1,150 miles of major transmission lines, not to mention the large deliveries of coal, oil, and nuclear fuel that would be necessary. Only in the low-growth case, based on the assumption that there would be no per capita increase in energy use and no net increase in population from immigration, would Florida be able to get by with a relatively modest expansion of power generating facilities—two new 1,000-megawatt generating plants and 50 additional miles of major transmission line would be sufficient. Although this essentially zero-growth case was perhaps as unrealistic as the high-growth case, it seemed to point up a compelling reason for Florida to seek to have the rate of population increase significantly reduced.

9. Florida Energy Committee, *Energy in Florida* (Tallahassee, March 1, 1974), pp. 96–113.

Some Floridians, especially if inclined toward traditional boosterism, scoff at the very suggestion of reducing population growth, as though to accomplish this would require a fence, border guards, and check points at the state line. What a controlled growth policy would in fact involve, however, would be to have new development in any particular place or region occur only at the pace, and to the extent, that it can be accommodated without endangering that elusive thing referred to as the "quality of life."

PRESERVING A SENSE OF PLACE. Defining "quality of life" necessarily has to do with philosophy and esthetics, yet, in Florida as in other states, people have had a tendency not to ask the fundamental question: "What kind of place do we want this to be?" Public concern is rarely expressed in terms of seeking some particularly desirable way of life, but rather in terms of alarm about things going wrong—water or energy supplies running low, the bay being polluted, once familiar species of plants or animals disappearing, urban life becoming congested, and so on. There is also sometimes the worry that tourists may be put off by the loss of amenities and decide to stay away. But, again, seldom is there an effort to define what kind of Florida would please the tourist most. Nevertheless, from all the talk of this or that place being despoiled and of a "paradise" being lost, one can arrive by inference at what Floridians, or certainly many of them, would like Florida to be. They want an environment in which the natural and the man-made are treated as complementary, with the choice wild places preserved and the cities becoming more gardenlike.

In achieving this, the Floridian, new arrival as well as native, would gain something else that could be precious to him—what architects and planners call a "sense of place." Florida is the only subtropical part of the continental United States, and thoughtful Floridians want it to remain distinct and different. They are angry and dismayed when characteristic features—lakes and citrus groves, pine and palmetto flatwoods, dome-shaped "cypress heads," tidal marshes and mangroves—are erased from the landscape by heedless urbanization and technology. Or when the resort atmosphere found in some of their better cities—an atmosphere characterized by a certain openness, lightness, and freedom—is lost to massive high-rise development which, if it belongs anywhere, is more appropriate to urban centers of the North.

With the land crisis proclaimed, and the 1970s advancing, Floridians still grope for a policy to guide growth and land use that will play strongly to their state's natural attributes, including its climate, land and seascapes, specialized subtropical agriculture, and its gateway location with respect to Latin America. Such a policy would, of course, have to encourage the intensive urbanization or other development of some lands, while either prohibiting or limiting development of other lands. It would also take account of the compatibility of various economic activities—tourism, retirement living, agriculture, manufacturing, and so forth—one with another, with the basic habitability of Florida, and with the enjoyment of a sense of place. The classification of land as suited or not suited for development and the evaluation of the impact of economic activities on the land are critical considerations. These I come to now.

A UNIQUE AND DELICATE ENVIRONMENT

A map prepared at the Red Flag Charrette (see figure 1–6) held by the Florida architects and environmentalists shows not more than a third of the land in the entire state as having "high tolerance" for development, and the greater part of the land so classified is not on the peninsula but in the uplands of north Florida and the panhandle. An area relatively intolerant of development—the definition here is my own, but it is not one with which many of the participants in the charrette would quarrel—is one

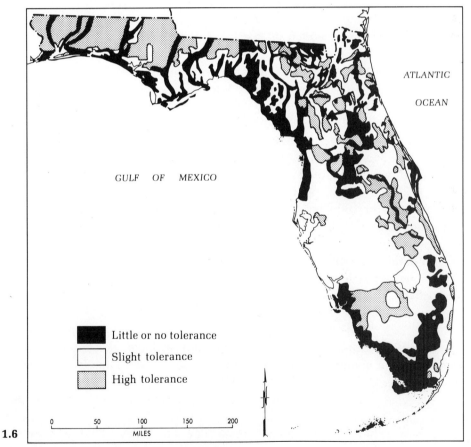

1.6

Areas of differing development tolerance

15 THE LAND AND THE CRISIS

where development, or any development that is not carefully limited and controlled, will cause the loss or degradation of one or more of the following: a regionally significant watershed or area of aquifer recharge; a natural feature such as a sandy ocean beach, scenic bay, or freshwater lake of high esthetic and recreational value; a habitat essential to maintaining a diversity of native plant and animal life—for instance, a coastal marsh habitat vital to wading birds and game fish; or an agricultural asset that contributes to the diversity of the regional economy, that is important for reasons of esthetics or aquifer recharge, and that perhaps represents a resource that is quite limited nationally—citrus, for instance, of which Florida groves account for three-fourths of the nation's total production.

AREAS OF SLIGHT TOLERANCE (OR NONE). Potential impacts on Florida's freshwater resources are of critical concern, and a few observations in regard to such resources are in order before areas considered intolerant to development are identified. Sizeable rivers such as the Apalachicola and the Suwannee flow into the Florida panhandle and north Florida from Alabama and Georgia. But no rivers flow into peninsular Florida from outside, and the region is wholly dependent on rainfall for its fresh water. As reckoned on the basis of an average of 50 to 60 inches a year, rainfall on the peninsula is abundant; but the average hides wide extremes, with the rainfall of some wet years being twice that of dry years. Furthermore, to store enough water from wet periods to meet the needs of agriculture and urban and industrial users during unusually dry periods is difficult in south Florida. The potential yield of the Floridan Aquifer, that great bed of water-bearing limestone underlying Florida, is large. In south Florida, however, this aquifer lies deep and its waters are brackish. Water users in this region are largely dependent on the several water-table or "shallow" aquifers, of which the largest is the Biscayne Aquifer. Lake Okeechobee, the only large lake in south Florida, is an important but by no means inexhaustible supplementary source of water for urban and agricultural users.

Wetlands are the places least suitable for development, especially when they serve as recharge areas for important aquifers, as is true of some of those to be described here:

The Everglades. This great "river of grass," up to 40 miles wide, once swept for 100 miles from the south shore of Lake Okeechobee to tidewater and the mangrove country of the Ten Thousand Islands and Florida Bay, uninterrupted by the works of either man or nature (see figure 1–7). The Everglades always has known periodic drought, but, prior to drainage of the upper glades early in this century, water levels in the Everglades usually were several feet higher than they are today. That is why the Seminoles—and white adventurers such as Lieutenant Willoughby—could usually travel by dugout or canoe across this wilderness of saw grass (a heavy sedge, its edges set with fine saw teeth) sloughs, and occasional "tree islands," even during the winter dry season. Now much of the Everglades is often so dry by late winter that the peaty, "muck" soils catch fire (muck fires occurred prior to drainage, but much less frequently than today) and sometimes burn all the way down to the limestone bedrock. The tortured history of Everglades drainage and water management is the subject for a later chapter. Here, it is enough to say that the hydrologic regimen of the upper glades is now maintained, after a fashion, by an elaborate system of canals, pumping stations, and dike-enclosed water

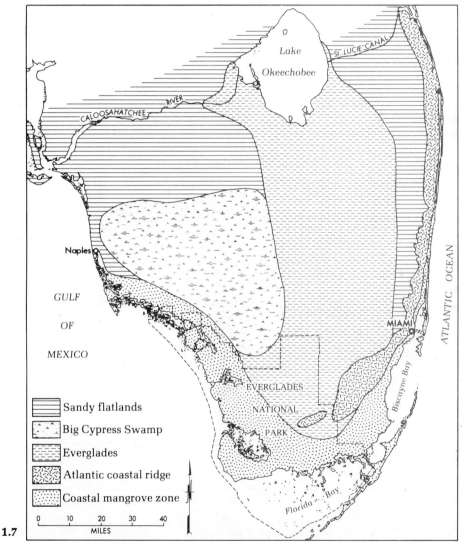

1.7

Ecologic zones of south Florida prior to development

Mangrove zone in the Everglades National Park

Patricia Caulfield

Citrus groves in central Florida

Soil Conservation Service—USDA

19 THE LAND AND THE CRISIS

conservation areas. Most Floridians now recognize that nothing is more important to the livability of southeast Florida than for what is left of the Everglades to be maintained unimpaired. The reasons for this are several. The Everglades is a place of beauty and recreation visited by over 2 million persons each year. In addition, this great interior wetland contributes to the biological productivity of the coastal estuaries by maintaining (though not so well as in the past) a "hydroperiod" that extends several months into the dry season. That is, fresh water in the Everglades, moving slowly southward on a virtually imperceptible gradient (dropping by as little as 2 inches per mile) in a thin, diffuse "sheet flow," continues to enter the estuarine zone for several months following the rainy season. Marine biologists have recently discovered that the brackish conditions caused by this inflow of fresh water facilitates the colonization of bacteria on mangrove leaves, the process whereby the leaf detritus is converted from cellulose to a supply of protein important in the marine food chain.[10] The Everglades also functions as a recharge area for the Biscayne Aquifer, into which sea water intrudes unless the necessary hydrostatic head is maintained. Preserving this vital recharge function of the Everglades is thus necessary if east coast well fields are to be kept from "salting up," a phenomenon that already has occurred from time to time under drought conditions.

The Big Cypress Swamp. This large watershed, some 2,450 square miles in extent, lies immediately to the west of the Everglades, from which it is distinguished by its slightly higher terrain, more complex drainage patterns, and markedly different vegetation. As much as 90 percent of the Big Cypress is flooded by seasonal rainfall for up to four months of the year. With the onset of the dry season, water drains from most of the land and collects in ponds and sloughs. In some places the Big Cypress is relatively open and savannahlike, with prairie grasses dominating. In others, dwarf or "hatrack" cypress coexist with the grasses; some of these trees, a characteristic feature of the Big Cypress, may be more than one hundred years old, but, rooted in shallow marl soils, their growth has been slight. Along the deeper sloughs, however, the cypress grows large and is found in long linear "strands," with the taller trees toward the center where the soils are deeper. The Big Cypress, like the glades, has its "islands" of higher ground of from a few acres to hundreds of acres in extent, and these are suitable for slash pine, palmetto, oak, and other plants that could not survive in a region of unrelieved swamp. The importance of the Big Cypress, like that of the Everglades, lies partly in its relationship to adja-

10. E. J. Heald, "The Production of Organic Detritus in a South Florida Estuary," Ph.D. dissertation, University of Miami, Coral Gables, Florida, 1969; W. E. Odum, "Pathways of Energy Flow in a South Florida Estuary," Ph.D. dissertation, University of Miami, 1970.

cent regions. The Big Cypress, like the Everglades, helps maintain the brackishness of the Ten Thousand Islands well into the dry season. Also, some of the more spectacular and interesting birds found in the Everglades National Park, such as the wood ibis (the only North American stork), use the Big Cypress either for nesting or feeding during parts of the year. Furthermore, the Big Cypress is the recharge area for the shallow aquifers from which the water needs of lower southwest Florida ultimately will have to be met. As in the case of the Everglades, the topography is so remarkably flat that during the dry season a drainage canal can lower the water table over a wide area, with damage to ecologic systems and fresh-water resources. The hammocks and pine islands of the Big Cypress have some tolerance for development, provided there is no disturbance of the sloughs, cypress "heads" (or ponds), and cypress strands interspersed among these enclaves of higher ground.

Salt Marshes and Mangrove Swamps. Florida still has, despite the encroachments of developers, more than 700,000 acres of prime estuarine habitat that serve as nursery and feeding grounds for a variety of important fish and shellfish species, such as sea trout, tarpon, snook, redfish (channel bass), and the pink shrimp. Marine biologists know, for instance, that the pink shrimp caught by commercial trawlers in the waters off Dry Tortugas spends part of its life cycle in the sheltered and nutrient-rich waters of the Ten Thousand Islands, at the northwest side of south Florida's mangrove cresent.[11] Furthermore, in visiting an undeveloped coastal estuary the sports fisherman or amateur naturalist may find a unique wilderness. The Ten Thousand Islands, for example, is a place of tide-washed mangrove islands and innumerable bays, channels, creeks, and short rivers. The red mangrove with its dark shiny leaves and spectacular system of prop roots, is a distinctive botanical feature of south Florida and is found nowhere else in the United States. Both the red mangrove flats and the lower salt marshes of the Florida coast are virtually at sea level and subject to daily tidal flooding; the so-called high marsh areas and the flats populated by the black mangrove and the white mangrove (species lacking the prop roots of the red mangrove) are inundated on periodic flood tides. Tidal lands of these various kinds are converted to waterfront real estate by dredge-and-fill methods, with finger canals or artificial lagoons often cut to depths of 20 feet or more as the fill is excavated to build up construction sites to minimum elevations required by local building codes. In the process, estuarine habitat is destroyed and conditions conducive to water pollution are created. The canals are usually poorly flushed by tidal action and are so deep that bottom conditions are anaerobic. Removal of

11. "The Big Cypress Watershed," a report to the Secretary of the Interior, by the Everglades-Jetport Advisory Board, an interagency task force of the U.S. Department of the Interior (April 19, 1971), p. 16.

mangroves also means the loss of a potential buffer against the devastating storm surge that may be generated by a hurricane.

The Florida Keys. On most of the keys buildable land is scarce and expensive. If dredge-and-fill methods are used—and this has been the common practice—to create additional land, mangrove and marine grass beds are destroyed, the normally limpid waters become turbid (at least temporarily), and silt is deposited on the offshore coral reef, the only such reef in the continental United States. In addition, when a key undergoes intensive development, wastes usually are disposed of either by septic tanks or by a small and usually inefficient treatment plant, with pollution of adjacent waters a possibility in either case. The terrestrial environment on all the keys linked together by Highway U.S. 1 has been severely altered already, often by shabby roadside development; but, up to this point, development in most places has been fairly light and the waters around the keys have largely kept their pristine quality.

River Swamps and Areas of Aquifer Recharge. A catalog of all such places is not possible here, but a few examples will suffice. First of all, there are the flood plains of rivers such as the Saint Johns, Oklawaha, Kissimmee, and Suwannee. The disturbing consequences of the channelization of the Kissimmee River and the destruction of half of the Oklawaha River swamp forest will be described in later chapters. Another place where development should be forbidden, or at least carefully restricted and supervised, is the Green Swamp of central Florida, headwaters for four sizable rivers and a recharge area for the Floridan Aquifer. Among numerous other significant inland wetlands found about the state are the Loxahatchee Slough near West Palm Beach, Paine's Prairie south of Gainesville, and Tate's Hell in the panhandle.

TOLERANT AREAS. Those parts of Florida *relatively* tolerant of development—the qualifier needs emphasis, for careless, uncontrolled development does harm wherever it occurs—are the higher lands and these are, for the most part, found in the panhandle and central and north Florida. As already indicated, a relatively small part of south Florida lends itself naturally to intensive urbanization—principally the Atlantic coastal ridge and parts of the Immokalee Rise or plateau, the latter being a sandy area southwest of Lake Okeechobee and north of the Big Cypress. Along south Florida's Gulf Coast, there is no pronounced coastal ridge comparable to the ridge along the Atlantic Coast. In fact, south of the Caloosahatchee River, even where there is a beach and dunes instead of mangrove swamp, the coastal strip lying between the Gulf and the Big Cypress is generally no higher than 5 feet above sea level and is often lower. Waterfront development there faces hurricane hazards, and, throughout this gulf coastal area, many places simply cannot be safely developed unless the land is raised several feet or more to bring it above flood levels. As for the Atlantic coastal ridge, much of it from West Palm Beach southward has been urbanized already but there remain some extensive tracts not yet developed, as in the areas north and west of Homestead in Dade County. Development is now proceeding rapidly on the several hundreds of thousands of acres, once part of the Everglades, that lie just west of the coastal ridge. This land, long since partly drained, is protected by a dike from any rise in the waters in the Everglades. Although altered irreparably from natural conditions already, such lands have tolerance for only limited, low-density development because of their importance for aquifer recharge.

The Immokalee plateau has not, except at the farm town of Immokalee, been urbanized, but has been used for farming and cattle ranching, with some of the lower places already having been drained. If the Okloachoochee Slough, (a tributary of the Big Cypress) is protected, development of the plateau might be allowed without harm to vital regional water supplies. Somewhat similar is the sand ridge extending north of Lake Okeechobee and separating the lower Kissimmee and upper Saint Johns basins.

Florida's lowland and upland provinces embrace extensive areas of pine flatwoods having some development tolerance. The flatwoods,[12] their virgin pine long since removed, are not of much esthetic significance, nor of high value for aquifer recharge. While often valuable as wildlife habitat, flatwoods are not a scarce resource—they constitute an abundant habitat type. Because these lands are almost level and typically have an underlying "hard pan" of impermeable soil, natural drainage is often poor and septic tanks can be unworkable. Such problems can only be overcome by construction of extensive water-control works and advanced waste treatment systems. Much of the Disney World site was originally pine flatwoods subject to seasonal flooding.

No part of Florida is more tolerant of development than the northwest uplands, extending from the Suwannee River through the panhandle. This is a region of gentle slopes, hardwoods and pine, well-drained soils, and numerous rivers. Florida's Central Highlands, on the peninsula proper, also are well drained and easily developed. But, here, several caveats are in order. The Central Highlands is one of the few places in Florida where, esthetically, man has improved upon nature: Orange groves on the rolling terrain, combined with numerous lakes, create an effect of rare beauty. That beauty, a unique Florida asset, is easily lost through poorly controlled

12. A term peculiar to the South, "flatwoods" refers in this instance to a plant association that occurs on flat terrain made up of poorly drained, fine, sandy soils. In south Florida flatwoods consist "chiefly [of] slash pine, which forms very open stands with little underbrush except for extensive mats of saw palmetto, huckleberry, gallberry, pawpaw, rosemary, and wax myrtle." From Frank C. Craighead, Sr., *Trees of South Florida*, vol. 1 (Coral Gables: University of Miami Press, 1971), p. 179.

development—a single ill-designed, misplaced structure can mar an entire landscape. Also, any of the many warm shallow lakes of the Central Highlands that are not highly eutrophic already will surely become so if polluted by domestic wastes or urban runoff. Furthermore, because rainfall percolates readily through the deep sandy soils of the citrus country, this highland region is far more important for the recharging of the Floridan Aquifer than is even the Green Swamp,[13] an area properly noted for its significance to water conservation. For these reasons, development in the Central Highlands is undesirable except where, in a given area, most of the ground surface is left unaffected by buildings, streets, or parking lots and hence is able to soak up rainfall.

THE IMPACT OF DEVELOPMENT

Viewed in a statewide and regional perspective, the heavy impact that development has had on the Florida environment appears disproportionate to the extent and kind of development that has occurred. Here, three related circumstances need to be pointed out:
• The population is highly urbanized, three-fourths of it living in cities and towns in 1970, a proportion comparable to that part of the national population that is urban. Almost 69 percent of Florida's population is found in seven metropolitan regions or, to use Census Bureau terminology, in Standard Metropolitan Statistical Areas; again, this is about the same as the proportion of the national population living in SMSAs. Florida has been a predominantly urban state since 1930 and the population on the peninsula has always lived largely in the cities and towns. Thus, most of the state has never undergone extensive rural settlement. A 1963 report of the U.S. Soil Conservation Service, *Florida Soil and Water Conservation Needs Inventory*, showed that, in 1958, only 1.1 million acres—or 3 percent of Florida, not counting large lakes and rivers—had been urbanized or "built up." (The latter term refers to villages, rural industrial sites, airports, and the like as well as to cities and towns.) By 1967, nine years later, there were still only 1.6 million acres in this category, or 4.6 percent of all land in the state, compared to the 61 million acres (or 13 percent) so classified nationally (excluding Hawaii and Alaska).[14]
• Intensive agriculture can have decidedly negative environmental side effects, especially as a cause of pollution and a high rate of water consumption. But the fact is that, in Florida, a relatively modest proportion of the land has been used for such farming. Florida's biggest cash crops—citrus

13. W. F. Lichtler, "Appraisal of Water Resources in the East Central Florida Region," Report of Investigations No. 61, U.S. Geological Survey (Tallahassee, Florida, 1972), pp. 5, 24–26.
14. *National Inventory of Soil and Water Conservation Needs, 1967*, Statistical Bulletin No. 461, U.S. Department of Agriculture (January 1971), p. 1.

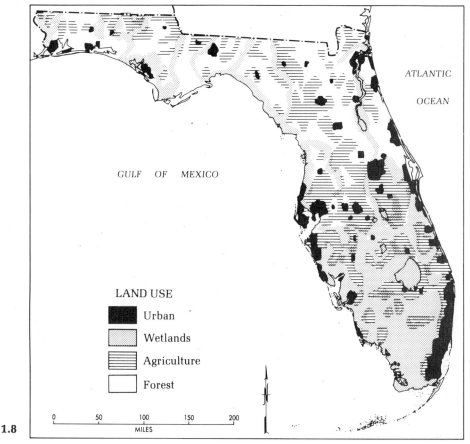

LAND USE

- ■ Urban
- ▦ Wetlands
- ☰ Agriculture
- ☐ Forest

GULF OF MEXICO

ATLANTIC

OCEAN

| 0 | 50 | 100 | 150 | 200 |

MILES

1.8

Land use in Florida

and winter vegetables—have a high per acre value, and the total acreages planted are modest. For example, less than 900,000 acres in Florida are devoted to citrus, even though Florida citrus represents three-fourths of the citrus grown in the nation. In 1958, only 17 percent of all nonfederal rural land in Florida—or about 5.27 million acres—was devoted to intensive agriculture, that is to say, for citrus, field crops, and improved pasture. By 1967, the proportion so used had increased to about 22 percent (6.65 million acres) compared to the 37 percent of nonfederal rural land devoted to such use nationally.[15] Thus, despite a significant agricultural expansion, more than offsetting the loss of farm land to urbanization, overall land use patterns in Florida were not much changed.

• Florida is still relatively nonindustrialized, certainly by national standards and even as compared to many other southern states. In fact, manufacturing accounts for only about 16 percent of Florida's total nonfarm employment, as against nearly twice that percentage so employed in the nation as a

15. Ibid., Table 2, p. 5.

whole. Furthermore, except for the mining and processing of phosphate, Florida's principal polluting industries—paper and chemicals—are not on the peninsula but in north Florida and the panhandle.

Strictly from an environmental standpoint, one should be able to take comfort in the fact that most of Florida is free of serious industrial pollution and that three-fourths of the state is still in coastal marshes, swamp and upland forest, grass lands, and wet prairies (see figure 1–8). Most of these lands, if used at all, are used only as unimproved cattle range or for commercial forestry (although the intensive management of a slash pine monoculture, now common on the some 3.1 million acres in north Florida and the panhandle owned by six large paper companies, itself poses environmental problems). It might appear, therefore, that man's incursions on Florida's natural environment are proceeding in a modest, incremental fashion. How is it, then, that environmental degradation has in fact become so widespread as to have given rise to a sense of crisis?

Although the urban communities occupy less than 5 percent of the land in a large state, the urbanized area includes most of the livable ground adjacent to both the Gulf and the Atlantic. The pattern has been for settlement to spread along the littorals in a series of resort-oriented cities and towns instead of to become more concentrated. In addition, there has been a tendency to build as close to the water as possible—a case of loving the amenity too much. Another and even more basic cause of widespread environmental degradation is that the construction of public works projects and utilities—roads, drainage and navigation canals, power plants, and the like—has often led to the unnecessary loss of pristine natural areas. For instance, where the construction of one highway across the Everglades should have sufficed, two have been built. And, as the story of the Cross Florida Barge Canal points up, planners deciding how and where such narrowly conceived projects shall be built have not cared about Florida's natural heritage or whether anyone might feel that there is something special about a small subtropical river.

For a further look at disruptive changes affecting the Florida environment, consider several broad categories of economic activity:

AGRICULTURE. The drainage of wetlands for agriculture has, beyond question, done more damage to the Florida environment than any other kind of development. Indeed, vastly more land has been drained for crop production and ranching than has ever been used for either purpose—as noted earlier, where the terrain is as flat and low-lying as it is in much of Florida, drainage canals dug to serve one property may lower the water table on adjacent lands for miles around. Also, the disposal of excess water from farm lands into adjacent waters contributes to accelerated eutrophication: clear, sandy-bottomed lakes filled with bass may quickly become algae laden and swarming with gizzard shad. Vegetable farms along the north shore of Lake Apopka have contributed heavily to the loss of this lake—Florida's third largest—for most beneficial uses. Similarly, farms in the Everglades Agricultural Area and in the Taylor Creek and Kissimmee watersheds are contributing to the eutrophication of Lake Okeechobee. In addition, the consumption of water by most crops requiring irrigation competes heavily with all other claimants for water, whether these latter are cities or wilderness preserves. Consumptive demand for water by agriculture in southeast Florida has been six times greater than municipal and industrial demand.[16] To be sure, agriculture can offer important environmental advantages, and especially is this true of the Central Highlands citrus groves, given their beauty and value for aquifer recharge. Even when grove owners in the highlands pump from lakes or the aquifer to irrigate their trees, the amount of water consumed is moderate.[17]

Economically, Florida agriculture ranks behind tourism, the retirement industry, and even manufacturing, but it is nevertheless important. Some 77,000 persons are employed in Florida agriculture (albeit many in low-paying jobs) and the state's annual farm output has a market value of about $1.3 billion. Besides being the leading producer of citrus, Florida ranks second only to California in the production of winter vegetables and ranks first among the states of the continental U.S. in the production of sugar— although, as I shall later explain, for the taxpayer this sugar does not come cheap. In sum, Florida agriculture is, in national as well as state terms, a unique and important activity—but one which, from an environmental viewpoint, is most acceptable when conducted on land lending itself naturally to farming as in the case of citrus land in the Central Highlands.

THE RETIREE-ORIENTED REAL ESTATE BOOM. Except for agriculture and related land drainage earlier this century, probably no other economic activity has had a greater and more widespread impact on the Florida environment than the land sales, site development, and housing construction associated with retirement living. Some of the housing development aimed at the retiree market represents appropriate land use, but much of it represents land abuse. So fundamental is this to the overall problem of shaping a land use policy conducive to environmental quality, a look at its various aspects and its origins is in order here. First, a few general observations about the retiree housing market:

• In 1970 there were almost 1 million persons of age sixty-five or older living in the state. They represented a disproportionately large part of Florida's total population—14.5 percent—whereas this age group accounted for just under 10 percent of the U.S. population as a whole. Furthermore,

16. Leach, Klein, and Hampton, Open File Report 71005, U.S. Geological Survey (Tallahassee, 1971), p. 34. The water-use calculations were based on the experience in the year 1965.
17. W. F. Lichtler, op. cit., pp. 24–26.

the elderly made up one-fifth to one-third of the population in twelve Florida counties, seven of these being Gulf coast counties such as Pinellas (St. Petersburg) and Sarasota, with the rest on the Atlantic coast or in the Central Highlands.

• The pension and social security income received by retirees represents an infusion of several billions of dollars into the Florida economy each year, and the market for retiree housing can offer rich profits. Even some national corporations not usually thought of in connection with real estate—U.S. Steel, Bethlehem Steel, ITT, Westinghouse, and the Chrysler Corporation, among others—are taking part, to one degree or another, in the Florida real estate boom. Developments usually are heavily mortgaged, and financial institutions in Florida and out of state are, of course, deeply involved. Workers in the building trades and their unions also have a significant stake in the market for retiree housing. What proportion of Florida's 165,000 construction workers owe their jobs to that market is not known, but it clearly is large.

• The retiree can live almost any place where the postman can bring him his social security and pension checks, for, unless he is trying to supplement his retirement income with earnings from part-time or full-time work, he is not tied to established job markets. This frees the land sales companies and the developer from the constraints that normally operate in the real estate market. From an environmental standpoint, the implications of this can be either positive or negative. Remote and ecologically valuable swampland, which in the past has been available at relatively low prices, can be drained to provide a site for a retiree-oriented development or land sales campaign. Even if the project is built on land tolerant to development, the local government having jurisdiction over the area may be backward and lacking in leadership and resources, and thus be unable to provide the waste control systems and other facilities needed for the thousands of new people who will be coming. Or, to cite still another example of negative impact, a high-density condominium development may be built in a place such as Miami Beach, which has long since fallen behind in trying to cope with the problems of rapid growth and development. On the other hand, the developer of a retiree-oriented "new town" could be urged—and, if necessary, required—to choose a site where the tolerance for development is high, where no unmanageable backlog of unmet environmental problems exists, and where public authorities are competent to oversee the development and provide necessary facilities.

The huge retiree market for Florida land and housing was discovered early in the postwar period and the rush to exploit it has been nearly as feverish as that of the wild days of the Florida real estate boom of the 1920s. In 1951, the Mackle brothers, who were already prominent builders in Dade County (they began the development of Key Biscayne), put a blind advertisement for retirement housing in a national magazine and, to their surprise, it drew 25,000 responses. A few years later the Mackles, in association with the General Development Corporation, began to pioneer in exploiting the retirement home market. A piece of promotional literature since prepared by the Mackles describes what happened:

> While running GDC, the three brothers inaugurated $10-down-and-$10-a-month installment terms for Florida lot sales, national advertising of Florida homesites, nationwide sales of homes sight-unseen, the sale of Florida property through an international network of franchised agents—and a host of other innovations since widely imitated. They built more than 5,000 homes and 100,000 homesites in Port Charlotte, Port St. Lucie, Port Malabar, Sebastian and Vero Beach Highlands, Pompano Beach Highlands, and other GDC communities which they launched. During the final four years that the Mackles headed General Development [the Mackles withdrew from GDC in 1961 and formed the Deltona Corporation], they racked up total sales of nearly a quarter-billion dollars. . . .

The out-of-state market for Florida real estate has continued to grow over the past two decades. In 1970 the state agency that regulates land sales promotions was registering almost 25,000 parcels each month! Some purchasers are retirees, others are persons approaching retirement, still others are younger persons making a long-term investment toward retirement, and some are out-and-out speculators (with quite a few Latin Americans and Europeans among them). Two principal kinds of real estate activity are aimed at the out-of-state market. One kind is where the purpose is to sell housing or, at the least, land improved for use as a homesite—this kind of activity being mostly the province of the larger, better financed companies. The other kind is the sale of "raw" or wholly unimproved land, an activity now carried on largely by smaller (and often fly-by-night) companies, wishing to turn a quick profit on a minimal investment.

As for the purveyors of raw land, they have been buying whole sections of wetlands and subdividing them into unsurveyed 5-acre, 2½-acre, and 1¼-acre parcels for resale in the raw, without roads or drainage. Some eighty subdivisions were marketed in the eastern half of the Big Cypress from the early 1960s through the early 1970s, with the result that this area of some 585,000 acres has come to be divided up into more than 30,000 individual parcels. Many of the sales—nearly always made by installment contract—have been made by high-pressure campaigns by arrays of telephone salesmen using Wide Area Telephone Service lines. So successful have these campaigns been that most of the available land in the Big Cypress and other south Florida wetlands has now been sold, and the land sales companies have had to move on to central Florida, where they are selling off acreage in places such as the Green Swamp. The subdividing of ecologically sensitive land for sale in small parcels is an inexcusable practice, but, until the new owners actually try to use the land (which, in many cases, will not happen for years), no environmental damage is done. (In fact, as will be more evident later from my account of the notorious Golden Gate Estates project in the Big Cypress, it may be far better to have no land use regulations at all than to demand improvements such as roads and drainage works without regard to their impact on ecologic and hydrologic systems.)

As for companies selling housing and improved homesites, they have clearly been underregulated and have in some cases contributed to a peculiarly undesirable kind of suburban sprawl. Indeed, some of the early projects built for the retiree market, such as Port Charlotte, have represented more nearly an effort at land disposal than community development. Port Charlotte, about half way between Fort Myers and Sarasota, covers 90,000 acres and much of it undoubtedly will still be vacant land several decades hence. The promotion of homesites in some of these developments would have been an outright fraud if state and county regulations did not allow septic tanks and individual water wells, for it would clearly not be economically feasible to provide central water and sewer service over a vast area where no carefully staged plan of development is imposed. The septic tank and individual well, together with the private automobile, have in fact made sprawl not only possible but perhaps inevitable, with developers following the familiar pattern of leapfrogging away from the perimeter of existing cities where land prices are high.

However, more recent projects undertaken by the Mackles, GDC, and certain other large developers appear to be designed and executed in expectation of creating pleasant and reasonably compact new communities. (The list presented in figure 1–9, prepared in June 1974 by *Florida Trend* magazine, shows some three score new community developments, not counting those large condominium projects that are not part of a new community.) An effort is now generally made to have the communities expand outward from a central core with sewers and water lines provided. From an environmental viewpoint, however, both good and bad projects are still being carried out, sometimes by one and the same developer. For example, Spring Hill is a new Mackle development some 40 miles northeast of Tampa, which appears to make appropriate use of what was recently a scrubby highland area. A second new Mackle development, Sunny Hills, in the Florida panhandle north of Panama City, is also being built on land well suited for development—and, furthermore, it is in a thinly populated part of Florida where growth is plainly to be desired. Yet the Mackles' Marco Island project is causing a massive and unnecessary loss of mangrove swamp and other estuarine habitat at the head of the Ten Thousand Islands. The ITT Palm Coast development north of Daytona—planned for ultimately 750,000 people—involves the construction of many miles of finger canals connected to the Intracoastal Waterway. These canals will no doubt become seriously polluted despite the bland assurances to the contrary offered by company officials.

Because of escalating real estate prices and changes in life style, the single family detached home once prevalent in the Florida real estate market has, in more recent years, been yielding to the condominium and the mobile home, each of which warrants special mention. As recently as 1971, prices for a house and lot in some new community developments began at less than $20,000, but, more typically, prices ran much higher—too high for many retired pensioners.

Condominiums. Builders have been selling condominiums at a wide range of prices, both as part of new community developments and (more commonly) as separate undertakings. A condominium apartment might have triple appeal to "empty nesters" without need for much space, with no desire to keep up a yard, and only modest ability to make a down payment and keep up monthly mortgage payments. The construction of condominiums, chiefly for retirees, first began on a large scale in the mid-1960s on the Gold Coast. But the condominium craze has since spread to other parts of Florida and, today, such dwellings represent most of the new housing being built.[18] In 1970 there were some 1,250 condominium complexes containing about 50,000 units, but by now these figures surely have increased manyfold. Many of the complexes consist of high-rise towers but others consist of garden-type clusters of moderate density. In 1973, prices went from $20,000 or less for a small unit in one of the less pretentious condominiums to $190,000 or more for something more ample in a place such as Fort Lauderdale's The Last Word. (An arresting peculiarity of some of the advertising pitched to the affluent retiree is the explicit emphasis, with no attempt at subtlety, on the high cost of the units offered. Combined with this gross appeal to the conspicuous consumer, is the promise of exclusiveness.) Condominiums make sparing use of land compared to single-family detached housing and they also make for efficiencies in providing public services, such as sewage collection. But condominiums for the affluent usually emphasize waterfront living and not a few are on filled land in areas once occupied by mangrove swamps or salt marsh. Also, some of the larger condominiums are huge warrens that might seem out of place anywhere, but especially in a seaside resort. Condominium construction has been proceeding at a frenetic pace along both the Atlantic and Gulf coasts. Environmentalists have been disturbed at the heavy new burdens put on already overloaded sewage plants, freeways, and the like.

18. The Census Bureau, in its March 1973 *Housing Authorized by Building Permits and Public Contracts,* reported that of the 280,976 units of new private housing for which building permits were issued in 1972, 176,846 units were to be in buildings of 5 units or more.

1.9 Inventory of large-scale developments

Name	Location	Developer	Acreage	Res. units	Ultimate pop.	Current pop.
North Golden Gate	Collier	GAC Corporation	2,500	6,000	26,000	
Cape Coral	Lee	GAC Corporation	61,000	100,000	300,000	16,371
Golden Gate Estates	Collier	GAC Corporation	112,000b	0	0	
River Ranch Shores	Osceola	GAC Corporation	6,427	15,000	40,000	
River Ranch Acres	Osceola	GAC Corporation	49,356b	0	0	
Remuda Ranch Grants	Collier	GAC Corporation	60,000b	0	0	
Barefoot Bay	Indian River	GAC Corporation	1,100	5,000	11,000	0
Ocala Springs	Marion	GAC Corporation	4,730	12,000	30,000	
Poinciana	Osceola/Polk	GAC Corporation	47,300	70,000	250,000	0
Golden Gate	Collier	GAC Corporation	2,500	6,000	26,000	
Port Charlotte	Charlotte/Sarasota	General Development	100,840	190,677	500,000e	28,500
Port LaBelle	Hendry/Glades	General Development	31,530	50,000	130,000e	10
Port St. Lucie	St. Lucie	General Development	48,480	83,100	220,000e	9,500
Port Malabar	Brevard	General Development	43,500	70,449	185,000e	6,750
Port St. John	Brevard	General Development	5,586	9,597	25,000e	1,400
Vero Bch. Shores/Hghlds.	Indian River (2)	General Development	1,556	2,329	6,000e	658
Sebastian Highlands	Brevard	General Development	4,958	13,195	35,000e	650
Julington Creek	St. Johns	General Development	4,630b	0	0	
Deltona	Volusia	Deltona Corporation	17,500	36,000	104,400	10,866
Marco Island	Collier	Deltona Corporation	9,100	25,800	75,500	5,330
Spring Hill	Hernando	Deltona Corporation	16,400	34,500	100,000	4,600
Citrus Springs	Citrus	Deltona Corporation	15,300	33,000	95,600	1,085
Sunny Hills	Washington	Deltona Corporation	17,100	34,000	98,500	175
St. Augustine Shores	St. Johns	Deltona Corporation	2,000	6,000	12,000	0
Pine Ridge Estates	Citrus	Deltona Corporation	9,584	5,000	14,500	0
Marion Oaks	Marion	Deltona Corporation	15,000	33,280	96,500	0
Royal Palm Bch. Village	Palm Beach	Royal P. B. Colony, Inc.	4,000	13,900	36,200	1,088
Royal Highlands	Hernando	Royal P. B. Colony, Inc.	8,000	19,000	66,000	
Holley-by-the-Sea	Santa Rosa	Royal P. B. Colony, Inc.	5,000	5,900	15,000	
Royal Trails	Lake	Royal P. B. Colony, Inc.	11,000	5,800	16,500	
Cypress Springs	Orange	Gulfstream Land & Devmt.	2,900b	0	0	
Switzerland Forests	St. Johns	Gulfstream Land & Devmt.	1,800b	0	0	
Gulfstream Plantation	Broward	Gulfstream Land & Devmt.	5,400	11,900e	33,300e	
Venice Gardens	Sarasota	Gulfstream Land & Devmt.	3,100	6,800e	19,000e	
Winter Springs	Seminole (PUD)	Gulfstream Land & Devmt.	3,500	7,700e	21,600e	
"Argyle Forests"	Duval/Clay	Gulfstream Land & Devmt.	8,000	17,600e	49,300e	

Development	County	Developer				
Coral Springs	Broward	Coral Ridge Properties c	13,000	53,000	130,000	6,715
Spring Lake	Highlands	Coral Ridge Properties c	6,400	18,000	50,700e	
Naples-by-the-Sea	Collier	Coral Ridge Properties c	2,100	4,600e	13,000e	
Sandestin	Walton	Evans & Mitchell c	2,000	6,000	18,000	
Halifax Plantation	Flagler	Evans & Mitchell c	5,600	16,800	50,000	
Perdido Bay C. C. Estates	Escambia	Cavanaugh Comm. Corp.	2,900	15,805	36,232	365
Rotonda West	Charlotte	Cavanaugh Comm. Corp.	26,000	65,688	164,000	520
Orangewood	Osceola	Florida Land Company c	4,500	17,857	48,000	100
Winter Springs (N. Orlando)	Seminole (PUD, 550 a.)	Florida Land Company c	2,250	1,664+	4,500	1,161
Killearn Estates	Leon	Killearn Properties c	3,485	5,630	15,500	2,600
Killearn Lakes	Leon	Killearn Properties	3,982	9,154	25,200	175
San Carlos	Lee	American Intl. Land Corp.	2,753	7,010	17,525	500
San Carlos Estates	Lee	American Intl. Land Corp.	1,160+b	0	0	
San Carlos "West 800"	Lee	American Intl. Land Corp.	720+b	0	0	
Peace River "West"	Desoto	American Intl. Land Corp.	3,000+b	0	0	
Peace River "East"	Desoto	American Intl. Land Corp.	2,306+b	0	0	
Hidden Lakes Ranch	Glades	American Intl. Land Corp.	3,545+b	0	0	
Lehigh Acres	Lee	Lehigh Acres Dev., Inc.	60,000	28,500e	80,000	4,394
Lake Buena Vista	Orange	WED Enterprises	3,580	9,650	27,000	18
Palm Coast	St. Johns/Flagler	IT&T c	100,000	250,000e	750,000	600
Crescent Estates	Polk	Florando Investment Corp.	2,821	20,000	52,500	50
Solana	Polk	Treasury Investment Corp.	2,200	15,260	35,000	0
Tomoka Springs	Volusia	Recreational Systems, Inc.	2,746	1,005	3,015	0
Placid Lakes	Highlands	Lake Placid Holding Co.	7,200	15,000	35,000	600
Wellington	Palm Beach	Breakwater Hsng. Corp.	7,400	14,800	37,000	0
Amelia Island Plantation	Nassau	Sea Pines Company	3,700	2,700	4,000	10
Compass Lake	Jackson	Compass Lake Dev. Corp.	12,000b	0	0	
Avon Park Estates	Highlands	Avon Park Estates Corp.	3,560b	0	0	
Rolling Hills	Marion	MRI Properties, Inc.	5,400b	0	0	
Miami Lakes	Dade	Sengra c	8,900e	25,000	25,000	
North Palm Beach	Palm Beach	(Ross Brothers) c	9,600	8,900e	25,000	10,923
Palm Beach Lakes	Palm Beach	Perini Corporation c	7,000	25,000e	70,000	
Palm Beach Gardens	Palm Beach	McArthur c	6,100	25,000e	70,000	7,620
Bay Port Colony	Hillsborough	Intervest, Inc. c	2,565	9,199	30,874	0
(Fletcher)	St. Johns	Fletcher Prop., Inc. c	5,300b	0	0	

b Held in undeveloped acreage; no plans for development currently
e Estimated by DSP
c Data from unverified sources

Mobile Homes. Retirees living in the numerous mobile home parks along the middle Gulf coast and the Gold Coast pass their last years meagerly, but in something of a campground atmosphere that many enjoy. *Florida Trend*, a business magazine, cites a University of Miami study which found that 77 percent of the inhabitants of mobile home parks were retirees and that the average annual income of mobile home owners was $5,702.[19] By 1971, there were some 231,000 mobile homes in Florida—undoubtedly more than in any other state—and the total was still climbing rapidly. Mobile home parks can be carefully designed and landscaped, but many are junky and nondescript. Some have been built on finger canals, now often polluted and made a worse liability by crumbling seawalls.

TOURISM. Tourist-related development has had a substantial effect on the Florida environment but its impact has been less than that of agriculture and probably less than that of the retiree-oriented land sales and housing industry. The opening of Disney World has made the potential environmental impact of tourism greater than anything seen in the past, however.

Tourism is the most important source of jobs and income for Florida residents. There are 60,000 hotel workers alone, and, just as Florida has proportionately fewer industrial workers than the United States as a whole, it has proportionately more workers in the service and retail trades. Over the past three decades the number of tourists has grown eightfold. The nearly 22 million visitors who came in 1969 spent $5.2 billion, and, when more up-to-date statistics become available, they will show large increases, for Disney World alone attracted 22.3 million visitors during the first two years after its opening in October 1971. In fact, the Disney World area of central Florida has joined the counties of the middle to lower Gulf and Atlantic coasts as one of Florida's great centers of tourist attraction. If current projections hold true some 60 million people a year will be visiting Florida by the year 2000.

Tourist attractions are of two kinds: those featuring natural amenities and those that are contrived. The 700 miles of ocean and Gulf beaches, together with an appealing climate and the generally excellent saltwater fishing, are the principal natural amenities that bring millions of tourists to Florida and bring them generally to coastal ridge areas that are more or less development tolerant. Admittedly, along much of the Atlantic coast and some of the Gulf coast, construction of hotels, motels, apartment buildings, marinas, or other tourist-related businesses or facilities has contributed to the beach erosion and to ugly strip development. Also, there are numerous instances where facilities contribute to the pollution of ocean,

19. "The Factory Built Home Becomes Florida's Newest Growth Industry," *Florida Trend*, August 1971. Increasingly, mobile homes are being manufactured within the state itself—by 1970 there were some seventy plants in Florida producing such dwellings, the total output approaching 26,000 units a year.

gulf, or estuarine waters—of this, Miami Beach is the classic case in point. Yet, given enough time and money, the pollution problems generally can be remedied, particularly where disposal of effluents by ocean outfall is possible after secondary treatment. Furthermore, some problems of beach erosion and strip development are not beyond remedy. And, in general, bad as much of the ocean or Gulf beach-front development may have been, it has not caused environmental problems as critical as those arising where coastal or interior wetlands have been filled or drained and then developed. Moreover, while the retiree and the tourist both come to Florida to enjoy many of the same amenities, the retiree makes greater demands on the environment than the tourist, particularly with respect to housing. By the nature of things, tourist accommodations lend themselves to compact development near natural or man-made attractions. By comparison with retiree living, the growth of tourist activity could be more easily directed to the Atlantic and Gulf beach areas where land is both relatively high priced and development tolerant. Because even the vacationer of modest means can be charged high rates for the short period of his stay, the developer of quality tourist facilities is not unduly hindered by high land prices and by restrictions against high density, whereas the developer of retiree housing faced with such circumstances will probably sell or rent only to the more affluent.

Tourist attractions in Florida's interior are chiefly the lakes, the larger springs, and productions such as Cypress Gardens (pretty girls on water skis), which have drawn tourists in numbers modest by comparison to the number visiting the more popular coastal resorts. Now overshadowing every other tourist attraction in central Florida is Disney World. With appropriate promotion, it could perhaps have been put almost anywhere in Florida and still have prospered, although its present highly central location may offer maximum business potential. Constructed at a cost of $400 million, Disney World offers a world of make-believe for the family trade. In its first year it attracted more than ten times as many tourists as all four of the countries in its immediate area (Orange, Osceola, Lake, and Polk) attracted in 1969. Welcome as are the benefits from this huge boost to the tourist economy, the environmental impact associated with the rapid growth and development that Disney World has helped stimulate in central Florida is cause for concern. One part of the region lies in the upper Kissimmee basin, where large lakes such as Tohopekaliga and Kissimmee are threatened by eutrophication. The other part lies in the Central Highlands where the possibility of a rapid conversion of citrus lands to urban uses threatens both water quality in the lakes and aquifer recharge. The escalation of land prices in the region around Disney World has been spectacular—grove land worth $2,000 an acre in the pre-Disney era is now often worth $6,000 an acre and in some cases may be worth $20,000 or even more. From December 1969 to December 1971 citrus acreage in

Orange County—the Disney World theme park is located in the southwest corner of Orange—declined by some 8 percent. Most of the citrus acreage that was lost is believed to have been affected by the severe freezes in the winter of 1970–71 as well as by the normal incidence of disease. But the fact that more of the grove land was not replanted after the freezes suggests that, given escalating land values, many growers have now decided not to invest capital in replanting slow-maturing groves and are instead waiting for the right moment to sell to a developer.

One of those apprehensively watching the situation is Henry F. Swanson, the Orange County farm agent. Swanson, an inveterate luncheon club speaker, has for some years now been going about to civic group meetings carrying an empty water barrel to dramatize his point that, if aquifer re-

Patricia Caulfield

At left, developers are busy near the Everglades National Park. *Below,* sugarcane fields with drainage layout in the Everglades Agricultural Area. *At right,* "Suburban Acres" housing project on flood-prone land at the edge of the Everglades National Park; mobile home park in south Florida; waterfront development south of Miami on filled land.

Agricultural Research and Education Center, Belle Glade, Fla.

Photos by EPA-DOCUMERICA—Fred Ward

charge is reduced through loss of citrus groves to urban development, the county will be in trouble. Swanson's sense of concern has, if anything, been heightened by what he has observed while serving on a county committee responsible for reviewing the steady stream of development proposals for land in the citrus belt region in western Orange, to the north of Disney. He fears that the experience of Orange County, California—the home, incidentally, of Disneyland—is about to be repeated. In the California county, citrus acreage declined by more than two-thirds in only fifteen years as urbanization spread.

In sum, with the advent of Disney World, Florida is witnessing a marked shift in patterns of tourist visitation—and in the environmental impact of tourism—as the result of wholly man-made entertainment. Other new central Florida attractions—Sea World, Bible World, and Circus World (a venture by Ringling Brothers and Barnum and Bailey Circus)—will further this new trend. Also, the land sales and community development enterprises aiming at the retiree market are taking full advantage of the fact that Disney World has made the central Florida interior's place on the map more conspicuous than it ever was before. GAC Properties' big new Poinciana development is just south of Disney, and this will no doubt be the forerunner of other such developments.

MANUFACTURING, MINING, AND OIL. Although industrial pollution is less of a problem in Florida than in many states, it is one that is extremely serious in some localities. In 1951 the Monsanto Chemical Company established a plant at Pensacola on Escambia Bay, and, subsequently, other plants were built there by Escambia Chemical Company and American Cyanamid. For a time, the bay seemed somehow to assimilate all the pollutants thrown at it, but by the early 1970s it had become a death trap for fish swimming into its warm, shallow, closely confined—and now heavily polluted—waters. In the first eight and a half months of 1971, there were eighteen major fish kills in Escambia Bay, with shoals of dead menhaden up to 16 feet deep found in some places. Similarly, paper mills in the panhandle and north Florida have severely polluted several rivers and tidal creeks, rendering them unfit for fish and wildlife or for any beneficial purpose other than that of serving as an industrial sewer.

The worst industrial pollution in central and south Florida probably has come from the mining and processing of phosphate in Polk, Hillsborough, and Manatee counties. But except for the repeated fish kills in the Peace River caused by escaping slimes, the environmental effects of the phosphate industry, though severe (from strip-mining and from air as well as water pollution), have been fairly localized. Sugar and citrus processors also have been polluters, and where citrus wastes have contributed to the overenrichment of lakes such as Apopka and Griffin, the consequences have been bad. In general, however, industrial pollution in peninsular Florida has been minor compared to pollution from domestic sewage and from nutrients running off farmlands. The more recent industrial growth in Florida has come largely in the form of large numbers of light— and relatively nonpolluting—manufacturing plants in fields such as electronics, aerospace, metal fabrication, fashion apparel, boat building, and the like. Much of this growth has occurred on the Gold Coast, and in the Tampa Bay and Orlando areas, coming as a welcome economic supplement to a tourist industry that offers mostly low paying jobs and is somewhat seasonal at best. There are now some 330,000 persons working in manufacturing enterprises of all kinds in Florida, for a total payroll of almost $2.2 billion.

A new environmental threat for Florida is now posed by exploration and drilling for oil. A 1970 report by the National Petroleum Council indicated that oil reserves in peninsular Florida and on the adjacent continental shelf could, to judge from geologic structures, amount to 7.8 billion barrels of crude (estimates of Alaska's North Slope reserves have begun at about 10 billion barrels). As for proved reserves, the discoveries to date have been comparatively modest. The most significant was the recent discovery of the Jay Field, on the panhandle, north of Pensacola. The first oil actually produced in Florida was at the Sunniland Field in the Big Cypress, where the discovery well was brought in in 1943. Oil recovery at Sunniland and the nearby Felda Field has been minor. Most drilling in south Florida thus far has produced dry holes.

SOME CONCLUSIONS

By way of recapitulation, these are the salient points to be kept in mind about Florida's land crisis and the challenge it presents to the state and local governments:

• First, the pressures of growth and development now experienced in Florida are more intense than those felt in any other state. Compounding the problems caused by those pressures is the fact that Florida's peninsular environment is extraordinarily delicate and susceptible to upset.

• Second, growth and development will continue largely uncontrolled, and with worsening environmental deterioration, unless the state government succeeds in asserting strong leadership and adopts and oversees the implementation of policies for controlled and directed growth.

• Third, to make growth and development compatible with environmental values requires a sensitive classification of all lands in Florida. In such a classification, possibly not more than a third to a half of all land in the state may be deemed more or less "tolerant" of intensive development— that is, developable without the kind of drainage, land filling, or the like that would cause serious environmental degradation.

• Fourth, the various kinds of economic activity found in Florida—tourism, the retirement industry, agriculture, manufacturing, and so on—each tends to affect the environment differently. Some require minimal alteration of the environment, whereas others require massive alteration, as in the case of the land drainage and reclamation associated with most farming activities in south Florida. Certain activities are plainly incompatible if placed in close proximity—for instance, tourism, on the one hand, and the manufacturing of paper or chemicals, on the other. Others are highly compatible, as in the case of tourism and the growing of citrus in the Central Highlands.

In a word, to enhance environmental quality and foster those economic activities for which the state is uniquely suited, Florida must have policies whereby state and local officials can influence and, when necessary, rigorously control the nature, location, and extent of all new growth and development. To adopt and carry out such policies will be no easy undertaking, with the greatest difficulties more likely to be political rather than technical.

Florida is a place where, until recently, the use of land has reflected an exploitative laissez faire philosophy. But this state may now be at the threshold of great changes, with Floridians beginning to acquire new attitudes toward land and developing methods of land use regulation that would bring conservation and development into a new harmony and creative tension. In the next chapter I describe some of the recent changes in Florida politics and institutions that give reason for hope.

The 2 fight against pork chop rule

A few years ago, before some encouraging changes began in Tallahas-see, one might have concluded that the government of the state of Florida could not possibly cope with an environmental crisis, or, for that matter, with any important and difficult problem. Up until the mid-1960s Florida was a political paradox. However different in population and economy from other southern states, Florida was locked into a political tradition which, in at least some of its essentials, belonged to a backward one-party South. This odd circumstance is understandable only in light of the state's peculiar history. Despite its pleasant climate and natural appeal, Florida was slow to be developed. In 1821 when Florida was acquired by the United States from Spain the territory was still largely unsettled and the Seminoles, whom the federal government would soon dispossess by raw force, owned most of it. Statehood did not come until 1845, after all other territories east of the

Mississippi River except Wisconsin had become states. Even then, Florida had only 55,000 inhabitants. The decisive blow in the Seminole Wars, which went on intermittently for more than two decades, was not struck until 1857, long after Indian wars in other eastern states had become a vague and distant memory.

For another half century or more Florida was to remain an out-of-the-way frontier state off the main line of westward migration. Land was cheap but about two-thirds of all land in Florida was swampy, at least seasonally; less than a tenth consisted of good Class I and II land tillable with a minimum of difficulty. Development was also impeded by a lack of convenient transportation. The construction of a railroad to Miami was not completed until 1896, almost three decades after completion of the first transcontinental railroad. Prior to the railroad, Miami's ties to Key West were closer than those it had with north Florida. And, within south Florida, the Everglades-Big Cypress wilderness made for an effective barrier to travel between the east and west coasts. In the year 1900 Florida as a whole had barely a half million residents, and south Florida was still largely uninhabited except for Palm Beach, the small town of Miami, and a few other settlements along the coastal ridge. Florida's population was not to reach one million until the boom times of the 1920s.

In fact, the twenties marked the beginning of a rapid change from the Old Florida to the New Florida—in everything but politics. The Old Florida was predominantly agricultural and most of its population was in the panhandle and north Florida (the antebellum culture based on cotton and slave-holding had never extended south of Ocala); it clearly belonged, politically and socially, to the Old South. The New Florida was to be, as we have seen, predominantly urban; its population would be largely on the peninsula and made up increasingly of people of northern and midwestern backgrounds; its economy would be tied chiefly to tourism, retirement living, light manu-facturing, and citrus. Events in Miami typified the transition: during the twenties Miami was discovered by large numbers of tourists, promoters, land speculators, and others, with the result that it more than tripled in size; by 1930, with a population of over 110,000, Miami had nearly the population of Jacksonville, Florida's largest city. But the Democratic party, still con-trolled by men brought up in the Old Florida tradition, continued to be the only vehicle of political preferment for men eager to win statewide office. The only real elections were the Democratic primary elections, and these tended to be fought on the basis of personalities rather than on substantive policy issues. A root cause of the backwardness of state government in Florida, as in many states, was the unwillingness of the rural politicians to reapportion legislative seats in keeping with population growth in the urban centers. Their instinct was to refuse stubbornly to yield power. By 1955, less than 18 percent of the voters in Florida could elect a majority of both the Florida House and Senate.

PORK CHOP RULE

In the 1950s the rural politicians who ran the legislature became popularly known as the "Pork Chop Gang." This group was well named, for when state appropriations were passed out, its members got the best cuts for their home constituencies. Racetrack parimutuel tax receipts, for example, were divided evenly among the sixty-seven counties rather than on a per capita basis. Also, rural counties were favored in the apportionment of road funds, and today one can find numerous monuments to Pork Chop rule, including a costly bridge far out in the Florida Keys between Big Pine Key and a small, uninhabited place called No Name Key. The rural legislators who controlled the Florida House and Senate belonged for the most part to the atmosphere of the small-town county seats, with their Confederate statues and brick courthouses. Yet the Pork Chop spirit was not confined to these legislators—indeed, it has ever been universal—and the term, as I use it here, characterizes the overall system of state government which prevailed up into the late 1960s. In fact, I should point out that there were some rural politicians who were fairminded and some urban ones who reeked of pork. Haydon Burns, the last governor of the Pork Chop era (in office, 1965–66), was a former mayor of Jacksonville; he quickly became discredited in the public eye by his particularly egregious way of favoring his campaign contributors with state contracts and by behavior such as accepting the loan of an airplane from a major grocery chain.

If the legislature had a saving grace it was that it was seldom in session. A legislator was once even reported to have suggested, only half facetiously, that, instead of meeting sixty days every two years, the legislature should meet two days once every sixty years. The legislature was truly a weak reed. Members had no staff; committees were incredibly numerous (fifty to sixty in each house) and anarchic (a chairman, holding his colleagues' proxies, would sometimes hold a "meeting" by himself); and much of the legislature's time was taken up with local bills and special acts passed on behalf of counties and municipalities simply because these local jurisdictions had not been vested with general powers of government or "home rule." For instance, of the more than 1,740 bills passed in 1955 about three-fourths were local measures having the scope of a county or municipal ordinance. Traditionally, city and county governments in Florida had lacked broad law-making authority and had found it necessary to go to the legislature with local bills on matters as small as the care and feeding of the sheriff's bloodhounds. The executive branch was no more effective than the legislative. There were more than 200 independent agencies and boards, these having been created haphazardly over the years by the legislature acting in response to problems of the moment. For instance, in the field of agriculture alone, besides an elected commissioner, there was a marketing board, a marketing bureau, an avocado and lime commission, a citrus commission, an egg commission, a milk commission, a plant insect and disease board, a livestock board, a soil conservation board, and a board of forestry. Furthermore, lines of authority were highly confused, with some 200-odd units of government reporting directly to the governor, others reporting to independent boards appointed by the governor, and still others reporting to that anomalous institution known as the Florida Cabinet.

The "cabinet system," which survives today (in somewhat modified form), goes back to the post-Reconstruction era of the nineteenth century and seems to have been designed deliberately to make the executive weak. The governor shares power with six other independently elected officials, namely, the attorney general, the secretary of state, the comptroller, and the commissioners of agriculture, education, and insurance (the latter also serving as state treasurer). These officials make up the cabinet and serve with the governor as the ex-officio members of various state boards, which control some important state agencies and decide some important questions in regard to use of natural resources. What is more, at the time of which I write, the cabinet and not the governor alone made up the annual state budget. The governor's position was further weakened by the fact that, while the cabinet members could succeed themselves (for a member to serve several four-year terms has been common), he could not. While a new governor was picking his way through the administrative and political thickets in Tallahassee, the older cabinet members, with their friends and allies in the legislature and the state bureaucracy, held an important advantage over him. The Florida cabinet system was, and to a considerable extent still is, a political scientist's nightmare.

Both the legislature and the cabinet were susceptible to overtures by lobbyists for industry and business, including large agricultural enterprises. Around Tallahassee the lobbyists were often referred to as the "third house," and the Florida House and Senate were frankly regarded by some of their own members as little more than conduits for the passage of special interest legislation. Lobbyists usually wrote the bills members would introduce and then helped grease the way to passage by doing favors for legislators—buying liquor and meals, picking up hotel bills, providing plane trips home and a variety of other "fringe benefits." The committees were usually shot through with conflicts of interest—bankers running the banking committee, insurance men dominating the insurance committee, and so on. The cabinet, also, was (and remains) vulnerable to lobbying. A particular member of the cabinet such as the commissioner of education or insurance is identified by the public chiefly with his own portfolio—that is to say, with education or insurance; yet this official votes on many questions far removed from his specialty. For instance, his vote may help decide whether a water resource project is included in the budget, whether an oil drilling permit is issued, whether a particular tract of state land is sold, or whether the dredging and filling of an estuary is allowed. Lobbyists and attorneys for interests seeking such things have traditionally cultivated the cabinet members and their aides. By voting "right" members have set themselves up for generous campaign contributions the next election year.

Perhaps the single most important reason why the state capital was lobbyist-dominated during the Pork Chop era was that some of the major interests represented were especially influential in the rural counties from which most of the legislators came. For instance, the pulp and paper industry is strictly a regional thing in Florida, but it has great influence in north Florida and the panhandle. The legendary Ed Ball, head of the Alfred I. DuPont interests in Florida, (which has included the largest chain of banks in the state, the Florida East Coast Railroad, and the St. Joe Paper Company) was a resourceful behind-the-scenes puller of political strings.[1] In central Florida, the citrus, the phosphate, and the cattle ranching interests had special influence both at the county courthouses and in Tallahassee. And in Florida, as in most states, the influence of the major utilities was pervasive inasmuch as their activities extended throughout the state. Florida Power and Light Company, the state's largest utility, was reputed to be especially potent. Associated Industries of Florida was established in 1920 by big business and industry to be a lobby permanently on the Tallahassee scene. The business lobbyists had legitimate interests to represent, of course; the unfortunate thing was that the competing voices—what few there were—were pathetically weak. Organized labor has never been strong in Florida outside of a few places such as Miami and Tampa, and it was no accident that Florida was the first state to enact a "right-to-work" law barring the union shop. Such conservation organizations as existed were primarily local groups oriented to local issues, and no collective voice for conservation was heard in Tallahassee. The predictable result of this state of affairs was improper exploitation of natural resources, a low level of public services in fields such as education and welfare,[2] and a regressive tax structure. For instance, in the matter of tax policy, a constitutional amendment adopted in 1924 prohibited the imposition of either an income tax or an inheritance tax. The principal sources of state revenue were the sales tax and gasoline tax, with significant secondary sources including

1. Ball, now in his eighties, is still active, and if he does not have the political clout he once did, he is still treated with respect and caution. Note, for instance, the fact that in February, 1974, the U.S. Army Corps of Engineers withdrew an earlier demand that Ball remove a fence erected to keep boaters from following the Wakulla River, a navigable stream traditionally open to public passage, upstream to his tourist attraction and wildlife sanctuary at Wakulla Springs.
2. This continues to be the situation today, although some improvement has occurred. Neal R. Pierce in his *The Megastates of America* (New York: W. W. Norton, 1972) reported that, on a per capita basis, Florida ranked forty-fifth in the United States in its expenditures for public welfare, forty-eighth in spending on highways, twenty-eighth in support of local schools, forty-first in support of higher education. In the late 1960s state and local tax collections represented only 3.2 percent of personal income, Florida ranking thirty-first in the nation in that regard.

taxes on liquor, cigarettes, and parimutuel betting. Except for a "homestead exemption" written into the constitution in 1934—exempting from local property taxes the first $5,000 of a home's assessed valuation—the Florida tax code offered small comfort for the ordinary citizen.

Even allowing for the understandable eagerness for growth and development in a state that only recently had been a frontier, the degree to which the legislature and cabinet favored resource exploiting interests was unseemly. A start toward establishing systems of state forests and parks was made in the 1920s and 1930s—the parks program gaining momentum from the activities of the federal Civilian Conservation Corps. And, in the late 1950s, an initial step was taken toward conservation of tidal and estuarine lands. But, for the most part, official attitudes towards Florida's natural resources favored more or less unchecked private exploitation. Between 1955 and 1967, the cabinet sold some 28,000 acres of state-owned submerged lands to developers. So freehanded was the cabinet in allowing dredging and filling, that in some instances entire estuaries were in danger of being converted to labyrinths of land fills and finger canals—Boca Ciega Bay near St. Petersburg being the classic example. The phosphate mining and processing companies, despite all the environmental damage caused by them in central Florida, were allowed to escape payment of a severance tax. Proposals for such a tax were introduced repeatedly in the legislature but got short shrift.[3] Industrial polluters of waterways were even allowed effective immunity from such antipollution laws as did exist. Under a 1913 law the state board of health was supposed to prosecute any party polluting public waters, but this statute was not enforced and was openly flouted for years by the chemical, pulp-and-paper, and citrus processing industries. For some polluters, even the mere possibility that the law might be enforced was removed. In 1941 the legislature declared that Nassau County (north of Jacksonville) was an "industrial county" and that henceforth discharges of sewage and industrial wastes into its tidal waters were to be considered as in the public interest. Thus, the subsequent defilement of the Amelia River and destruction of shrimp nursery beds by pulp mills operated by the Rayonier Corporation and the Container Corporation of America were, by legislative fiat, defined as acts of corporate citizenship instead of as crimes against nature. As if to demonstrate that the Nassau County act was no aberration, the legislature enacted a second such measure in 1947 and thereby classified the once beautiful Fenholloway River, in Taylor County on the Gulf Coast, as an industrial sewer for the use of the Buckeye Cellulose Corporation.

The legislature consistently put the interests of industry and private property ahead of the state's—and the public's—own interests. For example, while the state road department could exercise power of eminent

3. In 1971, after a twenty-year struggle over the issue, such a tax was finally imposed.

domain, this agency was required to pay the attorney's fees of property owners in condemnation cases (this law applies even today). And, incredibly, in south Florida where the state was establishing water conservation areas, it was sometimes acquiring only flowage easements even though the price of the easement might be nearly as much as what it would have cost to buy the land outright. Perhaps the most blatant instance yet of favoritism for a private interest occurred in 1965 when Governor Burns appointed Leonard Rosen, board chairman of the Gulf American Land Corporation, to the Florida Land Sales Board—this happening not long after Gulf American had been summoned before the board for deceptive sales practices. The Land Sales Act of 1963 had required that three of the board's five members be from the industry, but the legislature had not gone so far as to specify that a company known to be among the act's flagrant violators should be represented.

THE PORK CHOPPERS
OVERTHROWN

The first major blow to Pork Chop rule was the U.S. Supreme Court's 1962 decision in *Baker* v. *Carr* declaring the malapportionment of legislative seats to be unconstitutional. This ruling was not implemented in Florida until 1967, but, once it was, many able new legislators suddenly appeared in Tallahassee from long-deprived urban constituencies such as Miami, Orlando, and St. Petersburg. To have merely substituted a new legislative majority elected from urban areas for the old majority elected from rural areas and small towns would not, of course, have sufficed to bring about legislative reform. But the new urban legislators included leaders of exceptional ability. Men such as Frederick Shultz of Jacksonville, Ralph Turlington of Gainesville, and Richard Pettigrew and Marshall Harris of Miami set about to achieve important changes: the number of committees was drastically reduced; egregious conflicts of interest in the makeup of committees were generally avoided; competent, full-time committee staffs were established; proxy voting was abolished; the salary of legislators was raised from $100 per month to $12,000 a year; and (after a constitutional amendment) the legislature began meeting annually instead of biennially. The Florida Legislature, once one of the nation's worst, was now becoming one of the best and would soon be so recognized—in 1971 the Citizens Conference on State Legislatures ranked the Florida Legislature fourth in the nation (behind only the California, New York, and Illinois legislatures) on the basis of criteria such as representativeness and accountability.

Reform of the legislature, in makeup and procedure, was essential in the overthrow of Pork Chop rule but there were other almost equally significant developments. Consider the following:

The Break-Up of the One-Party System. The anomaly of a state with a population more nearly northern and midwestern than southern in background behaving politically like a part of the Old South finally came to an end in the 1960s. The erosion of the Democratic party's monopoly position began very gradually in the 1950s, and by 1962 there were two Republican congressmen from Florida. But the breakthrough came in 1966 when the governorship, a U.S. Senate seat, a third congressional seat, and a respectable number of seats in the Florida legislature were won by Republicans. This development had been inevitable in light of the massive demographic changes of the postwar years. In a political sense, peninsular Florida, or most of it except Miami and Tampa (both strongly Democratic by virtue of a big labor vote), was becoming a giant suburbia with decided conservative leanings and a tendency to vote Republican.[4] The victory won by Claude Kirk—the first Republican elected governor since 1872—was to be particularly significant in terms of conservation policies. For the erratic and at times demagogic Kirk, however great his faults, was probably as little beholden to resource-user interests as any governor Florida has ever had.

New Constitution and Executive. The newly constituted legislature, with Governor Kirk's encouragement, approved a new constitution to replace one going back to 1885 that had been amended more than 150 times. The new constitution, handily approved by the voters in 1968, provided for further governmental reforms: it allowed counties to opt for home rule, called for consolidation of the 200-plus state agencies and boards into not more than 25 departments, and permitted the governor to succeed himself. And whereas the constitution of 1885 had specified that the governor "shall be assisted" by the cabinet officers—this vague language having provided over all these years the constitutional sanction for a collegial form of executive—the new constitution left it entirely to the legislature to define what, if any, responsibilities the cabinet members would have beyond their individual portfolios as commissioners of education, insurance, or whatever. In the Executive Reorganization Act of 1969, the legislature retained the cabinet system but it increased the powers of the governor by giving him alone responsibility for formulating the annual budget and by placing some newly created departments—most notably, the departments of Administration and Transportation—under his exclusive control. The Department of Administration was, without doubt, potentially the most important in government because it contained both the budget division *and* the newly created Bureau of Planning.

4. See Manning Dauer, "Florida: The Different State," in William Havard, ed., *The Changing Politics of the South* (Baton Rouge, Louisiana: Louisiana University Press, 1972).

Government in the Sunshine. In 1967 the legislature enacted a law stating that all meetings of state and local governmental bodies at which business is conducted are to be public. Known as the "Government in the Sunshine" law, this statute has been interpreted by the attorney general and the courts to apply to virtually any conversation between elected officials in which public business is discussed. Officials violating the sunshine law can be fined or jailed, and some local officials have in fact been convicted for having met to talk over such things as firing the city manager. If the law goes a bit far, as some officials believe, it nevertheless has found widespread public acceptance. Nobody wants to see a return to the secrecy and frequent rumors of under-the-table dealings once endemic in Tallahassee and in Florida's city halls and county courthouses. By enacting the sunshine law, the legislature struck a hard blow at Pork Chop rule.

An Aggressive Press. The Florida press contributed substantially to reform of state government, both by exposure of the things that happened in Tallahassee and by force of editorial comment. Although the quality of regional newspapers in the United States is by no means uniformly high, Florida by good fortune has two of the better ones: the *Miami Herald* and the *St. Petersburg Times.* In addition, newspapers such as the *Miami News* and the *Tampa Tribune* do a creditable job. The political influence of the *Miami Herald* has been especially potent, in part because of the *Herald's* sway with the big Dade County legislative delegation, the members of which, having to run at large in a county of 1.2 million inhabitants, feel particularly dependent on favorable newspaper treatment. The vigor and independence of the press corps in Tallahassee was illustrated by an incident that occurred in 1967, when the legislature was meeting to consider reapportionment. The correspondents decided to rebel against the State Senate's common practice of meeting in closed session, ostensibly to consider state personnel matters. Led by *Herald* correspondent John McDermott, they refused to leave the gallery. They were then forcibly evicted, but the senators suffered enough embarrassment from this episode that never again have they chosen to meet in secret.

A NEW SET OF ACTORS

In the more favorable political and institutional setting that existed once the Pork Chop Gang lost its favored position, an important new set of actors emerged on the Florida scene and began influencing state policy with respect to the conservation of land and water resources. The new actors generally fell into three categories: there were (i) the conservation group leaders and their close allies, the professional environmentalists, usually either university-based or employed by a federal or state agency; (ii) a few individuals such as Nathaniel P. Reed, Governor Kirk's environmental adviser, who were either actually a part of the Kirk Administration or who were quite close to it; and (iii) a growing number of legislators, mostly from urban areas such as Miami and Orlando, who were greatly concerned personally at the increasing degradation of the Florida environment and conscious of a growing conservationist sentiment among their constituents. This sentiment was part of a gradually rising concern nationally about loss of environmental quality, but, because the problem in Florida was of a particularly aggravated kind, the concern among environmentalists there was assuming a special urgency.

ENVIRONMENTALISTS AND THE CONSERVATION GROUPS. The influence that a small number of biologists have had on public opinion in Florida cannot easily be overestimated. The interaction between these scientists and local conservation organizations was going on in a small way in the early 1960s and increased markedly toward the end of the decade. Arthur R. Marshall, a marine biologist who is now probably known to a larger public than any other environmentalist in Florida, had an early part in encouraging the Florida conservation organizations to take a more activist role. The U.S. Bureau of Sport Fisheries and Wildlife maintains a field office at Vero Beach, and, in 1960, Marshall became head of this office under discouraging circumstances. The U.S. Army Corps of Engineers, he felt, was undertaking water projects and granting dredge-and-fill permits with little regard for his office's assessments as to probable biological impact. Furthermore, because the Vero Beach office had almost no contact with the public, it was not influencing the decisions of the corps and local and state permitting authorities through public opinion. Marshall began looking for speaking opportunities, and made frequent appearances before small local conservation groups, especially the Izaak Walton League chapters. "I used to make speeches to as few as seven people," he told me. Marshall assiduously kept up his contacts with these groups and overlooked few chances to send scientific papers, news clippings, or other information that might help them mount protests against the continuing loss of biologically productive wetlands. Little by little, Marshall became an increasingly effective "biopolitician" (as one of his friends has described him) with a considerable personal following. In the late 1960s Marshall, in one of his last efforts before leaving government service to head an applied ecology program at the University of Miami, was one of the principal authors of the Interior Department report that had much to do with a White House decision to overrule Dade County's plans for a jetport in the Big Cypress.

The traditional conservation organizations themselves gained substantial new strength as the 1960s progressed, even though the number of people devoting substantial time to environmental issues was small then and remains so today. In the late 1960s the Florida Audubon Society became a very different kind of group from what it had been earlier. Although first established in 1900 to crusade against the slaughter of the plume birds, Florida Audubon had over the years lost its militancy and become dedicated chiefly to organizing field trips and establishing wildlife sanctuaries. Its membership in 1960 was less than 1,500, and nobody thought of it as a potent force for conservation. However, under the leadership of C. Russell Mason, formerly with the Massachusetts Audubon Society, Florida Audubon began to grow during the 1960s, in environmental and political sophistication as well as in membership (the latter would reach 25,000 by 1973). Audubon conventions came increasingly to focus on the distress of various regional ecosystems and the assaults upon them by private developers and public works agencies. Mason was to remain director of the society until succeeded in 1971 by Hal Scott, a leader who would further enhance Audubon's influence in Tallahassee.

A still more remarkable transformation occurred in the case of the Florida Wildlife Federation. About half of the federation's 30,000 members are hunters, and there was a time, not long ago, when the federation would brook no conservation proposal that might interfere with hunting. In 1957, S. H. Dubon, president of the federation, writing to oppose a proposed expansion of the boundaries of the Everglades National Park, advised the U.S. Senate's Subcommittee on Public Lands that "We feel the park at present has all the land they need for the birds and mosquitoes." In the late 1960s, however, John C. Jones, a West Palm Beach plumbing contractor, emerged as an aggressive leader who wanted the federation to have a voice in Tallahassee on a broad range of conservation issues, from protecting the alligator to stopping the channelization of streams and the drainage of wetlands. In 1972, Jones would give up his plumbing business and become the federation's full-time executive head and legislative lobbyist. Still another group that was eventually to emerge as influential in shaping public perceptions of environmental issues was the Florida Association of the American Institute of Architects (FAAIA) under the leadership of its commissioner on public affairs, Nils M. Schweizer of Winter Park. As previously noted, the FAAIA was a cosponsor of the Red Flag Charrette that called attention to the growing threat to various Florida ecosystems.

University-based environmentalists also had a major part in the late 1960s in bringing about the new awareness of an environmental crisis. Research and teaching done at the University of Miami's School of Marine and Atmospheric Sciences was especially useful in explaining the functioning and value of estuarine ecosystems. For instance, marine biologists had long been convinced that mangroves played a vital part in the estuarine system but it had remained for two graduate students, W. E. Odum and E. J. Heald, to show how mangrove leaves entered and enriched the food chain. As I shall later relate in detail, environmentalists at the University of Florida had a key role in beginning the opposition to the Cross Florida Barge Canal and in documenting the case against it.

THE GOVERNOR'S ADVISERS. The night that Claude Kirk won the 1966 Republican primary election for Governor he was dining at Hobe Sound with Nathaniel Reed, a young (then thirty-three) and quite wealthy Republican, who could be useful to him in raising money for the general election campaign. This was a significant encounter because, as a result of it, Nathaniel Reed was to emerge as an important figure in efforts to bring growth and development in Florida under control and to protect environmental quality. At that election night dinner Reed promised to help Kirk raise campaign money and also agreed to join with Lyman E. Rogers, the Republican chairman in Marion County (Ocala), in drafting Kirk's basic platform plank on natural resource management.

Reed is dynamic and exhibits the openness and self-confidence that one can look for in a man of good will, surefooted intelligence, and independent means. Reed felt a genuine commitment to conservation, a cause he came to partly from his enthusiasm for hunting and fishing. In the early sixties, for instance, Reed had been outraged by the siltation caused by flood control discharges from Lake Okeechobee. The silt was smothering the grass beds in the St. Lucie Inlet and lower Indian River, and ruining what up to then had been superb sea trout fishing. As Reed remembers it, he was once evicted from a hearing by the Flood Control District Board for speaking out of turn. Reed's family had developed Jupiter Island—a favorite wintering place for wealthy northerners—and he himself was active in the family real estate business. But, essentially, Reed represented old money and a new motivation: his real interest was in public life and Claude Kirk was to be the vehicle sending him on his way.

Kirk was able to win the governorship apparently with a minimum of commitments to campaign contributors. Despite some subsequent political and personal aberrations, he came to be regarded by many Floridians as the first and only "conservation governor" the state had had up to that time. And Reed, whom Kirk named as his $1-a-year environmental adviser and eventually also as chairman of the Florida Pollution Control Board, usually had the governor's ear. Reed, with Kirk's full approval, tended to dramatize environmental issues by his somewhat hyperbolic pronouncements, his constant comings and goings about the state in his private plane, and the stir and bustle that attended his movements. Among conservation leaders around Florida, whenever a problem arose that called for special attention, the byword was, "Call Nat."

A plank in the conservation platform prepared by Reed, Lyman Rogers, and other advisers called for Kirk to establish a Governor's Natural Resources Committee to be made up of prominent environmentalists and conservation leaders. Such a committee was in fact established with Rogers, a forceful individual with a messianic interest in "saving Florida," as chairman. Through the new committee and Nat Reed, conservation interests had excellent entrée to the executive branch of government, although there were important parts of it controlled by the cabinet and not by the governor alone. Where the conservation interest remained weakly organized and represented was in the legislature.

CONSERVATION '70s. One day in July 1969 some fifty-two persons, including Nat Reed, Lyman Rogers, most of the other members of the Governor's Natural Resources Committee and some sympathetic legislators, met in Orlando and established Conservation '70s, to serve as a conservation lobby in Tallahassee. At the same time, another important new group, the Florida Defenders of the Environment, was created, principally to support a court assault on the Cross Florida Barge Canal project—but, of this, I defer discussion until later. The unique thing about "C-70s," as it was called, was that half the members of its twenty-member board of trustees were senators and representatives and a few were heads of state agencies. Having legislators as trustees, of course, gave C-70s the advantage of being an insider to the legislative process. A disadvantage was that, while the legislators who served as trustees all had some conservation interests, some also had strongly conflicting development interests. For instance, C-70s was neutralized on the issue of the Cross Florida Barge Canal—a project most of the trustees opposed—because one trustee was a House committee chairman committed to defend the project. Yet, so much was needed in the way of basic conservation legislation on which wide agreement was possible, that the advantages to be gained from giving legislators a place in C-70s were perhaps compelling, at least for the short run. Because of leadership problems C-70s eventually faded as a presence in Tallahassee, but not before demonstrating that conservation could be a potent lobbying force.

FRUITS OF REFORM

In 1967, as the first governmental reforms were being accomplished, the legislature enacted two important conservation measures. One was a law which, as subsequently amended, has given Florida a policy and a mechanism for control of air and water pollution probably more effective than those of most states—admittedly a modest claim. A five-member board appointed by the governor has ultimate responsibility for issuing waste discharge permits and enforcing compliance with air and water quality standards. If not satisfied with a municipality's efforts to bring sewage effluents up to prescribed levels of treatment, the board can order that hookups of additional new buildings to the system be limited or stopped, although here the board faces formidable political constraints. As its chairman from 1969 until early 1971, Reed gave the Florida Pollution Control Board high visibility: three federal-state pollution abatement conferences were called at the state's request and a start was made in cleaning up Florida waters. Another landmark conservation measure enacted in 1967 was a statute requiring a biological survey as a prerequisite to any state and local decisions allowing alteration of tidal lands or the bottoms of state-owned lakes. This came as an amendment to the Bulkhead Act of 1957, by which local governments may issue dredge-and-fill permits and establish bulkhead lines defining the outer limits of waterfront development, subject in both cases to the approval of the governor and cabinet. In establishing a procedure for the issuance of permits for land use in tidal wetlands, the Bulkhead Act had been quite advanced for its time; its weakness, however, was that no conservation criteria had been prescribed to guide the decisions of local governing bodies and the cabinet. The 1967 law, known as the Randell Act after its principal sponsor, Representative Ted Randell of Fort Myers (who had become alarmed at the loss of good fishing from dredging and filling), in effect directed the cabinet to weigh the benefits the public might derive from a proposed waterfront development against the benefits to be lost from destruction of marine habitat. With passage of the Randell Act, owners of submerged lands could no longer assume that these lands were available to be filled or used as a source of fill. Governor Kirk, at Nat Reed's urging, frequently opposed applications for dredge-and-fill permits and thereby made it harder for the six Democrats making up the cabinet to vote for their approval.

The next big year for environmental legislation was 1970, the year C-70s, with a full-time representative in Tallahassee, began its lobbying effort. At the 1970 legislative session forty-one bills sponsored by C-70s were enacted. Most of these measures were noncontroversial and comparatively minor, as for instance the one making it illegal to remove pollution-control devices from vehicles; some others, such as the pesticide control bill, were enacted in an emasculated form; and certain important measures —the environmental inventory act is a good example—were not accompanied by the appropriations needed to carry them out. Nevertheless, taken overall, what C-70s had accomplished was impressive and at least a few of the measures passed were of real consequence. For instance, constitutional amendments permitting the issuance of sewer bonds and banning the sale of state-owned submerged lands *except in the public interest* (thus placing a heavy burden on parties seeking to purchase such lands) were approved for submission to the voters, who subsequently adopted them. Also, a law mandating minimum construction setback lines along Atlantic and Gulf beaches was passed. This act, like the Bulkhead Act, made the decisions of local governments subject to cabinet approval—a new affirmation of the state's role in the continuing evolution of policies governing growth and land use. In addition, a Coastal Coordinating Council was established and instructed to prepare a plan for the coastal area, a first step toward the zoning of coastal lands.

Another important year for environmental legislation was 1972, when Florida's land crisis was recognized in Tallahassee. The preceding year, Claude Kirk had been replaced as governor by Reubin Askew, a lawyer and former state senator from Pensacola who defeated Kirk by campaigning boldly on a platform calling for a corporate income tax. In Askew's first year in office, the legislature and the Florida voters (by referendum) did impose such a tax despite determined special interest lobbying—the clearest evidence yet that the era of Pork Chop rule was over. In 1972, after some compromises by his allies in the legislature, Askew won enactment of land and water management bills proposed by the task force that he had appointed after the alarming Everglades drought of 1971. This legislation, to be described later, is related intimately to the history of south Florida's settlement and development, dealt with in the next part of this book.

Land disposal and drainage

For the first century and longer after the attainment of statehood, Florida, as a frontier province, was shaped by men preoccupied with growth and development. Given the peculiarities of the Florida terrain, development necessarily involved making major changes in a complex natural environment that was still little understood. Moreover, the attitudes that prevailed during the state's first several decades were vastly different from those of today. The whole modern concept of "wilderness" as something worth preserving was scarcely thinkable then, for most of Florida *was* wilderness and many people regarded the Everglades, the Big Cypress, and the vast stretches of coastal mangroves as obstacles to progress. Wildlife was so common and abundant that few people thought of it as having value. Men with rifles and shotguns stood on the decks of the Oklawaha River paddle-wheelers, shooting at alligators, limpkins, and other creatures for amusement. In scenes of almost unbelievable wantonness, plume hunters "shot out" the bird rookeries of Florida Bay and the Ten Thousand Islands and left the starving nestlings for the vultures. The general failure to appreciate and better understand Florida's natural environment was in part a reflection of the ethical and esthetic sensibilities of the times, but it was also an indication of the fact that much basic information about the chain of life and complex hydrology of south Florida was then nowhere available. Drainage of the Everglades and dredging and filling in the coastal estuaries would, in time, bring major problems, but of this Florida officials and most citizens had no premonition, although there would be a few prophetic outcries.

The first fifty to seventy-five years of the state of Florida's history were of great importance in establishing trends in land use. The laws passed, the institutions established, and even the maps and surveys made were to be of enduring significance. In the beginning, the state and federal governments had full authority over most of the land in Florida, for they owned it. Yet, paradoxically, except in the case of Everglades drainage, government was to have a distinctly secondary role in Florida's early development, principally because all major sources of money were private. During this era, all government—federal, state, and local—was, of course, small and financially weak; industry, on the other hand, especially in the North and Midwest, was expanding rapidly and generating large amounts of investment capital. Half the nation was a newly opened frontier made up of new states vying to attract people and money; in bidding for Florida's share, state officials knew that the only major negotiable assets at their command were the public lands, and these they gave away recklessly. Among those regarded as figures of the first importance in Florida's early development there was but one politician—the liberal reform governor who began drainage of the Everglades. For this one politician there were a half dozen private capitalists and promoters. There were, for instance, the Philadelphia saw manufacturer who bought 4 million acres of Florida land and opened up the Lake Okeechobee region and the Kissimmee basin; the ex-Standard Oil Company tycoon who built a Florida railroad empire; the midwestern industrialist and promoter who built Miami Beach; and the streetcar advertising millionaire who bought up half the Big Cypress watershed and founded his own county.

THE CHALLENGE OF A
SWAMPY DOMAIN

SURVEYORS' ERRORS. At the coming of statehood, only a relatively small part of Florida was made up of privately held lands, that is to say, property (chiefly in north Florida and the panhandle) already sold by the U.S. government or disposed of earlier in Spanish land grants subsequently confirmed by the United States. More than three-quarters of Florida was still in public lands owned by the federal government. By early in this century, several millions of acres of the federal domain had been disposed of through sales, grants to homesteaders, and withdrawals for national forests and wildlife refuges. But some 24.2 million acres, or nearly 65 percent of Florida, had been given to the state.

The special federal land grants to the state included extensive reaches of submerged or "sovereignty" lands, but they need not and should not have. Under the Common Law such lands are held in trust for the people by the sovereign, or government, hence title to them vested in the state automatically once statehood status was attained. Surveying the submerged lands accurately was a manifestly impossible job under nineteenth-century conditions. These lands included all bottoms of navigable lakes and all tidal bottoms—and note here that, while Florida has 1,300 miles of *general* shoreline, it has 9,000 miles of *detailed* shoreline (the latter including all indentations and the shores of large and small islands), a shoreline longer by far than that of any other state except Alaska. While, under Common Law doctrines, a state may sell or permit the alteration of some limited part of its sovereignty lands, these must in general be kept open and useful to the public for navigation, fishing, and other purposes. Federal surveyors were assigned to prepare maps on which the coastal shorelines and the shores of navigable lakes would be shown by "meander lines"—that is, by lines showing the sinuosities of the shore. All tidal waters were considered as navigable, potentially or in fact; for freshwater lakes the test of navigibility was more complex, but a Federal Land Department manual of 1855 indicated that any lake of 25 acres or larger should be treated as navigable. Without modern aids such as aircraft and motorboats, a surveyor might have to venture out into vast swampy domains inhabited by mosquitoes, cottonmouth moccasins, and 12-foot alligators (which may have been harmless but looked otherwise). Only 190 lakes were "meandered" by the surveyors although even within a single central Florida county, such as Lake or Polk, lakes of 25 acres or larger exist by the hundreds. The result was the tragic loss of a public resource, for the fact that a lake had not been meandered led to the legal presumption that it was not navigable and, hence, that its bottom was not sovereignty land. The lakes not meandered were treated as swamp and overflow lands, to which (as will be explained shortly) the state was to gain title but then sell or give away. In this manner thousands of lakes, including some of great beauty enclosed by bell-bottomed columns of cypress, became private bodies of water on which the public would go only at the sufferance of the owners or by trespass. Similarly, extensive tidal bottoms, running to hundreds of thousands if not millions of acres, were lost to public ownership and control when federal surveyors made large errors in establishing meander lines representing the line of mean high water along the Florida coast. Thus, when meander lines were mistakenly established below mean high water, and sometimes well offshore, the boundaries described in deeds covering adjacent uplands actually took in sovereignty lands. Several generations of Florida attorneys have, by now, earned much

of their livelihood by helping clients interpret, defend, or challenge confused and cloudy titles to submerged lands.

THE SWAMP LANDS ACT OF 1850. Although there was no lack of naturally well-drained land to support the small Florida population of the early statehood era, state officials were even then contemplating Everglades drainage efforts which, when later undertaken, were to prove so costly, difficult, and controversial as to frustrate the plans of engineers, politicians, and settlers for nearly a century. Under the Swamp Lands Act passed by Congress in 1850, the state of Florida, along with all other states that had been carved from the federal public domain, was allowed to claim "swamp and overflowed lands" for the exclusive purpose of making them productive by drain-

At left, new railroads open up south Florida at the turn of the century; below, dredge cutting the first Everglades drainage canals; at right, Miccosuki Indians capitalize on their only remaining assets.

Patricia Caulfield

State Photographic Archives, Strozier Library, Florida State University

age and construction of levees. Florida claimed 20.3 million acres, most of this property truly being inland swamps and marshes, although there were indeed sovereignty lands included and some lands which were—a bit of fraud here—high and dry. The some 24 million acres in federal domain lands received by Florida under the Swamp Lands Act and other statutes was several million acres more than was received by the largest western states, such as California and Montana.

AN EARLY DREAM: "RECLAIMING" THE EVERGLADES. Contributing to the interest in Everglades drainage was the widespread belief, to which there apparently were few dissenters, that "reclaiming" the Everglades would be both easy and profitable. One of the legislators who had pressed for passage of the Swamp Lands Act was Florida's senator J. D. Westcott, Jr., who arranged for the government to commission a study of the feasibility of Everglades drainage. This study was made by Buckingham Smith, a St. Augustine attorney, who reported his findings in 1848. Smith said that the waters of the Everglades basin were at least 12 feet above sea level, and that the glades could be drained by giving Lake Okeechobee outlets to the Gulf and the Atlantic and by making drainage canals of streams such as the Miami and Hillsborough rivers. Smith described the Everglades as beautiful and awesome, and likely to engender a poetic mood in persons of "romantic imagination. . . . But if the visitor [to the Everglades] is a man of practical, utilitarian turn of thought, the first and abiding impression is the utter worthlessness [of the region] to civilized man, in its present condition. . . ."[1] Drainage of the Everglades, he added, would surely make possible the cultivation of tropical fruits that could be grown nowhere else in the union and might make possible the production of sugar and other important staples. Smith envisioned great prosperity for the Everglades region and possibly the creation of a new state, and his belief that the Everglades could easily be drained was shared by a number of army officers and surveyors familiar with the glades. For instance, General William S. Harney, who was in the Everglades during the Seminole Wars, said that "millions" of acres of highly valuable land could be reclaimed from the region, which otherwise would remain a wasteland "fit only for the resort of reptiles."[2] Furthermore, Harney said, success of this venture in tropical agriculture would make the United States largely independent of the West Indies and would in less than five years lead to the settlement of at least 100,000 persons in the Everglades region. "Our coast in south Florida is now extremely exposed in time of war," he said. "This population would protect it . . . and tend to the security

1. Buckingham Smith, *Report on the Everglades*, S. Doc. 242, 30 Cong. (1848), included in S. Doc. 89, 62 Cong. 1 sess. (1911), pp. 46–54. Senate Document 89 is a compendium of the reports and official correspondence pertaining to Everglades drainage written up to that time.
2. Ibid., pp. 56–7.

of the entire southern portion of the Union in an eminent degree." Harney's statement accompanied the Buckingham Smith report along with those by a dozen other individuals similarly optimistic about Everglades drainage. Only one of the statements solicited took a contrary view, and that one was by Stephen R. Mallory, the Key West customs inspector who later became a U.S. Senator and then secretary of the Confederate Navy. Mallory acknowledged that he had not made the careful studies necessary to know whether the Everglades could be drained or not. "But I have been in the glades and about them, from Jupiter to Miami, much. I have ate of its fish, drank of its waters, smelt of its snakes and alligators, and waded through its mud to my middle for weeks, and am *au fait* upon all these, besides possessing some little acquaintance with its mosquitoes and horseflies, both of which can be recommended. I have also, together with a friend, taken soundings with poles, marked for the purpose, from our boats for miles and miles; all of which labor might as well have been expended in surveying the moon. . . . My own impression is that large tracts of the glades are fully as low as the adjoining sea, and can never be drained; that some lands around the margins may be reclaimed by drainage or by dyking, but that it will be found wholly out of the question to drain all the Everglades."[3] Alone among the early "authorities" on the Everglades, Mallory displayed a becoming modesty in the face of the complexities of the Everglades environment, some of which still defy analysis today.

LAND DISPOSAL

THE "I.I. BOARD" IN RECEIVERSHIP. No Everglades drainage project actually was undertaken until the 1880s, and by then the drainage issue had become closely intertwined with questions of railroad construction. In 1851, the Florida legislature had established an Internal Improvement Board to manage all of the state's lands, especially the vast acreage of swamp and overflowed lands. Inasmuch as the encouragement of railroad and canal construction was a primary purpose of the new board, its members included two railroad presidents. In 1885, the legislature acted favorably upon a recommendation of this board to replace it with a new body—the Board of Trustees of the Internal Improvement Fund, which, along with its predecessor, will be referred to here as the "I.I. Board."

Prior to 1885, the I.I. Board had been made up of the governor and four of his appointees, the state comptroller, the treasurer, the secretary of agriculture, and the registrar of state lands. Under the new constitution, the board was made up of the governor and several independently elected cabinet officers. Part of the I.I. Board's mandate was to foster the construction of railroads through land grants and the issuance of bonds to cover the cost

3. Ibid., pp. 62–3.

of rails, rolling stock, bridges, and trestles. In the land grants, the railroad companies received not merely a 200-foot right of way but, also, for a distance of 6 miles out from each side of the track, they received each alternate section of land, in a checkerboard pattern. The bonds were to be paid off from the railroads' receipts, but, failing that, bond holders would receive state lands pledged against these obligations. Under this arrangement several railroad companies built or improved lines in northern and central Florida prior to 1861, but these companies were ruined by the Civil War and their property reverted to the state. The I.I. Board, short by nearly 1 million dollars of being able to meet its rail bond obligations, was eventually forced into receivership.

THE DISSTON SALE. With the I.I. Board in receivership and one creditor threatening court action to claim 14 million acres in exchange for his bond coupons, Florida faced a public lands crisis. This was the situation in 1881 when Governor William D. Bloxham, one of the first Democratic governors elected after Reconstruction, finally found a way out. Bloxham brought onto the scene the first of the northern capitalists who were to reshape Florida. Hamilton Disston, a wealthy young Philadelphia saw manufacturer who had visited Florida on fishing trips, was persuaded to buy 4 million acres of swamp lands for 1 million dollars, or twenty-five cents an acre, allowing the I.I. Board to pay off the rail bonds. This spectacular sale made Disston the largest landowner in Florida and possibly in the United States; his princely holdings were mostly in 10,000-acre tracts scattered from Duval County, in north Florida, to Lake Okeechobee. And, just as the state itself had selected some land from the federal domain which was neither swampy nor overflowed, Disston's own selections included some upland tracts. Besides the 4 million acres he had purchased outright, Disston was to receive title to half of all the swamp land that he could reclaim from the upper Kissimmee basin down through the Everglades. Altogether, some 9 million acres were supposed to be reclaimed. The Disston sale was to become a matter of continuing political controversy because the price per acre had been so low and because some of the land was naturally well drained and already partly occupied by squatters. Moreover, the objectives of the drainage plan soon proved utterly beyond attainment. Yet Disston would alter the landscape of southern and central Florida enough to offer a premonition of what ultimately was to come. A Disston dredge worked its way from Fort Myers up the Caloosahatchee River, a stream then rising in the marshes and shallow lakes west of Lake Okeechobee. Finally cutting a canal from the upper reaches of the Caloosahatchee to Okeechobee, the dredge gave the big lake a direct outlet to the Gulf. Disston dredges also made the meandering Kissimmee River more navigable, but without greatly altering it, and they cut canals between all major lakes of the Kissimmee basin, thus opening up the basin to steamboat traffic as well as draining some of its marshes. An attempt was made to dig a canal from Lake Okeechobee south across the Everglades to the Shark River, but after cutting less than 10 miles through deep muck the dredge encountered hard rock and could go no farther.

THE BOURBON ERA. With the I.I. Board's return to solvency after the Disston sale, the state was free to resume its prewar practice of making grants to railroad companies, only now the grants were to be more generous than ever. The period from the end of Reconstruction to the turn of the century is regarded as Florida's "Bourbon" era, the Bourbons having been the Democratic leaders who restored the political supremacy of propertied or well-to-do white Floridians (including what remained of the old pre-Civil War ruling class). This restoration of power was accomplished partly through an alliance by the Bourbons with newcomers who had large fortunes to invest, such as Disston and the major railroad builders. In his *A History of Florida*, Charlton W. Tebeau comments:

> The Bourbon blueprint for state development was fairly simple. Government activity and costs had to be kept at a minimum and taxes correspondingly low with no incubus of state debt. Government encouragement but never restraint was offered to those who would invest their money and look for their futures in the state. Bourbons maintained an image of economy and honesty in contrast to the previous regime [but] could be accused of extravagance . . . in the wanton fashion in which they offered the state's natural resources for development and exploitation.[4]

Wanton is indeed the word for the state's free-handed policy toward the railroad companies. By the end of the century the legislature and the I.I. Board had given to these companies more land than the state owned. The state was saved from this embarrassment only because the grants were conditional upon completion of the rail projects, some of which never materialized. The total amount of land actually deeded to railroad companies was about 9 million acres, or about one-fourth of all land in Florida. Because of erroneous coastal meander lines and the I.I. Board's failure to hold sovereignty lands for the public, in some cases tidal lands were deeded to railroads as swamp and overflowed lands. For instance, a deed issued by the I.I. Board on February 8, 1898, purportedly conveyed 14,000 acres of swamp and overflowed lands in the Florida Keys to the Jacksonville, Tampa, and Key West Railway, as part of the 550,000 acres due this company under a grant by the legislature conditioned upon the laying of 55 miles of track in north Florida. Yet the land granted was, by the terms of the act, supposed to be those lands "lying nearest the line of said road." The acreages specified in the deed were in fact not swamp and overflowed lands by any reasonable

4. Charlton W. Tebeau, *A History of Florida* (Miami, Florida: University of Miami Press, 1971), p. 274.

definition, but rather tidal or sovereignty lands in the Florida Keys, hundreds of miles away from the railroad line.

RAILROAD BARONS: PLANT AND FLAGLER. While it is not unfair that the Florida politicians of this early era should be judged harshly for their land giveaways, their policies in this regard were typical of what was going on elsewhere in the United States. Land grants to railroads by the federal government and the public lands states were to total over 204,000 square miles, an area nearly a third again larger than California. The lavish land grants by the State of Florida did add to the incentive for holders of surplus capital to invest their money in Florida. Two such capitalists were Henry B. Plant, principal owner of the Southern Express Company, who built a railroad and resort hotel empire on the Gulf coast; and Henry M. Flagler, former associate of John D. Rockefeller in the Standard Oil Company, who built a similar empire on the East Coast. By 1898, Flagler's Florida East Coast Railway, constructed at a cost of $30 million, reached from Jacksonville to Miami. The powerful influence of Flagler, Plant, and other railroad men on Florida politics was evident from the railroads' long immunity from effective public regulation despite undependable service, discriminatory freight rates, and the rebates made to favored customers. A regulatory commission was established by the legislature in 1887, abolished in 1891, and established again in 1897 but got little support from either the Bourbon politicians in Tallahassee or the state courts. Shortly before his death in 1913, at the age of eighty-three, Flagler completed his most daring venture by extending the Florida East Coast Railway another 155 miles, from Miami to Key West, 75 miles of it over tidal marsh and open water. This project cost $22 million and the lives of 700 workmen, who drowned in hurricanes. (The overseas railroad was itself swept away by a hurricane in 1935 and was later replaced by a highway.)

DRAINING THE EVERGLADES

NAPOLEON BONAPARTE BROWARD. By the coming of this century, the marked favoritism shown the railroads and other corporate interests by the Bourbon politicians at Tallahassee had provoked a strong reaction. The election of William S. Jennings, a liberal reform Democrat, as governor in 1901 led to a change in state policies which became quite evident two years later when the state received from Washington title to 2.8 million acres of swamp and overflowed land, one of the last large blocks to be transferred from federal to state ownership. Taking the position that their first obligation under both federal and state law was to have the swamp lands drained, Jennings and the I.I. Board refused to surrender this land to the railroads to satisfy outstanding claims. The railroads, including Flagler's East Coast Railway, which alone was claiming an additional 2 million acres, promptly

The Tamiami Trail   Patricia Caulfield

sued but failed to overturn the board's new policy. At this point, there arrived upon the scene a politician who was to become a singularly important figure in Florida history—Napoleon Bonaparte Broward, governor from 1905 to 1909.

Broward, like his immediate predecessor, Governor Jennings, was a liberal reform Democrat who profited politically from the agrarian discontent and populist sentiment of the times. Campaigning in 1904, Broward, who had first come to statewide attention in the 1890s by making daring (and financially profitable) smuggling expeditions on behalf of the Cuban rebels, accused the railroads of "draining the people instead of the swamps."[5] His biographer, Samuel Proctor, has recounted how Broward, armed with graphs, pictures, and a large map of the Everglades, went about the state advocating drainage. "Broward visualized great public benefits to be derived from the

5. Samuel Proctor, *Napoleon Bonaparte Broward* (Gainsville, Florida: University of Florida Press, 1950), p. 190.

drainage of the Everglades—'lands salvaged to men who wanted to build homes, plant crops, and tap the wealth of the fabulous muck.' Sometimes when Broward became hard pressed in a drainage argument, he took refuge in one of his famous phrases—'Water will run down hill!' Broward argued that the people of Florida should 'knock a hole in the wall of coral [the coastal ridge] and let a body of water obey a natural law and seek the level of the sea. . . .' "[6]

THE EVERGLADES DRAINAGE DISTRICT. After Broward's election the railroad companies and other interests holding large acreages in the Everglades became all the unhappier when he urged the establishment of an Everglades Drainage District empowered to levy taxes on lands within its boundaries. Although drainage would enhance the value of their properties these interests were not ready for the state to drain the Everglades with tax money collected from them. One of the parties with an important stake in this matter was the Southern States Land and Timber Company, a syndicate which had been formed by Herbert H. Lehman (later governor of New York) and others. This company, owner of 2 million acres around Lake Okeechobee, felt that far more technical investigation and planning should precede drainage. The legislature supported Broward's program, however, and created a board of drainage commissioners made up of the governor and the other four state officials on the I.I. Board. Because they were not represented on the new board, the big owners of Everglades land were especially displeased by the legislature's action.

By the time dredging actually got underway, the drainage program had become controversial and was under attack by many newspapers, including of course the railroad-owned press such as the *Jacksonville Times-Union*. Much of the editorial criticism was undoubtedly inspired by political partisanship and the selfish interests of companies resentful of the new tax or at the rejection of their land claims. Nevertheless, by the lights of later times, some of it had a prophetic ring: "The lands can't be drained . . . saw grass muck is a peat bog that will burn down to bedrock when drained. . . . We have countless thousands of acres of land which ought to be tenanted before attempting to open up other territory . . . ," said the *Ocala Banner*.[7]

In recent battles over water management in south Florida, corporate farms and big lands owners often have been properly regarded as bearing part of the responsibility for the overdrainage of wetlands that has occurred. It should not be forgotten, however, that, in the early 1900s, here was Broward, a liberal acting in the name of the people and against the "corporate interests," embarking on a drainage program that was to bring about a far greater man-made change in the Everglades environment than any such change happening before or since. When the drainage project began in the

6. Ibid., p. 191.
7. Ibid., p. 242.

spring of 1906, with the dredge *Everglades* chugging up the New River to begin cutting the first canal through from the Atlantic to Lake Okeechobee, a fundamental decision had been made, apparently without serious consideration of the alternative. Since the Buckingham Smith report of 1848, advocates of Everglades drainage had contemplated the draining of all, or at least most, of the glades over a very few years. This was Broward's objective—to bring under settlement and agricultural production all of the muck lands around Lake Okeechobee and much of those to the south of the lake. The alternative would have been to proceed piecemeal by diking off and draining the muck land as needed, which was precisely the approach that had been suggested in the report of a U.S. Department of Agriculture official who visited the Everglades in 1904.

FLORIDA FOR SALE

RICHARD BOLLES: THE FIRST SWAMP SALESMAN. Broward's ambitious program to reclaim the Everglades muck lands soon became mired in difficulty when landowners, through a law suit, prevented the levying of the proposed drainage tax. (In fact, not until after Broward had left office would the Florida East Coast Railway and other plaintiffs in the suit, no doubt reacting to the rising public interest in Everglades reclamation, finally agree to pay the tax.) Facing the prospect that the principal objective of his administration might have to be abandoned, Broward had recourse to the same kind of financial solution that he and other liberals had found odious in the Bloxham Administration—he resorted to sale of public lands. As it happened, Broward struck a deal with a man who was to become one of the earliest and most innovative salesmen of Florida swamp land. This was Richard J. Bolles, an ebullient New York-born promoter of diverse interests who first gained experience in the land sales business by subdividing a huge tract of mountain land in Oregon and selling 14,000 farm sites. The trustees of the Internal Improvement Fund sold Bolles 500,000 acres of Everglades land for 1 million dollars, half of which was to be used exclusively for drainage. The understanding was that payments for the land would be made over an eight-year period, during which Bolles would be reselling these marshy properties while the state would be draining and surveying them. In *Lake Okeechobee*, a regional history by Alfred Jackson Hanna and Kathryn Abbey Hanna, the Bolles land sales technique is described:

> The Florida Fruit Lands Company, first of the Bolles companies to be organized, introduced the contract method of land sales. Its holdings of 180,000 acres . . . in Dade and Palm Beach counties, were divided into 12,000 farms, varying in size from 10 to 640 acres; 8,000 farm tracts were 10 acres in extent; only two contained 640 acres. Within the holdings a townsite, called Progresso, was designated by the company; it

was to consist of 12,000 lots in addition to reservations for streets, factories, churches, schools, parks, public squares and public buildings. Twelve thousand 'contracts' were put on sale at $240 each for which payment could be made at the rate of $10 a month. Each contract holder owned a farm, the size and location of which was unknown (at the time of sale), and a town lot. . . .

Glib salesmen toured the rural communities of the Middle West, aglow with enthusiasm over the Everglades 'Tropical Paradise.' They called it the 'Promised Land,' the 'Poor Man's Paradise,' The 'Land of Destiny' and the 'Magnet Whose Climate and Agriculture Would Bring the Human Flood.' There, life was full and riches were to be had on every hand or, at least, a generous competence for old age. They conclusively proved that a 10-acre farm stocked with cows, hogs, and chickens could maintain a family and provide extras as well. . . .[8]

A NATIONAL SCANDAL. Bolles established additional companies to dispose of his other Everglades lands, while other parties, also hoping to turn a quick and handsome profit on such lands, set up companies in competition with his. For instance, the Florida Everglades Land Company, based in Chicago, subdivided 240,000 acres for promotion and sale. According to the Hannas, by 1911 Everglades land was being sold by no less than fifty Chicago real estate agencies or "swamp boomers." Inevitably, the Everglades land sales campaigns resulted in a national scandal. There were to be law suits, congressional investigations, grand jury indictments, and, of course, indignant articles in the press—indeed, the news stories about the Everglades promotions introduced the exposé of Florida land sales swindles as one of the hardy perennials of American journalism, like stories of the sex life of Hollywood stars. In one instance, a land sales promoter apparently arranged to have published as part of an official U.S. Senate document a report previously rejected as misleading by the U.S. Department of Agriculture's Chief of Drainage Investigations. The USDA employee who prepared that report would later become Drainage Engineer of Florida. In another instance, a Division of Drainage Investigation circular warning that draining and cultivating Everglades land was "largely problematical" was suppressed by the secretary of agriculture, apparently because of political pressures. Damning evidence of Everglades land sales swindles was produced when some of the promoters were tried for fraud. In November 1914, a Kansas City promoter who had sold 50,000 acres of Everglades land to some 20,000 persons in the Missouri Valley was convicted. The jubilant federal prosecutors declared, quite optimistically, that henceforth, land salesmen would be more honest. Fraud charges were brought against Bolles himself in 1913, but the original indictments were dismissed and the defendant died before the government

8. Alfred J. Hanna and Kathryn A. Hanna, *Lake Okeechobee* (Indianapolis and New York: Bobbs-Merrill Co., 1948), p. 139.

could again bring him to trial. In a sense, the state of Florida was on trial
along with the land sales promoters, for, by its sales contract with Bolles,
the state had helped to start the promotions. During the trial of the Kansas
City promoter, the then governor of Florida, Park Trammell, appeared as a
defense witness and laid bare the state's dilemma: Florida's only means of
raising funds for drainage was by selling state lands; yet the promotion and
resale of this land by others had brought on federal investigations and bad
publicity, thus stopping further sales and "very seriously crippl[ing] the
drainage fund."[9] The great majority of those people who already had bought
land either forfeited it by not meeting installment payments or not bothering
to pay taxes. This behavior, too, was to become a familiar part of the after-
math of subsequent Florida land sales campaigns.

SETTLEMENT FOLLOWS THE
CANAL BUILDERS

DRAINAGE ADVANCES, SLOWLY. The drainage program was in any
event taking longer and costing more than had been expected. Reformulated
by the legislature in 1913, the drainage tax now varied from ten cents to
$1.25 an acre, according to the proximity of any particular tract to the canal
system. But the funds provided by the tax were by no means enough. Yet
the state managed to sell $10.2 million in drainage bonds between 1917 and
1925 and to continue the reclamation effort. Altogether, between 1907 and
1929, the Everglades Drainage District spent almost $18 million and exca-
vated 79 million cubic yards of dirt and rock and built 440 miles of canals
and levees. The principal features of the drainage system that had been built
by the mid-1920s consisted of the Caloosahatchee Waterway, between Lake
Okeechobee and the Gulf; the St. Lucie Canal, between the lake and the
Atlantic; and four major waterways built from the south shore of the lake
across the Everglades, then through the coastal ridge to the ocean, these
being the Miami, North New River, Hillsboro, and West Palm Beach canals
(see figure 3–1). All of these canals followed, for part of their course, the
channels of the small coastal rivers. Improvements on the Miami River, for
instance, included the dynamiting of the rock sill over which the river had
tumbled in a short rapids; the sill and the rapids disappeared, and the silt
once trapped behind them could now pour freely into the once crystalline
waters of Biscayne Bay. Unfortunately, as events would ultimately show,
the new canal system had been built even below the drainage capacities
proposed in the naive recommendations of the Everglades Drainage District's
consulting engineers. These engineers had themselves not learned what a
really hard siege of rain over the Everglades is like, for, true to the char-

9. Ibid., p. 146.

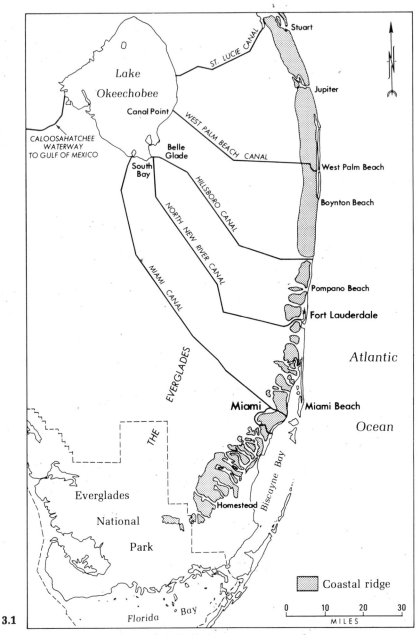

3.1

Everglades drainage canals built between 1907 and 1929

acter of the Everglades as a region of cyclical extremes, the years from 1910 to 1920 had been deceptively dry.

COMBATING "THE COMMON ENEMY." Feeding into the regional system of major trunk canals built by the state was a maze of subsystems, consisting of smaller canals and laterals, built at local initiative and expense for

72 SOUTH FLORIDA: AN EVOLVING LAND POLICY

the reclamation of particular areas. The legislature had, over the years, enacted a series of measures permitting these local drainage districts to be established. Most of the districts were authorized by special acts, but some were created under general laws, such as the remarkable Chapter 298 of the Florida Statutes, passed in 1913. Under this law, a majority of the landowners, or the owners of a majority of the acreage of any contiguous body of wet or overflowed land could form a drainage district, complete with power to levy a tax, simply by petitioning the circuit judge in their county and presenting a plan of reclamation. The drainage district's three-man board of supervisors, chosen in an election dominated by owners of the majority of the land, would enjoy sweeping powers. If necessary in carrying out the drainage plan, the supervisors could have canals and other works built not only inside the district boundaries but outside as well; stream courses could be altered and natural flows diverted; and flood waters—then regarded in Florida law as "the common enemy"—could be dumped into streams, lakes, and other water bodies. A circuit judge could reject a proposed drainage plan or order it modified if persuaded by dissident landowners or others that the public interest so required. Therefore, in principle, the petition and court review procedures prescribed by Chapter 298 offered an advantage over the legislature's practice of establishing drainage districts by special acts without any review of a drainage plan; actually, in their attitude toward these districts, the courts as well as the legislature were highly permissive.

THE EVERGLADES AGRICULTURAL AREA. The rich Everglades muck lands around the south shore of Lake Okeechobee were settled rapidly as drainage efforts finally made possible at least some of the rewards promised by land sales promoters. With the new trunk canals built and many new drainage districts established, a large Everglades agricultural area was coming into existence, and, over time, this area would become the single largest province of more or less contiguous agricultural land in Florida. Production of sugar cane, winter vegetables, and beef was beginning, though not without difficulties. Raw but vigorous towns, such as Pahokee, Belle Glade, South Bay, Clewiston, and Moore Haven, were developing along the lake, their growth stimulated by the extension of the Atlantic Coastline and Florida East Coast railroads to the south shore of the lake in the late teens and early 1920s. The custard apple swamps and moon vines so characteristic of the lake shore region even at the turn of the century were disappearing. Soon, however, two devastating hurricanes would reveal how precarious was the settlement of this upper Everglades region, and these storms were to be merely the first events in a series of natural calamities demonstrating the recklessness of the attempt by Napoleon Bonaparte Broward and his successors to drain the Everglades.

THE CREATORS OF
MIAMI BEACH AND
COLLIER COUNTY

CARL FISHER AND MIAMI BEACH. Concurrent with the drainage of the great Everglades marshes, developers elsewhere in south Florida were discovering that submerged tidal land can be potentially more valuable than dry land. The dredging and filling of submerged land on a large scale first began on that narrow sandy spit of land, bordered to its west by dense mangroves, which was to become known as Miami Beach. Carl Fisher, the extraordinary promoter from Indiana responsible for building this largely man-made island, could qualify as the patron saint of all subsequent developers, in Florida and elsewhere, who have profited from waterfront property made by filling in tidal marshes or mangrove swamps with material dredged from shallow bays.

Fisher was able to use to his own great advantage the obliging policies of a state eager to foster development. In the Riparian Act of 1855, the legislature, in order to encourage commercial navigation, had allowed owners of riparian property to fill the adjoining tidal land out to the channel for the construction of wharves, warehouses, and other facilities. The I.I. Board, interpreting the act more broadly than its language would seem to justify, did not limit the filling of submerged land just to purposes of navigation. In any event, the legislature, in the Riparian Act of 1921, declared as a matter of policy that the state benefits from waterfront development and stated explicitly that "warehouses, dwellings, and other buildings" could be built upon filled land.

Fisher first arrived in Miami in 1910, as another wealthy winter vacationer from the North. If Fisher was not as rich as Flagler, he was more colorful and flamboyant even than Richard Bolles, the dynamic purveyor of Oregon mountain tops and Florida swamps. He had made his money first by selling bicycles and automobiles, then by manufacturing a highly unstable gas for automobile headlights, which was profitable even though several of his plants blew up. Fisher had become a celebrity well before his arrival at Miami: he had, for instance, already flown 3,000 feet above Indianapolis in an automobile suspended from a balloon, built the Indianapolis Speedway, and promoted the construction of the first transcontinental highway.

After discovering how cheaply a protective arm of land had been dredged up around the boat dock at his new winter home in Miami, Fisher helped finance development of Point View, a Miami bayfront subdivision that involved dredging and filling. In 1913, he accepted 200 acres near the south end of what was to become Miami Beach in partial payment for a $50,000 loan made to a Quaker farmer named John Collins, who needed the money to complete a two-and-one-half-mile long wooden bridge across Biscayne Bay to the beach. In those years, before it knew either dredge or bulldozer, Miami Beach consisted of a continuous strip of sand, some 200 feet in width, sloping gently from a ridge of low dunes thrust up by storm tides. On the dunes were tawny patches of sea oats and dense green mantles of sea grapes. Toward the bay and to the west of the low ridge of dunes, sandy flats grown up in weeds and Spanish bayonet sloped imperceptibly to the salt mud of the tidal flats where the red mangroves stood, a maze of slender, arching trunks and prop roots supporting a thick canopy of dark green. Collins, who owned a five-mile-long stretch of this sand barrier island, was interested chiefly in the avocado plantation he had established on a piece of higher land west of the beach; others in his family, however, wanted to develop the ocean front as a major resort.

Through business arrangements worked out with the Collins family and others, Fisher was able, over a period of fifteen years, to fill in the mangrove swamps, which in places were up to 1 mile wide. In order to do this, he needed permits from the I.I. Board and the U.S. Army Corps of Engineers— the interest of the corps being limited solely to whether the project would obstruct navigation. These permits were obtained without difficulty. In *Billion-Dollar Sandbar*, Polly Redford, biographer of Miami Beach, says that to Fisher it was evident that filling in the mangroves would triple the usable land area, eliminate a breeding ground for sandflies and mosquitoes, and, as the result of the dredging, provide a basin deep enough for boating. She gives a vivid description of the dredge-and-fill operation:

> In the summer of 1913 new land began rising from the bay at the south end of the Beach where Fisher and [his business associates] spent $600,000 replacing a thousand acres of mangroves with six million cubic yards of fill. The forest was cleared by gangs of Negro laborers armed with saws and axes. They worked hip-deep in mud, a pall of smoke hanging over them because smudge pots and bonfires of palmetto fiber were the only available defense against clouds of mosquitoes and sandflies that made life miserable for men and mules alike. When the many-branched mangrove roots proved ruinously expensive to remove, they were cut off two feet above the mud and left there for dredges to cover later on. At the water's edge, steam shovels heaped the bay bottom into dikes while pile drivers sank rows of supports for a bulk-headed shoreline of wooden timbers anchored to pilings with steel cables. The shoreline alone cost $10 a running foot. Behind it, long pipe-lines reached from the mangrove stumps to the bay where suction dredges burrowed into the bottom, turning the water a muddy milky white. Fisher's largest dredge, the *Norman H. Davis*, could pump fill through a mile of pipe, and in places where this was not far enough, another dredge was rigged in tandem to boost the pressure. . . .
>
> So year by year a uniform, five-foot plateau spread northward along the bayfront. As it rose, the bay bottom fell, and what had been

hundreds of acres of turtlegrass flats covered with a foot or two of clear water became a deep, turbid pool running parallel to a smoothly bulkheaded shore. In this manner the original landscape was erased as if it had never been and a more saleable one built in its place.[10]

If people had thought Fisher was foolish to spend millions building land from bay bottom and mangrove swamps when plenty of dry land could be bought cheaply on the mainland, they learned better when, during the Florida land boom of the 1920s, he and his associates were making land sales totaling up to $23.4 million in a single year. Fisher's gamble in carrying out Florida's first large-scale dredge-and-fill operation paid off, and, as Polly Redford observes, "From Florida the notion spread northward, and eventually proved so profitable that today no marsh or mudbank between Boston and San Francisco is safe."[11]

In his Star Island venture of 1917–18, Fisher built an entirely new island, a half mile long and a quarter of a mile wide, out in Biscayne Bay. Evidently acting in anticipation of such projects, the legislature had, in 1913, enacted a measure vesting in the I.I. Board title to all shallow banks covered by not more than 3 feet of water at high tide and separated from the shore by a channel not less than 5 feet deep. This measure, applicable at first only to Dade and Palm Beach counties but made to apply statewide by 1917, was an important precedent because it marked the first time the I.I. Board was authorized to sell sovereignty lands. Accordingly, Fisher bought that part of the bay bottom on which the island was to be built, paying the state less than $17,000. Later, after bulkheading and filling this property, Fisher offered it at $200 per front foot. As part of the bargain, Fisher had gotten, at no extra cost, the huge volume of fill material that was pumped up from the bay to create the island. (He had paid nothing for that used in filling in the mangroves behind Miami Beach.) The success of the Star Island project encouraged other promoters, and man-made islands proliferated in the waters of North Biscayne Bay between Miami and Miami Beach (see figure 3–2).

Whatever the merits of Miami Beach and its satellite islands as tourist attractions or commercial assets, north Biscayne Bay's beauty and extraordinarily good fishing had been impaired. Moreover, for the sacrifice of the sovereignty lands that had gone into the making of this artificially created environment, the state had received virtually no direct return. But the state, as represented by the legislature and the I.I. Board, was aware of no sacrifice, for during the Fisher era and long afterwards neither state nor federal law recognized any public value in turtlegrass flats or mangrove swamps. Another half century would pass before the value of mangroves would be fully understood even by marine biologists.

10. Polly Redford, *Billion-Dollar Sandbar* (New York: E. P. Dutton, 1970), pp. 71–73.
11. Ibid., p. 70.

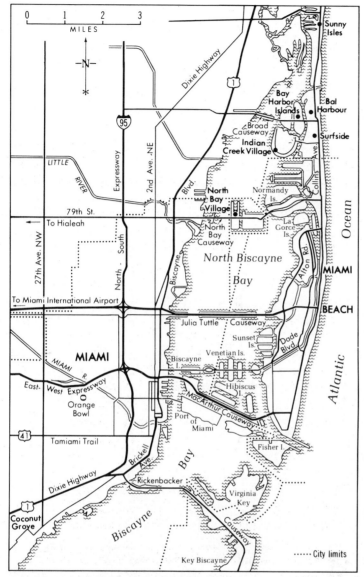

3.2

North Biscayne Bay and Miami Beach

BARRON COLLIER CREATES A COUNTY. As the state was completing the Everglades drainage work begun by Broward, and as Carl Fisher was converting more mangrove flats into waterfront lots, another extraordinary development was happening in south Florida. Barron G. Collier, of New York, many times a millionaire from his franchises in streetcar placard advertising, was founding a county and building a highway across one of the swampiest regions on earth. The highway was the Tamiami Trail (Tamiami being a contraction of Tampa-Miami) and the new county was Collier County, in the southwest corner of the Florida peninsula (see figure 3–3).

77 LAND DISPOSAL AND DRAINAGE

This was a region made up mostly of the "swamp and overflowed" lands of the Big Cypress watershed, lands which the state had disposed of in grants to encourage railroad and drainage projects. The grant recipients had, in turn, sold the property to timber and land companies, reportedly at prices of from twelve to thirty cents an acre. Barron Collier had first visited Florida in 1911 and he eventually bought a winter home near Fort Myers. In 1921, Collier began buying land, mostly in huge tracts, in what was then the southern part of Lee County. This property Collier purchased from land and timber companies, the state, and from local people, some of whom had been homesteaders. The legislature carved Collier County from Lee County in 1923, largely on Barron Collier's promise that the long delayed Tamiami

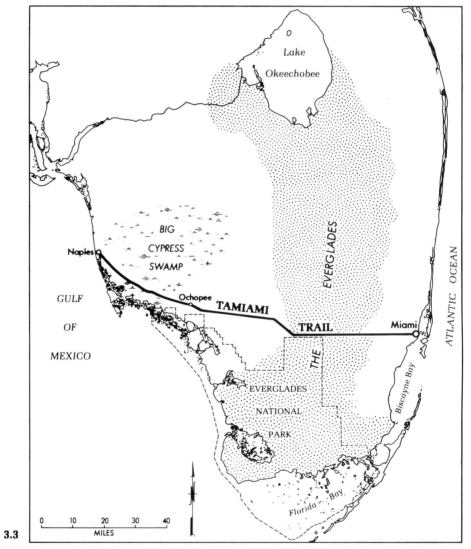

3.3

Tamiami Trail across the Big Cypress and the Everglades

78 SOUTH FLORIDA: AN EVOLVING LAND POLICY

Trail project would be completed. The new county embraced 1.3 million acres, and Collier owned 70 percent of it, or about 900,000 acres. The Collier holdings were extraordinary even in a state where large individual ownerships were common (even today some cattle ranches in the Kissimmee basin cover tens of thousands of acres). Tax records for the year 1926 indicate that the next three largest ownerships in the new county were: the 126,000 acres held by the Lee Tidewater Cypress Company, owner of two-thirds of the merchantable cypress in the county and a third of the pine; the 77,000 acres owned by the Empire Land Company; and the nearly 41,000 acres owned by the Atlantic Coastline Railroad.[12]

The Tamiami Trial. Up to this point, the Tamiami Trail project had had a discouraging history. In 1915 and 1916, when work on the trail first began, the construction of highways was still treated as largely a local responsibility, although before the end of the 1920s the state itself would assume the responsibility of building major highways. Dade County on the east coast, and two local bonding districts in Lee County, on the west coast, had undertaken the project, which called for building the road along a 136-mile route running from Fort Myers south to Naples, then east across the lower reaches of the Big Cypress into the saw grass Everglades and finally into Miami. No one yet had any conception of the engineering difficulties that would be involved in crossing this swampy wilderness. To have built the road on higher ground farther north would have been far easier and would have had the enthusiastic support of people in Fort Myers and the Caloosahatchee River valley. This was not done, however, because residents of Miami and the lower Gulf coast strongly favored the southern routing.

Adoption of the southern route meant not simply building a road but a continuous causeway. For most of the distance, the dredges extracting the fill material for the elevated roadbed would be working in hard limestone, behind blasting crews kept supplied with dynamite brought to the work site by oxcart. One of the first dredges used was a "walking dredge"; this primitive device, which had a puny one-cubic-yard bite, was mounted on rails and straddled the canal that was excavated as the dredge scooped up the limestone shattered by the dynamiting and heaped it onto the roadbed. Funds raised by the bonding districts were soon exhausted and the dredge that had been working slowly eastward from Naples came to a stop less than half way across the Big Cypress. After a hiatus of several years, due in part to the United States' involvement in World War I, work was resumed in 1923 by Collier County, which later sold $350,000 worth of road bonds on the strength of Barron Collier's financial standing. The state road department took over in 1926 and finished the last 12 miles, overcoming some of the most difficult rock conditions yet encountered. The dredge laboring

12. Ownership statistics cited by Charlton W. Tebeau in *Florida's Last Frontier: The History of Collier County* (Miami, Florida: University of Miami Press, 1966), p. 86.

eastward through the Big Cypress finally met one that was working west-ward across the glades from Miami, and, in 1928, the Trail was at last completed and opened to traffic.

For Barron Collier, the opening of the Tamiami Trail seems to have been only one part of a bold, if naive, strategy for inducing regional development. The Tamiami Trail alone obviously could not open up all, or even most, of his 900,000-acre personal domain. Accordingly, construction of what was to be State Road 29, a north-south crossing of the Big Cypress, also was undertaken concurrently with the building of the trail. A major justification for this road was that Collier had put the county seat at his new town of Everglades, built 5 miles south of the trail on a site created by dredge-and-fill methods from a mangrove swamp at the edge of the Ten Thousand Islands. State Road 29 connected Everglades both with the trail and with Immokalee, a farming community on the north side of the Big Cypress watershed. Without this road, Everglades, owned by Collier virtually in the manner of a company town, would have been left isolated. In choosing such a swampy out-of-the-way spot for the county seat, Barron Collier obviously intended to accelerate development in the Big Cypress.

THE MICCOSUKIS:
A COMMENTARY ON
PROPERTY RIGHTS

Apparently unmindful of the freehanded disposal of the Florida public domain lands to claimants and buyers who were often less than worthy, many Floridians today somehow think of property rights in terms of a revealed truth. There is, however, at least one small, isolated group of people that entertains no illusions about the fixed and sure nature of property rights. These are the Seminoles of Florida and Oklahoma, whose forebears ceded Florida to the U.S. government virtually at bayonet point. To this day, they have not received compensation for the nearly 30 million acres that was taken from them, although the fact that most of Florida once belonged to the Seminole nation was recognized by the U.S. Indian Claims Commission in 1964.[13] Moreover, the Miccosukis—the most defiant of the Seminoles who

13. In 1970, the Indian Claims Commission, having determined six years earlier that the Seminoles were once the lawful owners of most of Florida, ruled that the present-day Seminoles were due $12.2 million in compensation, less than a third the amount to which the Seminoles believed they were entitled. The ruling was appealed to the U.S. Court of Claims, and in early 1972 that court remanded the matter back to the commission for further review and elucidation. The commission had arrived at the amount of the award largely by estimating the market value of the Seminole lands in 1823 and 1832 when the treaties ceding them to the United States were signed. Payment of interest on that value could not be considered because, in similar Indian claims cases, such payments had been precluded by a ruling of the Supreme Court. As I write in the spring of 1974, nearly four years have elapsed since the commission's last substantive finding in the case, which remains under advisement.

retreated into the wilderness fastness of south Florida—cannot show title to any major part of the Everglades or the Big Cypress despite their long occupancy of the area. Compounding their misfortunes after the Seminole Wars was the fact that they were invisible men in the white man's world of property and legal conveyances. For about three generations they were allowed to subsist in the Big Cypress because this was a wild region for which the white man had found little use. After the road builders, loggers, hunters, and cattlemen came in the 1920s, the Miccosukis no longer could survive by hunting, fishing, trapping, and raising a few vegetables on the higher hammocks. Many perhaps did not want to.

Even before the Tamiami Trail was completed, most of the more remote Miccosuki camps were abandoned and new ones were built along the trail. The majority of the Miccosukis were to remain there, preferring the trail to the several reservations established in south Florida for Seminoles. For tourists, the Miccosuki camps were a curious novelty. Inside the open-sided, palmetto-thatched huts (or "chickees"), Miccosuki women, always shy and silent with white visitors present, worked at ancient hand-operated Singer sewing machines, preparing bright, multicolored garments. The faces of the men were dark, dignified, and philosophic, and as alien as the steppes of Asia. Survivors of the defiant ones who would not be shipped west, the Miccosukis were now in the tourist business as souvenirs of their tragic past.

The park and the flood control district

The year 1947 was important for south Florida because, during the course of it, steps were taken to protect what remained of the Everglades. Plans for the Central and Southern Florida Flood Control District (FCD) were formulated, and the Everglades National Park was established. Establishment of the park and the FCD were important for three reasons: 3,500 square miles of Everglades wilderness, mangrove forest, and shallow bays would be preserved, though not without severe modification in some areas; the old concept of "Everglades drainage" would begin yielding to a concept of multipurpose water management; and finally, for the first time since the swamp and overflowed lands were given to the state, a major federal interest and presence was reestablished in south Florida. This presence would be of decisive importance in several south Florida land and water management conflicts that would arise in the 1960s, including a major conflict between the park and the FCD.

HURRICANES, DROUGHT, AND FLOOD

Although otherwise different in origin and inspiration, the park and the FCD each represented a response to environmental changes and crises brought on in south Florida by the drainage and land reclamation begun in the Broward era. The troubles first began during the 1920s in the Everglades agricultural area, below Lake Okeechobee. Settlers in the lake region learned early that to tap the wealth of the muck lands would entail major hazards and difficulties. Those numerous purchasers of a few acres who had counted on making a living as small farmers invariably failed unless they increased their holdings. Farming in the Everglades was precarious at best, but the big farmers enjoyed a major advantage, for the cultivation of at least several hundred acres might be necessary for one to realize a profit despite the high costs of irrigating during dry months and removing excess water during the wet season.

Commercial farming in the Everglades had not begun at all until 1915, and as late as 1928 only about 96,000 acres were under cultivation, with probably not more than half that actually in production at a given time.[1] With proper preparation and water control the deep muck soils south of the lake could yield rich harvests of winter vegetables, sugar cane, and other crops in years of average rainfall. But torrential rains on the flat Everglades terrain can be ruinous to farmers. When the muck itself can absorb no more water, and all ditches, canals, and sloughs are full, then the fields become flooded and may remain in that condition for weeks or months. Such conditions occurred during the early twenties, and a precipitous 5-foot rise in the level of Lake Okeechobee in the summer of 1922 led the Everglades Drainage District to build a muck dike around the south shore.

YEARS OF GREAT HURRICANES—1926 AND 1928. Whatever complacency the dike may have encouraged was swept away by the hurricane of 1926. A great wind tide breached this structure at the southwest corner of the lake and at least 250 persons were drowned. Two years later, in September 1928, a second hurricane struck. One of the members of the FCD board today is C. A. Thomas, a large farmer at Lake Harbor on the south shore of Lake Okeechobee. In the 1928 hurricane Thomas, then a boy of thirteen, lost his mother, his three sisters, his two brothers, and an aunt and uncle. Frightened by the rising storm, Thomas and thirty-five others had crowded that night into the most substantial house available. "We were all in there together, white people and black people, and everybody was praying hard," Thomas has recalled.[2] What prayer could not provide was a substantial

1. John M. DeGrove, "The Central and Southern Florida Flood Control Project: A Study in Intergovernmental Cooperation and Public Administration" (Ph.D. dissertation, University of North Carolina, 1958), p. 104.
2. Pat Cullen, "Nature's Rule of the Glades," *Palm Beach Post,* June 20, 1971.

levee to resist the 12-foot wind tide that was rushing toward the south shore of the lake. The muck dike simply washed away and allowed a rapidly rising flood to sweep over the south shore settlements. The house in which those thirty-six souls were huddled in terror collapsed, and only Thomas, his father, and four others survived the swirling flood. Some 2,300 people of the lake settlements were drowned during the hurricane. To cope with the overwhelming stench and to prevent disease, many of the corpses, bloated and unidentifiable, had to be stacked in large cremation piles and burned. Nearly a half century later the memory of this catastrophe would remain a compelling factor in Everglades water management.

AN ENVIRONMENT UNDER STRESS. The disasters of the 1920s were, at bottom, caused not so much by hurricanes and high water as by the human invasion of the great Everglades flood plain south of Lake Okeechobee. The crises of the thirties and forties, though involving no catastrophic loss of life, posed a threat to the habitability of *all* of southeast Florida, including the coastal ridge. Arthur Marshall, the prominent Florida environmentalist, sometimes refers to what he calls the curve of stress: "The critical level comes abruptly, it is often beyond the range of human experience and can rarely be foreseen; there are great differences in the functioning of the system before and after the critical level; curative measures—if at all possible—must be drastic."[3] By the late thirties, the environment of southeast Florida had reached a point of stress that could be considered critical under anyone's definition. While the works of the Everglades Drainage District had not been adequate to prevent flooding after heavy and prolonged rains, they were more than adequate to cause overdrainage during dry periods. And, as it happened, during the period from 1931 through the first half of the forties several severe droughts occurred. Records as to the high and low stages of Lake Okeechobee, kept on a monthly basis, go back some fifty years, to the start of Everglades drainage. In 1912, the lake, probably for the last time, attained levels as high as 20 feet above mean sea level. Thereafter, with drainage and flood control, the lake would be kept at levels much lower than those that had obtained historically. During the drought of 1931–32, the lake level would fall to 10.2 feet, possibly the lowest ever up to that time. But this was only one of the signs that the changes then taking place in the Everglades from overdrainage were extraordinary and ominous.

MUCK FIRES. The most visible of these signs were the muck fires. From time immemorial, with the coming of winter and the dry season, fires (often started by lightning) have swept through the saw grass. When dry, the peaty muck from which the saw grass grows will itself burn readily,

3. Arthur R. Marshall, Statement given at Water Resources Conference, Tallahassee, January 26, 1971.

but, so long as the water table remains near the surface, the muck seldom ignites. Muck fires were not unknown under predrainage conditions, but after construction of drainage canals and laterals, they became the rule during droughts and even during the normal dry season. Not only the Everglades Agricultural Area south of the lake was thus affected, for the drainage works prevented the gradual southward flow of water that historically had helped protect the lower glades from drought. Consequently, raging, persistent muck fires broke out in both the upper and lower glades; the wild, inaccessible lands of the lower glades, especially, might burn for months, until finally quenched by a heavy rain. The dense clouds of smoke billowing up from these huge, uncontrollable fires frequently drifted over Fort Lauderdale, Miami, and other coastal cities. In the words of one Florida official, there were times when the pall of smoke over Miami "literally shut out the light of day."[4]

SOIL SUBSIDENCE. The fires were a nuisance and an impediment to tourism but they were much more than that. They were causing the destruction of irreplaceable muck and thus contributing to a complex array of environmental problems affecting all southeast Florida. And, spectacular as they were, the fires were by no means the most important destroyer of the muck. A characteristic of organic soils, wherever they occur, is their susceptibility to biochemical oxidation once they have been drained. To drain and farm the muck is to mine it. By 1940 the surface of the muck soils near Lake Okeechobee, which had had a depth of 12–14 feet in 1912, was now only 7 or 8 feet above the underlying limestone. In some places farther south, where the muck (and peat) never had been deeper than a foot or two, it had disappeared altogether.[5]

Subsidence of the muck lands in the farming area below the lake proceeded at a startling rate in the first years after drainage because of soil compaction as well as oxidation. Subsidence "valleys" began to form along the drainage canals, where the drop in the water table was most pronounced; thus reduced in depth, the canals could carry less runoff and gravity drainage became increasingly ineffective. For a time, the water table rose again and subsidence decreased. But pumped drainage became the rule after 1927 and subsidence resumed at a rapid rate. Every ten years about one foot of decayed organic matter that had taken at least 400 years to accumulate was being lost.[6] Wild, uncultivated muck lands that had been

4. Spessard L. Holland, U.S. Senator, appearing as witness before Subcommittee on Flood Control, Rivers, and Harbors, Committee on Public Works, Hearing on Central and Southern Florida Flood Control Project, April 8, 1970, p. 51.

5. J. H. Davis, "The Peat Deposits of Florida," *Florida Geological Survey Bulletin* 30: 1–247, 1946.

6. John C. Stephens, "Peat and Muck Drainage Problems," *Journal of the Irrigation and Drainage Division, Proceedings of American Society of Civil Engineers* (June 1969), p. 297.

Photos by Patricia Caulfield

drained subsided as rapidly as cultivated lands. Subsidence was causing the slow death of the land, but death is not a popular subject for contemplation and the Everglades farmers generally avoided the thought that the abandonment of most of their farms by the end of the century was perhaps inevitable.

THE DRYING UP OF THE 'GATOR HOLES. The continuing subsidence of the organic soil also meant an inevitable change in the Everglades ecology, for the saw grass marshes and much of the bird and animal life of the glades depend on the ability of the peaty muck to soak up water like a giant sponge during the rainy season and slowly liberate it during the dry season into the glades' sloughs and alligator holes. Where the glades dry up almost altogether, the encroachment of dry-land plants tends to occur; and, at the glades' southern edges, the salt tolerant mangrove becomes established along the banks of creeks and sloughs that once remained fresh in the dry season but that are now brackish. The 'gator holes, as they are known locally, are depressions in the limestone bedrock that alligators inhabit and keep clear of muck and choking vegetation. These were once nearly as common in the Everglades as was the alligator itself—prior to drainage and heavy poaching, these big reptiles probably numbered more than a million just in that part of the lower Everglades and Big Cypress lying

Patricia Caulfield

Agricultural Research and Education Center, Belle Glade, Fla.

Facing page, muck soil dries and cracks in south Florida; a survival hole for alligators created in the Everglades National Park by dynamiting. *Above*, Everglades 'gator hole. The alligator is swallowing a mudfish. *At left*, soil subsidence leaves palm tree with its roots exposed. Shown near the Everglades Agricultural Research Center, Belle Glade. Up to a foot of soil is lost each decade.

south of the present Tamiami Trail.[7] The 'gator holes served as places of survival for what Frank Craighead has called an "amazing biological assemblage": diatoms, algae, ferns, flowering plants, protozoans, crustaceans, fish and small reptiles such as turtles and moccasins, otter, and a variety of wading birds, including the wood stork, a species which—because it feeds not by sight but by groping with its bill—is peculiarly dependent on the dense concentration of organisms in closely confined waters. For wide reaches of the Everglades, the total ecological change brought about from these various causes—the declining water table, the loss of the muck, the precipitous drop in the alligator population, and the disappearance of most of the 'gator holes—has been both drastic and irreversible.

SALTWATER INTRUSION. For the residents of the Gold Coast the most directly threatening aspect of the environmental crisis that was rapidly developing in south Florida in the 1930s and 1940s was the intrusion of salt water into the municipal well fields. In fact, saltwater intrusion can make a low-lying peninsula one of the most vulnerable of terrestrial environments, as became evident once Everglades drainage was well advanced. The springs that had once flowed freely along the lower coastal ridge had dried up by the 1920s. The intrusion of salt water into the Biscayne Aquifer had begun because the head of fresh water in the Everglades, which had kept the heavier salt water out, was now much reduced. With the Everglades lying just above sea level, that head had been maintained by only a narrow margin even under predrainage conditions. Drainage had lowered the water table by as much as 6 feet in some places. This, together with subsidence of the muck and the lack of saltwater barriers in the canals that had been cut through to tidewater, had made saltwater intrusion inevitable. (Prior to its subsidence, the muck had been important in helping prevent such intrusion. When the underlying aquifer is full, 1 inch of rainfall absorbed by the muck raises the water table by half a foot, thus exerting a powerful hydrostatic leverage.)

In 1925, a City of Miami well field a mile and a half up the Miami River from Biscayne Bay "salted up" and was abandoned. By the mid-forties two more Miami well fields, still farther inland, had been abandoned. The situation was now critical: the salt front was advancing inland in some areas at the rate of nearly 900 feet a year and threatening both municipal wells and wells for farm irrigation. But this problem, brought on by drainage and drought, was soon to be relieved temporarily by the recurrence, for the first time since the twenties, of devastating floods.

---

7. Frank C. Craighead, "The Role of the Alligator in Shaping Plant Communities and Maintaining Wildlife in the Southern Everglades," The Florida Naturalist, vol. 41, nos. 1 and 2 (January and April, 1968).

EIGHT AND A HALF FEET OF RAINFALL. In 1947, unusually heavy summer rains were followed by hurricanes in September and October that brought torrential downpours. The average annual rainfall at Miami is about 58 inches, but the rainfall recorded near there from January through the fall of that year totaled 102 inches—8½ feet. Vast sheets of water, 20 to 40 miles wide, formed and spread beyond the Everglades into low-lying communities adjoining the coastal ridge or occupying breaks or low places in the ridge. In Dade County, communities such as Hialeah, Miami Springs, and northwest metropolitan Miami generally were inundated; damaging floods also occurred in Broward County, where 30 percent of Fort Lauderdale, including the downtown business district, was affected. Although there was no loss of life, total property damages were estimated at $59 million. Farmers as well as urban residents had suffered; canals and laterals had overflowed and crops were destroyed and cattle drowned.

THE FLOOD CONTROL DISTRICT

The 1947 flood, only one of a succession of environmental crises in south Florida, was what led finally to the formation of the Central and Southern Florida Flood Control District, an agency whose jurisdiction was to embrace an eighteen-county area of 15,673 square miles. Despite its name, the FCD was not a single purpose agency such as the old Everglades Drainage District but an agency of multiple objectives. The U.S. Army Corps of Engineers quickly worked up a proposal for the establishment of the FCD after the onset of the flooding, but here the engineers were fortunate in being able to make use of ideas and research findings already produced by others.

SEEDS OF AN IDEA. The concept of a comprehensive program of water management and land use for the Everglades region was first developed during the late thirties and early forties under the leadership of a few geologists and soil scientists, together with a few engineers long associated with Everglades drainage. An important step in this movement was the founding in 1939 of the Soil Science Society of Florida, with R. V. Allison of the state's Everglades Experiment Station at Belle Glade as secretary-treasurer. The influence of this group upon farm leaders and others was substantial because its members were widely known for their previous work. For example, Allison's discovery in 1927 that the muck soils were deficient in trace elements such as copper sulphate had permitted an enormous advance in Everglades agriculture. Through articles in the Soil Science Society *Proceedings*, Allison and others spread the idea that the objectives of water control in the Everglades should include flood control, irrigation for agriculture, prevention of soil subsidence, protection and enhancement of municipal and industrial water supplies, and maintenance of habitat for fish and wildlife.

Much of the data and research on which plans for the FCD were based began to be produced in 1932 when the Department of Agriculture's Bureau of Agricultural Engineering undertook studies of rainfall, temperature, evaporation and transpiration, and other factors related to water control in the Everglades. In 1939, the Southeastern Florida Joint Resources Investigation was established, under the sponsorship of the National Resources Planning Board—an invention of Franklin D. Roosevelt's New Deal—and its counterpart in Tallahassee, the Florida State Planning Board. Later, with the fading of the New Deal and the onset of a strong political reaction against "planning," the national and state planning boards were abolished. The cooperative research program for southeast Florida continued, however, with the Soil Conservation Service, the U.S. Geological Survey, the Florida Agricultural Experiment Station, and the Everglades Drainage District participating.

MAPPING THE GLADES. The research done by these agencies into the hydrology and soil characteristics of the region was of fundamental importance, and some of it was heroic. For instance, in 1939 when W. H. Speir, a new twenty-one-year-old employee of the Soil Conservation Service, received his first major assignment it was to help survey and map the Everglades-Big Cypress wilderness. With the few "outlaws and poachers" whom Speir says he was able to recruit as his assistants, he set forth, first on foot but later with crudely fashioned glade buggies that often broke down and sometimes sank into the marsh. In time, airboats and Navy "weasels" (a vehicle designed for the Arctic) were used to negotiate the saw grass and the marshy sloughs. Working year round, Speir and his crew remained in the wilderness seldom less than a week at a time and once stayed out a month and a half. They lived off the land, catching bass in the sloughs and shooting deer. Each night, if not rolled up tight in their blankets to escape mosquitoes, they soaked their feet in chlorox to combat "footrot" and drank whiskey to keep up morale. Between 1939 and 1947, with a wartime interruption, Speir ran thousands of miles of survey line and thus helped to produce the first topographic maps available for a large part of the Everglades, together with much information about the muck soils, their depth in various locations, and their suitability for agriculture.

BULLETIN 442. The findings and recommendations for the cooperative research program were first published in 1948 as Bulletin 442 of the Florida Agricultural Experiment Station, a major document in the history of Everglades water management. The basic information contained in the bulletin was available five years before that document actually appeared and it had an early influence. The Everglades Drainage District, acting on the important finding that the muck and peat soils were deep enough to support agriculture only in the upper glades within 25 miles or less of Lake Okeechobee, designated three water conservation areas to be made up of over 500,000 acres in the lower glades. These areas were to be carried over into the Corps of Engineers' plan for the Flood Control District and substantially expanded.

THE HURRICANE LEVEE. The Corps of Engineers had begun dealing with Everglades water problems in a limited way back in the early thirties when it had taken on the job of keeping Lake Okeechobee storm tides from spilling over again into lake shore settlements. The hurricanes of 1926 and 1928 had pointed up the bankruptcy, literally and figuratively, of the Everglades Drainage District and its efforts to cope with the Everglades water problem. After the catastrophic 1928 hurricane, President-elect Herbert Hoover toured the devastated lake region, and in 1930 Congress called upon the Corps of Engineers to intervene. (At the time, this represented an exception to the corps' general policy, for such missions would not become part of the regular program of that agency until passage of the Flood Control Act of 1936.) The corps built the "Hoover-Dike," a levee 34 to 38 feet high along the south shore of Lake Okeechobee and at low places farther north. It also constructed a 155-mile-long waterway across Florida—the first federally built cross-Florida canal project—by excavating a channel 80 feet wide and 6 feet deep (later deepened to 8 feet) from the mouth of the St. Lucie River, at Stuart, to the mouth of the Caloosahatchee River, at Fort Myers. The new works were first tested by the hurricanes of 1947. Fifteen thousand people evacuated the lake region in alarm before the first of these struck, but, with the new levee and lake regulating facilities in place, no water spilled over from the storm-whipped lake into the south shore communities.

AN INTRACTABLE PROBLEM. Although the Corps of Engineers had controlled the lake successfully against the hurricane hazard, it had answered but one of the complex Everglades water problems which, overall, had thus far proved intractable. The corps now faced something new in its experience. The usual flood control project is in a region with enough relief that the problem is confined to relatively distinct flood plains. But the topography of south Florida is so flat that a great part of the region is a flood plain. The south Florida water problem bears an odd, inverted resemblance to that found in the arid West, where land "reclamation" is undertaken by means of constructing reservoirs to catch runoff from the melting snow pack in distant mountains and building canals to carry the water to irrigable desert lands. In south Florida during June through October—the season when heavy rains are expected and hurricanes are possible—the problem is to remove quickly the usually abundant rain water from farm land in the glades or from low-lying communities by pumping part of it into Lake Okeechobee and the Everglades water conservation areas, and discharging the remainder into the Gulf and the Atlantic. The threat of hurricane tides imposes rigorous limits as to how much wet season runoff can be stored in the lake.

On the other hand, during the dry months, November through May, the problem is to transport and manipulate the available supplies of stored water to satisfy the demands of the various consumers: the farmers of the Everglades and the lower east coast, with their heavy requirements for irrigation and pest control (flooding fields for control of nematodes); the coastal communities, threatened by saltwater intrusion unless a head of fresh water is maintained in the Biscayne Aquifer; and the Everglades itself, threatened by muck fires, soil subsidence, and the loss of fish and wildlife habitat and scenic and recreational amenities. Although there seems to have been little awareness in the late 1940s that severe conflict might arise among south Florida's various claimants for water, the competitive situation even then beginning to develop in this region of abundant rainfall (as measured by *averages*) was not unlike that of the driest regions of the West.

THE PROJECT PLAN

The plan devised by the Corps of Engineers in 1947 was, for its time, a sophisticated response to south Florida's urgent need, though it did not resolve the water management conflicts then existing or foreseeable. A major feature of the plan was the levee that was to be built roughly paralleling the coastal ridge, though usually running some miles to the west of it (figure 4–1). This levee would provide flood protection for farms and communities situated on the eastern edge of the glades or in breaks or low places along the ridge. It would permit new agricultural and urban development on several hundreds of thousands of acres formerly subject to flooding. The perimeter levee would also be part of the network of levees enclosing the three FCD water conservation areas. Consisting of wild glades of little or no agricultural value, these areas would be far more than disposal basins for excess water. In addition, they would help protect about one half of the original saw grass Everglades from further degradation and permit this glades region to function as a more effective recharge area for the Biscayne Aquifer and as a reservoir of surface water for east coast farmlands and Everglades National Park.

Protection and enhancement of the Everglades Agricultural Area was second only to the protection of the lower east coast as a project priority. This was to be accomplished by establishing the conservation areas, improving existing canals within the Agricultural Area, and installing a system of eight powerful pumping stations capable of removing water from

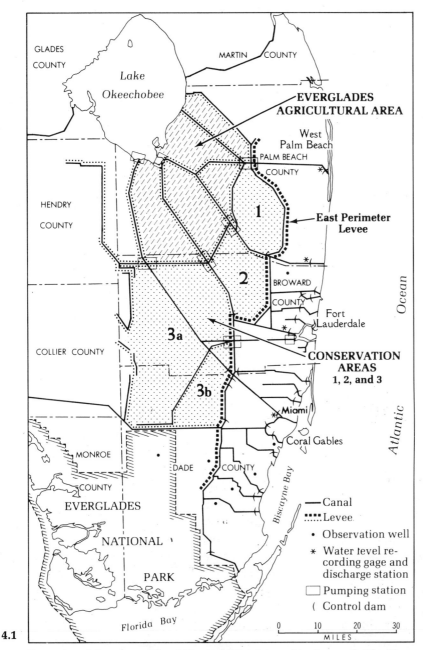

GLADES
COUNTY

Lake
Okeechobee

MARTIN COUNTY

**EVERGLADES
AGRICULTURAL AREA**

West
Palm Beach
PALM BEACH
COUNTY

HENDRY

COUNTY

1

**East Perimeter
Levee**

2

BROWARD

COUNTY

Fort
Lauderdale

COLLIER COUNTY

3a

**CONSERVATION
AREAS
1, 2, and 3**

3b

Miami

Coral Gables

MONROE

DADE COUNTY

COUNTY

EVERGLADES

NATIONAL

PARK

Biscayne Bay

Ocean

Atlantic

——Canal
▪▪▪▪Levee
• Observation well
✳ Water level re-
cording gage and
discharge station
☐ Pumping station
(Control dam

0   10   20   30

MILES

Florida Bay

4.1

Central and Southern Flood Control District system in south Florida

the Agricultural Area and discharging it into either Lake Okeechobee or the
conservation areas, or into both.

The project plan also called for building new canals and improving
existing canal systems along the lower east coast, plus completing the job
hurriedly undertaken by local interests during the 1943–45 drought of

93 THE PARK AND THE FLOOD CONTROL DISTRICT

installing saltwater barriers in some coastal canals. In addition, undertakings in drainage and flood control were planned for the upper Saint Johns River basin and the Kissimmee basin, looking especially to the reclamation of prairie marshes and other wetlands for agricultural use.

SOME SUCCESSES. *Combatting Flood and Drought.* This first attempt at comprehensive water management in south Florida had already become an important success by the 1960s. Completion of the perimeter levee at the eastern edge of the Everglades eliminated the threat of major floods along the lower east coast. Similarly, the works built for protection of the Everglades Agricultural Area allowed farming enterprises there an unprecedented (though not complete) degree of water control and helped them produce vegetables, sugar, and beef, which by 1970 would be valued at about $250 million a year (accounting for nearly a fifth the value of Florida's total farm output). From the start of the flood control project in 1950 through mid-1970 the flood damages prevented in the Everglades Agricultural Area and elsewhere totaled (according to Corps of Engineers estimates) more than $194 million. Moreover, the control structures built into many new and existing east coast canals, together with the perimeter levee and the new water conservation areas, reduced by about 20 percent the loss of fresh water from the Everglades to the Atlantic.[8] These measures made for higher water tables and lessened, though did not everywhere eliminate, the intrusion of salt water into the Biscayne Aquifer.

Opening the Glades To Recreation. Also, besides affording greater protection for much of the original saw grass Everglades, establishment of the water conservation areas was providing excellent public recreation. Vast reaches of glades previously accessible only to a few adventurers, poachers, and government surveyors were now accessible to tens of thousands of people by virtue of the new system of levees and the associated barrow canals created by the removal of spoil for the levees. Air boats and glades buggies (jerry-built contraptions with large airplane tires inflated at low pressure) were crisscrossing the glades in growing numbers. The Everglades always had been inhabited by a few white tailed deer adapted to the peculiar habitat of open glades and occasional hammocks or tree islands. With drainage of the upper glades and the lowering of water levels throughout the Everglades, the deer population had greatly increased. So now glades deer hunting was becoming popular—a sport which, with appropriate regulations on seasons and kills, put the herd in no jeopardy, even though it often featured the sorry spectacle of dogs being turned loose on the tree islands to drive the deer out into glades where they would be

8. Leach, Klein, and Hampton, *Hydrologic Effects of Water Control and Management of Southeastern Florida,* Report of Investigation No. 60, U.S. Geological Survey, Tallahassee, Florida, 1972, p. 57.

pursued and finally shot by hunters whooping and yelling from their buggies or airboats.

Phenomenal Bass Fishing. The really important recreational opportunity created along with the conservation areas was the fishing—largemouth bass fishing so astonishingly good that it was the best in Florida and perhaps the best anywhere. The general rule has been that man-made changes in Florida have reduced or destroyed fish and wildlife populations. But where canals in the glades adjoin the saw grass marshes, with no levee or spoil bank intervening, conditions are optimum for the propagation and growth of bass. By good luck, many of the barrow canals in the conservation areas were freely joined to the marsh. In the rainy season the marshes, teeming with life, provide the bass an abundance of bait fish, insects, and other food. In the dry season waters recede from the marshes into the canals, with the bass now not only plentiful but confined to narrow stretches of water where even novice fishermen can fill their stringers. If the best of this fishing is available especially for the sportsmen with special equipment such as airboats, there are still plenty of fish to be caught along roadside canals by bank fishermen and many blacks from Miami's inner city do catch them. (By 1970, visits by individuals to the three conservation areas were totalling—as estimated from traffic counts—more than 750,000.) Still more of this excellent fishing would have been created had Corps of Engineers planners, either in their innocence of fishery biology or in indifference to it, not needlessly separated certain canals from the marshes by a levee.[9]

SOME FAILURES. Although the achievements of the flood control project during its first ten years or so were very real, so was the failure of the Corps of Engineers, the state of Florida, and the Congress to face up to or even to recognize the project's several important shortcomings. These were (i) the lack of cost-sharing arrangements that would be equitable for all and encourage better use and conservation of land and water resources; (ii) the failure to give higher priority to works for the storage and delivery of the water necessary to meet user demands already foreseen, including the demands of the newly created Everglades National Park; and (iii) the

9. This was pointed out to me by Larry Shanks, formerly chief field biologist of the Florida Game and Freshwater Fisheries Commission and now with the U.S. Bureau of Sport Fisheries and Wildlife. An even more remarkable instance of such naivete arose in 1964 when the Central and Southern Florida Flood Control District, the state agency involved in the project, financed an experiment by a Florida Atlantic University scientist to see whether the manatee or "sea cow" could be used to control the water hyacinths that infest project canals. Five of these creatures were captured, the largest weighing over a ton, and then confined to half-mile segments of canal. The manatees ate some of the hyacinths all right. But these marine mammals are not really cows to be penned and pastured, and several caught pneumonia and died before the experiment was abandoned.

lack of policies to keep land reclamation, for agricultural and urban expansion, from increasing water demands beyond the project's ability to increase water supplies, and encouraging overexpansion of development in a region of limited development tolerance. As will later be made evident, these several failings are all closely related and their effects overlap.

Inequitable Cost Sharing. According to the benefit-cost ratio initially computed for the project in 1948, there would be $2.05 in benefits for every dollar spent, a ratio which, given subsequent recomputations of benefits and the counting of benefits not originally included (such as recreation) would increase to 5.3 to 1 by 1973. About 35 percent of project benefits were attributed to flood control, navigation, and preservation of fish and wildlife, and the cost of attaining these benefits was an expense to be borne by the federal government alone. The remaining 65 percent of benefits and costs was attributed to increased land use. The federal government was to bear 40 percent even of these costs, the theory being that increased land use is of benefit to the nation as well as to the state and region. Large benefits for agriculture were foreseen. Project works were expected to permit more profitable use of 1.57 million acres of existing crop land and pasture, and to allow some 726,000 acres to be put to agricultural use for the first time. Of the virgin farm lands, there would be some 530,000 acres in the vicinity of Lake Okeechobee, mostly in the Everglades Agricultural Area, and 128,000 acres in the coastal area east of the perimeter levee.

It is not too much to say that the cost sharing for the $529 million[10] FCD project has favored agricultural interests—and especially the corporate farming enterprises of the Everglades Agricultural Area—in an outrageously unfair way. This seems especially true in light of the other government subsidies available to these enterprises. The plain intent of Congress with respect to Bureau of Reclamation irrigation projects has been to limit the size of individual family holdings eligible for irrigation to 320 acres, even though loopholes in this policy have allowed large corporate farms to be irrigated from bureau projects. From the outset of the flood control project, there was not even a pretence of limiting the size of the individual holdings to be benefited, which was just as well because the high capital cost of farming in the Everglades Agricultural Area had made large corporate farming inevitable there. It would have been enough simply to have the farming interests in this area pay in keeping with benefits received. With 61 percent of total project costs to be borne by federal taxpayers, clearly there was no reason why these interests—receiving the exclusive direct benefit of many project works—should not pay a substantial part of the

10. This figure represents the latest (1973) estimate of project costs, past and projected, for land acquisition and construction; these are the so-called first costs. Included in the project's total costs are operation and maintenance expenses. The federal government has been bearing 82 percent of first costs, 61 percent of total costs.

remainder. This they were able to avoid, however, because farmers and ranchers held political control in the rural counties largely making up the FCD project area and had potent influence in the legislature. In a decision without precedent in the history of Everglades drainage and land reclamation, the legislature decided that the state itself would contribute funds to project construction out of its general revenues. Over the years these construction funds, together with other state contributions, have represented about 43 percent of the total nonfederal spending for the FCD project. The remaining funds have been raised within the seventeen-county project area by an *ad valorem* tax of up to one mill of assessed valuation, the same rate applying to all property owners regardless of benefits received. Urban property in Dade and other Gold Coast counties, much of it situated on the higher lands of the coastal ridge that are not subject to flooding, have accounted for the overwhelming majority of assessed valuations. If urban residents have not vigorously protested the glaring inequity of FCD cost sharing it is probably because the millage rate has been quite low.[11]

Partly because cost sharing for the flood control project has favored agriculture, vast areas have been designated for future agricultural use, whereas, for both economic and environmental reasons, much of this land should have remained as undisturbed wetlands or been restored to a wetland condition. The drainage of the marshes of the Kissimmee River Valley, which I come to in a moment in a somewhat different connection, has been

11. Of all the interests in the Everglades Agricultural Area favored by egregiously unfair public policies, the United States Sugar Corporation provides the prime, if somewhat outsized, example. In 1948, this company controlled 128,000 acres around the south and west shores of Lake Okeechobee and controlled two-thirds of the total of 48,000 acres that had been planted to sugarcane by all growers. The inadequacy of the water-control regimes then serving growers had been made all too clear, and, without the FCD, the future of farming in the Everglades Agricultural Area would have been uncertain at best. As it was, success was to be assured not only by protective FCD works obtained at small cost but also by a national system of quotas to keep sugar prices up, plus federal payments made for compliance with that system and for such good corporate behavior as not hiring child labor and not flouting fair-wage requirements. In 1969, there would be 160,000 acres planted in cane, about two-thirds of it grown by the ten largest producers. Of the $5,094,000 in federal subsidy payments received by area growers for that year, the United States Sugar Corporation, with 37,400 acres in cane, got about one-fifth of the total. Incredible as it might seem, this company will receive still another handsome subsidy. Some $2.5 million worth of improvements in a 32,000-acre local drainage district are to be made by the U.S. Soil Conservation Service, with half to three-fourths of the benefits to accrue to United States Sugar. Seventy-three percent of the costs will be borne by the federal taxpayer. Arthur D. Little, Inc., Final Draft Report, Volume II, Part I, on *Channel Modifications, An Environmental, Economic, and Financial Assessment*, submitted to the Council on Environmental Quality, March 31, 1972. See Field Evaluation No. 11. South Florida Conservancy District Watershed Project (proposed), pp. 11–1 to 11–11. (The Sugar Act under which the quota system has operated expires January 1, 1975, and at this writing, there is little likelihood that Congress will extend it. The world market for sugar today, unlike in times past, is highly favorable to producers.)

Flooding in downtown Fort Lauderdale, 1947; *at right*, drought fire in the saw grass of the Everglades

a major case in point. Another has been the fact that the status of half the land in the Everglades Agricultural Area has been left in an unfortunate state of limbo with the land managed neither for agriculture nor as part of the system of Everglades water conservation areas. There was an early expectation that all of the 700,000 acres in the Everglades Agricultural Area would be farmed, even though, at the time the FCD was established in 1947–48, only 168,000 acres were under cultivation. Yet, today, twenty-five years after the start of the project, the total amount of land cultivated has increased to no more than 400,000 acres. Conditions in the farm economy, together with the fact that the muck already is so shallow in some

Fred Ward—Black Star

areas as to be marginal for farming, kept the expansion from occurring to the degree expected. Because it has been partially drained ever since the Broward era, the land that remains uncultivated, like the land actively being farmed, is undergoing subsidence and gradually losing its potential productiveness. Had all land in the Everglades Agricultural Area been subject to a FCD tax consistent with fair cost sharing principles, things might have been different. If, under those circumstances, all of the land had not been brought into production, the land owners perhaps would have demanded that the uncultivated land be bought by the state, consolidated through land swaps into a single large tract, and diked off for

99 THE PARK AND THE FLOOD CONTROL DISTRICT

reflooding and conservation management. As it was, the FCD tax on the uncultivated land was trivial and nothing was done.

Failure in Setting Priorities. The problem of working out project priorities to provide for an early expansion of the FCD's water storage and delivery capabilities was no better met than the problem of cost sharing. As past droughts had demonstrated, demand for water already could exceed supplies, and the corps' 1948 project report made it clear that large increases in demand by the farming areas and the urban communities could be expected. Indeed, had cultivation in the Everglades Agricultural Area developed as prophesied, the water shortages experienced in south Florida in the sixties and early seventies would have been worse than they actually were. Studies by the U.S. Geological Survey have shown that, with the limited expansion of farming in the Everglades Agricultural Area that did occur, consumption of water by agriculture in Palm Beach County—this county embraces most of the Agricultural Area—has been four and a half times greater than *all* municipal and industrial consumption for the entire Gold Coast.[12] The corps' 1948 report also took note of the water needs of the newly created Everglades National Park. It included the letter of an official of the U.S. Department of the Interior who cautioned that, in the case of the park, the concern was not that there might be too much water, but that there should "not be too little."[13] The corps, for its part, had declared that project plans had been "developed in full recognition" of the importance of the park and that releases of water from conservation storage would help preserve it.[14]

The only way that surface storage of water can be substantially increased in south Florida is to restore Lake Okeechobee to levels more nearly approaching historic conditions. But the problem of controlling the lake presents a dilemma. Because the hurricane and rainy seasons coincide, the lowering of the lake for purposes of hurricane protection may mean the sacrifice of water that will be needed during the dry season. For instance, if rains at the beginning of September bring the lake up to 15½ feet—the level above which hurricane tides might overtop the levee—the gates in the St. Lucie and Caloosahatchee canals must be opened and the lake drawn down to make room for additional safe storage. Furthermore, this action must be taken immediately, because to lower the lake one foot takes about two weeks, and neither hurricanes nor the heavy rains that are capable of raising the lake rapidly above safe levels can be forecast two weeks in advance. Yet, a one-foot drawdown means discharging to the Gulf and the Atlantic 450,000 acre-feet of fresh water, equal to the amount

12. Leach, Klein, and Hampton, op. cit., p. 20.
13. *Comprehensive Report on Central and Southern Florida for Flood Control and Other Purposes,* H. Rept. 643, 80 Cong. 2 sess (1948), p. VII.
14. Ibid., p. 4.

used annually during the sixties by all of the Gold Coast communities combined and better than a third again as much as is needed to meet the annual minimum requirement of the Everglades National Park.[15]

There is but one way the FCD project can possibly resolve the dilemma of having to choose between a possible hurricane disaster and a water shortage—to increase safe storage in the lake by raising the height of the levee. A supplemental measure is to enlarge some of the primary canals in the Everglades Agricultural Area to allow the pumping stations to work at full capacity transferring water from the lake to the new conservation areas. In the early fifties the FCD Governing Board urged the Corps of Engineers to raise the levee and enlarge the canals. The corps decided against enlarging the canals at that time, but, by 1959, the Chief of Engineers had approved a plan to raise the levee by 2 feet, from 15½ feet to 17½. This vital work could surely have been accomplished within five years if given priority, but it was actually to take more than fifteen (not before the mid-1970s at the earliest). In part this was because congressional appropriations for the FCD project were smaller than requested. But it was also because those funds that were provided were not spent according to clear and defensible priorities. The extreme fuzziness of project priorities seems to have been the result of an odd mix of factors of geography, water law, politics, personality, and inequitable cost sharing. First, there was the sheer size of the project area—about a fourth of Florida—and the understandable desire of the Corps of Engineers, the FCD, and the Florida politicians to have most parts of the district share from the beginning in project benefits. Because all waters and lands affected by the flood control project are within Florida, the state has regarded the allocation of water as its sole prerogative. The Corps of Engineers believed that its own responsibility for water management was limited to the safe disposal of flood waters, hence its willingness to dig canals and build levees throughout a 15,000-square-mile area rather than to focus on a few endeavors of high priority. Frank Nix, now a hydrologist at the Everglades National Park, worked at the corps' Jacksonville District office in 1953–55 and worked on the flood control project. "I didn't even know there was a park down here," Nix told me. "Nobody ever mentioned it."

By law, the Florida Cabinet, sitting as the State Board of Conservation, had overall management responsibility for the state's water resources, and, given its authority to review the FCD budget, the board could have influenced flood control project plans and policies. But not until the 1970s

15. The sacrifice of fresh water by such drawdowns is made as a precaution against hurricanes which, on the average, will come once every three to four years although as many as sixteen years have elapsed without a hurricane's passing over or near Lake Okeechobee. The frequency of these storms and the paths they have taken are set forth in *Memorable Hurricanes of the United States Since 1873*, National Oceanic and Atmospheric Administration Technical Memorandum, NWS SR-56, 1971.

would the cabinet begin, in a limited way, to intervene decisively in FCD project planning or execution. In fact, cabinet oversight of water resources programs throughout the state was so casual and permissive that not until the early sixties was there a serious effort to establish some coordination and control over the annual fund requests made to Congress for water projects in various parts of Florida. Thus, in effect, the state's power to manage water for purposes other than flood control was in the hands of the FCD staff and governing board, a less than perfect instrument for setting rational priorities. The Corps of Engineers had the responsibility, the money, and the technical staff to do the planning and design work for the project as well as the letting and supervising of contracts. But the FCD, as the "local cooperator," could negotiate with the corps over plans and priorities, for its concurrence in such matters was necessary.

The FCD board was not a body to accept long deferral of benefits for those powerful agricultural interests that had managed to put the FCD tax burden largely on the back of urban residents. Indeed, those interests were potently represented on it. The board and its staff were based at West Palm Beach and, by law, each of the five members was appointed by the governor from a different county. Early, it became customary for men with farming and ranching interests to be named to the board and for them sometimes to hold a majority of the seats. A former executive head of the Everglades Drainage District, W. Turner Wallis, became general manager of the FCD in late 1952 and set about developing an aggressive constituency by promoting the formation of county water management committees throughout the district. These committees, on which local agricultural, real estate, and chamber of commerce interests were strongly represented, became the medium through which demands for drainage and reclamation in particular areas were pressed. Additions were made to the project by the following sequence of events: a county government would endorse a proposal for some local works, usually on the recommendation of the county water management committee, then send it to the FCD board. Lacking the resources to make its own feasibility study of the proposal, the board would request such a study of the Corps of Engineers. Should the corps determine the proposed work to be feasible according to the engineering and economic criteria which it considered relevant, the proposal then would be submitted to Congress for authorization, which invariably would be granted. This chain of procedures amounted to a default by the FCD as the state agency responsible for overall water management.

Lack of Land Use and Growth Policies. Another fundamental difficulty about the FCD project is that it has been carried forward in a vacuum insofar as a state or regional land use and growth policy is concerned.

The FCD perimeter levee on the eastern edge of the Everglades, together with such other project works as the expanded and improved system of east coast canals, have opened to agriculture and urban development tens of thousands of acres of formerly flood-prone land. Indeed, the new town of Coral Springs, being built by a Westinghouse subsidiary in Broward County, is situated immediately adjacent to the levee. This all means faster population growth, greater demand for water and electric power, and, possibly, both more urban sprawl and more urban congestion. The problem of a growth policy vacuum obviously is much bigger than the FCD and has not been the fault of that agency but of the state government itself. Not until recently has there been any move by the state toward policies that would keep south Florida's growth and development from exceeding the region's resources.

A TRAGIC BLUNDER: THE
KISSIMMEE CHANNELIZATION

The channelization of the Kissimmee River is the preeminent example of how the several basic problems mentioned—inequitable cost sharing, misconceived priorities, and the policy vacuum with respect to growth and land use—all can combine to produce a tragic and costly blunder. This project, on which some $34 million would eventually be spent, has changed the Kissimmee from a stream of 90 meandering river miles to a "wide, broad superhighway" (to quote the FCD's 1964 annual report) of 52 miles. Seasonal flooding of 65 percent of the river's natural flood plain, which had an average width of about 1 mile, was eliminated and most of 25,500 acres of marshland destroyed. In effect, the Kissimmee has disappeared and in its place is Canal "C-38." The unfortunate consequences of this project, which only in the last few years have been fully perceived, are still being added up. That the channelization would result directly in the loss of substantial fish and wildlife resources was known from the beginning, but it is now evident that a greater cause for worry lies with the project's collateral effects on water quality, both in the lakes of the Kissimmee basin and in Lake Okeechobee. Prior to channelization, heavy rains in the Kissimmee basin would cause the basin lakes and the Kissimmee River to rise and flood adjoining marshes, with water levels thereafter falling only gradually over a period of weeks. Under this natural hydrologic regime, the marshes helped maintain water quality by absorbing part of the phosphates and nitrates borne by storm runoff—in a word, they functioned as a "natural filter." With channelization, the river was largely cut off from the marshes, and, because of the channelized river's greatly increased capacity for receiving storm runoff, the lakes of the upper and middle Kissimmee basin could be kept at lower maximum levels, again with less flooding of marshlands. As the Environmental Information

Center at Winter Park has pointed out in a perceptive discussion of the Kissimmee project,[16] the average monthly flow into Lake Okeechobee from the river is about the same now as it was before channelization, but the rate of peak discharges into the lake has increased enormously. During the great hurricane of 1928 as much as 16 inches of rain fell at some localities, as at St. Cloud in the upper basin. Following this major storm, the Kissimmee's discharges into the lake peaked at a rate of 20,000 cubic feet per second (cfs), which is lower than the rates recorded today—with channelization—after storms of much less magnitude. For instance, a 4 inch rainfall in 1969 resulted in a peak discharge of 23,500 cfs. Lake Okeechobee now receives from the channelized river about 40 percent of the nitrogen and nearly 38 percent of the phosphate in its highly over-enriched nutrient budget. Thus, there is now the prospect that Lake Okeechobee will indeed go the way of Lake Apopka, with an excellent sports fishery collapsing, with periodic and massive kills of gizzard shad and other trash fish occurring, and with water quality declining. If, under such

16. ENFO Newsletter of February 1973, published by the Environmental Information Center of the Florida Conservation Foundation, Inc., Winter Park, Florida.

Flood Control District canals and pumping station in Everglades Conservation Area 3. *Facing page, top,* Everglades sugarcane field. Flood control project has made possible a thriving agriculture. *Below,* Everglades vegetable farming is done on a large scale. Shown here is a ten-row mechanical celery harvester and a mechanical in-field packing house or "muletrain."

Patricia Caulfield

Agricultural Research and Education Center, Belle Glade, Fla.

Agricultural Research and Education Center, Belle Glade, Fla.

105 THE PARK AND THE FLOOD CONTROL DISTRICT

conditions, Lake Okeechobee remains a recreational asset, it is likely to be one only for those people who never knew the lake as it once was.

Yet the channelization of the river will not keep the Kissimmee basin lakes from overflowing into developed areas the next time the basin is visited by truly exceptional rains. The channelized river and related works are designed to cope with a 10-year flood, but not the greater floods that can be expected to occur at intervals of up to 50 to 100 years. Thus, the Kissimmee project in a sense represents a mischievous invitation to developers to encroach upon historic flood plains that can be developed only at considerable risk. Benefits will be realized from converting marshes to improved pasture and sites for urban development, but these will probably be more than offset by large if infrequent flood losses, not to mention the disappearance of marshes important to fish and wildlife and to maintaining water quality.

The mere fact that the Kissimmee channelization has been completed while the work of raising the Lake Okeechobee levee remains unfinished is enough to make this project remarkably perverse. Without the higher levee, flood waters suddenly discharged from the Kissimmee into Lake Okeechobee often cannot safely be stored there and may have to be discharged into the Gulf and the Atlantic.

The U.S. Fish and Wildlife Service once proposed a way to increase the rate of flood discharges from the Kissimmee basin without destroying the river marsh. Its plan featured the concept of a Kissimmee "floodway." Several variations were suggested, but the one preferred by the service would have involved some minimal straightening and deepening of parts of the river together with constructing levees along the two edges of the marsh. But the adoption of such a plan would have meant less new pasturage for cattle men and less flood plain land open to development. The floodway concept was rejected by the Corps of Engineers, as was the service's recommendation that a public hearing be held on the prospective loss of the river marsh. Some features for "mitigation" of damages to fish and wildlife were included in project plans, but these were to prove largely unsuccessful.

By the time the Kissimmee channelization was completed at the start of the 1970s, many Florida political leaders as well as environmentalists were deploring its consequences, present and foreseeable. Environmentalists contended that the inflow of nutrients into Lake Okeechobee could be reduced to acceptable levels only by stringent land use and pollution control throughout the Kissimmee basin and by the reflooding of some or all of the Kissimmee marshes. In November 1972, the FCD board, by now reformed in makeup and philosophy, recommended establishment of an accelerated program of land and water use regulation for the basin. Looking beyond a FCD staff plan for a limited restoration of the Kissimmee marshes, the board proposed that the possibility of an even more ambitious restoration—one looking to the dismantlement of all or part of the Kissimmee River project—should at least be investigated. Inasmuch as dismantling the project and bringing the river marshes under public ownership could cost $88 million or more, there is no real likelihood of a total or near-total marsh restoration. That such an idea can be entertained at all, however, is a measure of how reckless the Kissimmee channelization was. The "Kissimmee Ditch," as the channelized river is often called, stands not only as the FCD's worst mistake, it has become a symbol of water resource management gone awry.

THE EVERGLADES NATIONAL PARK

Some of Florida's boosters of growth and development began to fear in the late 1960s and early 1970s that the water needs of the Everglades National Park might interfere with the expansion of the population and economy along the Gold Coast. As a prominent environmentalist characterized the attitude of one advocate of more or less unrestrained growth, the park was regarded as "another country, and an unfriendly country at that."[17] In fact, the park was anything but alien in its origins. The campaign that went on between the mid-1920s and the late 1950s to establish the park and enlarge its boundaries was one waged chiefly by Floridians and was as indigenous to Florida as Governor Broward's earlier campaign to drain the Everglades. At the time the Everglades National Park was created, new parks always had been established either by withdrawals from the federal domain or by gifts from either a state or a wealthy private benefactor. In 1903, President Theodore Roosevelt, by a withdrawal from the federal domain, had established in Florida the first national wildlife refuge in the United States—the Pelican Island Refuge along the Indian River. And, in 1908, Roosevelt, again by withdrawals from unallocated federal domain lands, had created the first of the national forests east of the Mississippi—the Ocala National Forest, in the Big Scrub east of the Oklawaha River, and the Choctawhatchee National Forest, in the Florida panhandle.[18] But by the 1920s, when establishment of the Everglades Na-

17. These words were used by Nathaniel P. Reed, environmental adviser to the Governor of Florida and later Assistant Secretary of the Interior for Fish, Wildlife, and Parks, to describe the attitude of Randolph Hodges, director of the Florida Department of Natural Resources, a development-oriented state official who had consistently opposed a water guarantee for the park. They aptly describe an attitude by no means rare among people who see any diminishing of Florida's growth as bad for business. Reed's remark was quoted in the Miami Herald of March 12, 1971.

18. The establishment of the national wildlife refuges and national forests in Florida represents, on the whole, one of the brighter aspects of resource management in the state. By 1972, there were twenty Florida units in the National Wildlife Refuge System. Some of these are of less than 50 acres in size, but others are large, such as the 64,000-acre St. Mark's Refuge (drawn partly from the federal domain) on the Gulf coast below Tallahassee and the 145,000-acre Loxahatchee Refuge, which makes up one

tional Park was first being proposed, there remained no possibility of a withdrawal from the federal domain for that purpose. Land within the proposed park area had long since passed from federal to state jurisdiction under the Swamp Lands Act, with much of it having been disposed of under state grants to private interests such as Flagler's Florida East Coast Railroad and Model Land Company. As for the idea of the federal government's *buying* land to establish a park, this was at that time a concept wholly without political currency. It was not until 1961, when Congress authorized the establishment of the Cape Cod National Seashore, that the government first actually undertook to establish a new unit of the national park system by purchase of private lands (although it had in some earlier cases supplemented state and private donations of land through purchases). For an Everglades National Park to be established, the state of Florida would have to press for it in Congress and give extensive tracts of land to get the park started.

A long struggle was to ensue, however, between those Floridians who envisioned a large Everglades park as the means of preserving a precious piece of the state's natural heritage and those who felt that such a park would obstruct progress. Perhaps because they owed their election to a statewide constituency, a succession of governors during the 1940s and 1950s sought to have a sizeable park established, while the legislature, still a body of generally parochial attitudes, waxed and waned in its support of the proposal.

ERNEST COE, A MAN OBSESSED. The first steps toward creating the park go back to the second decade of this century. In 1916 the Florida Federation of Women's Clubs persuaded the legislature to designate a verdant tropical hammock in southwest Dade as the Royal Palm State Park, with the understanding that the park would be managed by the federation itself. In the twenties Ernest F. Coe, a landscape architect of Coconut

---

of the FCD conservation areas in the upper Everglades. For the most part, the refuge properties are made up of lands purchased with funds appropriated under the Duck Stamp Act of 1934, or of lands obtained for refuge management by agreement with either the state (the agreement for the Loxahatchee Refuge being the major example) or with the National Aeronautics and Space Administration, as in the case of the 83,800-acre Merritt Island Refuge near Cape Canaveral. There are now three national forests in north Florida and the panhandle, not counting the Choctawhatchee Forest, which was transferred to the War Department in 1940 to become the site of Eglin Air Force Base. The Ocala National Forest was more than doubled in size through purchases under the Weeks Act of 1911, a statute which has had much to do with the establishment of national forests in the eastern United States, and today the Ocala Forest covers about 366,000 acres. In 1931, the Osceola National Forest, of 157,000 acres, was established in north Florida with land purchased under the Weeks Act; in 1936, the Apalachicola National Forest, which would eventually cover 557,000 acres, was established, again with Weeks Act funds and later with purchases made under the Bankhead-Jones Farm Tenant Act of 1937, a measure for the buying up of submarginal farm land for soil conservation purposes.

Grove, began promoting, like a man obsessed, the idea that much of the lower Everglades and the coastal mangroves and bays below the glades should be preserved as a national park. Marjory Stoneman Douglas has described him: "Gentle-mannered, soft voiced and mild, a man on fire with the passion of the idea that would possess him for the rest of his life. No one ever wrote more letters, paralyzed more people with his insistent talk, was considered more a fanatic, than Ernest Coe."[19]

Coe gradually won some influential supporters for the park idea and these included Gilbert Pearson, the National Audubon Society leader who had played a major part in stopping the slaughter of plume birds; David Fairchild, horticulturist (and son-in-law of Alexander Graham Bell) who often entertained visiting scientists at his Coconut Grove estate; and Miss Douglas's own father, Frank B. Stoneman, editor of the *Miami Herald*. The park proposal gained sufficient support to be politically respectable, particularly inasmuch as it came along at a time when prospects for development in the lower glades were scarcely bullish. The land and water areas being discussed for inclusion in the park were mostly below the right of way of the Tamiami Trail, then under construction in a region served by no drainage canals and remote from the farming area below Lake Okeechobee. The Florida real estate boom ended in the fall of 1926 and land prices in the Everglades and the Big Cypress, as well as in Miami, were plummeting, not rising. If anything, the establishment of the national park was expected to aid in the economic recovery of south Florida by attracting more tourists.

THE WILBUR REPORT. By 1926, Florida's U.S. senators were calling for a study by the Department of the Interior of the possibility of establishing the park. Such an investigation was finally made in 1930 by a team that included among its seven members Horace Albright, then director of the National Park Service. The study team toured the lower glades, the Ten Thousand Islands, Florida Bay, and the upper Florida Keys by all means available—foot, automobile, skiff, even dirigible. Its report, delivered to Congress by Secretary of the Interior Ray L. Wilbur, was strongly in favor of establishing the park to preserve a piece of the United States' only subtropical wilderness. Two years later, in a prophetic letter to Albright, Wilbur expressed concern about the proposed park's supply of fresh water and said that a wide area to the north of the park should be kept as a natural watershed.

On the face of it, the Everglades National Park proposal would have seemed assured of quick congressional approval. The park bills introduced in Congress by Florida members stipulated that the federal government was to spend nothing toward acquiring land for the park, all of which

19. Marjory Stoneman Douglas, *Florida: The Long Frontier* (New York: Harper & Row, 1967), pp. 281–2.

would be donated by the state. In 1929, the legislature had established an Everglades park commission and given it the authority—but not the money —to acquire the park lands. Ernest Coe was named commission chairman, and, in 1931, the I.I. Board was authorized to turn over to the Coe Commission several hundred thousand acres of state-owned land in the lower glades. The park bills encountered no serious trouble in the Senate, where such measures were passed in 1930, '32, and '34. But the House of Representatives refused to authorize the park until 1934, when finally the park legislation was passed over strong Republican opposition.

"A SNAKE SWAMP PARK." The very fact that the state was willing to give land for the park had caused the Republicans to raise their guard. The park proposal was viewed by them as an attempt to trap the federal government into building expensive roads and other improvements in south Florida in return for nothing better than, as one member put it, a "snake swamp park on perfectly worthless land."[20] It was even suggested that the park would promote the land holdings and financial interests of Barron Collier, who happened to be a prominent Democrat. It was pointed out in rebuttal that the park proposal had the endorsement of national conservation organizations and scientific societies as well as that of the Department of the Interior.

Although the country was in the fourth year of the Depression, with nearly 8 million people still unemployed, this circumstance did not appear to everyone as an argument against creating parks for people to enjoy. Willis Robertson, Democratic congressman from Virginia, spoke to this point during the House floor debate by quoting Wordsworth's "The World is Too Much With Us."[21] The vote in favor of the bill was 222 to 145.

With this measure's enactment, the park would be established once the state donated the necessary land. The maximum boundaries set forth in the bill embraced 2,164,500 acres of land and water, and included most of Key Largo, all of Florida Bay, and some 300,000 acres in the Big Cypress to the north of the Tamiami Trail as well as roughly three-quarters of the great crescent of coastal mangroves and most of the saw grass Everglades to the south of the trail (see figure 4–2). Except for the northwest reaches of the Ten Thousand Islands, between Marco Island and the vicinity of the town of Everglades, no important part of the wilderness below the trail had been overlooked.

UNSETTLED BOUNDARIES. The maximum boundaries were not necessarily meant to be the boundaries, however. U.S. Senator Duncan U. Fletcher of Florida, in a statement on the Senate floor, observed that "The bill

20. Lehlbach, U.S. Representative, *Congressional Record*, 73 Cong. 2 sess. (1934), p. 9497.

21. Willis Robertson, U.S. Representative, ibid., p. 9500.

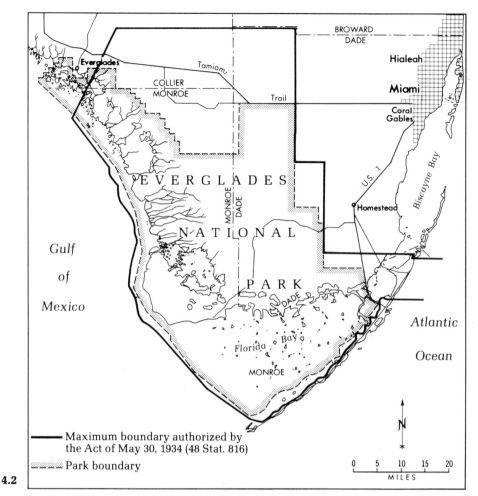

4.2 1934 maximum boundaries of the Everglades National Park and more restrictive actual boundaries of 1958

merely provides for the establishment of a national park within [the maximum boundaries]. We do not yet know the size of it." As matters turned out, twenty-four years would pass before the park boundaries were fixed. The major cause of delay was the state's ambivalence, for Florida officials were now beginning to hedge on the generous commitments the state had made earlier. Lamar Johnson, who at the time was one of the top ranking engineers with the Everglades Drainage District (which held title to some 6,100 acres in the lower glades), followed park developments closely. "On the one hand," Johnson told me, "the state wanted the park as a tourist attraction and was promoting it. On the other hand, it was playing the reluctant dragon when it came to providing the land."

SPECULATION IN OIL LEASES. Widespread speculation in oil leases and a general rise in land prices as economic conditions improved were partly responsible for the state's reluctance to deliver the land, Johnson believes. The state itself had encouraged the speculation by selling mineral leases on hundreds of thousands of acres to parties who then subdivided these lease holdings, often in 40-acre parcels, and resold them at a large profit. In the Murphy Act of 1937 the Florida Legislature had provided that vast acreages on which tax payments were in arrears could be sold to anyone willing to pay the taxes due. Because of the excitement over oil leases many owners of such properties decided to pay up their taxes and hold the land for speculation; further, much of the land that was sold under the Murphy Act was bought by speculators. The oil strike made in 1943 at Sunniland in the Big Cypress, heightened the speculative fever.

FLORIDA MEETS ITS COMMITMENT. Nevertheless, the commitment by the state to provide land for the park, was never repudiated, and during the wartime administration of Governor Spessard L. Holland the state began to meet it. From that point on, establishment of the park would be accomplished in two tortuous phases, extending over about fifteen years. The first phase involved: (i) an agreement between the Florida Cabinet and National Park Service officials for park boundaries much reduced from the maximum Congress had allowed; (ii) the conveyance of 850,000 acres of state property—much of it being a remnant from the federal grant of swamp and overflowed lands—to the National Park Service, plus an appropriation by the legislature of $2 million for the purchase of additional lands by the Park Service; and (iii) a formal dedication of the park in 1947 at the town of Everglades, with President Harry S Truman attending. The second phase involved still other boundary changes that would have the net effect of a further substantial reduction in the size of the park from what Ernest Coe had dreamed.

THE BIG CYPRESS EXCLUDED. In 1944 Holland and the cabinet reached an agreement with Park Service officials to exclude from the park all land above the Tamiami Trail. This decision, along with some of the other boundary changes agreed to, meant that the park would have no control over the important part of its watershed that was in the Big Cypress. But it also meant that plans to set up the park would not be opposed by the Collier interests, for now none of Collier County would be within the proposed boundaries. Far from seeing a financial advantage in the park, as some congressional Republicans had suggested, Barron Collier, who died in 1939, had been much opposed to any of his holdings being taken for the park, and this policy was continued for some time after his death by his successors in the Collier Corporation. Barron Collier had expected major development to occur in the Big Cypress. "He thought fabulous things were going to happen out there, but they didn't and he died broke [or rather land poor]," Walter P. Fuller, a St. Petersburg realtor who was a business associate of Collier's, told me.

Governor Holland also agreed to the exclusion of some farm lands in west Dade from the park and made some major boundary concessions to Monroe County. State Representative Bernie C. Papy of Key West, influential member of the legislature and the man-to-see in Monroe, was able to have excluded from the boundaries most of that part of the Big Cypress lying south of the Tamiami Trail, plus all of the higher, more habitable keys, including heavily forested Lignum Vitae Key and Shell Key (in 1972, these two keys would finally be acquired by the state at a cost of $1.9 million, of which $200,000 would be raised by the Nature Conservancy).

POKER AT HORSESHOE LAKE. The $2 million the state was obliged to give as one of the conditions for the park's establishment was believed to be sufficient for purchase of private lands within the park boundaries. Yet to obtain that much money for such a purpose from the ultra-conservative, rural-dominated Florida Legislature might have seemed impossible. But the *Miami Herald* was a force in Florida politics, and John Pennekamp, the *Herald*'s editorial director and member of the Everglades National Park Commission, had been campaigning for the park. When the need for a lawyer arose and the commission had no money to hire one, Governor Millard F. Caldwell (Holland's successor) suggested that Pennekamp seek the help of the Florida Power and Light Company (FP&L). FP&L would be a useful ally in any event, for in those days, especially, FP&L could influence politicians as readily as it could generate electricity.

What followed was a subtle, casual exercise in power, by Pennekamp, by the head of the power company, and by the key legislators who controlled appropriations. McGregor Smith, FP&L's board chairman, not only provided an attorney, he also arranged a meeting between the legislative leaders and Pennekamp at the company's fishing camp on Horseshoe Lake near Ocala. A poker game followed a chicken and rice dinner at the camp, and Pennekamp, who says that when winning he is insufferable, raked in pot after pot with high elation and much joking at the losers' expense. Finally, one of the state senators said, "Why don't we just give Penny that $2 million when the legislature meets? Maybe he'll lay off us."[22] This was a firm commitment, and the money was duly appropriated.

Of the $2 million, $400,000 went to buy 200,000 acres, at $2 an acre, from the Flagler heirs' Model Land Company, which had been set up by Henry Flagler to manage the swamp and overflowed lands granted by the state to his Florida East Coast Railway. The remainder of the money did not go as far as had been expected, for some land owners had begun sub-

22. Quoted in Nixon Smiley, "Poker Game Helped Found Everglades Park," *Miami Herald*, December 3, 1967.

dividing their holdings and selling them off in small parcels to anyone gullible enough to buy. For instance, as Pennekamp later told a congressional committee, the park commission once received a pathetic appeal from an elderly couple who were searching for the nine lots for which they had paid $3,440—lots which the commission determined to be in a remote area where land was probably worth not more than $1 an acre.

BOUNDARIES MEETING THE PARK'S "MOST VITAL NEEDS." In his efforts during the 1950s to fix the park boundaries, Spessard Holland, now a senator, had vexing problems with the legislature and the I.I. Board. In 1951, the I.I. Board had, at the request of the Park Service, adopted a resolution agreeing to extend the boundaries to the northwest to take in that part of the Ten Thousand Islands around the town of Everglades. The upper 30,000 acres was being given by the Collier family, which now had visions of Everglades becoming the park's "western gateway," with an influx of tourists giving a lift to this out-of-the-way and languishing little county seat in the mangroves. But the "Northwest Extension" included a stretch of mangrove islands and mainland marshes in Monroe County as well as in Collier, and others besides the Park Service had plans for the area in Monroe. In 1953, the legislature, in one of the "local bills" for which it was noted, enacted a measure that would have prohibited the I.I. Board from donating any more land in Monroe County for the park. This measure was vetoed by the governor. Later that same year the I.I. Board sold a lease for a 17,000-acre tract within the Northwest Extension, at 50 cents a year per acre, to a company that planned to begin cutting the mangroves for the manufacture of textile loom shuttles—a venture, which, fortunately, was never carried out. In early 1954, the I.I. Board actually rescinded its 1951 resolution agreeing to the new park boundaries. Senator Holland protested these actions strongly, calling them a repudiation of past commitments. Apparently unmoved by his protests, the legislature in 1955 adopted a resolution stating that that part of the Northwest Extension through the Ten Thousand Islands in Monroe County should be confined to a narrow inside passageway, between the islands facing the Gulf and the mainland marshes. Officials of Monroe County and some owners of land in or adjacent to the Northwest Extension wanted freedom to build drainage canals to tidewater, and they wanted nothing to prevent conversion of the tide-washed mangrove islands facing the Gulf into developable land.

Opposition to the park boundary bill came not only from Monroe County officials but also from sportsmen's groups whose perspectives on conservation seemed limited to what could be seen over a shotgun barrel. Hunters had been barred from venturing into the park in their airboats and swamp buggies and many were against extending the park boundaries. Commercial fisherman who used the Ten Thousand Islands—sometimes deliberately stirring up suffocating, gill-clogging clouds of silt from shallow bay bottoms to drive schools of mullet into their nets—also protested any extension of the park boundaries.

Senator Holland had, however, the support of Governor LeRoy Collins as well as that of the *Miami Herald* and other influential newspapers. In 1958 the boundary bill was enacted, with the I.I. Board having given a grudging assurance that the state lands necessary for the Northwest Extension would be provided. Altogether, the park would embrace about 1,337,000 acres of land and water—a very large area, even if some 827,000 acres smaller than that defined in the "maximum" boundaries of the 1934 act. But some potentially serious problems remained. With nearly all of the Big Cypress excluded from the boundaries, the entire northwest arm of the park now extended only a few miles inland from the coastal mangrove zone.

Nevertheless, passage of the 1958 act was regarded as a signal achievement by the park's supporters, because now the park boundaries had been fixed and the Department of the Interior had, in a euphoric moment, proclaimed them adequate to meet the park's "most vital and essential needs."[23]

23. Hatfield Chilson, Under Secretary of the Interior, in a letter of June 11, 1957, to Senator James E. Murray of Montana, chairman of the Senate Interior Committee.

The years of drought and the land and water laws of 1972

In a real sense the progenitor of the 1972 land and water management legislation that marked Florida's first attempt to cope broadly with its land crisis was the severe south Florida drought of 1971. This drought, however, was but the latest in what seemed a cyclical series that had begun in the early 1940s. The recurrent droughts ultimately were to give rise to increasing speculation that south Florida was going to "run out of water" and that the growth of its population and economy would be limited because of it. Therefore, the story of how the new land and water management laws came to be enacted begins not in 1971 or '72 but much earlier.

Periodic water shortages have, of course, been but one manifestation of south Florida's deepening environmental crisis, and perhaps not the worst of them. If willing to make the hard choices, the residents of this region need never find themselves desperately short of water. For one thing, a choice can be made between more people and less agriculture inasmuch as the consumptive demand for water by agriculture is several times greater than that of all other users. Even without any reduction in agricultural activity, a population substantially larger than the existing one could get along on the water now available in south Florida if the growth were properly planned and if rationing were ordered in time of shortages. To have to stop watering lawns or washing cars temporarily may be an inconvenience but it is not a crisis. Just to reverse existing schedules of water rates by charging more as use increases rather than less would in itself reduce per capita demand if the schedules were made steep enough.

THE PARK SUFFERS, CONGRESS RESPONDS

Nonetheless, for a growing number of Floridians the region's emerging "water crisis" had, by the early 1970s, become symbolic of the larger problem of growth and the decline in quality of life in south Florida.

THE FCD FAILS TO DELIVER. The drought of the early to mid-1960s produced the first widespread public awareness that competition for water might become severe. The Everglades National Park was in a particularly bad situation because it was at the lower end of the new FCD system. The flood control project, especially through the establishment of the water conservation areas, had helped protect the Gold Coast from saltwater intrusion and to mitigate effects of the drought in that part of the Everglades above Tamiami Trail. But, below the trail, in the park, effects of the drought were disastrous and, for a time, the project works actually aggravated them. Although the park normally receives about 80 percent of its water directly from rainfall, the overland flow into the park can be vitally important. This flow comes mostly from the Big Cypress and from those parts of the Everglades lying to the north of the trail and to the east of the park (figure 5–1). The completion of levee 29 in late 1962 closed off the park from Conservation Area No. 3—that is, from most of the upper Everglades. Although this levee, which runs along the north side of the trail, was equipped with gates for releases, none were made. The policies of the FCD and the Corps of Engineers, then governing the project, contemplated such releases only when the water in storage was at or near the area's maximum capacity. Despite the vague assurances contained in the Corps of Engineers' 1948 Project Report, there were no plans to meet the park's minimum needs. And given its slow progress in increasing regional water storage and delivery capacity, the FCD was not prepared to release water to the park except during wet years when all of the park's water needs might in any case be more than satisfied by rainfall directly within the park boundaries. Thus, although parched and "burning up" from the extended drought, the park received no significant amount of water from the project from 1962 until 1965. The point is disputed, but Frank

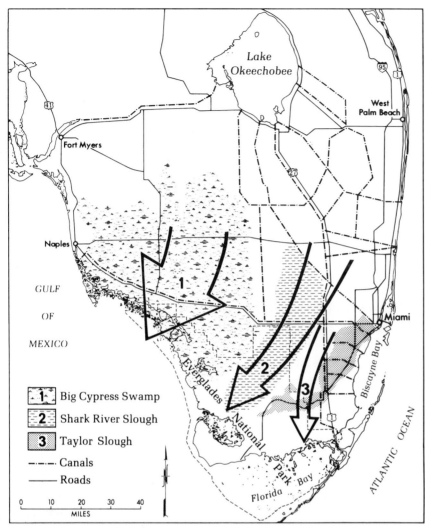

5.1

Three major natural drainage systems of the Everglades-Big Cypress region

Nix, the park hydrologist, contends that enough rain occurred over the conservation areas to have permitted the release of 100,000 acre-feet of water during one of the drought years and smaller releases in other years. Yet, had more water been released to the park, less would have been available for recharging the Biscayne Aquifer and protecting the Gold Coast well fields from salt intrusion. The Flood Control District governing board had been unwilling to make such a sacrifice. As one board member is reported to have put it, "People come before birds."[1]

The Everglades National Park is sometimes referred to as a "biological" park famous principally for its bird and animal life, whereas western parks

1. Verne Williams, "The Glades Are Parching," *Washington Post*, March 13, 1966.

such as Yellowstone and Yosemite are noted more for their geological features. The drought struck hard at the park's biology. In 1962, rookeries at East River and Cuthbert Lake, where some 20,000 wood ibis and egrets had nested each year from February to May, failed to form for the first time in memory; when this was repeated in 1963 and 1964 there was concern that the rookeries might be lost forever. The drying up of the 'gator holes contributed to the nesting failures and also caused losses of the other creatures dependent on these dry-season refuges, including of course the alligators themselves. Some of the alligators left stranded without water were captured by rangers and moved to water holes elsewhere in the park. In some cases where no survival hole was available, rangers would blast one from the limestone bedrock with dynamite. The marine life of Florida Bay was also threatened by the prolonged drought; with no fresh water entering the bay from the glades, its shallow waters were at times becoming twice as salty as sea water.

THE 1968 WATER RESOURCES REPORT. For the largely federally supported flood control project not to provide for its only major federal client, the national park, was a situation that obviously should not continue. As early as May 1962, Senator Spessard Holland, as vigorous an advocate of the project as he was of the park, called for a study to see if the park's water needs could not be met. Subsequently, a $400,000 investigation by

Game warden patrolling by airboat in Everglades Conservation Area; *at right,* deer abound in Everglades conservation areas.

the Corps of Engineers, culminated in the five-volume water resources report of 1968.[2] This report concluded that the project as then authorized could not, even if completed promptly, meet all water needs of central and southern Florida beyond 1976. Moreover, a 90 percent increase in agricultural acreage was projected for the some fifty years covered by the report and a better than fourfold expansion of the population.[3] Urban water needs, covering municipal and industrial use and the water needed for salinity and pollution control, were expected to increase from 780,000 acre-feet in 1970 to 1.84 million acre-feet in 2020; the water required for farm irrigation in the Lake Okeechobee and lower east coast regions would increase by a half million acre-feet, the total rising from 1.1 million to 1.65 million. To meet these growing water demands at least through 2004, the report outlined a $70.3 million solution, consisting of these three major elements:

(i) Raise the Lake Okeechobee levee sufficiently to permit 21½ feet of safe storage—4 feet higher than the 17½-foot maximum that was still years from being achieved.

(ii) "Back pump" some of the storm runoff entering east coast canals into the conservation areas rather than discharge it into the Atlantic.

2. U.S. Army Corps of Engineers, Jacksonville District, *Water Resources for Central and Southern Florida* (1968).

3. U.S. Army Corps of Engineers, *Water Resources for Central and Southern Florida* (1968). Main Report. See page 12 for population projections and page 30 for expansion of agricultural acreage projected.

(iii) Improve and extend the project canal system, permitting better conveyance and distribution of available water supplies.

The comments that the Corps of Engineers received from other agencies about the report signified that a controversy was in the making. A primary objective of the corps plan was to deliver each year to the park at least 315,000 acre-feet of water, the volume requested by the National Park Service on the basis of known historical flows. Mindful that the corps had not delivered on the promises of 1948, Park Service officials this time wanted a legally binding guarantee. Accordingly, in a letter to corps head-quarters, Harthon L. Bill, the Park Service's deputy director, said the delivery of water to the park should be established as a primary purpose of the project.[4] His position was that, while the park's needs would not receive priority over the *existing* needs of other users, its needs should be satisfied before any water went to meet new demands resulting from further growth of the region's population and economy. State and Flood Control District officials, on the other hand, took exception to the Park Service viewpoint. Randolph Hodges, director of the Florida Board of Conservation (and later head of the new Department of Natural Resources), said that the park was a "creature of Nature's adversity" and "just one of several customers" seeking project water.[5] The Park Service should share adversity cheerfully, he added, and "refrain from inciting the public either directly or indi-rectly . . . against the Flood Control District or against the state. . . ."[6] Hodges emphasized that it was the state's prerogative to allocate project waters as it chose.

The FCD's executive director, G. E. Dail, Jr., in his comments on the corps report, noted another matter of concern. The corps' projections, he observed, indicated that, even with construction of the proposed new works, south Florida would again be "running out of water" at the turn of the century. Dail indicated that so "pessimistic" a view could not be justified for a region with an average annual rainfall of more than 53 inches. "You must recognize the importance of the development of adequate surface water both in sustaining the economic growth of our area and in preserving the value of the national park," he wrote the corps.[7] In sum, the attitude expressed by water management officials was that the growth of the region could be expected to continue indefinitely and that the corps' pessimistic supply and demand curves with respect to water was not reason enough to interfere with that growth.

Yet, if anything, the Corps of Engineers had been more optimistic about the prospects of expanding regional water supplies than the facts

4. U.S. Army Corps of Engineers, op. cit., Appendix III.
5. Ibid.
6. Ibid.
7. Ibid.

of the situation warranted. Although the new corps plan was approved by Congress in the public works authorization act of 1968, to obtain the appropriations needed to carry it out was quite another matter. The exigencies of the federal budgetary situation were such that, even if the plan engendered no controversy, the funding of it would probably be long stretched out. And the fact was that, except for the proposed improvements in the system of conveyance canals, the plan was controversial. One possibility disturbing to many people was that the works proposed might aggravate conditions already contributing to the overenrichment and eutrophication of Lake Okeechobee. The Florida Game and Fresh Water Fish Commission had warned that to raise the lake level much above the long-standing goal of 17½ feet above sea level would decrease the extent of the shallows where rooted marsh and aquatic plants thrive and take up nutrients.[8] Less vegetation would mean that more nutrients would be available to support the algal blooms that could reduce water quality, alter the ecology of the lake, and destroy much of the lake's recreational value. There was also the possibility that, while the high lake levels contemplated might cause ecological damage when they did occur, they would not occur regularly enough to provide dependable insurance against water shortages. To pump agricultural runoff from St. Lucie County into the lake—another feature of the corps plan—would increase the inflow of nutrients and probably of pesticides and other pollutants. Similarly, the backpumping of surplus water from the east coast canals into the conservation areas could dump heavy loads of nutrients and pollutants into those areas, especially under the conditions of rapid agricultural expansion and urban growth that the corps had postulated. The corps was looking to more stringent and better enforced water quality standards to overcome this problem. Yet the efficacy of pollution control efforts had not yet been demonstrated, and prospects were (and are) particularly doubtful for controlling diffuse, "nonpoint" forms of pollution such as the pesticides borne by the runoff from farmland.

A WATER GUARANTEE FOR THE PARK. Against this background of a developing water shortage for which no clearly acceptable solution had been proposed, Congress in 1970 provided the water guarantee for the Everglades National Park that the Park Service wanted. Although the legal right to allocate water is vested in the states, Congress could get around that by making its support of the flood control project conditional upon the park's getting its share of project water. Senator Gaylord Nelson of Wisconsin, sponsor of the water guarantee measure for the park, seized upon that very possibility. The fund authorization for the flood control project was to carry

8. Ibid.

the proviso that, as soon as improvements in the system of conveyance canals permitted, the park would receive 315,000 acre-feet of water annually, or 16.5 percent of total project deliveries, whichever is less. Nelson, with help from Senator Edmund S. Muskie of Maine, succeeded in having the measure adopted despite Senator Holland's opposition. In this, Nelson had the encouragement and support of the increasingly influential national conservation groups, which were showing special concern for the park both because of past droughts and because of the threat to it from the proposed south Florida regional jetport.

The congressional hearings held on the proposed water guarantee brought a collision of ideas as to what Florida should do about population growth. Although devoted to the park, Senator Holland could not envision somehow limiting growth—and hence water demand—in south Florida. "The ever-increasing population will continue to demand an ever-increasing amount of fresh water, and ways and means will have to be found to use and reuse this precious resource," Holland said.[9] While the Senator was hopeful that the park would never suffer, he emphasized that the water demands of the Gold Coast population, present and future, held first priority. Nelson and Muskie, on the contrary, took the view that there was no valid reason to risk the destruction of the park when water supplies in south Florida could in any event be stretched only so far. "The point has to be emphasized," said Senator Muskie, "that when you have come to the end of your resources, you have come to the end of your resources."[10] In a colloquy with Holland's Florida colleague, Senator Edward J. Gurney, Nelson made the point more explicit:

> GURNEY: Is your answer that we should deny people water if we come to the crunch between people and the park?
>
> NELSON: My answer is you can have as much growth in the area as its resources will support. . . . I would not destroy the park for the purpose of creating some more industries and another town. . . . If [people] know that they can't have [the water needed by the park], the growth that would depend on it would not occur.[11]

The enactment of Nelson's proposed water guarantee was gratifying to the Park Service and its allies, but there was every possibility that that guarantee would ultimately prove hollow. As Senator Muskie observed during the hearings, without a policy of controlled growth, "The pressures for making this water available to people rather than wildlife in case of a drought will be overwhelming, whatever policy we write here."[12]

9. *Rivers and Harbors Subcommittee.* Hearings before the Senate Committee on Public Works, 91 Cong. 2 sess. (1970), p. 44.
10. Ibid., p. 117.
11. Ibid., p. 116.
12. Ibid., p. 112.

MORE DROUGHT AND THE
GOVERNOR'S WATER
CONFERENCE

The issue of uncontrolled growth and rising water demands was, as it turned out, to be brought forcibly to public attention by one of the worst droughts ever recorded in south Florida. From the end of October 1970 through April of 1971 the rain gauge at Miami International Airport measured a total of 2.04 inches, less than a third of that ever previously recorded for that period. By the end of April, fires had swept over more than 400,000 acres of the Everglades. Smoke from these muck and saw grass fires created severe driving hazards for motorists, on one occasion tying up rush-hour traffic over a forty-block stretch of Dade's Palmetto Expressway. "We can't give a report because we can't see," came the word from a radio station's traffic helicopter. The City of Miami had to shut down eight of its water supply wells because of saltwater intrusion. The water table in south Dade dropped below sea level and farmers had to install stronger pumps and make other costly changes in their irrigation equipment. Some south Florida cattle ranchers were appealing for federal emergency funds for the digging of wells and ponds for their endangered livestock. With the drought still in progress at the beginning of May, the FCD ordered those farm irrigation districts that were drawing water directly from its canals to cut their withdrawals by a third. Although lacking authority to order farm interests or municipalities to reduce withdrawals of groundwater, the FCD exhorted all water users to lower their consumption. Some municipalities promptly enacted ordinances to stop or reduce lawn watering and the like, but other cities did little or nothing. Fortunately, just as the water shortage was becoming critical with less than one-half foot of usable storage left in Lake Okeechobee, late spring rains finally arrived and the drought ended.

Governor Askew, looking for a way for south Florida to break the trend toward recurrent and worsening water shortages, called the South Florida Water Management Conference. For this conference, held in September 1971, some 150 professional and lay people were assembled who had either special knowledge of the water problems of south Florida or a special political interest. They included conservation group leaders, local government officials, some key state legislators, and a number of scientists and engineers from Florida universities and state and federal agencies. In his opening speech, the governor made clear that he wanted the conferees to address themselves squarely to the problem of south Florida's almost uncontrolled growth. "It's time we stopped viewing our environment through prisms of profit, politics, and geography or local and personal pride," he said. "Already the cities, the farms, and the Everglades National Park are engaged in a fierce competition for Lake Okeechobee's dwindling supply of water. As the population expands and the supply [of water] continues to diminish, then that competition becomes critical."[13]

"We must build a peace in south Florida," the governor said, "a peace between the people and their place. . . ." The chairman of the conference, John M. DeGrove, then dean of the College of Social Science at Florida Atlantic University (a new state institution at Boca Raton), believes that it was the governor's frank recognition of the growth problem that caused the conferees to respond in kind. "It was the first time any high state official in Florida had questioned the goodness of growth," DeGrove told me.

The report of the conference called for limiting population densities within the region according to a comprehensive land and water use plan developed and enforced by state and regional boards, which the governor would appoint.[14] This proposal was entirely out of keeping with Florida and U.S. tradition, and for anything even resembling it to be approved by the legislature and then effectively implemented would not be easy. Indeed, a true consensus even of the large and diverse group of conference participants probably cannot be claimed for all of the report's more far-reaching recommendations—this I suspect from conversations I have had with some of the conferees. Yet one can infer that most conferees were agreed that the solution to south Florida's recurrent drought problem would have to involve land use control measures and could no longer be found primarily in the manipulation of available water resources. The conference report flatly opposed raising the maximum level of Lake Okeechobee above the 17½ feet already authorized, and, although the backpumping of water from the east coast canals into the lake and conservation areas was not opposed as such, treatment of *all* such water was recommended—a condition probably impossible to meet economically.

NEW LAWS ARE PREPARED
AND ENACTED

The governor followed up the conference by appointing a fourteen-member Task Force on Resource Management to prepare a land use control bill for consideration at the 1972 session of the legislature. This task force was, in its makeup, symbolic of the new people and currents of opinion coming to bear on the land use issue. Having been chairman of the water manage-

13. Quoted in Mike Toner, "Gov. Askew: Cure Water Problems Before Disaster," *Miami Herald*, September 23, 1971. Also, see the *Water Management Bulletin* of the Central and Southern Florida Flood Control District, vol. 5, no. 2, October–November 1971, article entitled "Five Major Problems Listed by Governor."

14. The Governor's Conference on Water Management in South Florida, *A statement to Reubin O'D. Askew*, Miami Beach, September 1971.

ment conference, DeGrove was a logical choice to head the task force and he was in fact chosen for this role. As a Ph.D. candidate in political science at the University of North Carolina in the late 1950s, DeGrove had written his dissertation on the flood control project,[15] and he understood better than most the need to have water management respond to broadly conceived strategies of regional growth and development instead of to the narrow economic aims of big farmers, land developers, and local chambers of commerce. Or, to put the matter another way, DeGrove felt strongly that water management should no longer be a largely independent, loosely controlled determinant of patterns of land use, but rather should be the servant of land use policies developed in a regional and statewide perspective.

Another key member of the task force was Arthur Marshall of the University of Miami's new Center of Applied Ecology, the "biopolitician" who had done much to alert Florida to its environmental crisis. Marshall had been vice-chairman of the Water Management Conference and was one of the principal authors of the conference report. The several state legislators on the task force included Senator D. Robert Graham of Dade County, an outstanding example of the kind of able young legislator increasingly being sent to Tallahassee in the new era of reform. Graham, who was then thirty-six, is one of the principal officers in the Graham family corporation that has created Miami Lakes, a pleasingly designed new town situated to the west of Miami on part of the Grahams' extensive Florida land holdings.[16] Never identified with a narrow prodevelopment outlook, Graham had been selected by the Florida Association of the American Institute of Architects several years before as the public official who had contributed most to the advancement of planning and design in Florida. He, too, wanted water management, pollution abatement, and transportation policies used to guide—not respond to—development and thus help bring about fulfillment of regional plans. But Graham, while he favored controlling growth, was clearly not of the same mind as Marshall and some others on the task force about sharply limiting growth. In his view, regional planning should be directed at replacing the old pattern of sprawl and uncoordinated growth with the development of new towns, of which, in south Florida alone, he

15. John M. DeGrove, "The Central and Southern Florida Flood Control Project: A Study in Intergovernmental Cooperation and Public Administration," (Ph.D. dissertation, University of North Carolina, Chapel Hill, 1958).

16. Originally floodprone, the Miami Lakes site is a good example of south Florida land developed with the benefit of the protection afforded by the flood control project works and contemporary landfilling techniques. As for the latter, the buildable land at Miami Lakes has been raised above flood level with fill obtained in creating the "lakes," the amenity feature that contributes to this new community's special character. To be acceptable from a water management standpoint such projects must be carefully designed and not too large, too numerous, or too densely populated.

Above, nesting bald eagles; *below*, bittern in Everglades' saw grass; *at right*, a profusion of wading birds.

Photos by Patricia Caulfield

129 YEARS OF DROUGHT AND THE LAWS OF 1972

could foresee the need for possibly as many as twenty-five by the year 2000, each with 100,000 inhabitants or 2.5 million altogether.[17]

Also playing significant roles in the work of the task force were two legal scholars, Gilbert L. Finnell, Jr., professor of law at Florida State University and himself a task force member, and Fred P. Bosselman, a Chicago lawyer (of the firm of Ross, Hardies, O'Keefe, Babcock, and Parsons), who became a task force consultant. Bosselman, together with an associate, had just completed a study of land use control in selected states for the President's Council on Environmental Quality.[18] Still more significant was the fact that he had been associate reporter in the preparation of the latest draft of the American Law Institute's Model Land Development Code,[19] a document that refers to total localism in land use control as "anachronistic" and calls for the state governments to play a major role in such regulation. The CEQ already had looked to the ALI draft *Model Code* for the major concepts incorporated in the national land use policy legislation that the Nixon Administration had submitted to Congress in early 1971. Finnell was the first to conclude that the ALI code was the right model for the governor's task force to follow, and it was he who proposed that Bosselman be hired as a consultant.

A COMPREHENSIVE OR A SELECTIVE APPROACH? Working independently of the task force, John White, an aide to the Speaker of the House, was drafting some legislation along the lines of Hawaii's Land Use Law. The Hawaiian statute, enacted in 1961, is by far the earliest state land use control measure of broad scope. Under it, Hawaii has been divided into four districts—conservation, agricultural, rural, and urban. In the urban district, land use remains under local control; but, in the other three districts, land must be used in compliance with state regulations emanating in part from a new Land Use Commission responsible for preventing the loss of farmland to urban sprawl. To model a law for Florida on the Hawaii law was one of perhaps several ways the task force could have pursued a *comprehensive* approach to land use control, and White's draft legislation was indeed considered.

Alternatively, if a more *selective* approach to land use control were to be pursued, the task force would recommend that state intervention be limited chiefly to certain places and to development of certain kinds or magnitude. This is the approach advocated in the ALI draft *Model Code*, and the one ultimately chosen by the task force. According to Richard F.

17. D. Robert Graham, "An Urban Development Plan for Florida," *The Florida Architect*, March–April 1971.

18. Fred P. Bosselman and David Callies, *The Quiet Revolution in Land Use Control* (Washington, D.C.: Council on Environmental Quality, 1971).

19. The American Law Institute, *A Model Land Development Code*, tentative draft no. 3 (April 1971).

Babcock, the Chicago attorney who was the prime mover in the code's development, a state applying it would be involved "only in the big cases." "Probably 90 percent of the local land development decisions have no real state or regional impact," Babcock has said. "It is important to keep the state out of those 90 percent, not only to preserve community control, but to prevent the state agency from being bogged down in paperwork over a multitude of unimportant decisions."[20] Specifically, the draft *Model Code* recommends that state involvement be limited to:

(i) *Districts or areas "of critical state concern,"* which the state itself would designate. These would include areas "containing or having a significant impact upon historical, natural, or environmental resources of regional or statewide importance," and also areas significantly affecting (or being affected by) a major public project such as the construction of a jetport or an interstate highway. Finally, potential sites for new communities could also be so designated. Development in areas of critical concern would be regulated by the local governments, but under special standards established by the state and subject to state review.

(ii) *Large-scale development,* or, to use the language the task force would adopt, "Development of Regional Impact" (DRI). A project falling in the DRI category could be either public or private, running the gamut from the construction of a jetport or power plant to the development of a large new residential subdivision. As in the case of an area of critical concern, regulation of a DRI would be left to the local governments, subject to state standards and review. Factors to be considered in evaluating a proposed DRI would include its environmental and economic impact and its effect on such things as housing and transportation and waste treatment facilities.

(iii) *Development of regional benefit.* This could include projects, such as low income housing, that might be discriminated against by exclusionary local zoning. In such matters, the state could override the local government. This potentially controversial provision would not appear as a separate item in the task force bill, but the provision pertaining to DRIs is perhaps broad enough in scope and intent to be used against improper exclusionary practices.

In opting for the selective approach of the *Model Code,* the task force had several major considerations in mind.[21] As DeGrove has told me, it felt that "a state as large and complex as Florida simply was not amenable to the [comprehensive] approach followed by Hawaii." Also, it did not want to see created a large centralized state bureaucracy that would be con-

20. See testimony of Richard F. Babcock in *National Land Use Policy,* Hearings before the Senate Committee on Interior and Insular Affairs, 92 Cong. 1 sess. (1971), 2:394.

21. Gilbert L. Finnell, Jr., "Saving Paradise: The Florida Environmental Land and Water Management Act of 1972," in the *Urban Law Annual* (St. Louis, Mo.: Washington University Press, 1973).

stantly interfering in local decisions. What it wanted was a new land control process wherein the state, intervening in the "big cases," would ensure that decisions were reached only after a "balanced consideration of all the competing environmental, economic, and social factors."[22] Later, as floor manager of the land use legislation, Senator Graham would emphasize that the task force proposals should not be construed as weighted in favor of preservationists.[23]

Whatever its advantages, the task force's selective approach was not in itself sufficient to meet the Water Conference's goals of keeping growth and development from straining resources or lowering environmental quality. By definition, a state land use control policy that focuses on the big cases and ignores the vast majority of local land use decisions is one which at best cannot have more than an indirect effect on the growth and development that comes in innumerable small increments. Construction of, say, 100 new 250-unit condominiums on the Gold Coast next year will, in the aggregate, accommodate another 75,000 inhabitants or so (year-round and seasonal), even though no individual one of them is a DRI. Furthermore, incremental development obviously can lead to either an improvement or a deterioration in environmental quality depending on its location, design, relation to open space, and access to adequate waste treatment and transportation facilities. To cope with incremental growth as well as the big cases obviously requires growth and land use policies that cover all development, whatever the scale, although those policies need not call for direct state control of decisions in the Hawaiian manner.

Actually, according to what Finnell has told me, the draft legislation initially submitted by the task force to Governor Askew contained a lengthy section aimed at having all local governments undertake comprehensive planning. As Finnell recalls, the governor, while not rejecting the idea that a legislative mandate for such planning was in order, felt that this section should be dropped from that particular bill so as not to ask the legislature to take on too much at one sitting. There was indeed reason for such caution. Even as submitted to the legislature, the task force proposal would encounter strong opposition. If these proposals became law, the governor could come back later with a comprehensive planning bill that would be the essential complement to selective land use controls affecting DRIs and areas of critical concern.

WHAT THE LEGISLATION PROVIDED. After Governor Askew accepted the task force proposals, all those of concern to us here were finally enacted by the 1972 legislature, although not without compromises. The new laws included:

22. Ibid.
23. D. Robert Graham, "A Quiet Revolution/Florida's Future on Trial," *The Florida Naturalist* (October 1972).

• The Environmental Land and Water Management Act, based on the concept of joint state-local regulation of areas of critical concern and developments of regional impact (see figures 5–2 and 5–3).

• The Water Resources Act, establishing five regional water management districts which, supervised by the Department of Natural Resources and the Florida Cabinet, would regulate—in a manner not yet clearly defined—local drainage districts, county water management boards, and, where needed, the consumption of water. This act (see figure 5–4) holds promise of finally bringing to an end the near anarchy that has characterized land drainage and other water management activities in many parts of Florida. (Although endorsed by the governor's task force, the Water Resources Act was actually drafted by a special House committee chaired by Representative Jack Shreve of Merritt Island.)

• The Land Conservation Act, authorizing—subject to a vote of the Florida electorate—the issuance of $200 million in state bonds for the purchase of "environmentally endangered lands" and $40 million in bonds for outdoor recreation lands. At the November 1972 election, Florida voters approved these bond issues by a 70 percent majority.

• The Florida Comprehensive Planning Act. Despite its title, this act would not appear to meet the need for comprehensive planning referred to earlier. The "plan" prepared under it would not be strictly a land use plan. It would provide long-range guidance for the orderly social, economic, and physical growth of the state by setting forth goals, objectives, and policies. The plan would become official once approved by the governor, who is designated under the act as the chief state planning officer, and by the legislature, to the extent that new laws are required. The Department of Administration, together with its new planning division (now upgraded from bureau status), would coordinate state agency budgets and actions in keeping with the plan. But the Planning Act does not provide for the state to override local decisions where they conflict with the state plan.

NECESSARY COMPROMISES. The compromises that proved necessary to obtain the enactment of Senate Bill 629—the Environmental Land and Water Management Act—show what a politically difficult task the sponsors of this measure set for themselves. Consider the following:

• *Arbitrary limits were placed on designation of areas of critical concern.* As first drafted, SB 629 would have made it relatively easy for the state to designate ecologically sensitive areas wherever they might be and limit and regulate development in them through protective orders. As the bill was finally passed, the opportunity for protecting such areas was restricted in several ways. First, the amount of land that could be designated as of critical concern was limited to 5 percent of the state's land area (or about 1.7 million acres)—a clearly arbitrary restriction. Less than half of the land

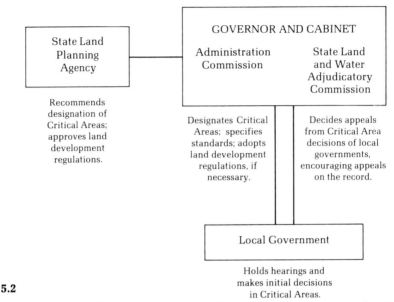

5.2

Decision-making structure for regulation of critical areas under 1972 Land and Water Management Act

Source: Gilbert L. Finnell, Jr., "Saving Paradise: The Florida Environmental Land and Water Management Act of 1972," *Urban Law Annual* (St. Louis, Mo.: Washington University, 1973). Reprinted by permission.

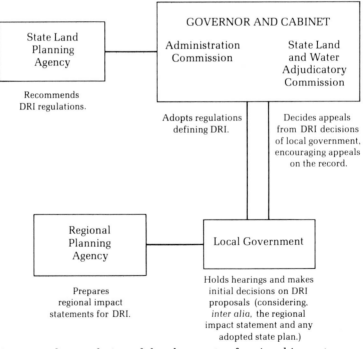

5.3

Structure for regulation of developments of regional impact

Source: Gilbert L. Finnell, Jr., "Saving Paradise: The Florida Environmental Land and Water Management Act of 1972," *Urban Law Annual* (St. Louis, Mo.: Washington University, 1973). Reprinted by permission.

in Florida is suitable for intensive development and, if one accepts the estimates of the Florida architects and environmentalists who participated in the Red Flag Charette, only 35 percent of Florida is suitable for such use.[24] Second, a grandfather clause was written into SB 629 whereby any development authorized prior to the designation of an area of critical concern embracing it shall be exempt from regulation. This is a major loophole because numerous subdivisions have been officially platted but not yet developed in places such as central Florida's Green Swamp. Still another significant compromise was that the areas-of-critical-concern provision was not to become effective unless Florida voters first approved the $200-million bond issue for purchase of "environmentally endangered lands." Although the bond issue was to be approved the next fall, the legislature, by imposing such a condition, may well have encouraged property owners and their attorneys to argue all the harder that a compensable development right adheres to all lands affected by protective orders issued under the act.

• *The Florida Cabinet instead of appointive officials are to make the ultimate decisions.* SB 629 originally would have had areas of critical concern designated by the state planning agency, with that agency also establishing "principles" to guide development in those areas. Similarly, appeals from local government decisions in regard to areas of critical concern and DRIs would have been heard by a five-member state "adjudicatory commission" named by the governor. The task force felt that to leave such matters to an appointive body would give the new program of land use regulation a degree of insulation from political pressures and would result in better decisions. But this would have reversed the trend toward giving the Florida Cabinet broader powers in land use regulation. Also, there was a strong feeling in the legislature that land use control questions were too important to be left to appointive officials. Accordingly, the sponsors of SB 629 agreed early to have the cabinet vested with the major powers of decision. This amendment giving such power to the cabinet was not necessarily a weakening change in the legislation, but it was so regarded by its sponsors.

HARD LOBBYING BY BOTH SIDES. Even with the compromises, passage of SB 629 did not come easily. Leading the fight against the bill was the Florida Association of Homebuilders. During one committee hearing, Perry Odum, the association's director, attacked the measure as one of the most "far-reaching and devastating" ever considered. A lobbyist for the General Development Corporation and the ITT Corporation (the developer of Palm Coast) tried, unsuccessfully as it turned out, to have the provision for control of DRIs removed from the bill. On the other hand, the Arvida

24. *Florida: The Seeds of Crisis*, report of the Red Flag Charette, March 3–5, 1972, sponsored by the Florida Association of the American Institute of Architects and the Florida Defenders of the Environment.

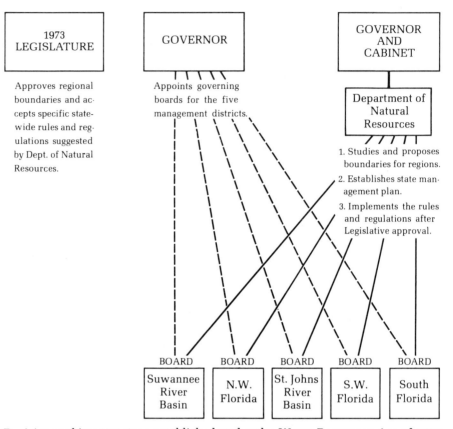

5.4

Decision-making structure established under the Water Resources Act of 1972

Source: ENFO Newsletter, April 1972, Environmental Information Center, Winter Park, Florida. Reprinted by permission.

Corporation, a developer with major land holdings along the Gold Coast, saw an advantage in more orderly and controlled development and strongly supported the bill all the way. Some other large developers, such as the Deltona Corporation and the GAC Corporation, at least kept a discreet distance from the legislative battle.

The lobbying for the bill was equal to the lobbying against it. The Conservation 70s lobbyist, Ben Phipps, was working the capitol corridors full time. Other Florida conservation groups were also busy generating support for the measure. The Florida architects and the Florida Defenders of the Environment held the Red Flag Charette as the fight over SB 629 was reaching a climax, and their report may have convinced some senators and representatives that enactment of land use control legislation was essential. Consideration of the bill continued for several months and the measure was more than once nearly killed in committee or on the floor. As Senator Graham, who served as the bill's floor manager, told me SB 629 would have been lost had it not been for the environmentalists' "tenacity and diligence . . . in keeping the issue alive through letters and personal contact with legislators." Another factor behind the bill's passage was the strong support it received from the state's major newspapers, including the highly conservative *Orlando Sentinel*. Indeed, long before SB 629 was introduced and even before the Governor's Water Management Conference had been held, the *Sentinel* had carried a lead editorial entitled "State Land Management Law Needed as Basis for Intelligent Growth."[25] Yet, even with all of the foregoing working for SB 629, it very likely would have failed had Governor Askew not pressed continually and fervently for its passage.

A MODEL FOR THE NATION? When SB 629 was finally signed into law by the governor, its sponsors and the Florida environmentalists who had lobbied hard for it were jubilant. There was a belief among many that Florida had stolen the march—that no other state of comparable size and complexity had enacted so strong and potentially effective a law. In an article in *Urban Law*, Gilbert Finnell, of the governor's task force, suggested that the Florida Environmental Land and Water Management Act might become a "model for the nation."[26] Whatever the merit of that claim, it was true that a beginning had been made, which subsequent legislatures could build upon. Moreover, the new statutes recognized certain principles of high importance, namely that Tallahassee's primacy in land use regulation was not confined to only a few special problems such as the protection of tidal lands. A two-tiered land use control system involving the local governments and the Florida Cabinet was emerging, and, even if this system had many limitations and imperfections, it represented progress.

25. "State Land Management Law Needed as Basis for Intelligent Growth," *Orlando Sentinel*, September 19, 1971.
26. Finnell, op. cit.

6 Dade County: The mini-state

Nearly every major aspect of Florida's problem of controlling growth and protecting environmental quality can be found in Dade County. Dade is itself a sizeable region, part developed and part undeveloped, covering 2,054 square miles, an area almost exactly the size of the state of Delaware (see figure 6–1). Its still burgeoning population of almost 1.4 million residents is nearly twice as large as that of any other Florida county and represents a seventh of the state's total population. Dade's problems are, broadly speaking, of three kinds:

• First, there is that of checking the decline in the quality of life in Greater Miami through the control of population densities and other measures, while at the same time maintaining and enhancing a healthy economy.

• Second, there is the problem of controlling Greater Miami's expansion from beyond the few hundred square miles of north Dade that is already heavily urbanized. South Dade is the county's frontier area where land speculation is rampant and extensive development is beginning.

• Finally, there is the problem of preserving Dade's valuable remaining

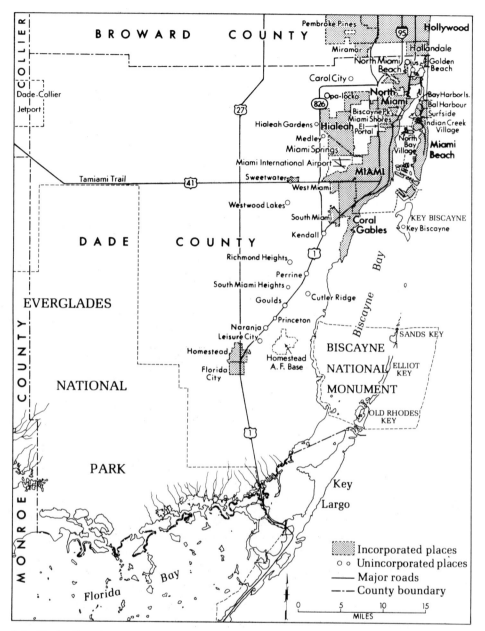

6.1 Dade County

natural areas, no small matter inasmuch as these include part or all of the Everglades National Park, FCD Conservation Area No. 3, and Biscayne National Monument, plus some extensive areas that are not under public ownership and protection.

Policies for controlling land use and guiding growth are not likely to succeed in the rest of Florida if they do not succeed in Dade County. Indeed, state officials will have much to learn about appropriate strategy from Dade's experience and its current groping for effective policies. In 1972, the elected officials of Metropolitan Dade County (or "Dade Metro") began seriously to look for a growth policy and strategy. The undertaking of a major revision of the county master plan, together with the declaring of moratoriums on new construction in selected areas pending zoning studies and possible "rollbacks" to lower densities, was evidence of that search. So also was the proposal by Dade Metro's new mayor, John Orr, that Metro should establish limits on population density for *all* parts of the county, even overriding the municipalities in this critical matter whenever necessary.

RICH AMENITIES AND A GATEWAY. Greater Miami's rapid growth is easily explained. Even more than most parts of Florida, Dade County is richly endowed with natural amenities. The average January temperature of 70°F. is about 10° warmer than that found in north Florida. Summer weather can be uncomfortably warm and humid, but peak temperatures in Miami are less than those experienced in cities such as Washington, Chicago, and New York. The warm climate and generally abundant, if uneven, rainfall allows Miamians—wherever they take the pains—to make the urban landscape a lush, year-round tropical garden. A large variety of native and exotic trees, shrubs, and flowers thrive here, such as palms, banyan trees, bougainvillea, hibiscus, poinsettia, and flowering oleander, to name but a few. Opportunities for outdoor recreation are outstanding. Although Dade County's oceanfront has been abused from overdevelopment, there are still good public beaches to be enjoyed, especially on Key Biscayne. The Gulf Stream, just offshore, affords fine fishing for species such as sailfish, dolphin, and kingfish. In the FCD's Everglades water conservation areas the freshwater fishing is, as described earlier, sometimes unequaled. South of Miami, Biscayne Bay remains in good if not pristine condition, its crystalline waters appearing under the tropical sun as a shimmering aquamarine. While still in sight of the Miami skyline one can catch bonefish and large permit over the bay's luxuriant turtle grass beds. For the increasing numbers of people who are discovering the pleasures of snorkeling, there is the coral reef east of the line of narrow keys separating South Biscayne Bay from the Atlantic. The reef seems almost a fantasy: it is a place of brain coral, elkhorn and staghorn coral, sea fans and sea feathers where spiny lobsters and stone crabs hide and brilliantly colored angelfish and butterfly fish flash in the sunlit waters.

Besides its amenities, Dade County enjoys another important advantage that has contributed to Greater Miami's growth. Being farther south than any other place in the mainland United States, it is at the gateway betweeen North America and Latin America, an advantage which the advent of large commercial jets has made fully apparent. In fact, Miami International Airport ranks among the world's ten busiest airports, and, among U.S. airports, is second only to New York's Kennedy in the volume of international passengers accommodated.

Although the combination of strategic location and exceptional amenities has caused Greater Miami to develop rapidly, the topographic and other constraints on Dade County's growth are very real. As pointed out early in this book, the naturally habitable or development "tolerant" land base in southeast Florida is limited chiefly to the coastal ridge (see figure 1–7). This low ridge, from 10 to 25 feet above sea level, is rarely more than 5 miles wide in north and central Dade, where it generally follows the coast closely; in south Dade, where it swings inland in a shallow arc, the ridge widens in places to 8 or 10 miles, but peters out altogether just below the town of Homestead. During the 1947 flood most of Dade County west of the ridge was inundated, not to mention the flooding that occurred in the numerous breaks or low places in the ridge itself. In that part of south Dade east and south of Homestead, the land is only a few feet above sea level even 10 miles or more from the coast, and the mean high tide mark extends in some places several miles inland from the seaward edge of the mangroves. Storm tides whipped up by hurricanes have been known to overtop U.S. Highway 1, 10 miles west of Biscayne Bay (see figure 6–2). Of course, as I have pointed out, low-lying coastal and inland areas in Dade can be made habitable through massive engineering. Yet the more coastal wetlands converted to urban use by dredge-and-fill methods, the more the remaining wetlands are critical to the preservation of estuarine ecosystems. Also, the mere fact that drainage, diking, and land filling permits settlement of wide areas that were once a part of the Everglades does not mean that all or most of this land should be settled. Development of these areas will lower the volume and quality of water recharged to the Biscayne Aquifer at the same time the demand for water is increased. Moreover, about half of the land in Dade County has been put off limits to most kinds of development by the creation of the Everglades National Park and the Flood Control District's Water Conservation Area No. 3. (The park seems secure from virtually all development, public and private alike; this is less true of the conservation area, witness the south Florida regional airport project discussed in the next chapter.) Also, establishment of the park, together with the creation of Biscayne National Monument (which I shall come to later), has tended to lead to constraints on development even well beyond the boundaries of these important federal preserves.

THREE WAVES OF GROWTH

The growth of Dade County and Greater Miami has come in three major waves, each made possible partly through environmental manipulation that

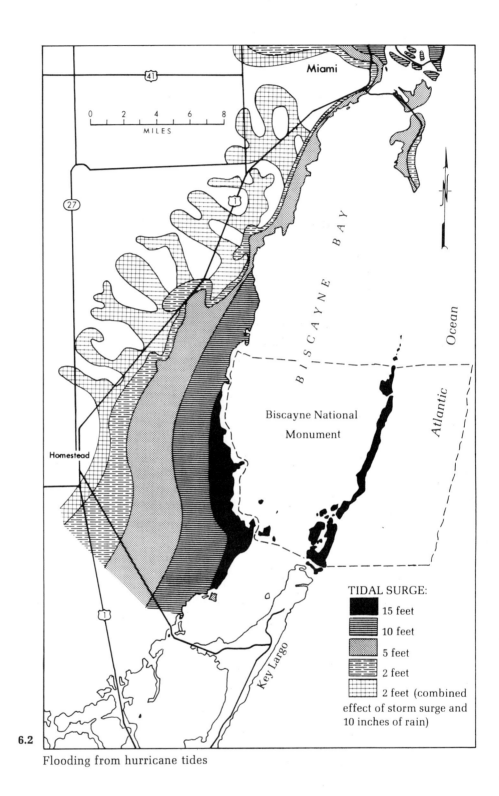

6.2 Flooding from hurricane tides

eased somewhat the immediate constraints of topography. The first wave began in 1896, when Henry M. Flagler extended the Florida East Coast Railroad to Miami, and continued up through World War I. Construction of the railroad did not itself substantially modify the Dade environment, but, by opening the county to rapid settlement, it contributed to such alteration, for better or worse. Not only did Flagler bring in the railroad and build the first major resort hotel, engineers back at his headquarters in the old Spanish colonial town of Saint Augustine actually laid out downtown Miami's pattern of narrow one-way streets. From a village of several hundred people when the first train arrived, Miami became a city of several tens of thousands by 1920. Except for the small towns of Homestead and Florida City in south Dade, Miami still represented almost the sum total of development in Dade County. Occupying mostly ridge and hammockland, it covered only a few square miles along Biscayne Bay and either side of the Miami River. There was also, however, the beginnings of Miami Beach, which Carl Fisher in 1913 had begun to raise from a sandbar and mangrove swamp. Fisher's project involved a major modification of Dade's pristine coastal environment at a time when development of almost any kind was regarded by the state government and by most citizens as progress. Yet, even by today's lights, such sacrifice of mangroves and some natural bay bottom for the development of an ocean beach resort in one of the few places in the county where such development is possible would not be unreasonable if the rest of the county's coastline were to be left largely undisturbed. Miami Beach in time became Florida's most popular destination for tourists (at least until the opening of Disney World) and a mainstay of the Dade economy.

Dade's second great wave of growth occurred during the boom of the 1920s, a time of national prosperity when Florida was discovered by the great American middle class, which was enjoying a new affluence and (given the mass production of relatively cheap automobiles) a remarkable new mobility. Despite feverish land speculation and fictitious values, the growth and development during this period was quite tangible and would not disappear with the collapse of the boom. The population of Miami grew severalfold during the decade, and, by 1930, the city was losing its provincial look and even had a clutch of modest skyscrapers along Biscayne Bay. Miami Beach had also developed rapidly, with some fifty-six hotels and numerous substantial Mediterranean-style villas (stuccoed walls and red-tiled roofs) built along the oceanfront.

In terms of the evolving patterns of land use, a significant change was that urban development was now no longer confined to the coastal ridge and hammocklands but was spreading westward, onto lands once part of the Everglades. As the reader will recall, the drainage project first undertaken after the turn of the century by Governor Broward and continued by his successors had, by the 1920s, lowered water levels in the

Everglades by as much as 6 feet. Wide areas along the glades periphery had been entirely drained, although the 1947 flood would show devastatingly the inadequacies of the early drainage works. Coral Gables, one of the first totally planned communities in the United States, was begun by promoter George Merrick on pinelands west of Miami, on the coastal ridge. But other new developments were being laid out wholly or partly in places that not many years previously had been saw grass marsh. These included new communities such as Miami Springs and Hialeah, the latter ultimately to become Dade's second largest city (with a 1970 population of 101,000). The entirely unrestrained, freewheeling nature of the land development process in the Florida of the 1920s was evident from the very pace of events in Dade. In this one county, during the peak boom year of 1925, 481 hotels and apartments were built, 271 subdivisions were platted (though most of their would-be developers were soon to be broke), and 174,530 deeds were recorded.[1]

The third wave of development, which continues today, began after World War II. Although its primary source was the nation's booming postwar economy and Dade's natural amenities and gateway location, the new wave was facilitated by two governmental initiatives. One was the establishment of the Dade County Port Authority (DCPA) in 1945, while the other was the launching of the Flood Control Project in 1948. The DCPA, together with several of the major airlines, promptly began the development of Miami International Airport on a site just south of Miami Springs and Hialeah. The location was convenient to downtown Miami, only 5 miles away, if poorly chosen from the standpoint of the potential noise nuisance that would be caused. There were to be two major thrusts to the development of commercial aviation in Miami. One was to take advantage of MIA's gateway location for international passenger and cargo traffic. The other was to encourage the affluent and even the not-so-affluent of the big northern cities to fly south for a winter vacation. In enticing tourists, the airlines—with their heavy advertising budgets—were to be perhaps as important as the spectacular array of big, showy oceanfront hotels, which during the 1950s replaced the villas along the Miami Beach oceanfront. The general use of air conditioning, another technological development of the 1950s, also furthered tourism. Air conditioning allowed the airlines and hotels to tap the tourist market in summer as well as winter and to accommodate people in tolerable comfort in huge, warrenlike hotels.

The flood control project facilitated the growth of Greater Miami by taking the worst risk out of the continuing encroachment upon the Everglades flood plan. Construction of the Everglades perimeter levee, improvement of existing canals, and the building of new canals as part of the

1. *Profile of Metropolitan Dade County: Conditions and Needs* (Metropolitan Dade County Community Improvement Program, Office of the County Manager, October 1972), p. 24.

project minimized the possibility of a recurrence of the kind of flood disaster experienced by Hialeah, Miami Springs, the west side of Miami, and other communities in 1947.

As it happened, the rapid growth of light industry that took place in Dade during the 1950s and 1960s largely occurred west of the coastal ridge on what had been naturally flood prone land. By 1973 the county would have some 4,000 manufacturing plants, mostly small ones producing electronic equipment, metal and wood products, leather goods, boats, and a variety of other things. Dade's good weather, its expanding labor market, and the improved access to national markets that had come with the development of commercial aviation and better highways, all contributed to this industrial growth and increasing diversity of economic activity. Also, drainage and the FCD protective works had made it feasible for much of the new industry to be built in the Hialeah and the Miami Gardens-Sunshine State industrial districts, where land for plant sites and for housing for workers was readily available and relatively cheap. This pattern of land use offered the advantage of having most industrial activity occur away from downtown Miami and amenities such as Biscayne Bay, Key Biscayne, and Miami Beach. (In downtown Miami there is, however, a garment district.)

During the 1950s Dade's population grew from a total of about 500,000 to nearly 1 million, more than three-quarters of the increase due to immigration from out of state.[2] Many of the newcomers were retirees, but most were younger persons coming to take advantage of the growing job market and superior climate. Vast tracts of single-family homes were built during the 1950s, such development encouraged by the availability of mortgage insurance from the Federal Housing Administration and the Veterans Administration. These new subdivisions were too often characterized by an excessive sameness, with great numbers of homes all built of concrete block and stucco in a rectangular ranch style. Some subdivisions were built in the remaining vacant land in the northeast corner of the county, either on the coastal ridge or, more commonly, on cheaper land to the west of it. Others were built to the south and southwest of Miami. Just as the county's population almost doubled in size during the 1950s, so had its urbanized area, if indeed that area had not more than doubled.

In the 1960s, the county's population rose to 1,267,000, having increased by 36 percent during the decade (modest only by comparison with the 89 percent increase for the 1950s), with migration of people into Dade again accounting for most of the growth. But, whereas in the 1950s the majority of new people had come from other states, 71 percent of the net migration into Dade in the 1960s was accounted for by Cuban refugees.[3] Altogether,

2. *Population Projections, Metropolitan Dade County 1970–2000*, Metropolitan Dade County Planning Department, August 1972, p. 30, table XIII.
3. Ibid., p. 15, table VI.

these refugees numbered some 178,000, most of whom came by airlift. The refugees generally made do with what old existing housing they could find, hence the sudden burgeoning of Little Havana in downtown Miami and the emergence of sizeable Cuban communities in Hialeah, West Miami, and elsewhere. The Cuban influx represented an exceptional short-term factor making for increased population densities in existing municipalities rather than for growth of new suburbs. Yet there was in any event a developing trend in Dade toward more intensive use of land. More than two-thirds of the new housing built during the decade was in multifamily buildings, in striking contrast to the predominance of single-family homes in previous decades.[4] The appearance of high-rise condominiums, along South Bayshore Drive, Miami Beach, and north Miami Beach was very much a part of this new trend. Increasing construction costs and changing life-styles were contributing to the new popularity of multifamily housing.

DECLINING QUALITY OF LIFE

Dade's 1973 population of about 1.4 million was almost ten times larger than the population of 1930 and nearly three times that of 1950! Such rapid growth, though allowing some individuals to enjoy higher incomes and a better life-style, has brought a marked decline in the overall quality of life. It has also given rise to plaintive expressions of nostalgia by "old" Miamians, such as the following by Ben Funk, an Associated Press writer who has lived in Miami for the past two decades:

> It was January 1951. Our destination was Miami, that special haven of Northerners seeking respites from the cold and grime back home. We hoped to remain all our lives. . . .
> We were struck by the sight of seaside towns spread out in pastel colors over white sands. And in Miami we found everything we sought. The waters were pure, the air free of man's contamination, the fishing great, the life jolly and unhurried. The ten-mile drive home from the office was a fifteen-minute breeze over roads and streets shaded by spreading banyan trees and flowering poincianas. Key Biscayne was a wild coconut plantation inhabited by raccoons and a small colony of humans who had settled on the island to get away from it all. . . .
> We could stroll through hardwood hammocks teeming with wildlife, swim in any body of water, walk a lonely beach and watch the moon rise. . . .
> In those days, the tourist "season" was December to March. The rest of the year, most of the hotels closed and the town belonged to the "natives". It was one great place to live. But the drumbeaters were busy. Resort owners and land promoters, cities, airlines, counties, and

4. Metropolitan Dade County Improvement Program, op. cit., p. 33.

the state were spending huge sums of money to lure people to this unique corner of the continent. They were coming in rapidly growing numbers. . . . More and more people meant more garbage, more trash, more sewage, more hotels, more automobiles. Human wastes poured in an ever-increasing flood into the canals, the Miami River, the bay, and the ocean. Fumes from automobile exhausts and jet planes fouled the once pure air. Hammocks were flattened by the bulldozers. Dredges mangled the shorelines. Mile after mile, hotels and motels marched up the beaches—gaudy monuments to the tourist dollar—hiding the oceans behind a concrete wall. . . .

And one day we took a good look around. Suddenly we knew that we had kissed the good life goodbye.[5]

Local politicians are more inclined to be boosters than are local journalists, but, in Dade, even some of the politicians have voiced the paradise lost theme. Hardy Matheson, a member of one of Dade's pioneer families and until early 1972 a county commissioner, told me, "This was a pleasant place to live in the 1930s, even though we were all broke. Now we are affluent and nobody wants to live here."

Those who reminisce perhaps make the old Miami appear somewhat better than it was, and the new Miami worse than it is. Yet the essential truth of the impressionistic observations by people such as Ben Funk and Hardy Matheson can be abundantly documented. The report *Profile of Metropolitan Dade County: Conditions and Needs*, released in October 1972 by the office of the County Manager, showed that much of the county was experiencing a loss of environmental quality and other problems related to rapid growth. The *Profile* describes serious problems of pollution, transportation, housing, and, more generally, of land use conflict and development practices that have deprived metropolitan Miami of its potential amenities. It is a detailed and graphically illustrated document to which I make only passing reference here. Suffice it to say that the *Profile* and certain other documents[6] that describe conditions in Dade give no cause for complacency. For instance, consider the following:

Pollution. Dade's backlog of pollution problems, largely from domestic sewage, is such that a public investment of at least several hundreds of millions of dollars in sewers and treatment works will be necessary to remedy it. All inland waters in north and central Dade, which is to say the Miami River and the major canals, have been grossly polluted. Also, some pollution of ocean waters has resulted from outfalls discharging raw or

5. Ben Funk, "Miami: Kissing the Goodlife Goodbye," *Tallahassee Democrat*, March 21, 1971.
6. Especially relevant here are the *Proceedings of the Federal-State Conference in the Matter of Pollution of the Navigable Waters of Dade County* (Federal Water Quality Administration, October 20–22, 1970).

inadequately treated sewage. As recently as 1970, almost 40 percent of all housing units in the county were still served by septic tanks, and 5 percent of all housing had *both* septic tanks and individual water wells— a dangerous combination. In early 1973 an outbreak of typhoid fever among migrant farm workers in south Dade and a temporary panic at Miami Beach over contamination of the city's water supply came as reminders that water pollution can lead to serious public health problems as well as to waters being rendered esthetically revolting and unfit for fishing, swimming, or other sports.

Dade does not yet have severe air pollution. But, if the use of motor vehicles in the county should continue to increase (there were 823,000 vehicles registered in Dade in 1971), a now incipient problem of smog could eventually become a crisis. As for noise pollution, Miami International Airport by itself creates a serious problem. Aircraft from this facility impose a 20-square-mile "footprint" of noise on the metropolitan area, the intensities ranging from teeth-grating to merely annoying.

Inadequate Transportation. At peak hours, traffic on expressways and thoroughfares serving Greater Miami generally either approaches design capacity or exceeds it. Traffic jams are very much a part of many Dade

Above, housing development in South Miami Heights; Saga development beginning south of Miami. *Below*, Turkey Point power station; C-111 canal built for the Aerojet Corporation, which threatened extensive salt-water intrusion.

motorists' daily life. Furthermore, even the construction of a modern system of mass transit cannot offer more than partial relief from this problem. Such has been the suburban sprawl, with many people living at considerable distances from their places of work, that no transit system can directly serve the greater part of the population now dependent on automobiles. The traffic tie-ups and the wasting of gasoline associated with an extensive and complex pattern of commuting may continue for many years. The present system of transportation, heavily oriented to the private car, also constitutes a major disadvantage for the poor living in downtown Miami and elsewhere who cannot afford automobiles and for many elderly persons who do not drive.

Shortage of Housing and the Segregation of Population by Race, Age, and Economic Condition. Not even Dade's usually hyperactive building industry has kept up with the demand for new housing. Such is the housing shortage that 41 percent of the people in the county pay more for their housing than they can afford. Fourteen percent of all dwellings are overcrowded, with more than one person living in each room. Also, in 1972, less than 12 percent of the more than 80,000 households (families and elderly individuals) eligible for public housing were being accommodated in such housing. Besides the housing shortage there is the fact that all too many of Dade's blacks, Cubans, and poor, elderly Jewish people live in blighted ethnic enclaves. Most of the county's 190,000 blacks (making up about 15 percent of the total Dade population) and the majority of the 300,000 Spanish-speaking people (representing almost a fourth of all county residents) live in the Miami inner city, each group keeping largely to itself. South Miami Beach has an astonishing concentration of the elderly poor. Seventy-two percent of this area's 41,650 residents are age sixty or older and most are living precariously, depending on social security checks and small pensions.

Conflicts in Land Use and Loss of Esthethic Appeal. A land use problem index map presented in the *Profile* shows serious conflicts occurring over a substantial part of urban Dade. These include problems such as homes located too near busy, noisy streets or too near industrial or commercial areas. A widespread problem in metropolitan Miami is the commercial strip development along major streets and some highways. A land use survey conducted in 1960 showed that, even then, more than 120 miles of streets and highways were lined with commercial development.[7] Strip development erases much that might be distinctive about the Dade scene. Anyone seeing the ubiquitous hamburger drive-ins, fried chicken places, and pizza parlors along such highways could readily imagine him-

7. *Zoning Handbook*, Metropolitan Dade County Planning Advisory Board and Harland Bartholomew and Associates, September 1965.

self to be in Atlanta, Richmond, Tulsa, or any one of a dozen other American cities. Another reason for metropolitan Miami's failure to convey a strong "sense of place" is that landscaping has been generally neglected. Authors of the *Profile* observe that, "Dade County's urge for rapid and sometimes uncontrolled growth has allowed it to neglect the finishing touches which are so important to the overall quality of the residential environment. Many subdivision developers totally ignore the landscaping of the homes and streets. . . . Dade County's unfinished appearance is not only detrimental to the life style of its permanent residents, but to the tourist economy as well. It has been reported many times that tourists are disappointed to find metropolitan Miami rather ordinary and not as tropical as expected."[8]

THE POLITICS OF GROWTH

Of the means available to Dade's county and municipal governments for guiding growth and preserving the quality of life, control of land use according to a well-thought-out master plan is clearly the most important. The first municipal zoning ordinance in Dade was the one adopted by Miami Beach in 1930, four years before the City of Miami adopted such an ordinance.[9] It was not until 1938 that the Dade commissioners adopted a zoning ordinance for the county's unincorporated areas. Ultimately, all of Dade was to be covered by some form of county or municipal zoning. Yet, inasmuch as there was no enforceable county plan, the principal good that could be expected to come from zoning was that gross conflicts of land use within particular parts of the county might be prevented, and even that modest aim was to be frequently thwarted.

Across the nation generally, local government has served largely to provide certain minimal service and police functions. Using the powers of local government to achieve a high quality of urban and suburban life—to make the environment appealing and gardenlike—has, oddly enough, rarely been emphasized. Where a local government has established a system of public parks—Dade County today has numerous parks, some of them excellent—the parks often exist as oases, or incongruities, in an otherwise unappealing setting. In Dade, as elsewhere, local government has not only generally failed to encourage and express a creative interest on the part of the community in achieving a better quality of life, it has served too often as the manipulative device of crass commercial interests and self-serving, sometimes dishonest politicians. Indeed, several Dade municipalities appear to have been created for no other purpose. For instance, during the late 1940s, the legislature allowed the incorporation of the new municipalities of Hialeah Gardens, Medley, and Pennsuco—all

8. Metropolitan Dade County Improvement Program, op. cit., p. 137.
9. Metropolitan Dade County Planning Advisory Board, op. cit., p. 4.

situated west of the coastal ridge in areas then naturally subject to severe flooding—despite the fact that there was scarcely anyone living in any of them (in 1970, the combined population of these three communities was still less than 1,000). According to Edward Sofen, author of *The Miami Metropolitan Experiment*, the factors contributing to the establishment of these and other new municipalities in Dade "included the 'imperialism' of the land promoters, the expectation of escaping zoning restrictions, the quest for inexpensive land, and the desire to obtain liquor licenses and other benefits."[10] The abuse of zoning powers by some local politicians in Dade would, over the years, repeatedly come under attack by the *Miami Herald*. "[Zoning] is where the payoff is these days," the *Herald* observed in 1972. "Politicians no longer can make out on paving contracts and street-car franchises. Zoning is the place to work out the deals in attorney's fees, insurance premiums, and other hiding places for cash payoffs."[11]

THE BEGINNINGS OF
DADE METRO

The establishment of Metropolitan Dade County in the late 1950s can be seen in retrospect to have been a step that could help make local government more accountable and creative in the enhancement of the quality of life, even if progress in that direction was to be slow.

A Dade County Coordinated Planning Council was formed as early as 1944, showing that leaders of the various local governments had some sense that long-range planning for Dade's overall economic and physical development was needed. The council accomplished little because the interest of those leaders in general planning was not sufficient to keep more parochial or immediate issues from diverting their attention.[12] But some steps toward metropolitan government were in fact taken in the 1940s, with substantial gains in efficiency and economy realized from the consolidation on a countywide basis of services in the fields of public health, education, tax assessment and collection, and airport and seaport development. Such consolidations plainly were in order because, of the county's more than a score of municipalities, all but a few of the smaller ones were clustered around Miami. Further, as Sofen has pointed out, urban Dade was so new that it was in many respects "one big suburbia," with the differences between the core city and its satellites probably not as great as those in most metropolitan areas.[13] Simply as a matter of self-survival, office-holders and employees in Dade's municipalities felt a strong identity with their

10. Edward Sofen, *The Miami Metropolitan Experiment* (Indiana University Press, 1963), p. 16.
11. Editorial, "Stop the Zoning Manipulators," *Miami Herald*, November 20, 1972.
12. Sofen, op. cit., p. 20.
13. Ibid., p. 71.

city governments, but, in Miami as well as some of the other cities, most citizens were not hostile to further consolidations. This was perhaps especially true of people who had only recently migrated to Dade. Furthermore, the fact that, in the early 1950s, Miami city commissioners were suspected of having ties to illegal gambling interests did not add luster to city government. In 1953, to the great alarm of municipal officials, Miami voters only narrowly rejected a proposal to abolish their city and transfer its functions to the county. Shortly thereafter, the idea of creating a federal system in which the city governments would retain their identity and many of their functions began to be looked upon with favor by Miami officials and leaders of the Dade League of Municipalities. Sofen observes: "Strategically, 'federalism' in Miami appears to have been an accommodation to both groups of antagonists: A shelter for localists against the 'terror' of total consolidation, and a half-way house toward integration for the centralists."[14]

In 1956 Florida voters approved a Dade home rule amendment to the state constitution that would allow Dade voters subsequently to adopt a charter establishing the new "metro" government. That a consensus of sorts had been achieved was evident from the fact that in Dade the amendment was approved by 71 percent of the voters. This consensus would vanish the next year, however, when municipal leaders were unwilling to accept the terms of a metropolitan Dade charter giving the new countywide government powers that they unfairly characterized as "so general as to permit the complete extinction of all the municipalities without their consent."[15] The coalition behind the Metro proposal—a coalition that included the Miami-Dade Chamber of Commerce, the Dade delegation to the legislature, the League of Women Voters, the *Miami Herald*, and the *Miami News* —was able to prevail by only a slender majority in a referendum on the Metro charter. Indeed, without the support of substantial majorities in Miami and Coral Gables, the charter proposal would have lost. Thus, the new Metro government began life under a political mandate much weaker than the powers formally invested in it. This discrepancy between Metro's charter powers and its political strength hindered its performance in a number of fields, including planning and the regulation of land use.

METRO'S CONCESSIONS TO THE MUNICIPALITIES. Under the charter, the Metro commission[16] was authorized to "prepare and enforce comprehensive plans for the development of the county" and to "establish, coordinate, and enforce zoning and such business regulations as are necessary for the protection of the public." Municipal boundary changes and the

14. Ibid., p. 85.
15. Ibid., p. 65.
16. Initially this body had five members, but later it would have nine. All but the chairman, or mayor, must reside in separate districts, but all are elected at large.

establishment of new municipalities would require Metro's approval. The commission also had authority to build roads, bridges, and tunnels, and to build or regulate public transportation facilities. In addition, it could either provide and regulate water and sewer systems or delegate these functions to the municipalities.[17]

If vigorously used, these powers over planning, land use, and related activities would have enabled Metro to guide and control growth and development throughout the county. The cities were to argue that it was not intended for Metro ever to override municipal zoning. But the charter is quite explicit in assigning such power to Metro, although it does permit the municipalities to prescribe zoning standards more exacting than any established by Metro. For development to follow an orderly, rational, and coherent pattern, minimum zoning standards and development guidelines obviously would have to apply countywide. To exclude from this regime Dade's twenty-six municipalities would make no sense at all because two-thirds of the county's 1960 population of nearly 1 million lived within city boundaries (in 1970, 58 percent lived in the cities).

As soon became evident, the Metro Commission had no firm commitment to controlling Dade's growth, and it would in any case have found such a commitment difficult to live by. Besides the recalcitrance of municipalities unwilling to yield old prerogatives, there was the formidable pressure for development by both local and outside interests. Any interference with growth and development would have encountered powerful resistance from contractors and labor unions. Local mortgage lenders, notably the banks and savings and loan associations, would no doubt also have perceived a strong interest in seeing development continue at a fast pace. In addition, a whole host of outside interests—eastern banks and investment houses, major insurance companies, and large industrial corporations—were eagerly joining in the Dade real estate boom, and some were not beyond blatant attempts at political manipulation to get their way.

The Metro Commission at first actually approved ordinances making Metro responsible for enforcement of zoning and building regulations countywide. It also enacted a public works ordinance making municipal as well as county public works projects subject to minimum standards. But the municipalities objected to these ordinances so vehemently that Metro, concerned about its thin political mandate and unsure of its survival, repealed the zoning and public works ordinances in 1958. Thus, almost at the outset, Metro surrendered its putative authority to control land use in the cities. If Metro was to accomplish anything at all in guiding Dade's future development, much would depend on its performance in the county's still largely unincorporated frontier area of south Dade.

17. Sofen, op. cit. Significant parts of the charter are reprinted in Appendix G, p. 240.

LAND USE DECISIONS IN
SOUTH DADE

Metro's early policies governing land use in south Dade tended to be indiscriminately prodevelopment. In 1958, the Metro Commission, in one of its first major land use decisions, fixed the bulkhead line for South Biscayne Bay (or "South Bay," as it is often called) 700 feet off shore! Had developers been ready to build along the South Bay shore in the early 1960s, this exceedingly liberal bulkhead line (which the Florida Cabinet approved) would have permitted the destruction of South Bay's productive estuarine ecology. Mangroves would have disappeared and thousands of acres of turtle grass flats would have been destroyed.

THE CITY OF ISLANDIA. Another action by Metro that could have been severely damaging to South Bay was it decision in 1961 to charter the proposed new city of "Islandia," to be made up of the string of narrow keys lying between the bay and the Atlantic (see figure 6–1). The incorporation procedure in this case was a charade: as prescribed by law, a voting machine was set up on these isolated, virtually uninhabited keys to permit about a dozen persons, all at least nominally residents of the keys, to decide whether they wanted Islandia incorporated as a city or not. Yet the incorporation of the new municipality was a serious matter. It would give the landowners and promoters who were seeking to develop Islandia control of zoning on the keys, and, of more immediate importance, it would allow them to issue municipal bonds for the construction of a causeway. Under the best of conditions, the development of a resort city on the keys—which even today remain accessible only by small boat—would have been likely to degrade South Bay. To have allowed such a development to occur largely under the control of promoters with a selfish interest would have all but ensured such degradation.

THE LAND USE MASTER PLAN. A general land use master plan for south Dade and the rest of the county was prepared during the first half of the 1960s by the Metropolitan Dade County Planning Department, with the Metro commission giving the plan its preliminary approval in 1963 and final approval in 1965. Some of the policies reflected in the plan are difficult to quarrel with, but, too often, the plan evaded hard choices and embraced incompatible goals. For instance, although calling for the preservation of South Bay as an amenity, the plan also contemplated—at least in its 1963 preliminary version—the construction there of a deepwater port and oil refinery-petrochemical complex, to say nothing of the new city of Islandia and the three causeways to connect this resort to the mainland and Key Biscayne. It also called for the enhancement of agriculture in the Homestead area, yet made it clear that agriculture would have to yield whenever it stood in the way of residential, commercial, and industrial development. Indeed, according to the plan, the future of agriculture in Dade over the long term would depend on drainage projects opening up land presently unusable for farming. The plan alluded to pending Flood Control District reclamation projects for south and southwest Dade although oddly enough, in view of the severe droughts even then occurring, there was no reference whatever to potential water shortages or the need for water conservation. Continuation of the extraordinarily rapid rate of growth of the 1950s was assumed. The population was expected to more than double by 1985, rising to 2.5 million, a total which Metro demographers now do not expect to be reached until sometime after the year 2000. Indeed, an essential weakness of the master plan was that it was based chiefly on projections of past trends of population growth and land use practices instead of on conscious political choices by Metro officials and their constituents. It was an extension of the past rather than a vision of the future.

Another fundamental policy weakness related to the master plan lay not in the plan itself but in the fact that Metro too often ignored it in making decisions on zoning, building permits, and public works projects. The Metro commissioners were especially lax in regard to living up to the master plan's laudable concept of having new residential development occur within well-planned community and urban units, each unit to have its own complete system of sewers. As early as 1961 Metro developed a sewer plan for the entire county, but, because of its high cost, essentially nothing was done about implementing it until the mid-to-late 1960s when the Florida Board of Health and the Federal Housing Administration began refusing to approve septic tanks for some new construction in north Dade. Prior to that, and even afterwards, much new development in south Dade to the east and west of the Dixie Highway (U.S. 1) had relied on septic tanks and had taken the form of just the kind of urban sprawl regarded in the master plan as undesirable.

Yet several important issues of conservation and development in south Dade were resolved during the 1960s and early 1970s in a manner more or less satisfactory to Dade conservationists. In some cases the conservationists succeeded in exerting strong political pressure, and in others they obtained favorable court decisions. Their success sometimes turned partly on sheer good luck, however. Furthermore, most of the controversies had to be resolved in an ad hoc manner whereby developers were put to much trouble and expense that might have been avoided had potential conflicts been worked out earlier through an appropriate planning process.

MIX UP ON SOUTH BAY. For a time it seemed that development would come in a rush to South Bay. Major projects initiated there between 1960 and the end of 1970 included the Islandia development, the Seadade deep-water port and oil refinery, the huge power plant complex at Turkey Point,

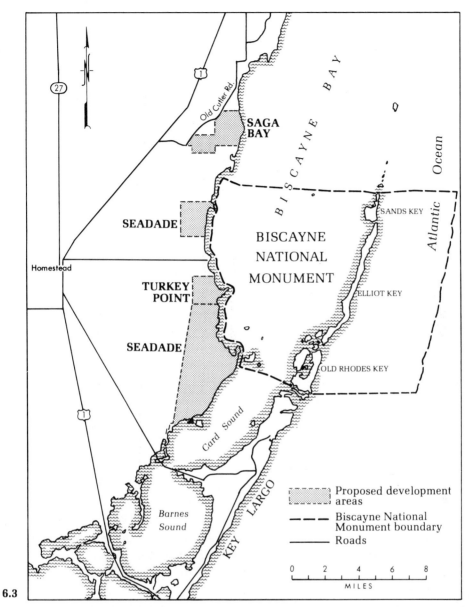

6.3

Proposed development projects—Biscayne Bay area and Biscayne National Monument

and two large new deluxe communities (see figure 6–3). With the exception of the power plant, and one of the two new community developments, these undertakings were to be entirely frustrated—in several instances one would collide with another. The proposed Seadade port and refinery was the first of the South Bay projects to provoke intense public controversy, and it contributed to the birth of a potent Dade County environmental movement.

In the Seadade controversy, environmentalists seeking to protect the quality of life in their home region had to challenge the priorities held by wealthy outside interests and by local political and business leaders (the latter motivated in part by an economic slump). In 1959, Daniel K. Ludwig, one of America's super entrepreneurs, began buying up large acreages in south Dade, with the immediate goal of building the deepwater port and refinery on a bayfront site east of Homestead Air Force Base. Ludwig, as head of National Bulk Carriers, Seatankers, Inc., and Universe Tankships, Inc., and a major shareholder in American-Hawaiian Steamship Co. and the Union Oil Company, has been referred to as the "American Onassis".[18] He was a resident of Darien, Connecticut, whose own personal life-style would not be affected if, by some mischance or failure of technology, the limpid waters of South Bay should become polluted with oil from his tankers or the clear skies of south Dade should be smeared with emissions from his refinery or related petrochemical plants. However earnest and sincere Ludwig's assurances that the port and refinery operations would cause no pollution, one could reasonably suspect that his main interest would not be in the quality of life in Dade County but in the amplitude of the profits from his investments there.

As it happened, when rezoning for the port and refinery project was unanimously (though conditionally) approved by the Metro commissioners in early 1962, the only opposition to the rezoning had come from a few articulate but for the most part obscure individuals. A prime mover behind the opposition was Lloyd Miller, an employee of Pan American Airways at Miami International Airport and an enthusiastic fisherman and outdoorsman. The son of a labor leader in Reading, Pennsylvania, and godson of socialist Norman Thomas, Miller was not afraid of colliding with some pillars of the establishment if that is what it would take to keep South Bay from being despoiled. In the mid-1950s, Miller had organized the Mangrove Chapter of the Izaak Walton League, but, because of the league's strictures against political activity, in 1960 he organized a new group, this one to be called the Safe Progress Association (SPA). Others joining with him now in the fight against the port and refinery included people such as Lain Guthrie, an Eastern Airlines pilot; Ed Corlett, a local trial lawyer; Jim Redford, who at previous times had been a ship's officer, a writer for the Chicago *Sun Times*, and who now managed to combine his work as a real estate broker with a passion for conservation causes; Redford's wife, Polly, a gifted writer; Belle Scheffel, a tiger on the garden club circuit; several marine biologists at the University of Miami, including especially Donald DeSylva; author Philip Wylie, whose *Look* article of the late 1940s entitled "Florida: Polluted Paradise" had shamed local officials into stopping the discharge of raw sewage into North Biscayne Bay. (If there was anyone

18. Polly Redford, "Small Rebellion in Miami," *Harper's* magazine, February 1964.

among the SPA people who was already a "name" to be reckoned with, it was Wylie.)

The SPA had little money with which to wage a campaign against the Seadade project—it started with $11.05 in its treasury and spent less than $4,000 during its first two years—but it had arguments that would ultimately prove persuasive. Its cause would also be helped by a conflict between plans for the Seadade project and those for the proposed new city of Islandia. Essentially, its arguments were these:

• First, that Biscayne Bay is a warm, shallow, poorly flushed salt lagoon that can be easily and irreversibly harmed as an important amenity by industrial pollution.

• Second, that while in theory it might be possible for operation of the port and refinery to be more or less pollution free, the probability was that there would be pollution, especially in light of the vagaries in the enforcement of air and water pollution control laws (laws which, in any case, were then quite weak). The likelihood of severe pollution was all the greater inasmuch as Ludwig was plainly expecting a large complex of petrochemical plants to spring up around the new refinery. If not, SPA spokesmen asked, why had Ludwig acquired a 2,200-acre industrial site when a 250-acre site would have sufficed if a port and 50,000-barrel refinery were all that he had in mind? Given such a complex of smokestack industries, residents of Miami, Coral Gables, and other cities in north and central Dade could expect the prevailing southeasterly trade winds to spread the effluents over their communities.

• Third, and this was implicit in everything the SPA people said, Dade County could not escape choosing the kind of life it wanted for its present and future populations. If it was to emphasize living amenities, then those economic activities that were to be allowed would have to be such as not to cause unmanageable pollution or seriously degrade the environment in any other way. A SPA bumper sticker, spelled out in bright red peanut letters, said, "NUTS to Dirty Industry."[19]

When the SPA began its campaign against the port and refinery project it stood virtually alone, whereas Ludwig and company had the active support of the Greater Miami Chamber of Commerce and both Miami newspapers as well as that of the Metro commission. Yet, between early 1962 and late 1964, public support for the port and refinery was gradually to fade, and by the end of this period the project would be certifiably dead. An improvement in economic conditions together with other circumstances and events (some carefully stage-managed by the SPA) contributed to its demise. Often, irreversible environmental damage is already done by public or private projects before effective political action can be mounted against them. This was not the case with the

19. Ibid.

port and refinery, however, because of a delay in Metro's issuance of a building permit pending preparation and adoption of a countywide pollution ordinance and because of Seadade's difficulties in obtaining a channel dredging permit from Metro, the Florida Cabinet, and the Corps of Engineers. The developers of Islandia raised questions about the dredging permit because they did not want the channel passing between their keys and thus necessitating construction of an expensive high-level bridge.

Airing their views before every possible forum, SPA spokesmen gradually succeeded in turning public opinion against the port and refinery project. In little more than a year the SPA won over to its position the *Miami News*, the governing bodies of the cities of Miami and Miami Beach, citizens associations in nineteen unincorporated areas and thirty-five clubs and civic organizations. What finally proved critical in the campaign against the Seadade project was the fact that the future of South Bay became a hot issue in county politics at just the time a proposal was emerging to preserve most of the South Bay as the Biscayne National Monument (see figure 6–3). Lloyd Miller was the first to conceive of having most of South Bay placed under some kind of federal park status. In April of 1963, the Metro commission, though by no means committed to the idea, asked the U.S. Department of the Interior to investigate it. Miller, with the help of national leaders of the Izaak Walton League in Washington, met with Interior Secretary Stewart L. Udall and engaged his personal interest in the proposal. Still, the idea might have died had Udall not found Representative Dante Fascell, Democratic congressman from Dade County, warmly receptive and cooperative.

Next, a team of researchers from Interior was assigned to prepare a report on the South Bay area. Appointed to lead the study was Arthur Marshall, the very same field supervisor from the U.S. Fish and Wildlife Service's Vero Beach office who for several years had been trying assiduously to help local conservation groups become more effective in fighting to save estuarine areas such as the South Bay. Marshall and his colleagues surveyed the resources of the South Bay—the marvelous coral reef, the luxuriant turtle grass beds, the tropical hardwoods (lignum vitae, mahogany, Jamaica dogwood, and other species are found on Elliott Key),[20] and the rich variety of birds and fish—and proclaimed the area to be of national significance. Polly Redford, writing in *Harper's* magazine, reported that even the SPA had never dreamed that the resources of South Bay were so rich. "Dade County reacted like someone who just discovered a dusty Rembrandt or Stradivarius in the attic," she said.[21] Secretary Udall, after a personal visit to South Bay, was virtually won over to the national monu-

20. G. L. Voss, et al., *The Marine Ecology of the Biscayne National Monument*, NPS Contract Study, (Coral Gables, Florida: Institute of Marine Science, University of Miami, 1969).
21. Redford, op. cit.

ment idea, and the next year his Advisory Board on National Parks, Historic Sites, Buildings, and Monuments endorsed it. But, before the monument could be established, the assent of the Metro commission, the Florida Cabinet, and the U.S. Congress would have to be obtained. Getting Metro's assent was critical because, without it, the cabinet probably would have been unwilling to give the federal government title to the 92,000 acres of submerged lands within the boundaries of the proposed national monument. Furthermore, without Metro's support, Representative Fascell, already hearing plenty from some constituents who wanted nothing to interfere with plans for Islandia or with the port and refinery, might well have found the political burden of sponsoring legislation establishing the monument too much to bear.

It was therefore fortunate for the SPA that Hardy Matheson, member of a prominent Dade County family that had once owned all of Key Biscayne, ran for the Metro commission in the fall of 1964 on an anti-port and refinery platform and won by a stunning majority. With his election, along with that of two other new commissioners who had more or less climbed on Matheson's anti-Seadade bandwagon, the Metro commission stopped vacillating and voted to deny Ludwig the building permit which he had been awaiting for three years. In 1965, the national monument proposal received a further boost when Herbert Hoover, Jr., (of the Canton, Ohio, Hoovers known for their vacuum cleaners) sponsored a large luncheon in Miami to promote it and announced that the Hoover Foundation would give $100,000 toward establishing the monument. Later, the Metro commission endorsed the Fascell bill creating the monument and, at length, the cabinet, on a four to three vote, agreed to donate the submerged land. As a gubernatorial candidate in 1966, Claude Kirk had actually opposed the national monument proposal, but the urgings of his environmental advisers and pressure from Dade conservationists helped bring him around on this issue.[22]

Passed by Congress in 1968, the Biscayne National Monument Act established a preserve of 96,000 acres (4,000 acres of keys, the rest bay and ocean bottom) extending from the outer edges of the coral reef on the east to within several hundred yards of the south Dade mainland, stopping short of the imaginary bulkhead line Metro had fixed in 1958 to mark the outer limit for waterfront development. From beginning to end, at each critical turning point at the local, state, and federal levels in the fight to stop the Seadade and Islandia developments and establish the

22. Nathaniel Reed, Kirk's environmental aide, told me that, in the hope of converting Kirk to the cause of saving the bay, he made sure that a sailing trip for the governor-elect took place within the boundaries of the proposed national monument. After the trip, Kirk called Reed in, and, as the latter remembers it, said: "The bastards aren't going to tear up that beautiful bay. Now go find a way to save it." Another thing said to have helped turn Kirk around on the monument issue was the fact that his Natural Resources Committee urged him to support the monument proposal.

monument, the SPA leaders and other Dade conservation leaders, such as Alice Wainwright and Joe Browder of the local Audubon Society, had campaigned furiously. Polly Redford told me that what the situation required—and what conservationists delivered—was a "strong showing at public hearings, thousands of letters and telegrams from conservation club members, bumper strips, etcetera, etcetera—the whole paraphernalia of a modern political campaign. This built up Miami's conservation movement so that, later on, when the jetport and Turkey Point controversies got underway, we had a small, disciplined fighting force able to take on big-time opposition."

With the establishment of Biscayne National Monument, there would be no new city of Islandia, no causeways across South Bay, no pollution emanating from development on the South Bay keys, no new resort to compete with Key Biscayne and Miami Beach. And, although its boundaries did not extend to the mainland shore, the monument would almost inevitably have a restraining effect on what happened there as well. Certainly the port and refinery project could never be revived as long as the local, state, and federal governments remained committed to preserving the monument's resources. In fact, no other intrusive and disturbing development could be allowed—as would later become evident in controversies over the Turkey Point power plant and the proposed new town of Saga Bay. Yet, important as it was, establishment of the monument had not come about in the context of a deliberate planning effort. Instead, it had stemmed from the piecemeal efforts of a few conservationists who simply did not want to see South Bay despoiled. "The monument idea came along at an opportune time," Jim Redford, one of the SPA leaders, told me. "With the fight going on between Islandia and the Seadade oil refinery people, the monument proposal was a *deus ex machina*. All of a sudden people saw it as an out: 'It serves those bastards right.' Once we got it going, why it built up and the bay was a sanctified thing. It represented the only thing in town that people had really been trying to preserve. As a result, we got a lot more out of the bay than we would normally. There was a certain accidental quality about the way it worked out."

TURKEY POINT. At the very time that the establishment of Biscayne National Monument was burying the Seadade and Islandia controversies, other events, moving along quite separate tracks, were occurring and posing new threats to South Bay and creating new confusion as to the region's future. One such event was the construction by the Florida Power and Light Company (FP&L) of a huge power generating facility at Turkey Point, a low-lying promontory 15 miles south of metropolitan Miami. This project was to touch off a controversy pointing up, perhaps even more clearly than the Seadade and Islandia controversies, the difficulty public officials can have in dealing with specific questions of development in the absence of a growth policy and land use plan—a plan which, even at an early stage of formulation, could be expected to classify land and water resources according to their development tolerance. As matters were to turn out, the unfortunate Seadade Industries, which had seen its plans for a port and refinery frustrated, was again to suffer from Metro's lack of such a policy and plan. This time, the Seadade plans that were to be upset would be primarily for a large waterfront residential development.

Faced with rapidly mounting power demands, FP&L acquired the original 3,200-acre Turkey Point site in 1964 after having been denied permission the preceeding year to expand its oil-fired generating plant at Cutler Ridge, near Coral Gables. Metro, which had objected to the proposed expansion at Cutler Ridge for fear of air pollution, readily granted the "unusual use" permit required under the zoning code for construction of power facilities at the new site. Apparently, it occurred to no one that the construction of the power facility might interfere with Seadade's use of the 20,000 acres of salt marsh and scrub mangrove, which it owned to the south of Turkey Point.

The Turkey Point project was, of course, getting underway long before enactment of the National Environmental Policy Act of 1969. The site was picked by FP&L, then sanctioned by Metro and the Atomic Energy Commission (and, at least indirectly, by the Florida Cabinet), all without any overall analysis of environmental impact.[23] Initially, FP&L planned to build only two oil-fired units generating a total of 864,000 kilowatts, but the company soon decided to add two nuclear units of 760,000 kilowatts each. A once-through cooling system was to be used, the initial plan calling for the discharge canal to enter the bay less than 2 miles south of Turkey Point.

A cooling system of this kind may be ecologically acceptable when used in places where deep waters and strong tides or currents keep temperatures from building up over a large area around the point of discharge. Such a system is not acceptable on South Bay because, given its shallowness, its weak and erratic tides, and poor flushing characteristics, a large input of heat from a power plant will not be readily dissipated. In the case of the 2,384-megawatt Turkey Point facility, the normal peak discharge of heat was to be truly immense, running to 39 million BTUs per second.[24] Were that discharge to be made into the bay, the injury to the subtropical marine life could be enormous. Much of this marine life is not adapted to as wide a range of temperatures as is the marine life of

23. The cabinet, though it was never to become deeply involved in the Turkey Point controversy, could have exercised a strong voice because no cooling water intake and discharge canals from or to the bay could be built without its concurrence.

24. *Conference Proceedings in the Matter of Pollution of the Navigable Waters of Biscayne Bay and Its Tributaries in the State of Florida*, vol. 1 (Federal Water Pollution Control Administration, 1970), p. 38.

Above, hotel row along Collins Avenue in Miami Beach; *at right,* Miami Beach after the hurricane of 1926; *below,* pinelands in Dade County.

temperate zones. For some species, such as shrimp and crabs, the critical maximum is 91°F. or 93°F., and in August, when the mean monthly temperature of South Bay waters can be as high as 87°, they are living perilously close to that threshold even under natural conditions. Turtle grass, which is vital to the bay's ecology, shows stress even before temperatures reach 90°.

By late 1969, Dade conservation leaders managed to bring about a situation where FP&L was under strong pressure not to carry through its plans for the cooling system. Believing that Governor Kirk had close ties with FP&L, these leaders had concluded that Nathaniel Reed, who was board chairman at the Department of Pollution Control as well as the governor's environmental aide, was being forced to stall. "Finally, when we hinted we might have to sue, Nat passed the buck by having the governor call a federal-state water pollution conference," Polly Redford told me. "This got him off the hook, and the federals—who didn't give a damn about FP&L—were quite willing to make an example at Turkey Point."

The upshot of the conference, and of a law suit brought against FP&L by Secretary of the Interior Walter J. Hickel, was that the power company had to provide a cooling system that would avoid thermal discharges into either Biscayne Bay or the bay's connecting waters to the south, Card Sound. The company considered several alternatives, but all except one it deemed unacceptable. For instance, to build cooling towers and establish a closed cycle system using bay water to make up for evaporation losses was ruled out because salt would become concentrated rapidly in the system. If fresh water were used, the amount that would have to be pumped from the Biscayne Aquifer would total 58,000 acre-feet a year—enough for a city of 280,000 inhabitants! Or, if cooling towers were used as part of a "once-through" system—with bay water to be pumped through the plant, then cooled on the towers before being returned to the bay—there would be highly visible vapor plumes from the towers and some deposition of wind-borne salt over an area of 3–10 square miles.

The alternative judged by FP&L and its consultants to involve the least uncertainty as to environmental side effects, system reliability, and ease of maintenance was a harp-shaped closed-cycle system of numerous parallel and interconnected cooling canals. Enormously demanding in terms of land, this system would cover about 7,000 acres and would reach from just below Turkey Point almost to Card Sound. In September 1971, after frequent meetings between representatives of FP&L and the state and federal pollution control agencies, the Turkey Point dispute was settled in the U.S. District Court in Miami, with all parties accepting the proposed closed-cycle cooling canal system as the ultimate solution, to be achieved within a five-year period. During that period, FP&L would be allowed to discharge the cooling water to Card Sound via a new "Six-Mile Canal," but, except during emergencies, the Turkey Point plant would operate at less than normal power output.

This settlement dispelled any hope that Daniel Ludwig might still have had that Seadade Industries would be able to develop its holdings below Turkey Point. Seadade had been preparing plans to convert much of the uplands, salt marsh, and mangrove swamp that it owned in this region to waterfront sites for homes, hotels, condominiums, and the like. According to press reports, a new town of 24,000 dwelling units and 100,000 people was contemplated. The plan was said to include a seaport (possibly for shallow-draft vessels) and an industrial park for light manufacturing. In preparing these plans Seadade had had no assurance that Metro would accept them, but there had been some encouraging indications. The county's

1965 master plan showed a "Bay Urban Area," taking in all of the Seadade tract, as likely to emerge sometime after 1985. Perhaps still more pertinent was the fact that the boundaries of Biscayne National Monument had been carefully drawn to permit the dredging of a ship channel from Card Sound to the open Atlantic, the channel to pass between the monument and the John Pennekamp Coral Reef State Park. Now, however, Seadade was helpless to keep use of its lands from being preempted by FP&L.

Seadade finally sold the entire 20,000-acre tract to FP&L for $16.8 million, some $10 million more than Seadade had bought it for but only a fraction of what the company might have made from its proposed development. For its part, FP&L gave the state of Florida 2,500 acres of mangrove flats and salt marsh extending along nearly all the south Dade coast below Turkey Point. In return, the state gave the company assurance of undisputed ownership of its remaining land, clearing a clouded title that stemmed from the difficulty of delineating the mean high water line where state-owned submerged lands begin. This property may have to accommodate not only the radiatorlike grid of cooling canals but still another set of generating units—which FP&L almost certainly will have to build unless the company's projections of future demand prove to have been much exaggerated. In sum, one outcome of the Turkey Point controversy was that most of the lower south Dade coastal area has been set aside for what, in effect, may become a large power plant park.

THE SAGA NEW TOWN PROJECT. As the events described in the foregoing suggest, at the start of the 1970s Metro still had no clear overall land use policy for the South Bay region and continued to make major decisions on an ad hoc, case-by-case basis. This was true not only in the Turkey Point case affecting the lower south Dade coastal area, but also in the case of the Saga new town development affecting part of the South Bay coast above Turkey Point. As I intend to show, Metro's confusion in dealing with the Saga project was further evidence of the shortcomings of the ad hoc approach—an approach which, incidentally, today characterizes proceedings related to "developments of regional impact" under the Florida Environmental Land and Water Management Act of 1972.

The Saga controversy was unusually significant because the outcome would be important in itself and as a precedent possibly affecting the outcome of proposals for other large bayfront projects. The Saga Development Corporation, a firm owned by Connecticut interests, had bought 2,800 acres along 2 miles of bayfront for a new town which, to judge from the original plans, might have accommodated up to a quarter of a million people. Saga's request in late 1969 for Metro to rezone the land for commercial and residential use (much of it high density) covered what at that time was the largest single tract ever to have come up for rezoning in Dade County. Called for in the Saga plan were closely ranked waterfront high-rise apartments and commercial structures, with the public to be—as Juanita Greene of the *Miami Herald* put it—"walled off" from the bay, as at Miami Beach. Even as later modified and improved, the Saga plan was to encounter strong opposition from a loose coalition that would eventually include the professional societies of architects and landscape designers, the League of Women Voters, Zero Population Growth, the traditional conservation groups, and several activist groups with names such as Survive and Ecocommandos.

What Metro badly needed was a clear policy, well understood and supported by the public, against which to measure the Saga proposal. But all that it actually had was (i) a newly drawn South Bay bulkhead line fixing the outer edge of the mangroves—or the "vegetation line"—as the farthest point bayward that development could extend; (ii) the county's 1965 general land use master plan showing that that part of the bayfront within the Saga tract was designated for high density development (thirty-six living units or more per acre); and (iii) a commitment to South Bay's preservation, as manifested in Metro's support of the legislation establishing Biscayne National Monument. These several policies were grossly inconsistent, because the bay could not be preserved as a pristine resource if the mangroves were to be destroyed. Furthermore, the Metro commission had reason to know, after all the past battles over South Bay, that any policies or development proposals threatening the bay probably would be politically unacceptable.

THE BULKHEAD LINE. The original bulkhead line, set 700 feet offshore, had been rendered obsolete by the Randell Act of 1967 demanding that bulkhead lines not be established until after the potential ecological consequences of development had been determined by competent surveys. At Metro's request, state biologists made the necessary survey of the South Bay region and recommended that the bulkhead line be moved far inshore, to the mean high water mark. To follow this advice to the letter would not have been easy because not only does the mean high water mark in some places extend inland several miles from the outer edge of the mangroves, but it is also very poorly defined. Indeed, a wise decision as to where the new bulkhead line should go would have to involve many different considerations—scientific, esthetic, social, economic, and political. The record on which the Metro commission acted obviously should have contained detailed testimony about which mangrove areas have the highest ecological value and which have the least, about the best locations for marinas and possible rights of way for a bayshore parkway, and about other questions such as how much population is desired along the bay in the light of hurricane hazards and available or planned facilities for such services as transportation and waste control. Ultimately, the decision reached would have to be in part a political judgment, and, ideally, it would reflect the wishes of an informed public as to what the South Bay region should become. Yet, critical as the new bulkhead line would be to South Bay's future, the Metro commission had given short shrift to many of the above considerations in deciding that the vegetation line was to be the new bulkhead line.

THE SOUTH BAY AREA STUDY. Although the 1965 master plan clearly was outdated and not relevant to an evaluation of the Saga project, the Metro commission did not, in the first instance, regard adoption of a new plan for the upper South Bay area as a prerequisite to acting on the Saga proposal. For its part, however, the Metro Planning Department in 1969 had selected a 14.5-square-mile area, adjoining South Bay and including the Saga tract, and laid out a general land use plan. Under this plan, the number of dwelling units to be allowed would have been slightly higher than the 17-per-acre-average for Miami Beach, but the greater part of the bayfront would have been saved for public use, as in marinas, a scenic drive right-of-way, and areas for the preservation of mangroves. Although crude by current standards of environmental analysis, the department's study, which was presented to the Metro commission in early 1970, gave some emphasis to the importance of preserving the bay's ecology. Had the commission invited public comment on the study's recommendations and then adopted a South Bay plan that commanded broad support, the developers of Saga would have known early what had to be done if their project was to win acceptance. But the commission chose not to do this, with some commissioners even expressing the curious view that it would be unfair to "prejudice" the decision against Saga by adopting basic new policies with which Saga would have to comply.

By early 1970, opposition to the Saga plan had grown so intense that the developers' original proposal was withdrawn. Mortgages on the Saga property were held by several prominent local people, including a circuit judge, and the developers had first believed that the necessary zoning changes could be obtained through political influence. Finally disabused of that idea, Saga had sought the help of Darrey Davis, a prominent Miami lawyer and former county attorney. Davis agreed to represent the firm on condition that the development plan be redone by a planner of recognized competence. "The first Saga plan overloaded the land and should have been turned down," Davis told me. John O. Simonds of Pittsburgh, one of the nation's most prominent planners, was hired by Saga and he persuaded the company to stop seeking conventional residential and commercial zoning. Simonds wanted higher population densities in certain parts of the development than conventional zoning would permit, thus leaving more open space elsewhere and achieving economies that would permit more amenities overall. Accordingly, Simonds and Davis prepared an "Agreement for Land Development," legally binding on Saga and on

Live oaks are spared to provide living amenity in this development in Coconut Grove, Miami

any party to whom the land might be sold. Stipulated were such things as the maximum allowable number of dwelling units and the amount of land to be reserved for parks and open space. Within such constraints Saga would be allowed considerable freedom in the arrangement of buildings and densities on the site. In a word, Saga was now proposing what is commonly known as a planned unit development or PUD. The maximum overall population was to be reduced from the quarter of a million in the original plan to about 120,000. And now about half of the bayfront was to be preserved, and, throughout the project, a number of special amenities such as neighborhood parks and walkways along the interior canals and lagoons (to be created in excavating fill material) would be provided.

Moreover, the new plan was in harmony with the Metro Planning Department's proposal for a scenic bayshore parkway and it had that agency's endorsement.

Saga brought its new plan before the commission in late June of 1970, but, although this was a far better plan than the earlier one, public sentiment was now even less favorable to Saga than before. The problem lay in Metro's failure to come to grips with the two basic policy issues raised by South Bay development—what was to happen to the bayfront and how much population density was to be allowed? Under the circumstances, Saga did not have a chance. Polly Redford, whose husband Jim was one of the leaders in this latest fight over South Bay, neatly summed up what happened: "The coalition of conservation troops stepped in and, in a loud, spectacular, well-prepared public hearing before the Metro commission, threw Saga's plans right out the window. These battles are not won by impersonal forces. They are won by people—housewives, lawyers, businessmen, and students who get out and campaign on a person-to-person basis. My god, how we lobbied those commissioners!"

The commission did not reject the Saga plan out of hand, but denied it "without prejudice" so that it could be resubmitted as soon as revised. Shortly thereafter, the commission did what it should have done months before and established general policies with respect to bayfront development and maximum population density within the 14.5 square-mile region that had been the subject of the Planning Department study. No development was to be allowed immediately along the bay and the population was to be limited to 150,000, or some 330,000 less than the maximum contemplated in the study. The Saga officials, though at first shaken and dispirited by the rejection of their second plan, came back to the commission in the fall of 1970 with a third one. It conformed to the new policy guidelines and was approved. The new plan excluded all development along the bay except for a marina and it limited overall population to 51,000, or about one-fifth what was contemplated in the first Saga plan.

The settlement in the Saga case was generally viewed as an indication of the policies Metro would apply to subsequent proposals for development along South Bay. Yet, while Metro now had a policy of sorts for the region, this policy still lacked clarity, consistency, and a fully rational basis. For one thing, the population ceiling of 150,000 fixed for the study area seemed to represent a largely intuitive judgment and, had it been challenged in court, might well have been ruled arbitrary. Any legally defensible population ceiling or "cap" fixed for the South Bay region probably will have to bear a clear relationship to such factors as the maximum design capacity of various public facilities such as waste treatment plants, water supply systems, highways, mass transit services, and recreation areas. A second difficulty with the new policy was that Metro had not made it clear what, if any, development rights the owner of bayfront property could assert. Although Saga was not to be allowed to develop its bayfront, Metro had agreed to take a five-year option to buy the bayfront land at cost plus interest. Furthermore, at Metro's urging, the Florida Cabinet had already accepted the outer mangrove edge as the bulkhead line for the South Bay. Yet, in essence, the settlement in the Saga case indicated that an owner of bayfront land could be made to surrender whatever right he might have to develop that property in return for permission to develop adjacent property further inland. But, if this were indeed the policy, why had Metro not frankly said as much? The confusion surrounding Metro's policy in regard to the bayfront deepened in July 1971 when a Dade County circuit judge declared the new bulkhead line to be invalid. In deciding a case brought by some local environmentalists and users of the bay, the court in effect held that Metro and the cabinet could not fix a bulkhead line that compromises estuarine values without a showing of major offsetting public benefits to be gained. The issue in dispute would not be finally resolved until 1974 when the legislature designated Biscayne Bay as an aquatic preserve—thus mandating the preservation of mangroves up to the line of mean high water.

THE GROWTH ISSUE AND
METRO'S NEW LEADERSHIP

The Saga controversy was a consciousness-raising event and was one of the last before Metro began to turn the corner and face the growth issue. For by 1972 Metro had begun consciously trying to cope with growth through efforts to achieve better planning, improved land use controls, and stronger political institutions. The history of droughts (and especially the drought of 1971), the South Bay controversies, the jetport controversy (which I come to in the next chapter), the general decline in environmental quality in north Dade, and the endless battles over zoning, all contributed to the new state of mind. The hard evidence that most people in the county were fed up and would be willing to see some exceptional land use controls instituted came in the most politically meaningful way—in an outpouring of votes, first in a referendum on a proposed ordinance authorizing temporary freezes on new construction in selected areas, and second in the election of a Metro mayor and three other new Metro commissioners committed to better control of growth.

The campaign for the proposed ordinance allowing selective building moratoriums or freezes began in mid-1971. A thirty-three-year-old Miami Beach attorney, Harvey Ruvin, representing the Key Biscayne Property Owners Association, asked the Metro commission to declare a six-month moratorium on the issuance of building permits for new multiple-unit structures on Key Biscayne. This key, where former President Nixon maintains his Florida home, is one of the most desirable places to live in Dade County.

More than half of the island has been dedicated as county and state park-
land, and about half of the rest is given over to expensive and luxuriantly
landscaped single-family homes. The most valuable of the remaining vacant,
developable land is on the key's ocean side and has long since been zoned
for high-density hotel and apartment construction. A Metro planning department study made public in January 1971 indicated that this oceanfront area might soon be going the way of Miami Beach, with an unbroken
row of huge high-rises encroaching on the beach, blocking the view of
the ocean, impeding public right-of-way, and destroying the island's easy
tropical atmosphere.[25] The six-month building moratorium that Ruvin was
seeking was intended to maintain the status quo while Metro prepared a
detailed land use plan that would, in effect, prescribe a rollback of allowable densities to much lower levels. The Metro commission flatly rejected
Ruvin's proposal, although it did later approve in concept a "land intensity
plan" intended to guide the arrangement of densities within the existing
limits in such a way as to avoid walling off the oceanfront. The commission's attitude could be fairly characterized as basically oriented toward
upholding the rights of the developers, as Metro understood those rights.
The commission clearly could not pretend to take a purely disinterested
view. One commissioner was the owner of valuable commercial property
on the island, two others were contractors, and another was a labor leader
representing the building trades. The Metro mayor, Stephen P. Clark, one
of the contractors, was a former mayor of Miami, where zoning had had
what many Dade countians regarded as a particularly sorry history of
abuses.

Yet Ruvin was able to prevail in the matter of the building moratorium
because he was leading an increasingly popular cause. In many parts of
the county people were interested in freezing development pending possible zoning rollbacks. In early 1972, when the commission voted six to
three to reject the proposed moratorium ordinance for a second time,
Ruvin was ready to force the issue, having already obtained almost 17,000
signatures on petitions calling for a referendum. Prior to that referendum,
an all-out effort to defeat the proposed ordinance was made by the construction industry and the building trades unions. Herschel V. Green, past
president of the Builders Association of South Florida, predicted in a
Miami Herald article that "Moratoria for long periods [would result] in
large unemployment in an industry important to the well being of all people
living in Florida." With 31,500 persons, or about 6 percent of the total
work force,[26] employed in contract construction in Dade, such cries of
alarm could be expected to influence many people. The fact is, however,

25. Metropolitan Dade County Department of Planning, *Key Biscayne Environmental
Design Study*, January 1971.
26. Florida Department of Commerce, *Dade County: Labor Market Trends*, December
1972, newsletter no. 324.

the building moratorium ordinance was approved by a substantial majority of the voters.

ENTER JOHN B. ORR, JR. The outcome of the Metro election of October 1972 represented another clear gain for those people in the county who believed that growth should be brought under better control. Several weeks before this election, Jim Redford of the Izaak Walton League and other local conservation leaders, following their tactic of setting up ad hoc groups to meet the demands of special situations, formed the "Committee for Sane Growth," and under its letterhead sent out 6,000–7,000 letters that in effect endorsed four candidates for the Metro commission. The committee expressed particular concern at the need to control and limit growth in south Dade, and, in its letter, observed, "[We have] joined solely to defend our declining subtropical life-style. We seek to solve the paradox of 'the more people who come to share our good life, the less good it becomes.' "[27] The four Sane Growth candidates were pledged to oppose any zoning change that would allow development in situations where adequate highway capacity or water supplies might be lacking, or where dredge-and-fill permits had not been obtained. All four won election. One of these candidates was Harvey Ruvin. Another was John B. Orr, Jr., who defeated incumbent Stephen Clark and won election as mayor.

Jack Orr was no newcomer to Dade politics. As a liberal Democratic member of the Florida House of Representatives in 1956, he was the only legislator to vote in favor of racial integration of the public schools—a stand that won him the acclaim of human rights organizations and the displeasure of his constituents, who voted him out at the next election. More recently, Orr was an assistant state attorney in Dade responsible for rooting out malfeasance in local government, and, in this assignment, he had seen how easily land use zoning can be corrupted. Orr defeated Mayor Clark only narrowly, but he immediately began transforming his modest office (nominally, the mayor is limited chiefly to being the Metro commission's presiding officer and its representative at ceremonial occasions) to a position of political leadership.

Mayor Orr began championing a variety of reform proposals, several of which either directly involved the control of land use or affected the moral climate in which such regulation is carried out. He soon saw to the adoption of a strong conflict of interest ordinance,[28] which was made to apply to officials and employees of the municipal governments as well as

27. Robert D. Clark, "Ban Asked on Rezoning in South Dade," *Miami Herald*, September 5, 1972.

28. The new ordinance forbids any Metro commissioner, employee, or advisory board member from conducting any business with the county or from profiting in any way from present or past association with county government, with the same prohibition applying equally to anyone in the immediate family of any such official, advisor, or employee.

to those of Metro itself—this being an early move by the mayor to invoke Metro's neglected charter powers and prescribe minimum standards of conduct and performance for the municipalities. As for zoning practices within Dade's unincorporated areas, Mayor Orr, together with other commissioners and County Manager R. Ray Goode, proclaimed a new day. The high densities allowed on land zoned for multiple-unit dwellings was sharply reduced, with the maximum number of units per acre allowed under apartment zoning cut by more than a third and with at least 40 percent of all sites to be left in open space unencumbered by either buildings or parking lots.[29] The practical effect of Metro's new attitude toward land use control could best be seen on Key Biscayne, where the building moratorium movement had begun. By the fall of 1973, a general scheme of controls had been negotiated by Metro, the major interests with developable land along and near the oceanfront, and spokesmen for the key's residents. Whereas the prospect in 1971 had been for this property to become dominated by high rise structures of eighty-seven units per acre or greater, the prospect now was for an overall density of thirty units per acre or a bit more if the developers would provide special amenities. County Manager Goode declared moratoriums in several other areas besides Key Biscayne during 1972 and the first half of 1973, and zoning rollbacks could be expected in most of those areas, too.

DEVELOPMENT OF A NEW MASTER PLAN

The most far-reaching reform of land use regulation sought by Mayor Orr and his colleagues related to the development of a new Dade County general land use master plan. The 1965 master plan was primarily the product of the county's professional planners; citizens groups had relatively little part in its preparation. Partly for this reason, this earlier plan was a document of small political consequence and small practical effect. The Metro commission realized that, if more was to be expected of the new master plan, citizens drawn from a wide range of age groups, occupations, ethnic backgrounds, and the like should be involved in its development from the very outset. Accordingly, Metro had its Planning Advisory Board appoint a citizens' task force for each of six topics of study—land, population, economy, environment, public services, and plan implementation.[30] A total of almost 140 persons were to serve as members of these several groups, each of which was chaired by a Planning Board member. Liaison with the

---

29. Dade County Ordinances nos. 72–91 and 72–92, adopted December 5, 1972, by the Board of County Commissioners.

30. *Proposed Metropolitan Development Policies for Metropolitan Dade County*, Part One of the Comprehensive Development Master Plan. The Citizens Advisory Task Forces. December 1973.

Dade County League of Cities was achieved by having a representative of that organization serve on each task force. All of the task forces were to approach their assigned topics from the standpoint not of what could be expected based on a simple projection of past trends but of what is most desirable. They were to consider future growth and patterns of development, the distribution of services, and governmental regulation and administration. Background papers on existing conditions, trends, and policy issues were prepared by the Department of Planning to help the task forces in their deliberations. From March through July 1973 the groups met frequently (collectively putting in about 2,500 man-hours of work) and produced numerous tentative recommendations, many of them overlapping and some conflicting. The next step came during the fall when the six task forces met together in five workshop sessions and agreed on a common set of 410 recommendations that were then summarized in a preliminary statement made public in late 1973.[31] This document was of great potential importance because, once ratified by the Metro commission, it would be *the* official statement of metropolitan development policies and serve as the foundation of the new master plan's two remaining parts, namely the *Environmental Protection Guide* and the *Metropolitan Development Guide*.

THE DEVELOPMENT POLICIES

Some of the highlights of the statement of policy deserve mention here, despite this document's preliminary nature. Consider the following:
• In general, the new Metro policy would represent a sharp turning away from the old emphasis on growth and development. Conservation objectives would figure prominently in all planning. Specifically, the policy would prohibit further drainage of wetlands; preserve aquifer recharge areas; preserve agriculture as an economically viable activity (to rezone farm land for development would require a two-thirds majority vote of the Metro Commission); and seek harmony between natural and "manmade" environments through landscape standards, open space requirements, and other means such as planned unit development.
• Population growth would be restrained. Allowed densities would be fixed at levels much lower than those common in the past. A ceiling for the county as a whole would be set after a study by the Metro commission to determine the county's "carrying capacity . . . based on criteria such as water supply, costs of services, and the preservation of natural areas." Any project to augment water supplies—and hence to ease constraints on population growth—by technologies such as desalination and reverse osmosis would require approval in a referendum. Insofar as the county can influence economic growth through public investment or other means, it

31. Ibid.

would deliberately foster activities expected to employ people already living in the county rather than activities likely to further stimulate immigration.

• Development would not be permitted to outpace the provision of such essentials as public transportation, schools, waste collection and treatment facilities, and recreation areas. No longer would such facilities be planned and provided piecemeal and long after the need for them arises. Instead, they would be developed in a coordinated fashion intended to encourage and bring about growth and development at the times, in the places, and in the manner contemplated in the plan. "The general configuration of metropolitan growth should emphasize concentration around centers of activity, rather than directionless sprawl."[32] These centers could be either "specialized," as in the case of an education and research center featuring university and industrial facilities, or "diversified," as in the case of a center having various regional shopping, cultural, entertainment, and governmental facilities and high density residential development.

• Developers and landowners would, in effect, pay handsomely for development permits and for the public services that make their undertakings feasible. Besides the dedication of open space, school sites, and the like, they would be required to offer a diversity of housing types, with some units to be priced for families of low to moderate income. In addition, windfall gains resulting from various governmental actions (such as a rezoning action or a decision to build a road or major sewer line) might be subject to a special tax.

• The master plan would be "tied to a zoning map for implementation purposes" and, where a developer seeks a zoning change, he would bear the burden of proving that his project is in fact in conformity with that plan. Furthermore, Metro would adopt an "environmental impact ordinance" requiring all who undertake "significant developments" (with "significant" left, for the moment, undefined) to submit impact statements. No project involving dredging and filling of Biscayne Bay would be allowed unless shown to be of "overwhelming public benefit."

• In implementing the master plan, the Metro commission would oversee the municipal governments, as the Metro charter seems to allow. The municipalities' own land use plans would have to conform to the county plan. Moreover, minimum zoning standards established by Metro would apply throughout the county.

NEW DIRECTIONS FOR GROWTH

If adopted, the policies recommended by the advisory task forces would represent a radically new departure. Yet Dade's growth problems are such

32. Ibid.

that nothing less than strong, unprecedented measures are likely to suffice. In any case, it is well to consider the pattern of conservation and development that could take shape over the next few decades if policies of the kind recommended by the task forces are pursued.

REJUVENATION OF URBAN DADE. By sharply restricting the development of low-lying coastal and inland areas, the new policies would tend to place a premium on the redevelopment of areas already urbanized. This would ease development pressures in places such as south Dade while at the same time making the urban environment more attractive and satisfying. As a matter of fact, some major commitments already are being made to improve and enrich urban life. For instance, in 1972, voters in the City of Miami approved a $40-million parks development program that will preserve some of the remaining open space along the bayfront and elsewhere. Also, efforts are underway by the city to make the Miami River a major asset of downtown Miami, in the way that the San Antonio River has become a principal amenity of San Antonio. This once beautiful stream has long been grossly polluted and used as the graveyard of numerous derelict hulks. Once the river is cleaned up, it can become an important amenity lined by plazas, walkways, shops, and waterfront restaurants.

Long awaited improvements also appear at hand in housing and public transportation. In 1973, the Miami city commission began considering a proposal to have a sixteen-block downtown area designated for a high-density new town development, and a Metro committee recommended a $100-million program of housing for low-and-moderate income families. Downtown Miami and much of the remainder of the county should benefit from the Dade Area Rapid Transit (DART , an $805-million system of elevated trains which Metro is now committed to build. DART will operate on a large rectangular loop serving downtown Miami and Miami Beach, with spurs extending to Miami International Airport and to the periphery of metropolitan Miami in south Dade.

MORE INDUSTRIAL GROWTH IN NORTHWEST DADE. Industrial growth should probably continue to occur largely in northwest Dade where such activity already is centered. One major advantage which this area offers is that it is near Miami International Airport and the major highways leading out of the county. Also, it is convenient both to Miami and metropolitan Fort Lauderdale-Hollywood. To accommodate an expanding labor force some enclaves of high-density, low-to-moderate income housing could be appropriately built in this same area. This is not to say, however, that truly massive new growth would be desirable in northwest Dade, which includes a significant part of the land in Dade that is still undeveloped and highly useful for aquifer recharge. Nor is it to suggest that it would be inappropriate for nonpolluting industrial plants of small to moderate size to figure in new community development in the county's frontier area, south Dade.

A STRATEGY FOR SOUTH DADE. *Development on the Coastal Ridge.* Clearly, the best place for new development in south Dade is along the coastal ridge to either side of the Dixie Highway and the planned route of the mass transit system (see figure 6–4). Some of this region has been developed already, but considerable land remains vacant or is being farmed. Besides the two new highways (the South Dade and the West Dade tollways) and the DART system that will serve it, this area is within convenient reach of a proposed 50-million-gallon-a-day regional sewage treatment plant and deep-well effluent disposal system. This disposal system requires special mention because a federal-state pollution abatement conference that was first held in the fall of 1970 and later reconvened several times led to the conclusion that deep-well injection is the only way to get rid of sewage effluents satisfactorily in south Dade.[33] Discharge of even highly treated effluents either to canals or to Biscayne Bay is considered unacceptable, as is discharge to the Everglades National Park. Disposal by ocean outfall is the preferred method in north and central Dade, but in south Dade this method is not practicable because direct access to the open Atlantic is lacking and because extending a large sewer up to an outfall in central Dade or across Biscayne Bay to the ocean would not be acceptable. The approved deep-well disposal method involves pumping sewage effluents, after secondary treatment, down into the Boulder Zone, a cavernous region some 2,900 feet below sea level that now contains only brackish water. It involves some risk of contaminating the Biscayne Aquifer, and the U.S. Geological Survey has recommended that the first disposal well be built not far from tidewater, where the aquifer is in any event salty.[34] What this means is that all new development should be built within economical reach of the experimental well until the deep-well disposal method has been certified as safe.

Hurricane Hazards in the Lowlands. If the foregoing explains why new development should be on the coastal ridge, the reasons why such development ordinarily should *not* occur elsewhere in south Dade can also be readily noted. Development of the low-lying land to the east and south of the coastal ridge, besides causing ecological problems, could expose thousands of people to disastrous hurricanes. Since 1886, thirteen hurricanes with winds of up to 125 miles per hour have passed over or near south Dade, and four "great hurricanes" with winds of even higher velocity have visited the region. Computer studies by the National Hurri-

33. *Final Environmental Impact Statement: South Dade County, Florida,* C120377, Environmental Protection Agency, Region IV, Atlanta, Georgia, 1973.
34. Ibid., p. 182.

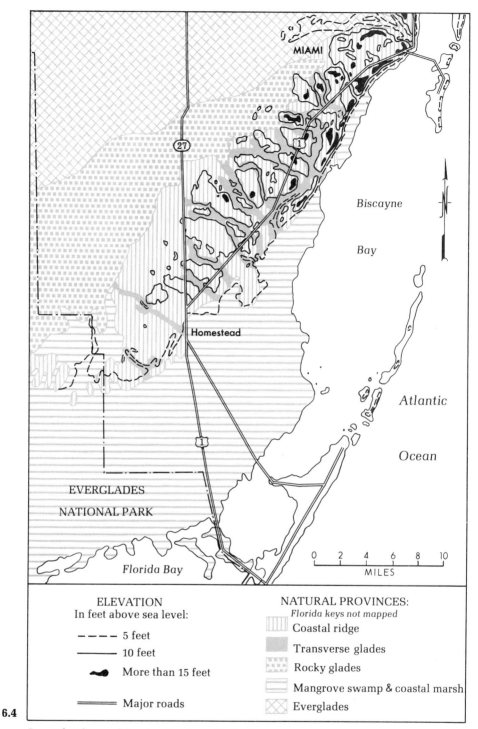

MIAMI

27

1

Biscayne

Bay

Atlantic

Ocean

Homestead

EVERGLADES

NATIONAL PARK

Florida Bay

0   2   4   6   8   10
MILES

ELEVATION
In feet above sea level:

- - - - 5 feet

———— 10 feet

More than 15 feet

===== Major roads

NATURAL PROVINCES:
Florida keys not mapped

Coastal ridge

Transverse glades

Rocky glades

Mangrove swamp & coastal marsh

Everglades

6.4

Coastal ridge and lowlands of south Dade

cane Center in Miami indicate that a great hurricane sweeping across Biscayne Bay into south Dade would generate a "storm surge" 15 feet greater than normal high tide. This mighty surge of water could sweep inland for up to 10 miles, with areas even as much as 18 miles from the coast inundated to depths of 5 feet.[35] With advance warning and effective emergency plans, residents of threatened areas in south Dade might use high-rise buildings as places of safe refuge. But, should this region ever be heavily developed, the property losses from a hurricane would be calamitous because it simply is not economically feasible to construct ordinary homes or commercial buildings to withstand a 10-to-15-foot storm surge. Furthermore, given the incidence of hurricanes in the region, such calamities would not merely be likely, they would be inevitable. In light of the hurricane menace and the environmental drawbacks associated with residential development in the coastal region, FP&L's preemption of Turkey Point and the large area to the south for its generating facilities and cooling system seems not inappropriate.

Water Problems from Lowlands Drainage. Still another powerful reason why development in the south Dade coastal area should be either greatly restricted or forbidden altogether is that the construction of more drainage canals there would lower the water table on adjacent lands of the coastal ridge. In fact, during the 1971 drought, some prominent farmers protested that the construction by the Flood Control District of three new south Dade canals below Homestead would have precisely such an effect. FCD officials disputed this, but the Florida Cabinet, acting partly on the advice of a Metro commissioner from south Dade, nevertheless saw fit to have two of the canals kept plugged to prevent drainage and to have work on the third stopped altogether.[36] Since the 1971 drought and the political response it engendered, the FCD has revised its thinking about undertakings such as the south Dade canals project. Both that project and the southwest Dade project (calling for drainage of the area between Homestead and the Everglades National Park for winter farming) now appear

35. *Resources and Land Information,* South Dade County, Florida. U.S. Department of the Interior, Geological Survey Investigation I-850, 1973.

36. The two canals that had almost been completed, C-109 and C-110, were to have discharged into the notorious "Aerojet Canal," or C-111. This latter canal, on which the Aerojet General Corporation had hoped to barge rocket motors from a testing area in south Dade out to the Intracoastal Waterway for shipment to the Kennedy Space Center, gave rise several years ago to a suit by the National Audubon Society against the construction agency, the U.S. Army Corps of Engineers. As a result of the suit, the Corps agreed to leave C-111 blocked at its lower end with an earthen plug. Had this not been done, salt water would have intruded into that part of the Everglades National Park lying immediately south of the canal and caused major ecological changes. As matters turned out, Aerojet was not to suffer from this decision because the expected space contracts failed to materialize and the modest facilities built by the company in south Dade have remained idle behind closed gates most of the time.

dead beyond all chance of resuscitation. Southwest Dade is the largest remaining aquifer recharge area in Dade County, lying outside both the Everglades National Park and FCD Conservation Area No. 3, that has not been affected by drainage, saltwater intrusion or at least localized pollution of the ground water.[37]

Saving Dade Agriculture. Although the coastal ridge is the best place in south Dade for urban development, it is also the place most suitable for the cultivation of the county's principal fruit crops: avocados, limes, and mangos. Winter vegetables grow well on the marl soils to the east and south of the ridge, but not the fruit crops. The some 11,000 acres devoted to fruit production at the time of a 1969–70 survey was down by about a third from the acreage of a decade earlier, and, without a more or less consistent Metro policy against their conversion to urban uses, the commercial groves could disappear within another decade or two. Accounting for less than 1 percent of personal income earned in the county,[38] Dade agriculture is a very minor economic activity by comparison with activities such as tourism, manufacturing, and commercial aviation. Nevertheless, it seems well worth preserving as a highly specialized type of farming that is in some respects unique. The south Dade avocado is quite unlike the California variety, and this fruit, along with some of the other subtropical speciality crops grown in the county, can be produced nowhere else in the United States. Also, farming has long been a part of the Dade tradition—Homestead, which still has not altogether lost the atmosphere of a farming community, is one of the county's oldest towns—and might be worth retaining simply for cultural diversity. In addition, fruit groves can serve admirably as the green space needed to set off one community from another and help keep overall regional population densities within desired levels.

THE MUNICIPALITIES REMAIN IMPORTANT. Although the role of Metro in establishing policies for growth and land use is emphasized in the foregoing, the role of the municipalities will remain important. Miami's situation is revealing on this point. This city now offers its residents basic services in only five fields—police and fire protection, sanitation, parks and recreation, and planning and zoning. As Maurice Ferre, the city's new mayor, has observed, if still more services should be taken away

37. James H. Hartwell (former U.S. Geological Survey hydrologist) and others, *Implications of the 1971 Drought Upon Dade County's Water Resources and Management Policies* (Report prepared under the sponsorship of the Mangrove Chapter of the Izaak Walton League with a grant from the Hoover Foundation, May 1973).

38. Data from *Survey of Current Business*, U.S. Department of Commerce, May 1972. Reported by the Metropolitan Dade County Planning Department, July 1972.

from Miami, "the city really ceases to exist."[39] But no one is proposing that Miami and Dade's other cities surrender all authority over their growth and development. Indeed, Mayor Orr has stated that he is firmly committed to a two-tier system of local government. Orr has in fact expressed regret that much of Dade is unincorporated and thus only under Metro or single-tier government.[40]

In a county as big and fast-growing as Dade, all of the planning and land use decisions probably could never be properly made by a single countywide government. Perhaps the most Metro can do effectively is to establish the county general land use master plan with the benefit of advice from the municipalities, citizens' groups, and other sources, and then see that subsequent county and municipal decisions conform to that plan, with no exceptions allowed without its express approval. Metro is unlikely to abuse its powers often in dealing with the municipalities. If the cities have developed their land use plans with the participation and support of their citizens, those plans will carry political weight and will not be lightly regarded.

METRO'S COMMITMENT IS
BEING TESTED

In the spring of 1974, as this is written, preparation of the new master plan is still some months from completion. A series of hearings has been held on the citizen task forces' preliminary statement of new development policies. Generally, the public attitude seems to remain strongly supportive of the concepts of controlling growth and keeping development from exceeding the "carrying capacity" of natural and man-made systems. Nevertheless, it is too early to say that the plan ultimately approved will in fact be an adequate blueprint for a new and better day in Dade County. Much less can it be said that, once adopted, the plan will be faithfully implemented.

TASK FORCE PROPOSALS UNDER ATTACK. Many storms will have to be weathered. Some of the proposals by the citizen task forces have been denounced as extreme. "There's going to be court suits if some of these recommendations stay in," commented William Safreed, executive director of the South Florida Builders Association, shortly after the proposals were made public.[41] The recommendation that new housing include units for families of low and moderate income was one that many developers

39. John McDermott, "Ferre and the Future: Renew Downtown Miami," *Miami Herald*, November 11, 1973.

40. Sam Jacobs, "Solve Your Zoning Mess First, Cities Tell Metro," *Miami Herald*, November 18, 1972.

41. Quoted in Frank Greve, "Mixed Income Housing Urged in Developments," *Miami Herald*, November 17, 1973.

particularly disliked. More fundamental is the disagreement over the concept of establishing a growth ceiling or "population cap." The hearings revealed substantial opposition to the fixing of a growth ceiling, and it is unlikely that the master plan finally adopted will prescribe one. The Greater Miami Chamber of Commerce has, predictably, opposed a growth limit, but so has the *Miami Herald*. The *Herald* has repeatedly scoffed at the very idea of such a limit. It is in fact probably true that any growth ceiling established for a county as large and complex as Dade would be arbitrary and legally indefensible. On the other hand, it is feasible to arrive at reasonable growth limits for particular projects or places by considering the present conditions in the area, the plans for providing essential public services, and the appropriate environmental and quality-of-life standards. Such limits, though provisional, will be meaningful. To abandon the idea of growth ceilings at least in this limited sense would be to abandon all serious effort at controlling growth.

WHERE METRO SHOWS ITS RESOLVE. In some significant respects, Metro's commitment to controlling growth appears to have deepened over the past year and a half since the election of a new county commission majority. Consider, for instance, the fact that Metro now has a better grip on the extension of public services that influence growth than ever before. This is so because of the consolidation under a new Miami-Dade Water and Sewer Authority of systems formerly run separately by Metro and the City of Miami (the old Miami Water and Sewer Board supplied more than a quarter of the Dade population with sewer service and about half of the population with water). The new authority, headed by a board appointed by the Metro Commission, is under the commission's budgetary control and is required to make its plans conform to the county master plan.

In two other instances, Metro is asserting or defending its powers under the county charter to oversee actions of the municipalities in land use and boundary changes. The Metro Commission has formally designated all of Biscayne Bay as a "county aquatic park and conservation area." This will allow Metro to review all dredge-and-fill projects proposed in the future, including those affecting submerged lands that adjoin municipalities.[42] In the other instance, the commission is appealing to the Florida Supreme Court a disturbing decision by the Dade Circuit Court to allow the town of Homestead to annex a 3,305-acre tract over the commission's objections. It happens that the tract in question embraces the site of a proposed housing development disapproved by Metro but favored by Homestead. (The suit may become moot if Metro and Homestead reach agreement on what development is appropriate for the tract.)

42. Steve Sink, "Biscayne Bay is now a Park," *Miami Herald*, April 3, 1974.

Metro's Mayor Orr continues to articulate the issues related to growth and to advocate useful innovations. He would, for example, have Metro require the preparation of an impact statement for any proposed housing project of more than 250 units. This requirement would do much to ensure better review of projects, including those proposed for places where no detailed planning has been accomplished. It would also underscore the fact that the county and its municipalities may be even more affected by growth coming in modest individual increments than they are by the large projects that are subject to reviews under the Environmental Land and Water Management Act of 1972. Finally, it would give Metro a new way of influencing what happens in the cities, because, under the mayor's proposal, an impact statement would be subject to county review even though it pertains to a project within a municipal boundary.

One of the boldest actions yet taken by Metro was its decision in March 1974 to impose a moratorium on all new building in a 310-square mile area of west Dade extending from Broward County almost to the extreme south end of the county. The moratorium, intended to preserve the status quo pending the completion of the county master plan, was approved despite vehement protests by some eighty land owners. So tumultuous was the meeting at which this action was taken that Mayor Orr ordered one man ejected by the sergeant-at-arms.[43]

WHERE THE COMMITMENT WAVERS. Metro has not, however, shown complete fealty to the concepts characterizing the kind of master plan likely to be adopted. Especially questionable is its decision approving the selection of a site for a pilot training airport (and ultimately for a large commercial airport) deep within Water Conservation Area 3B—a matter to be fully discussed in the next chapter. Also, two large new community projects in west Dade, Doral Park and The Hammocks, were approved on split votes by the Metro Commission against the advice of its planning department. In each case, the decision was made in the face of strong arguments that, if the projects were not to be disapproved, action should at least be deferred pending completion of the county master plan. Metro's approval of The Hammocks, a project conceded by the county planners to be of outstanding design, was understandable, especially as it included some units for low income families. Its approval of the Doral Park project, however, was clearly open to severe criticism. Designed to accommodate 16,500 people on a 2-square-mile site, this new community would be built in a wet prairie area several miles beyond the industrial area along the Palmetto Expressway, which generally defines metropolitan Miami's western periphery. Developable land would be created by building up the low-

43. Steve Sink, "Metro Extends Freeze on West Dade Building," *Miami Herald*, March 20, 1974.

lying prairie with fill from a series of twenty-one lakes dug to a depth of 40 feet. As pointed out in the staff report of the South Florida Regional Planning Council, storm runoff from the development would flow into these lakes, where there would be direct exchange between ground water and surface water, without the latter passing through the natural cleansing processes of the wet prairie ecosystem. Other negative aspects of the project include the fact that, being several miles from the nearest spur of the proposed DART system, it would generate much automotive traffic —an estimated 56,000 trips a day. Also, the developer expects 60 percent of the dwelling units of this luxury-type project to be occupied by families who will migrate to Dade County, with most of these to be new migrants to Florida. Although the project would be convenient to Dade's most important industrial area, it would not offer housing priced within the reach of the average worker with a family. "I plead [that we] hold off on this type of large-scale development until we have an overview [the county master plan]," said Harvey Ruvin, addressing fellow members of the Metro Commission.[44] "We're putting a blindfold on ourselves if we approve this."

DADE AS A POTENTIAL MODEL

To sum up, Dade County, Florida's largest and most populous county and the first to devise a two-tier metropolitan government, has recently seen the emergence of what appears to be a political majority behind concepts of land use and growth control that answer to humanistic, esthetic, and ecological considerations as well as to economic interests. Metro's new leadership has responded to this new attitude and helped to shape it.

There seems no reason yet to doubt Metro's commitment to controlling growth, despite the questionable decisions made with respect to a few matters such as Doral Park and the jetport. The critical test for Metro may come in the middle to latter part of 1974 when the new master plan comes up for adoption and its implementation begins. If implementation of the plan does safeguard vital resources and ensure a better quality of life, the consequences could be highly significant not only for Dade but for Florida as a whole. There is much groping on the part of the citizens of a number of Florida's metropolitan regions for a way to reorder the confused relationships existing between county and municipal governments. Given a successful demonstration of its two-tier system in coping with the challenge of growth and land use, Dade may become a model of great importance and influence.[45]

44. Steve Sink, "Doral Park Approved," *Miami Herald*, April 10, 1974.

45. The reform and improvement of local government was set back in July 1974 when Mayor Orr died of cancer. On October 1, 1974, Dade voters chose Orr's successor—Steve Clark, the incumbent mayor whom Orr defeated in 1972. However, in the same election two strong advocates of controlled growth, Jim Redford and Clara Oesterle, won seats on the Metro commission from the countywide electorate.

The jetport: Misplaced responsibility

The controversy over the plans of the Dade County Port Authority to build a south Florida regional jetport first arose in late 1968. Now, as I write more than five years later, the question of where to put this facility still has not been satisfactorily resolved, although most of the parties to the controversy believe that it has, albeit with varying degrees of conviction. Initially, the jetport problem developed partly because many people still were not sufficiently aware of either the value or the fragility of the Everglades and Big Cypress, and this despite the fact that water management had been an issue in the region for more than half a century. Another major cause of the controversy, and the one that I shall emphasize here, was the fact that the Port Authority was allowed the initiative of deciding where to put a large facility affecting Everglades National Park, the Flood Control District, and other interests that it could not conceivably represent. In a later phase of the jetport problem, after the Port Authority finally agreed to abandon the first site chosen, the U.S. Departments of Interior and Transportation and the governor of Florida would join in a pact with the authority to find a replacement site. But, again, by no means all of the interests at stake would be represented in the new process of site selection. The essence, therefore, of the story that follows is a mismatch between action and political responsibility.

THE FIRST SEARCH FOR A SITE

THE PORT AUTHORITY AND AVIATION IN DADE COUNTY. In 1967 and 1968, when the Port Authority began acquisition of a site in the Big Cypress for its new jetport, Dade County officials understood very well indeed commercial aviation's important role in their county's money economy even if they understood poorly the role of the Big Cypress in the natural economy of south Florida. Thirty-two scheduled airlines were flying out of Miami International Airport, including many of the major American airlines (such as Eastern, Pan American, National, and TWA) and better than a score of foreign airlines, mostly Latin American. Miami International was accommodating almost ten million passengers a year and nearly 500 million pounds of air cargo. About a third of the tourists coming to the Gold Coast were arriving by air. Furthermore, aviation was a major source of jobs in metropolitan Miami and in southeast Florida: some 35,000 persons worked at airports in the region, most of them at Port Authority facilities (which included several busy general aviation airports as well as Miami International), and another 47,000 persons held jobs directly dependent on the aviation industry. One fifth of the population of Dade County—or about 240,000 people—was, and is, supported by aviation, making this industry second only to tourism in importance to the local economy. From the time of its establishment by the Florida Legislature in 1945, the Port Authority was to have a special status. Enjoying a large income from rental and user fees, the Authority was not and is not dependent on Metro's general revenues. Furthermore, its executive director was for years answerable only to the Board of County Commissioners—not until 1973 was the Authority finally reconstituted as a department of the Metro government and placed under the control of the county manager. The Authority could even condemn land in counties other than Dade, provided the consent of the county affected was obtained.

As early as 1949, Miami International, profiting from its "end-of-the-line" position for domestic flights and from south Florida's good weather and large, uninhabited land and sea areas, had become an important base for maintenance and overhaul of commercial airliners and for pilot training. The possibility of establishing a new airport to accommodate increasing numbers of pilot training flights was first proposed by a Metro commissioner in 1952. But it was not until the mid-1960s that the Port Authority decided that such a facility had to be built, both in view of the airline companies' large investment in support facilities at Miami International and the

Authority's contract with those companies to accommodate pilot training. Yet training flights necessarily took second priority to commercial flights, and total operations already exceeded the airport's theoretical design capacity of 437,000 flights a year. The training flights made up a fourth of all operations at Miami International, but, even if all these were diverted elsewhere, air traffic at the Miami Airport was expected to reach saturation levels again before the end of the 1970s.

Construction of more runways at this airport almost on the edge of downtown would have been a poor solution, if it were possible at all. The problem of aircraft noise was already severe. Furthermore, establishment of a new jetport had long been seen by the Port Authority staff and Metro commissioners as the key to the long-term expansion of commercial aviation in south Florida. These officials in fact entertained the dream that this jetport would ultimately become one of the world's largest and divert international passengers from airports in New York and elsewhere. The new facility was thought of as an "airspaceport," for both supersonic and subsonic jets,[1] which would take advantage of south Florida's strategic location as a hub for flights between the United States, Europe, and Latin America. Miami International, by far the most important airport on the eastern seaboard south of Atlanta, was already handling a significant amount of traffic between the Americas and had some service to Europe. The new jetport, without near rivals, would be the only jetport in Florida with frequent long-haul as well as short-haul domestic and international service.

The Port Authority's plan was for the new jetport to have from four to six huge runways, with two of them to be possibly 30,000 feet long—nearly 6 miles! At the outset, however, only two runways would be built, with their use limited to pilot training for the first five years or so. Then, once traffic at Miami International finally reached the saturation point, commercial flights would begin. The Port Authority, together with its engineering consultants, Howard, Needles, Tammen, and Bergendoff (HNTB), was clearly competent to find a site in south Florida which, from the standpoint of air traffic requirements and economic criteria, would lend itself to the phased development of such a jetport. And no one seemed much worried about the fact, if indeed they even thought about it, that

1. In the Dade Port Authority's 1968 annual report the proposed Big Cypress jetport was billed as "Miami's international skyway crossroads." An official of the Port Authority of New York was quoted as saying that, unless relief for air congestion at New York was soon coming, many Latin American travelers would be shunning airports in that area and flying to Europe via Miami. Arthur H. Patten, Jr., a Metro commissioner during the period 1958–1970, once summed up the Dade Port Authority's aims: "We plan the greatest jetport man has ever envisioned—We should be flying half of the passengers in the eastern United States out of Miami. We can handle the international flights better than New York. We've just passed the mark of ten million passengers a year at (Miami International). We'll be flying sixty-five million by 1985." Patten was quoted by Howard Bloomfield, "The Everglades/Pregnant with Risks," *American Forests*, May 1970.

the Authority could not represent all of the interests that this huge new facility would affect for better or worse. Nor was it clearly perceived that, as a local entity jealous of its prerogatives yet powerless to establish facilities outside Dade except through agreement with another county, the position of the Authority was weak and anomalous. Commercial aviation, still hardly a half century old in the United States, has been nurtured through its infancy and adolescence into adulthood by the municipalities and other local government entities that now own and manage several hundred airports that serve commercial jet aircraft. With the advent of big commercial jets and large new airports, the child was growing too big for the parent to handle alone, but this was still to be recognized.

The only existing airport considered to have possible potential for development as a large commercial jetport for south Florida was Homestead Air Force Base, below Miami in south Dade. Upon further inquiry, Homestead was found to be neither suitable nor available. Although there was a vast amount of undeveloped land in south Florida, the Port Authority was from the outset to encounter difficulty acquiring the jetport site. Together, the FCD conservation areas and the Everglades National Park extended for about 100 miles north to south and from 15 to 40 miles east to west. Some large tracts of land were available east of the FCD's perimeter levee and west of the coastal ridge, but this land, originally part of the Everglades, was near enough to the Gold Coast to raise the possibility of problems such as high land prices, air traffic conflicts, and aircraft noise complaints, which the Port Authority was trying to escape. The only other places where the Authority could build the jetport within 50 miles or so of Miami would be the lower Everglades Agricultural Area, where the muck had been partly drained but not tilled; "Immokalee Island," the low, sandy plateau that begins just to the west of the Agricultural Area; and finally, the eastern Big Cypress.

The Port Authority considered building the jetport east of the FCD levee in Broward County on a site previously identified by the Federal Aviation Agency as conveniently near the center of the Gold Coast population. This idea was abandoned, however, when Broward County officials emphatically rejected the proposition that Broward have no part in running the jetport and receive none of the user fees. When the Port Authority first turned to the vast Everglades-Big Cypress region west of Miami in its search for a site it met rebuffs there too. It considered two sites in the Flood Control District's Conservation Area No. 3, but the FCD was not willing to sacrifice the water storage and wilderness values that construction of a jetport in that area would have required. Consideration of a third Everglades site, this one below the Tamiami Trail and next to the Everglades National Park, was abandoned after the Park Service raised objections—objections which, at that time, had mainly to do with concern about aircraft noise and loss of wilderness solitude. Another site in this same general area, but farther west and wholly within Monroe County, was discarded as a possibility after Monroe County officials, as a condition, insisted on a redrawing of county boundaries that would put the Islandia keys in Monroe in exchange for Dade's getting some 30 square miles of Everglades and Big Cypress swampland. The proposal to establish Biscayne National Monument not yet having won acceptance, the Monroe officials were of course thinking of Islandia not as a park but as a rich new city.

THE SEARCH ENDS IN THE BIG CYPRESS. The Port Authority's search finally ended in the Big Cypress wilderness, in an area about 45 miles from Miami and about 6 miles from the Everglades National Park (see figure 7–1). This area was considered suitable for the jetport site despite its distance from the Gold Coast. To have the pilot training facility well away from Miami would be an advantage because it meant no conflict with the dense Gold Coast air traffic. And, as for passenger access to the commercial jetport eventually to be built, there was the possibility of having the facility served by a high speed ground transit system as well as having the south Florida segment of Interstate 75, then in the early planning stage, routed so as to give the jetport a high speed highway link to Miami. The site chosen was roughly the same distance from Naples as it was from Miami, but the west coast area was not expected to contribute much to the volume of passengers using the airport, at least not for many years. Less than 7 percent of south Florida's population of 2.4 million (the 1970 census figure for the seven counties below Lake Okeechobee) lived in the southwest counties of Collier, Lee, and Hendry. More than 91 percent lived in the three Gold Coast counties of Palm Beach, Broward, and Dade, with the two latter counties having better than three-fourths of the total and with Dade alone having more than half.

About a third of the 39-square-mile site which the Port Authority had identified was in Dade County, but the remaining two-thirds was in Collier. At first it appeared that the Collier commissioners, like the commissioners in Broward, would refuse to permit the Port Authority to condemn land within their county for a jetport that Dade alone would own and operate. What finally seemed to overcome their initial resistance was the promise of residential and commercial development associated with the jetport project. Construction of this facility could be expected to enhance property values and stimulate development throughout the eastern Big Cypress. Alan C. Stewart, then director of the Port Authority, had prophesied that a city would inevitably spring up around the jetport.[2] And it was not until after extensive discussions between representatives of the Greater Miami Cham-

2. Stewart was quoted in the Miami *News* of April 14, 1969, as follows: "If the conservationists want to stop industrial and commercial development, they are going to have to save their pennies and buy the land. What they're saying is that they don't want a city to rise up around the airport, but everywhere I know about, that's what's happened."

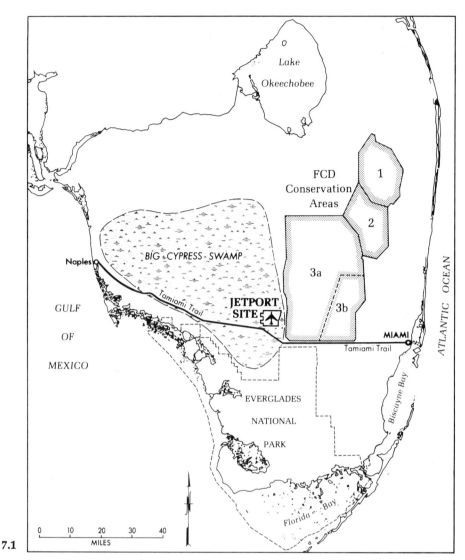

7.1

Original site for south Florida jetport

ber of Commerce and the Greater Naples Chamber of Commerce that the Collier County commissioners began to see the jetport as an important potential asset. A final agreement was reached in June 1968 between the two counties: the "Everglades Jetport"—as the Port Authority first unwarily named it—would be built in the Big Cypress just west of Conservation Area No. 3 and immediately north of the Tamiami Trail. The Dade-Collier agreement was silent on the question of regional land use controls except for a provision stating that all land within 3 miles of the jetport boundaries would be zoned "with due regard to the function and purposes of the airport."

Conservationists would later accuse the Port Authority of indifference

192 SOUTH FLORIDA: THE PROBLEMS OF GROWTH

to environmental considerations and of failure to consult properly with state and federal agencies. Yet Richard Judy, who at the time was deputy director of the Port Authority (he would later succeed Stewart, whom the Metro commission wanted out) told me, quite accurately, that his agency was proceeding in something of a state and federal "policy vacuum" with respect to land use. The Authority was nevertheless careful to consult all state and federal agencies that had an interest in the Big Cypress. The Federal Airport Act of 1946 requires that airport projects approved by the Federal Aviation Agency be "reasonably consistent" with such regional plans as planning agencies might have prepared. Of course no agency had ever made any plans for the Big Cypress, but the FAA, either on its own initiative or to acknowledge steps the Port Authority was taking in any event, made its approval of the Big Cypress site conditional upon the approval of state agencies whose interests might be affected.[3] The Port Authority and its consultants several times discussed the site selection with representatives of the Everglades National Park, the Flood Control District, the Game and Fresh Water Fish Commission, and other agencies. The usefulness of these discussions was limited, however. This was 1967 and 1968, when it was far less common than it is today even for professional conservationists to be thinking in broad "environmental" terms. Before the Dade-Collier agreement on the Big Cypress site was finally signed, the State Board on Conservation (soon to become the Department of Natural Resources), the Internal Improvement Fund (which owned land in the vicinity of the jetport), the Flood Control District, and the Game and Fresh Water Fish Commission all informed the Port Authority in writing that they had no objection to the site. The director of the Game and Fish Commission was even enthusiastic about the project; he could envision part of the extensive jetport property becoming a public hunting and fishing area.[4] Officials at the Everglades National Park were to show increasing concern that development activities stimulated by the jetport might destroy the Big Cypress as a wilderness watershed, but they actually had suggested that a site be found above the Tamiami Trail, somewhat away from the park in that part of the Big Cypress where the jetport now was to be located. And, in June 1967, a Park Service official had written the Federal Aviation Agency to say that the choice of the new site was "very heartening to us."[5]

3. Although there appears to be no correspondence or other written record available to confirm it, this explanation of what happened is based on the best recollection and surmise of Richard Judy of the Port Authority and Robert F. Bacon, chief of the FAA's Systems Planning Division, Airport Services.

4. Letter of March 6, 1968, from O. E. Frye, Jr., director of the Game and Fresh Water Fish Commission, to Alan C. Stewart, Director of the Dade Port Authority.

5. Letter dated June 8, 1967, from Charles S. Marshall, acting director, Southeast Region, National Park Service, to William J. McGill, chief, Airports Division, Federal Aviation Agency, Atlanta, Georgia.

The groundbreaking for the jetport was held on September 18, 1968, and from that ceremony one would have assumed that the project was to be without controversy. Colorful, hand-sewn jackets were worn not only by the Miccosukee Indian leaders who were present but also by officials of the Port Authority as well—an ironic touch inasmuch as the Authority was now invading the last sanctuary to which the Miccosukees were driven during the nineteenth century by U.S. Army troops. An official proclamation from Governor Kirk was read, which praised the Port Authority for its "new vision" and "superlative planning." Secretary Alan Boyd of the U.S. Department of Transportation could not be present for the groundbreaking, but he participated by telephone. A former Miamian, Boyd also praised the Port Authority, and he even ventured to say a few words in Miccosukee, though these were drowned by static. The ceremony came to a climax when, at Boyd's command, a charge of dynamite was detonated, hurling muck and pieces of limestone into the air. This ceremonial gesture was no more than a small detail in the busy day of a high-ranking Washington official, but symbolically it was significant. A remote federal bureaucracy was given its blessing to a huge intrusive project in south Florida—and this without observing the letter and spirit of existing law and in virtual isolation from some powerful forces that would soon be at play. As later analysis would reveal, the cost of the commercial jetport would exceed $1 billion (not counting the cost of rapid ground transit) and the expected federal contribution would be as much as $300 million. The FAA already was preparing to make a grant toward construction of the first training facility runway. Section 4(f) of the Urban Mass Transportation Act of 1964 says that the secretary shall approve no project requiring the use of publicly owned park, recreation, or wildlife areas unless there is "no feasible and prudent alternative." The act calls for a special effort to preserve such areas. Neither Boyd nor his successor, John A. Volpe, would be advised by the FAA that these provisions of the Transportation Act would apply to a jetport on the Big Cypress site if the project were carried beyond the stage of a training facility to full commercial development. Construction of any new ground transit system leading from this site to Miami would require taking land either from the park or from FCD Conservation Areas 3A and 3B, which are managed partly for outdoor recreation and conservation of fish and wildlife.

THE JETPORT CONTROVERSY UNFOLDS

AN FCD OFFICIAL RAISES QUESTIONS. Some five weeks after the groundbreaking ceremony, with construction of the training facility proceeding rapidly, an incident occurred that helped generate a national controversy over the jetport. Robert W. Padrick, the Fort Pierce automobile dealer who was chairman of the Flood Control District's governing board, discovered while attending a meeting regarding highway access to the jetport that the State Road Department was still actively considering a plan for a road and general transportation corridor that would cross Conservation Area No. 3. Padrick felt betrayed because, as he has since related, Richard Judy of the Port Authority had told him a few weeks earlier that this routing was "Just a line on a map, it is out, not being considered."[6] He called on conservation organizations in Florida, and nationally, to help him defeat this "abominable proposal."[7] More than a dozen persons representing state, federal, and private conservation interests were invited to meet with the FCD board in December. At that meeting what before had been misgivings about the jetport began to harden into opposition.

Represented there were several agencies of the Department of the Interior, the Corps of Engineers, the Florida Game and Fresh Water Fish Commission, and the State Department of Natural Resources. Present also were Arthur Marshall, for Interior's Bureau of Sport Fisheries and Wildlife; Nathaniel Reed, from the governor's office; and two young conservation group leaders who were to play major roles in encouraging national conservation organizations to oppose the jetport project—Joe Browder, then southeastern representative of the National Audubon Society, and Gary Soucie, then eastern representative of the Sierra Club. Among the Park Service people attending was Rodger W. Pegues, a former Sierra Club regional representative who was now an attorney in the Park Service director's office and who was beginning to serve as an unofficial liaison between his agency and the national conservation groups. Pegues had shrewdly reasoned that to try to block the jetport would take no more effort than to try to build safeguards into it; and, further, that if the project could not be blocked, the safeguards obtained would be stronger than they might be otherwise. Of course, neither Pegues nor his colleague, Manuel Morris, a water resources specialist in the Park Service's Washington headquarters, who was also in close touch with national conservation groups, was in a position to advocate that the jetport project be stopped or moved to another site. But, in this matter of the jetport, an unofficial alliance between the Park Service and the conservation groups was in the making, with the latter taking positions that the Park Service and its employees could not take, certainly not publicly.

The jetport project itself was not directly challenged at Padrick's meeting, however. Only Soucie insisted that moving or stopping the project should be seriously considered; Marshall and Pegues agreed with him, but,

6. Letter dated November 5, 1968, from Robert W. Padrick to Jay W. Brown, Chairman of the State Road Department, Tallahassee. Text appears in Everglades National Park, Hearings before the Senate Interior Committee, 91 Cong. 2 sess. (1969), p. 87.
7. Ibid., pp. 87–88.

for the moment, both kept silent on the point. Most of those present are said to have felt that construction of the jetport at the Big Cypress site was inevitable. What principally emerged from the meeting was a decision to call on Port Authority officials to address publicly the question of the project's environmental impact at a public hearing.

The hearing was held in late February 1969, with Padrick presiding. The long list of questions brought up had to do with both the direct environmental effects of the jetport and related ground transportation facilities and with the indirect effects from the private development likely to occur around the jetport. The Port Authority's spokesmen repeatedly had to plead ignorance or say "studies are under way" to questions such as how much drainage the project would entail, where flood waters would be discharged, and how detergents and chemicals used in washing aircraft would be treated and disposed of. When Nathaniel Reed and Joe Browder began pressing the Port Authority for answers, Dade Metro Mayor Chuck Hall labeled them "white militants."

The Port Authority's confession that the Big Cypress site was selected without careful evaluation of environmental effects made the jetport project more vulnerable later to a direct attack, with Governor Kirk among those leading it, saying that his earlier support of the project had rested on the mistaken assumption that there had been such an evaluation. Furthermore, the Port Authority's confession helped lay the basis for a possible challenge of the project under Section 4(f) and related provisions of the Transportation Act. In fact, at the hearing, Arthur Marshall stated that Interior definitely had a responsibility to investigate the jetport's impact on the Everglades National Park and the environment of south Florida. Yet, if Padrick had not taken the leadership and called the Port Authority to account, timely opposition to the jetport might not have developed. Indeed, in a report to his superior, a representative of the Bureau of Outdoor Recreation, the Interior agency assigned the leadership on matters arising under Section 4(f) of the Transportation Act, later expressed relief that Padrick and not himself or someone else from BOR was taking the initiative. "We are avoiding the onus of a federal agency trying to tell the local folks what to do," he wrote.[8] Already, National Park Service people felt frustrated because, on the jetport issue, their official channel to the Secretary of the Interior's office was through BOR.

THE EVERGLADES COALITION. By mid-April 1969, an "Everglades Coalition" of nearly all of the national conservation groups was demanding that construction of the jetport be halted. Among the prime movers behind the coalition's formation were Soucie of the Sierra Club and the two Park Service employees previously mentioned, Pegues and Morris. They had

8. Letter of December 19, 1968, from L. G. Hendrickson, Jr., to Roy Wood, director of the BOR southeastern regional office in Atlanta.

met with Elvis Stahr, head of National Audubon, in New York, and Stahr, seeing the need for concerted action by the national conservation groups, had put the coalition together.[9] Once formed, the Everglades Coalition, which was made up of twenty-one conservation organizations and two labor unions, addressed an appeal to Secretary of Transportation John A. Volpe, urging that the jetport project be stopped. Otherwise, the coalition did little else, but the mere fact of its formation was important because it alerted officials and politicians in Washington, Tallahassee, and Miami that the jetport issue was one of high priority to conservationists.

SECRETARY HICKEL AGAINST THE PROJECT. Besides the establishment of the Everglades Coalition, three other events in the spring of 1969 contributed to making the Big Cypress jetport a national issue of concern to two cabinet secretaries and ultimately to President Nixon himself. The first was a trip by Secretary of the Interior Walter J. Hickel to the Everglades; the second, the public hearings held by the Senate Committee on Interior and Insular Affairs on the jetport and other Everglades issues; and the third, the announcement just prior to those hearings that the departments of Interior and Transportation would jointly conduct a study of the jetport's environmental impact. Secretary Hickel became exposed intensively to the jetport issue for the first time on his Everglades trip in March, but it was not that problem but rather the plight of the alligator that brought Hickel to Florida. No presidential appointee had ever got off to a worse start than had Hickel. His first disastrous press conference ("A tree looking at a tree really doesn't do anything" and other gaffes) and his Senate confirmation ordeal left a public relations problem of large magnitude. Hickel's dashing off in an airboat—with newsmen trailing along behind—to show his determination to bring every last alligator poacher before the law inspired some cynical comment about public relations gimmickry and image-building. Yet, whatever the motivation behind the

9. Although his role in the council's formation may not have been crucial, the support for this initiative given by Frank Masland, Jr., a Carlisle, Pennsylvania, carpet manufacturer, reveals how an environmental issue can sometimes excite individuals found anywhere along the political spectrum. A former member of the John Birch Society's National Council and once a director of the National Association of Manufacturers, Masland is a stalwart of the political right wing. However great his abhorrence of many governmental activities, he is a dedicated supporter of the Park Service. He has served as chairman of the Park Service Advisory Board, and has made it his habit to spend part of each winter at Flamingo, in the Everglades National Park. One day in the winter of 1969, Joe Browder, doubtful of his own influence as a young National Audubon field representative, urged Masland to call on the national conservation groups to make a fight over the jetport. Shortly thereafter, Masland made a series of calls from the office of John Raftery, the park superintendent, with Raftery present, to leaders of several major conservation groups, among them Charles H. Callison, executive vice-president of National Audubon and Browder's boss. His message, as Masland now remembers it, was that "an antijetport coalition was essential, that a concerted effort was required, and that there was no time to be lost."

trip, Joe Browder, Nathaniel Reed, and officials at the Everglades National Park eagerly seized the chance to tell the secretary why the jetport project had them alarmed. Hickel's party camped out on Lostmans River in the park, and, as one member of the group related off the record, "The secretary was exposed to some hard lobbying. The first politically sensitive environmental issue which Hickel had encountered was this Everglades issue. He was really sharp and immediately saw the political potential and the low costs involved in taking the right kind of Everglades position. He understood the water issue, the jetport issue, the Everglades mystique. And that accomplished a very necessary thing—it [protection of the Everglades] became a true secretarial level issue, and there aren't many of those." Hickel later told me that it was on this trip that he concluded that the jetport should not be built in the Big Cypress. He said that he made his mind up about this the minute he was flown over the site, where runway construction was proceeding. "Having been in the construction business all my life," he explained, "I saw the problem immediately. In order not to obstruct the water flow, the jetport would have to be built on pilings, like a bridge. That wouldn't be possible economically." In any case, several weeks after his return from Florida, Hickel wrote Secretary Volpe to express concern about the jetport and to ask what "feasibility" and land use studies had been made in connection with it.

Meanwhile, staff members of the Senate Interior Committee had conceived the idea of holding hearings on the jetport issue and other Everglades problems after talking with Manuel Morris, the Park Service hydrologist specializing in Everglade matters. William J. Van Ness, the committee's special counsel, saw the jetport issue as generic to a whole class of land use problems involving state, local, and federal decision makers. At the time, Senator Henry M. Jackson of Washington, chairman of the committee, was developing the National Environmental Policy Act of 1969, whereby environmental impact studies would be required for all important projects built with federal support or under federal permit. The need for land use policy legislation was also beginning to receive his attention. Senator Jackson announced his intention to call the jetport hearings while speaking before a National Audubon convention in late April. On June 2, the day before the hearings began, the departments of Interior and Transportation announced that they were jointly undertaking a study of the jetport's impact on the Everglades National Park. "I am seriously concerned over the potential threat to the Everglades that might result from uncontrolled land use in the areas surrounding the proposed new jetport," Secretary Volpe said. The calling of the hearings, like the formation of the Everglades Coalition, had helped to make the jetport question a national issue with which the Nixon administration was now trying to cope.

The idea for the impact study had been conceived in the office of Under Secretary of the Interior Russell E. Train. According to Boyd Gib-

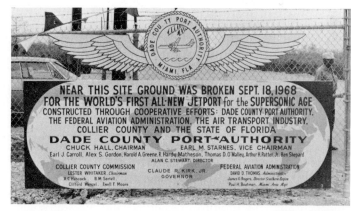

Aerial view of the jetport, and sign
announcing abortive jetport project.

bons, Train's deputy, what led to the environmental study was a memorandum that had come to him in early 1969 from an old personal and political friend, John D. Ehrlichman, the powerful (but still relatively obscure) top White House aide on domestic affairs. The note, which Gibbons has since framed as a memento, merely said, "I have a letter with regard to the impact of a proposed airport on the Everglades National Park. Do you have any information on it?" As an attorney formerly deeply involved in real estate and zoning matters in Seattle, Ehrlichman was familiar with land use questions. The environmental study prompted in part by his casual inquiry was to be a major factor in the White House decision that the Big Cypress site should be abandoned.

The under secretary's proposal for a study gave Governor Kirk a chance to slip out of his now embarrassing commitment to the jetport project. Accordingly, when Nathanial Reed and the governor got word of it, they were eager for the study to start and they helped Train obtain Hickel's support for it. Train had been a frequent visitor to Hobe Sound, that wintering ground for wealthy easterners, and he and Nat Reed knew one another socially. After flying to Washington one spring afternoon, Reed and the governor were warmly received. "We went to Russ Train's house," Reed told me. "The governor and Russ sat on the floor and I gave a briefing on what I saw of the Big Cypress, on water flow, water quality, the impact of the jetport on the surrounding land mass. They asked a lot of questions. I think we must have briefed for almost three hours. The jetport was a hot issue by now. Russ was thoroughly committed to the idea that this type of thing could not continue in the United States, that an independent environmental study had to be made, and, depending upon the results, the Executive Branch would have to decide whether to proceed or not [with federal financial support of the jetport project]. The governor agreed wholeheartedly with that approach. And the next day we sat down with Secretary Hickel and [the final decision to make the study was made]."

LUNA LEOPOLD AND THE IMPACT STUDY. Government studies are frequently so cautiously hedged and qualified in their conclusions that policy makers receive no clear guidance, but this was not to be the case with the report on the proposed jetport's potential environmental impact. Luna B. Leopold, senior research hydrologist with Interior's U.S. Geological Survey, was the scientist assigned by Under Secretary Train to lead the study for Interior. And, inasmuch as the Department of Transportation's contribution was never included in the report, the entire study as publicly released bore the imprint of Leopold and his study team. By his upbringing, personal inclinations, and professional accomplishments, Leopold is a remarkable man. His late father, Aldo Leopold, one of the organizers of the Wilderness Society and the founder of scientific wildlife management in the United States, had a generation earlier been an important figure in the conservation movement in the United States. Luna Leopold grew up in a home atmosphere of unusual freedom. "My father always respected the idea that young people were very independent people and shouldn't be told what to do," Leopold now recalls. As a talented researcher and member of the prestigious National Academy of Sciences, his position of senior hydrologist in the Geological Survey was one of exceptional independence. "I do as I please, absolutely as I please," he told me.[10]

Leopold was making field studies in Wyoming when the under secretary's office finally reached him to ask that he head the jetport study. "I knew that I could do the job as well as most people, and I wanted some concessions," Leopold says, recalling his discussions with the under secretary. One was that he would have his pick of people to work with him on the study; a second was that the report would represent only the views of the authors and not be a statement of their agencies' positions. And, at least implicitly, it was understood that the report would not be subject to review by Geological Survey or Interior Department officials because Leopold told Train he would deliver the final report by mid-August in order that he could then be off to Europe on other professional business.

At a meeting with Department of the Interior personnel in Washington, Leopold met Arthur Marshall, who (as we noted in Part I) in his deep concern about the rapid deterioration of the Florida environment, had been rattling the chains for nearly a decade. Leopold quickly decided that Marshall would be Florida coordinator for the study. Knowing little about the south Florida environment himself, Leopold conceived of his own role as primarily that of orchestrating the work of others. After the initial meeting with the study team, he returned to Wyoming whence he had been summoned. Later, in mid-July, Leopold went to Florida where he spent a few days traveling about Everglades National Park and the Big Cypress with Park Service people, and then met with the study team. In the days that followed, the team's report was prepared but there remained the possibly troublesome problem of incorporating into it the material to be furnished by the Department of Transportation. Officials of that department, seemingly little aware of the report's potential impact, were to make their contribution so late that little time would be left either to reconcile

10. Leopold was one of six federal civil servants given Rockefeller Public Service Awards in 1971 worth $10,000 each. Leopold's award was in recognition of his overall contribution as a government scientist. "His concern for preserving the quality of the nation's environment spans more than three decades," the citation said. In 1969, Leopold had become significantly involved in the then emerging controversy over the trans-Alaska pipeline as well as in the one over the jetport. Shortly before being called into the jetport controversy, Leopold went to Alaska at the request of the USGS and spent a week investigating the route of the proposed pipeline. His report from that trip led to studies by other USGS scientists which influenced the Secretary of the Interior's decision to delay issuing permits for construction of the pipeline. Leopold left the USGS in 1972 to join the faculty of the University of California at Berkeley.

the different points of view held by the Interior people and themselves, or, more likely, to have the report point out the extent of agreement and disagreement.

A central conclusion of the report was that the western arm of Everglades National Park was vitally dependent on the long seasonal wet period and the thin, diffuse "sheet flow" of water overland that characterize the natural functioning of the Big Cypress Watershed. The 39-square-mile jetport tract itself represented less than 4 percent of the part of the Big Cypress tributary to the park. But the report held that in the absence of adequate land use regulation, the eastern Big Cypress would suffer drainage, pollution, and other adverse environmental affronts as commercial, industrial, and residential activities were encouraged by development of the jetport and related ground transport facilities. What it clearly implied was that control of land use would be as weak in the future as in the past. The failure of the state and the south Florida counties to make a serious effort at land use regulation in the Big Cypress was all too apparent. The Port Authority had found the jetport site, prior to acquisition, to consist of 2,800 individual ownerships, many of these having come about from the freewheeling operations of land sales companies that had subdivided larger tracts and sold parcels out of state and abroad. One 640-acre section in Collier County had 385 owners—all Brazilians. Unless land fill methods were used to build up the land, or unless it were drained by construction of a network of canals, all of the jetport site would be subject to seasonal flooding. Parcels were still being sold in and around the jetport site as late as 1969 when the Port Authority had begun condemnation proceedings. In their advertising, the land sales companies, supposedly regulated by the Florida Land Sales Board, were allowed euphemistically to describe the flooding as "ponding."

Moreover, the fear that the eastern half of the Big Cypress would be destroyed by uncontrolled land use practices was fully justified in the light of what already had occurred in the western half where, as will be more fully described in the next chapter, Collier County officials had been allowing a huge and devastating land development project to proceed unchecked since the early 1960s. And there was perhaps even less reason to hope for effective land use controls in Monroe County than in Collier. The still dominant clique of Pork Chop politicians in Key West could not have cared less for the county's almost uninhabited Everglades and Big Cypress country on the mainland if that region had been on the moon. On the unpaved "Loop Road" below the Tamiami Trail is the tiny, ramshackle community of Pinecrest, "the place the law forgot." From Pinecrest, the refuge of several professed ex-poachers who say they no longer slip into the park with jack light and gun to kill alligators, the nearest Monroe County deputy sheriff is, by road, nearly 100 miles away. The county building inspector apparently travels the Loop Road no more often than the sheriff, for dozens of homes have been built along that road without any-one bothering to apply for a building permit.[11]

Thus, the odds against either Collier or Monroe County protecting the Big Cypress Watershed through land use controls were overwhelming. Dade County was more likely to exercise such controls effectively because of its greater sophistication in land use matters and because of the Dade conservation groups' political clout. Yet Metro's still wavering perform-ance in the South Biscayne Bay region suggested that even Dade could not be counted on.

As for the prospects of *regional* land and water management capable of protecting the Big Cypress, the only development that could be regarded as even a hesitant step in that direction began in May 1969, when repre-sentatives of Collier, Monroe, and Dade counties met to discuss the forma-tion of a Tri-County Jetport Planning Council. The meeting was held at the urging of the State Bureau of Planning, but this weakly led, weakly supported planning agency had neither the inclination nor the authority to demand that the south Florida counties establish adequate land use regulations. The jetport council would later take in (for a time) all seven counties below Lake Okeechobee and be renamed the South Florida Regional Planning Council. It would have to surmount more than the usual parochialism endemic in such planning bodies. Early, there was suspicion on the part of some leaders in the still lightly populated south-west Florida counties that the council might try to restrain their growth and economic development. The council could not achieve unanimity even as to establishing a two-year moratorium on zoning changes in the jetport area. Dade and Collier would declare such a moratorium, Monroe County would not.

Taking account of the foregoing, the report[12] by Interior's study team identified three possible courses of action and set forth what the authors viewed as the likely consequences of each: (i) Proceed with staged develop-ment of training, cargo, and commercial aviation facilities—and see the south Florida ecosystem destroyed from the effects of widespread collateral development beyond the jetport boundaries; (ii) proceed with construction of a one-runway training facility and obtain an alternative site for the commercial jetport—and thus reduce, but by no means eliminate, pres-sures for development around the jetport and possibly allow time for establishing effective land use regulations; and (iii) obtain an alternative site for both the training facility and commercial jetport—and "inhibit greatly" development forces and give impetus to establishment of land

11. James Malone, "No Permits, But Homes Built Near Jetport," *Miami Herald*, October 28, 1969.

12. Released in September 1969 under the title *Environmental Impact of the Big Cypress Swamp Jetport*, by the U.S. Department of the Interior, 155 pages. The report's major findings, paraphrased above, appear on pp. 1–2.

use controls. The report declared, moreover, that "so long as the training airport is in use, pressures for its expansion will continue and will inexorably and surely lead to ecosystem destruction completely."

On about July 21, 1969, Leopold gave Oscar Gray, acting director of the Department of Transportation's new Office of Environmental Impact, a copy of the report as then drafted and informed him orally of the conclusions at which his study team was arriving. Not until August 19, however, did the Department of Transportation finish revising the report and return it to Interior; it was now four days past the deadline Leopold had insisted upon, yet the two versions of the report presented differences not to be easily resolved. The viewpoint of Oscar Gray and others at the Department of Transportation was that, while there was indeed a threat to the park from future development in the Big Cypress, this threat would exist even without a commercial jetport and related ground transport projects.[13] Operation of the pilot training facility would not stimulate land development in the region, and, because of aircraft noise, could actually deter development, authors of the Department of Transportation draft report observed. Construction of a commercial facility would encourage collateral development, they acknowledged. But this effect, they added, could be reduced by adoption of a "satellite terminal concept" by which employment at the facility would be held to a third of what it would be with conventional development. In general, what the satellite concept envisions is to have many services—for instance, ticket sales, some baggage handling, and aircraft maintenance—done at terminals and airfields situated in or near the urban centers that generate most of the passenger traffic rather than at the regional jetport itself. The authors observed that their report did not "consider the losses that might be imposed on the human environment if the Training Airport [were] removed from its present wilderness location and . . . developed nearer to south Florida's urban areas."

In discussions with Leopold, Oscar Gray had first suggested that the federal government should buy as much of the Big Cypress as necessary to protect the Everglades National Park. Later, he suggested still another alternative: that the government make its financial support for the jetport contingent upon state and local action to institute effective land use controls, again with federal help. For his part, Leopold agreed that the jetport, even as a fully developed commercial facility, would not in itself affect a large enough area to destroy the south Florida ecosystem.[14] But he felt that Gray's proposals for avoiding collateral development were unrealistic. If the government had not yet seen fit to buy various small private holdings within the park, he argued, how could one expect it to buy hundreds of square miles of the Big Cypress. As for federal encouragement of land

13. *Environmental Impact of the Big Cypress Swamp Jetport*, Department of Transportation, revised August 18, 1969. This draft report has never been made public.
14. Letter of August 22, 1969, from Leopold to Under Secretary Russell E. Train.

use controls, it was Leopold's view that anything done by the government to help the jetport project move toward full development "will so spur the land sales and the escalation of prices in the Big Cypress that whatever measures the state and federal governments might take toward improved land planning and land use controls would be entirely negated."[15]

On August 22, seven days after the report was to have been completed, Leopold lost patience and submitted the report to Under Secretary Train with the Department of Transportation's name scratched off the cover. When the draft by that department arrived later that day, it was sent along separately to Train. In a letter to the Under Secretary, Leopold observed:

> I think that the fact that we spent a great deal of effort in compiling the report gives us some advantage in that they are going to have to argue against what we have written down. They have no report of their own, but will be in the position of trying to break down the statements that we make.
>
> I suspect that they underestimate the effect which our report will have on local people, both in Florida and elsewhere. I rather suspect that they are somewhat sorry now that they did not cooperate actively with us in working toward a joint report which better states their point of view.[16]

Leopold was suspected by Department of Transportation officials of letting the report leak out some three weeks before it was officially released to the public, but, in fact, the leak occurred in Florida where this document was largely prepared. Nathaniel Reed had obtained a copy before the end of August. "Claude [Kirk] is not a [willing] reader, but he read the entire report," Reed told me. "That, plus disturbing rumors about who was involved in land deals and who hoped to sell for $2,500 to $5,000 an acre land purchased for $200, made him decide to oppose the jetport."

THE WHITE HOUSE FORCES THE ISSUE. Reed and Kirk were off to Washington again where they met with Train and Secretary Hickel. Memories are hazy as to what happened next, but it is evident that one of the two top Interior officials went to the White House and got the support of the President's aides to look for a way to end the threat to the park, and if necessary have the jetport moved to a new site. Meetings later took place between Hickel, Kirk, and Secretary of Transportation Volpe. James D. Braman, Volpe's Assistant Secretary for Urban Systems and Environment, recalls that Kirk, "all aflutter" about the jetport, was promising to find another site for the facility, and possibly on state-owned land below Lake Okeechobee in Palm Beach County. The catch was, as Dade

15. Ibid.
16. Ibid.

officials always had made clear, the Port Authority would not think of moving the jetport to any county where it could not enjoy exclusive control of the facility and its revenues.

As Leopold had predicted, the Department of Transportation officials, with no carefully developed report and position of their own, had either to agree that an alternate site should be found or to challenge the alarming conclusions reached by the Interior study team in its report. Secretary Volpe offered no such challenge; indeed he was himself convinced that the park was in jeopardy. The Interior report helped John Ehrlichman and his deputy for environmental matters, John C. Whitaker, to conclude that the park and a commercial jetport in the Big Cypress probably were incompatible. The report was "extremely important," Whitaker told me, although he had never read the report, but was briefed on it. "It was the scientific foundation for the administration's position." That position was not reached in a political vacuum. The national news media, which by now had fastened onto the "environment" as a public issue, were—with much adroit encouragement from Gary Soucie and Joe Browder—singling out the Big Cypress jetport for special treatment. *The New York Times, Look, Life, Time,* NBC-TV's "Today Show," and television personality, Arthur Godfrey, all were taking up the jetport question. Furthermore, as it was the first big environmental controversy with which they had to deal, the White House and the Department of the Interior were according the jetport issue a high priority. As one former Department of Transportation official observed to me, "Russ Train was displaying Interior's environmental flag down in the Big Cypress Swamp." As for Governor Kirk, he was a sure candidate for reelection the next year, and the following he had acquired among conservationists with Nat Reed's help was among his dwindling political assets. Notwithstanding the momentum of the campaign against the jetport, the major airlines operating out of Miami, such as Eastern, Pan American, Delta, and National, might well have had sufficient political influence to persuade the White House not to interfere with the jetport project. Gary Soucie believes that a meeting he and Joe Browder held in the spring of 1969 with high officials of several of the airlines at Eastern's headquarters in Miami caused the airlines not to throw their weight around. As Soucie has related it to me, he and Browder told the airline officials essentially this: "If you want an airport in south Florida, you'd better not fight for the present site. If you take a 'here or nowhere' approach, it'll be nowhere."

On September 10, 1969, at a joint press conference, Volpe and Hickel, with Governor Kirk present, said it was "very doubtful" that a commercial jetport could be constructed in the Big Cypress and that alternative sites would be sought. This was announced before the official release of the Interior impact study and also before the appearance of two other reports on the jetport question. The Interior report and a report by a National

Academy of Sciences (NAS) summer study group were both released about a week after the Hickel-Volpe press conference.[17] The academy report recommended that state, federal, and local authorities develop a comprehensive regional plan for the Big Cypress and that the eastern Big Cypress be made a "natural water conservation district," possibly under the jurisdiction of the Central and Southern Florida Flood Control District. According to the report, the training jetport would not pose severe environmental problems for Everglades National Park provided that safeguards, such as the prohibition of low-altitude flights over the park, were instituted. The environmental impact of a commercial jetport was, however, held to be unpredictable. The report said that it should not be taken for granted that such a facility need be built on the Big Cypress site. Much research was said to be needed for an effective program of land use management in south Florida. Policies required to preserve the park would be complementary if not identical to those required to ameliorate environmental conditions throughout the region, the academy report suggested. The third report on the jetport question was by a new consulting firm retained by the Port Authority, Overview Group, which had been established by Stewart L. Udall, Hickel's immediate predecessor as Secretary of the Interior. This report set forth the concept of a "satellite terminal" (or "clean enclave") jetport first mentioned in the Department of Transportation's stillborn version of the report prepared by Oscar Gray and his team.[18] Further, it proposed vaguely that an "environmental surcharge" tax could be levied against passengers and cargo to finance the purchase and preservation of land in the Big Cypress Watershed. But, by the time this Udall proposal—which was consistent with what Oscar Gray and James Braman of the Department of Transportation had been proposing—was made public in December, the jetport question was almost at a critical new turning.

THE JETPORT PACT

On January 15, 1970, representatives of Interior, the Department of Transportation, the governor's office, and the Port Authority, after weeks of negotiations, signed the Jetport Pact, an agreement without precedent. It

17. Cochairmen of the NAS study group were two distinguished physical scientists, Marvin L. Goldberger of Princeton University and Gordon J. F. MacDonald, then vicechancellor of the University of California at Santa Barbara, and later to be among President Nixon's first appointees to the Council on Environmental Quality.

18. The report, "Beyond the Impasse: The Dade Jetport and the South Florida Environment," dated December 10, 1969, cited Dulles International Airport in Washington, D.C. as an example of how the satellite terminal concept had already been applied. At Dulles, the terminal is physically separated by about a mile from the aircraft landing areas, and the connecting link between the two is the mobile lounge. For a south Florida regional jetport, the Udall report suggested, the terminal and landing areas could be fifty miles apart, rather than one mile, and the connecting link, instead of the mobile lounge, could be a rapid relay transit system carrying passengers, baggage, and air freight.

provided for the abandonment of the Big Cypress site once an acceptable replacement site could be found, acquired, and then developed to a stage comparable to that of the existing training facility. This would all be done at no cost to Dade County. The pact also contained provisions important to preserving the Big Cypress Watershed, but these we pass over for the moment. The working out of the federal position for this "extraordinary agreement," as Secretary Volpe called it, had involved numerous conferences between top officials of the departments of Interior and Transportation, who for the most part met in harmony. Volpe had hoped that the training facility, at least, could continue to be operated, but there was renewed pressure from Hickel to abandon the Big Cypress site entirely and the White House supported him. "One of Hickel's great strengths," Nathanial Reed observed to me, "was that when he got down to an issue he really believed in, such as moving the jetport, he wouldn't give an inch. He took no prisoners." Kirk's role in bringing about the Jetport Pact was also important, if not critical. For Kirk, as governor and a Republican governor at that, to advocate removal of the jetport made it easier for Hickel and Volpe to intervene. In addition, National Audubon's Miami attorney, Dan Paul, had filed petitions under the Transportation Act demanding that Secretary Volpe investigate alternatives to placing the jetport in the Big Cypress. If denied an administrative remedy, Paul was ready to bring a law suit. These various pressures that had helped produce the Jetport Pact were resented by Port Authority officials, leaders of the Greater Miami Chamber of Commerce, and some people in the Department of Transportation. But, for all concerned, the pact ended a controversy that had gone on too long.

The Jetport Pact marked the beginning of a third and possibly final phase in the evolution of the decision-making process by which a site for the jetport was to be designated. Here, it is useful to recapitulate highlights of the two preceding phases. In *Phase One* the Port Authority, with some policy guidance from the Federal Aviation Administration but none from the State of Florida, set forth independently to find a site for a jetport that would affect interests going far beyond Dade County. Under FAA requirements, the authority was obliged to consider plans adopted by regional planning agencies but there were no such agencies or plans. There was consultation, much of it after-the-fact, with state and federal conservation agencies but this turned out not to be meaningful. The state and federal officials who reviewed the project were generally thinking in terms of their particular agency's narrow interests and not of the project's overall effects, both direct and indirect, on the regional environment. Under Section 4(f) and related provisions of the Transportation Act, the Department of Transportation was supposed to keep the jetport project from harming or encroaching needlessly on the Everglades National Park or the FCD Conservation Areas; but, even after the choice of the Big Cypress site led to public controversy, months went by without any action by the department to protect these resources. Governor Kirk, without benefit of any overall evaluation of the jetport project from an independent source, had accepted the Port Authority's euphoric view of it.

In *Phase Two*, almost by chance, Robert Padrick, a gubernatorial appointee heading the regional water management agency, took the initiative and brought together an incipient coalition of state, federal, and private conservation interests to challenge the Port Authority by demanding specific answers to questions about the project's impact on the regional environment. At the time, no other official or agency was able or disposed to act as forcefully as Padrick. The governor had been coopted. The ability of National Park Service officials to move the heavy bureaucracy above them was doubtful. Numerous environmental problems about the country were competing for the attention of the national conservation groups. The jetport finally became a "secretarial level" issue by a fortuitous conjunction of circumstances and events: a top White House aide's note to the Deputy Under Secretary of the Interior, Hickel's visit to Florida on behalf of the alligator, the formation of the Everglades Coalition, and Nathaniel Reed's close rapport with Governor Kirk and Under Secretary Train. Then the report of the Interior study team, led by Leopold and Marshall, two of the boldest professional environmentalists in government, gave Reed, Train, Hickel, and others a rationale to press for the jetport's removal. Finally, the White House decided that the jetport must in fact be moved, thus raising the question of how a new site was to be found and who would approve it.

Ideally, in *Phase Three* the state and federal parties to the Jetport Pact negotiations would have demanded that a new site for the jetport be selected in a true regional and state perspective, through study and analysis directed at finding one reasonably convenient to most of south Florida and conducive to a well-balanced program of regional conservation and development. This would have meant participation by the State Bureau of Planning (now the Division of State Planning), the Florida Department of Transportation, the Flood Control District, and other south Florida counties as well as Dade, not to mention private conservation and development interests within the region. Also, it would have meant that the technical and analytical studies underlying the choice of a site would not be made under the Port Authority's sponsorship but under that of an agency free of parochial self-interest in the matter. The State Bureau of Planning could have qualified as such an agency, as perhaps could the Florida Department of Transportation. The problem was that the Port Authority might never willingly abandon its firm intention to operate the jetport under its exclusive political jurisdiction—yet, had the site been chosen on a true regional basis, the authority almost certainly could not have maintained such an exclusive hold. Furthermore, the principal objective of the federal and state officials involved in the site selection was the narrow one of bringing about the closing of the Big Cypress airport by finding a new site acceptable to the Port Authority but not offensive to the Department of the Interior and the Everglades Coalition.

The Jetport Pact provided neither the mechanism nor the philosophy by which the project could be treated as a matter of regional significance. To make matters worse, the purpose to be served by the new jetport, once it evolved from a training facility to a commercial airport, was not clearly defined. Was this jetport meant to serve all of south Florida? Or, rather, was it to serve primarily the Miami-Fort Lauderdale metropolitan area, or, at most, the upper as well as lower Gold Coast? Confusion resulting from this failure to spell out clear aims would soon be manifest as the site selection process got underway.

THE SEARCH FOR A NEW SITE

Richard Judy of the Port Authority instructed one of its consultants, Howard, Needles, Tammen, and Bergendoff (HNTB), to draft a plan for a site selection study and this plan was subsequently agreed to, with some modification, by parties to the pact. The study was ultimately to cost about $1.2 million, with the FAA paying two-thirds and the state and the Port Authority paying the remainder. In the fall of 1970 Judy also had the parties to the Jetport Pact appoint a Site Review Team. The review team was to receive reports from HNTB and other consultants on the site selection study, hold hearings and "public information" sessions, and, most important, screen the list of possible sites and finally recommend to the Port Authority the site deemed most suitable. The Authority, the FAA, the Secretary of Transportation, the Secretary of the Interior, and the governor of Florida each had a representative on the review team. There was little discussion among those on the review team as to whether or not the membership of that body should be broadened. The possibility of having a representative of the Everglades Coalition on the review team was mentioned, but rejected. One consideration was that, if the coalition were represented, why not also other interests such as the Greater Miami Chamber of Commerce, the airlines, and the tourist industry? The governor's man on the review team could try to represent the broad regional interest, but how would he determine what that interest was? (Indeed, the same question arises any time an individual is appointed to "represent" some broad, ill-defined group such as "consumers," or "conservationists," or, to cite the ultimate, "the public.") The site selection criteria were designed partly from the standpoint of environmental protection and partly from that of flight requirements. In addition, the site chosen was supposed to be consistent with the region's long-range comprehensive planning for conservation and development. The latter proviso was meaningless, however, because there had been no comprehensive regional plans when the Port Authority had moved into the Big Cypress and there were none now.

The site selection study actually began in the spring of 1971. HNTB had recruited more than a dozen research organizations such as Stanford Research Institute, TRW Systems Division, and Research Analysis Corporation to work on various aspects of the study. A list of some thirty-five sites (see figure 7–2) had been compiled from suggestions by interested

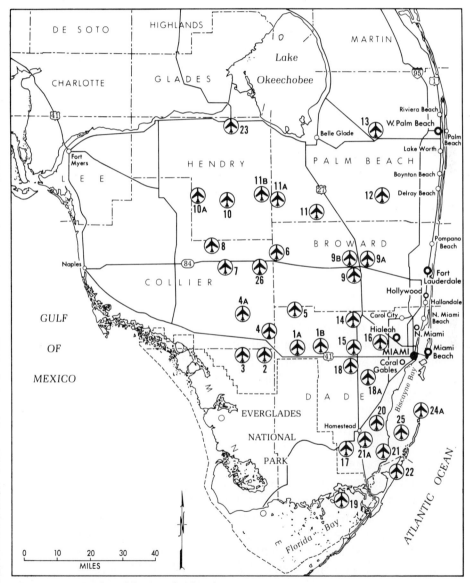

7.2 Sites considered for south Florida jetport

parties and the public. About half of these were patently unsuitable for environmental or other reasons, and were rejected out of hand. Most of the remainder either were just inland from the Gold Coast and east of the FCD perimeter levee or were in or to the west of the lower Everglades Agricultural Area. According to the approved procedure, the review team was to eliminate some sites periodically as the study progressed, with investigation of the remaining sites becoming increasingly thorough and intense.

FOCUSING ON DADE COUNTY. The Port Authority was frustrated when Secretary Volpe rejected its appeal to have the existing Big Cypress site studied along with the score of others that were to be investigated—a rejection, which although perhaps mandated by the Jetport Pact, was not altogether logical inasmuch as the Nixon Administration was even then developing alternative plans to protect the eastern Big Cypress from the uncontrolled development postulated in the report of the Interior study team. The Authority insisted therefore that the review team give high priority to finding a site in Dade County, either in southwest Dade or in that part of north Dade running westward from metropolitan Miami to Conservation Area 3B. To confine the search largely to Dade and thus avoid the complications of intercounty negotiations and the need for special legislative acts was attractive to the environmentalists, who wanted the Big Cypress site quickly replaced, as well as to the Port Authority, which wanted the jetport to be under its exclusive control. Joe Browder, Gary Soucie, the Everglades Coalition leaders, the governor's representative on the review team, and Department of the Interior officials favored early designation of a site in Dade. There was a strong suspicion on their part that the Port Authority wished to delay selection of a new site in the hope that, given time, the Nixon Administration or a succeeding administration could be persuaded to tolerate a jetport in the Big Cypress. A proposal by the Authority to extend the Jetport Pact beyond its January 1973 expiration date, and thus allow the site selection study to continue longer, contributed to this suspicion.

Although the search for a new site was soon narrowed essentially to Dade County, the information assembled in the site selection study illuminated the extraordinary scale and potential regional significance and impact of the proposed jetport. Early in the study, Joseph (Jay) Landers, Governor Askew's representative on the Site Review Team, had been convinced by projections of passenger traffic that a new jetport would indeed have to be built. The projections were such that most of the flights that would be generated could not possibly be handled merely through improvements to Miami International and other existing airports, even if one assumed that the airlines would be using many jumbo jets and would not be flying them half empty. (In 1972, however, the average "load factor" for nonstop flights from Miami International to points in the Northeast, Midwest, and far West was, with few exceptions, less than 55 percent and in one extreme case it was less than 30 percent.) Domestic and international passenger traffic at all four Gold Coast airports—Miami International, Fort Lauderdale, West Palm Beach, and the new regional jetport—were projected to total 68 million by 1990 and 156 million by the year 2000, with about three-fourths of the traffic to be at the new airport by the latter date. The year 2000 volume would be almost twelve times that of the Gold Coast airports in 1970. Somewhat more than a third of the passengers would be Gold Coast residents; nearly a third would be travelers passing through; and the remaining third would be visitors, mostly tourists. On the average, 3 million passengers would be arriving and departing from the four airports each week and 1 million of these would be tourists and other visitors, a remarkable number in light of the fact that, in 1969, tourists flying to *all* Florida destinations totaled only about 4.1 million. The projection for a huge rise in passenger traffic rested on the assumption that such traffic would increase at a rate nearly twice the rate of population increase for the lower Gold Coast (Dade and Broward). That assumption, in turn, rested in part on a belief that people would have more disposable income and leisure time and would show a growing tendency to take air trips casually and for short visits. (The consultants were making their projections in 1971 and early 1972, nearly two years prior to the energy crisis of the fall and winter of 1973–74.) Also, by the consultants' reckoning, aviation would become an increasingly important source of livelihood for Gold Coast residents. Whereas in 1972 this industry was supporting about 12 percent of the population, or about 271,000 people out of 2.2 million, the study projected that by the year 2000 about 17 percent would be so supported— or 771,000 out of 4.4 million! Activities either at or otherwise associated with the new regional jetport would of course largely account for the increase.

PALM BEACH COUNTY SITE IS ELIMINATED. All possibility that the review team might seriously consider looking beyond Dade County for a site was largely eliminated in the third month of the site selection study, which was to continue for nearly a year and a half. According to the minutes of the review team's meeting of June 11, 1971, Interior's representative on the team, Robert F. Gibbs, moved that three sites (shown in figure 7–2 as Sites 11, 11A, and 11B) south of Lake Okeechobee in Palm Beach and Hendry counties, and in and just west of the Everglades Agricultural Area, be added to the short list of sites being given priority consideration. As Gibbs has since told me, he regarded these sites, and especially Site 11 (on state-owned land in the lower Agricultural Area), as well placed for a south Florida regional jetport in that they were more centrally located than any of the others proposed. Furthermore, an airport at Site 11 would be conveniently located in relation to Interstate 75 (see figure 7–3). It would be directly in the path of I-75 if the State Department of Transportation followed the recommendation of its environmental advisory panel as to the routing of this highway between Fort Myers and Miami; but, even if the existing Everglades Parkway (or "Alligator Alley" as it is called) were chosen for the right-of-way, as a minority of the panel members recommended, I-75 would pass only 10 miles to the south of the jetport site. Although Site 11 was some 50 miles from Miami, a 1969 study by TRW Systems Group had already indicated that there was a possibility of building a high speed ground transit system capable of serving both as a jetport access facility and as a rapid transit system for the Gold Coast and perhaps even all of south and central Florida (see again figure 7–3).[19] However, again as shown by the minutes of the June 11 meeting, Ben Shepard, a Dade Metro commissioner and chairman of the review team, observed that the Port Authority had "agreed" to eliminate the Big Cypress site from consideration if the review team would confine its search for a new site to Dade County. Robert Bacon, the FAA representative, said the jetport was meant principally to serve the needs of the lower Gold Coast. A jetport built on a site in Palm Beach County would, in his opinion, be too remote to serve that area—a surprising attitude in light of views expressed by Bacon during this same general period as to the advantages the equally remote Big Cypress site would have offered (if served by an adequate regional transportation system) by virtue of its position midway between Miami and Naples.[20] The upshot was that Gibbs's motion

19. TRW Systems Group, *High Speed Jetport Access*, Feasibility Study of a Demonstration Project in Southern Florida, December 1969. This study, done under a $200,000 contract with the Department of Transportation, was begun after the jetport project had become controversial. Consequently, rather than confine the investigation to possibilities for a ground access system serving a jetport at the Big Cypress site, TRW extended it to five other possible sites as well, one of these being the site in Palm Beach County referred to above as Site 11. The cost of a system to serve a jetport at any of the sites would, by 1969 estimates, exceed a half billion dollars, perhaps half as much as the cost of the jetport itself. Therefore, if during the early years of a new jetport, passenger demand were relatively low, the access facility could not be made economically self-sustaining; either it would have to be subsidized or, more likely, its construction would be deferred. Thus, there would be a major advantage in combining a jetport access system with a rapid transit system linking the Gold Coast cities if, by so doing, early on the system could be made to operate profitably or at only a modest subsidy.

20. This opinion about the Big Cypress site was expressed to me personally by Bacon, then chief of the FAA's systems planning division (airport service), on September 22, 1971. The fact that Department of Transportation officials regarded the Big Cypress site as attractive for a regional jetport is also evident from remarks made by Secretary Volpe in a March 16, 1969, press release announcing that the TRW high speed ground travel study was to be undertaken. Volpe said that the Big Cypress site was "ideal . . . for the demonstration of a completely new ground access system." A jetport at the Big Cypress site actually could not be as readily served by a regional transportation system as one south of Lake Okeechobee. The lake area is more centrally located than the Big Cypress site, and, as I have noted, it will not be far from Interstate 75.

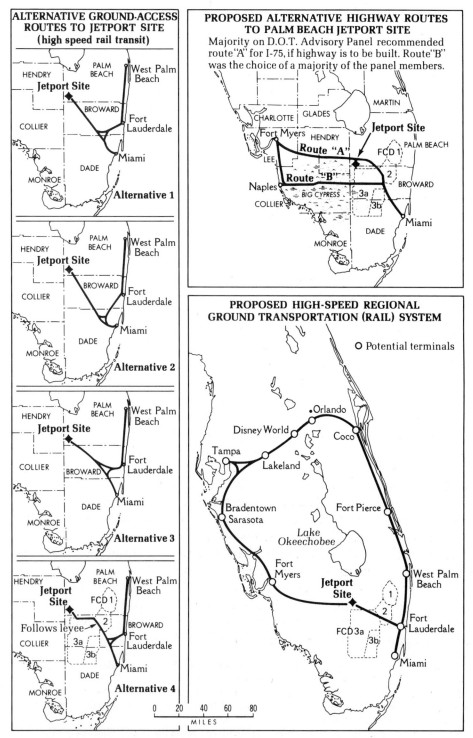

7.3 Alternative ground-access routes to jetport site

got the support of only the governor's representative and lost by a vote of three to two.

This narrowing of the search to Dade County and the lower Gold Coast brought no protest from anyone. Indeed, as I have indicated, neither Interior nor the Everglades Coalition wanted the selection of a replacement for the Big Cypress site delayed. The life of the Jetport Pact was for only three years, and half of that time had already elapsed. Unless a replacement site were agreed to within the next eighteen months the Port Authority would, in the absence of any extension of the pact (the pact was eventually renewed), be under no obligation to abandon the training facility in the Big Cypress. Yet, whatever the reasons for it, the review team's summary dismissal of the Palm Beach County site as a serious possibility undercut the integrity of the entire site selection exercise. Early in the jetport controversy, Ray L'Amoreaux, director of planning for the Florida Department of Transportation, had observed that, for the jetport to serve the most people, the best place for it would be near Lake Okeechobee.[21]

In December 1970, Arthur Marshall who had by then left Interior's Bureau of Sport Fisheries and Wildlife to join the faculty of the University of Miami, prepared—on contract with the National Park Service—a paper[22] that recommended several sites in the same general area as those which Gibbs later proposed for intensive study but which the review team rejected. In Marshall's view, the fact that these sites would be north of the conservation areas and either on or just to the east of the sandy Immokalee Island plateau would offer a major environmental safeguard. Little drainage would be necessary and treated waste waters could possibly be sprayed on the land rather than discharged to canals or other watercourses, he believed. Earlier, in a letter to Nathaniel Reed, Marshall had also suggested that a significant collateral benefit of having the jetport in this area would be that the facility could help keep the Everglades Agricultural Area from going into an economic decline.[23] He alluded to the fact that soil scientists knowledgeable about the area were predicting that continued soil subsidence would make farming impossible in much of it by the end of the century. Marshall advised the Park Service not to consider any site east of the FCD perimeter levee and adjacent to the Gold Coast. Construction of a jetport in that area, he said, would probably lead to drainage, pollution, and esthetic damage affecting either the Everglades National Park or the Conservation Areas. This would be contrary to both the National Environmental Policy Act and Section 4(f) of the Transportation Act, as Mar-

21. Ray L'Amoreaux quoted by the Associated Press in "Planner Sees Right Site for Jetport Near Lake," *Miami Herald*, September 24, 1969.

22. Arthur R. Marshall, *A Preliminary Ecological Survey of Some Potential Alternate Sites for the South Florida Jetport*, December 1970, (School of Marine and Atmospheric Science, University of Miami).

23. Letter of January 29, 1969, from Marshall to Nathaniel Reed, Environmental Advisor to Governor Kirk.

shall interpreted those acts. Marshall's contract with the Park Service provided that the report would be made public only at the service's discretion.
In March 1971, Marshall wrote George Hartzog, director of the Park Service,
to urge that the report be released and to express his discouragement at
writing "pigeon-hole reports."[24] The report was not made public, however,
at least in part because Park Service officials did not want to appear to be
prejudging the site selection. Almost a year later, Thurman H. Trosper,
a Park Service employee assigned to follow the jetport question, advised
the Office of the Assistant Secretary of the Interior for Fish, Wildlife, and
Parks—now headed by Nathaniel Reed—not to release the report:

> The Port Authority has made it very clear that they are interested
> only in sites in Dade County. Moreover, Palm Beach County commis-
> sioners are not interested in having Dade's jetport in their county and
> Broward will agree only if they are given a share of the action.
>
> Under the circumstances I do not feel any real purpose would be
> served by release of the report in the secretary's name. Furthermore,
> its release may even embarrass the Port Authority and members of the
> review team.[25]

Trosper, who has since retired from government and is now president of
the Wilderness Society, added that he saw no objection to Marshall's being
allowed to make the report public in his own name. Marshall never received permission to do this, however.

As the site selection study moved toward a conclusion there was little
indication of an awareness by the public in south Florida of all the issues
at stake. There was little serious analysis in the press of the site selection
problem and its broad regional implications. For its part, the review team,
consistently treating the jetport question as a matter chiefly of concern to
the lower Gold Coast, held hearings only in Miami and Fort Lauderdale, not
bothering even to go to West Palm Beach, much less Naples or Fort Myers.
Norman Arnold, the HNTB coordinator for the study, kept the fledgling
South Florida Regional Planning Council informed of the study's progress,
but this body was then so obscure that, as late as the summer of 1971,
even the editor of the *Miami Herald* had never heard of it. By the end of
1971, the review team had narrowed its choice to three sites (see figure
7–4), two in Dade County (sites 14 and 18) and one in Broward County
(Site 9). Because officials in Broward had already said that the Port Authority would not be permitted to operate an airport in their county, there was
virtually no possibility of the Broward site's being selected. The odds-on
choice was Site 14, covering 50 square miles of north Dade and lying mostly

24. Letter of March 19, 1971, Arthur R. Marshall to George Hartzog, director of the
Park Service.
25. Memorandum from Trosper to the Special Assistant to the Assistant Secretary,
January 14, 1972.

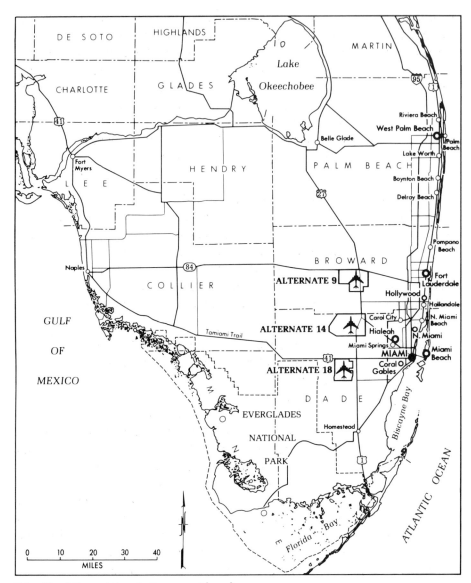

7.4 Final three jetport sites considered

in the FCD's Conservation Area 3B. In July 1972 the review team recommended this site and the Port Authority indicated that it would be accepted.

PROS AND CONS OF THE NORTH DADE SITE. The review team regarded the north Dade site as both an environmentally acceptable site and highly convenient to the majority of air travelers entering or departing south Florida. According to the projections made by Port Authority consultants, Dade and Broward counties' 1970 population of 1.8 million would grow to 3.5 million by the year 2000 and continue to represent approximately three-fourths of all the people in south Florida. The consultants concluded that air travelers would, collectively, save many millions of dollars annually in out-of-pocket costs and in time (reckoned at the rate of $3.00 per hour) if the jetport were built at the north Dade site rather than at a location more distant from the population center. Wherever the jetport was built in south Florida, there would be an impact on the natural environment. But, at the north Dade site, the jetport would be about 15 miles from the Big Cypress watershed and nearly as far from the Everglades National Park. Although the facility would encroach extensively on Conservation Area 3B, the Port Authority's consultants said that the adverse effects of the intrusion could be minimized by treating waste water effluents to Lake Tahoe purity and by realigning the levee to prevent any net loss in the amount of land available in Area 3B for water conservation. Major service facilities for the jetport, such as fuel tank farms, could be built to the east of the levee. Also, the site offered the advantage that no ground access roads or transit system would cross or impinge on the conservation areas.

Nevertheless, the north Dade site presented disadvantages not to be easily glossed over. The direct impact on the environment and air space of the lower Gold Coast area would not be negligible. Air traffic in the area was already extraordinarily dense. During fiscal 1970, FAA traffic control towers logged a total of 2,330,789 flights at the five major commercial and general aviation airports in the Miami-Fort Lauderdale area, and four of these facilities ranked among the United States' ten busiest airports, as measured by number of flights. "It is not surprising, therefore, that none of the sites under consideration [in the lower Gold Coast area] generate much enthusiasm in the hearts of the air traffic controllers," consultants observed in a report presented to the review team.[26] Development of a commercial jetport at the north Dade site would in fact eventually necessitate closing two of the general aviation airports.

Furthermore, even though the new jetport's runways would be inside the conservation area, the noise footprint of the aircraft operating from them would extend eastward to overlap the advancing edge of metropolitan Miami. Just counting the existing population under that footprint, some 14,400 people would be affected to varying degrees by aircraft noise. Several "noise sensitive activities"—the consultants' term for two schools, three churches, and two hospitals—might have to be soundproofed. The noise footprint would also extend westward into Conservation Area 3A, thereby lessening that area's recreational value (although noise from the airboats and half tracks used by many visitors to the area is itself hardly conducive to quiet contemplation).

To excuse the fact that the jetport would intrude on an FCD conserva-

26. Report prepared by HNTB for presentation to the Site Review Team on November 5, 1971.

tion area, proponents of the north Dade site have sometimes suggested that Area 3B is of little value for water conservation. They point out that, due to the porousness of the underlying limestone, this area is a poor reservoir for surface water. Yet Area 3B's tendency to "leak" makes it an important recharge area for the Biscayne Aquifer. With the jetport project, Area 3B and the land immediately to the east of it would undergo excavation work so massive that the amount of dirt and rock moved might be greater than the 79 million cubic yards that was excavated between 1907 and 1929 in constructing the original 440 miles of Everglades drainage canals and levees. According to the preliminary environmental impact statement prepared by consultants to the Port Authority,[27] this project would involve the disturbance of some 9,000 acres and the excavation of perhaps as much as 90 million cubic yards of material. Up to 60 million cubic yards of rock would be excavated and deposited on the lands designated for runways and other facilities to build them up above flood levels. The resulting rockpits, cut into the Biscayne Aquifer, would cover nearly 800 acres and would contaminate part of the aquifer itself if they should become polluted. In addition, some 15–30 million cubic yards of peat, which cannot be used as foundation material, would have to be removed in the excavation of the rockfill and the preparation of the construction sites. Disposal of peat in so immense a volume could itself present a major problem. In its natural condition, Everglades peat is water-laden and serves as a natural filter of pollutants. Once excavated, however, it dries quickly and can easily catch fire. Commenting on such problems, G. E. Dail, executive director of the FCD, has observed that "an airport just isn't compatible with water storage."[28]

According to Dail, however, the greatest cause of concern is that, by breaching the integrity of the FCD's system of conservation areas, the jetport would encourage still other intrusions. In his view, the system is too small as it is and represents the bare minimum necessary to provide southeast Florida with adequate fresh water. "They [the conservation areas] should have been larger, but, back in 1948 when they were planned, no one foresaw the tremendous urban growth that was going to take place here." There is also the fact that substantial acreages within the system of conservation areas are in a less than secure status. Of the 860,800 acres in the system altogether, almost 84,500 are privately owned and subject only to FCD flowage easements. In addition, private parties hold the mineral

27. Preliminary Environmental Impact Statement, South Florida Regional Airport Site Selection Study Program, the Dade County Port Authority, October 1972, pp. 31–32. The amount of dirt and rock excavated in the construction of the original Everglades drainage system was reported by John M. DeGrove, "The Central and Southern Florida Flood Control Project: A Study in Intergovernmental Cooperation and Public Administration," (Ph.D. dissertation, University of North Carolina, 1958), p. 79.

28. Mike Toner, "New Danger to the Everglades: Man and his Cities Expanding to the West," *Miami Herald*, September 30, 1973.

rights to 172,653 of the acres owned by the FCD. Some time ago, an enterprise called Everglades Assets Corporation, which holds mineral rights on 14,750 acres, obtained a court order affirming its right to mine limestone from its acreage. The court added, however, that the mining must not conflict with the FCD's water management objectives, a proviso that could be critical to the FCD's chances of preventing the limestone mining after all. But how will the agency argue convincingly that the digging of large rockpits in a mining operation is unacceptable if the same kind of activity is to be allowed for the jetport project?

Aside from the project's potentially harmful direct effects, establishment of a major jetport at the north Dade site would inevitably stimulate more growth along the lower Gold Coast. This alone gives many local people pause. As noted earlier, the projections by Port Authority consultants indicate that, by the year 2000, another half million people will be supported by aviation along the Gold Coast, mostly by activities at or related to the new jetport and Miami International. In the previous chapter I described an array of problems in Dade that have been exacerbated by rapid and poorly controlled growth, including jammed freeways, gross inefficiencies in transportation and energy consumption, a discouragingly large and costly backlog of pollution problems, and endless battles over zoning. Also, as a consequence of the fact that the north Dade site is near metropolitan Miami, the cost of its acquisition would be high, perhaps as much as $45 million.

Besides the foregoing disadvantages of the site, there are others related to the fact that, given its location in a corner of the region, it would not seem to fit as well as a more centrally located site into an overall system of public transportation for south Florida. To this point I shall return later.

The jetport site selection came to a point of decision just as Floridians and their elected officials were adopting a more cautious attitude toward growth. At Governor Askew's bidding, the 1972 legislature had enacted the new land and water management laws. An early consequence of this was an enlargement of the FCD board and the appointment to it of two men who had led in proposing those laws: Arthur Marshall, the south Florida environmentalist and coauthor of the Interior Department's impact report on the jetport, and John DeGrove, the Florida Atlantic University dean who had chaired both the Governor's Water Management Conference of 1971 and the subsequent legislative task force. Even before the change in its makeup, the FCD board had voted unanimously to oppose the location of a jetport "either wholly or in part" in any of the conservation areas.[29] The board was now certainly no less inclined than before to protect the con-

29. Letter of August 20, 1971, from G. E. Dail, Jr., executive director of the Central and Southern Florida Flood Control District, to Norman Arnold of Howard, Needles, Tammen and Bergendoff, coordinator of the site selection study.

servation areas. Marshall, DeGrove, and Padrick were even expressing open skepticism that a big new jetport was needed anywhere in south Florida.[30] In September 1972 the board did, it is true, adopt a resolution to "cooperate" with all other agencies with respect to plans for a jetport on the north Dade site. But the wording of this resolution had, at Marshall's suggestion, been made deliberately ambiguous. Without doubt, there would have been no resolution of cooperation at all were it not for the fact that the board members—six of whom were new Askew appointees—did not want to defy the governor and throw a wrench in efforts to reach the settlement at which the Jetport Pact had been aimed. "The state is between a rock and a hard place, or I'd never vote for it," DeGrove said at the time.[31]

METRO INITIALLY REJECTS THE SITE. As previously noted, the Dade Metro commission underwent a major change with the election in the fall of 1972 of Jack Orr, Harvey Ruvin, and two other candidates supported by the Committee for Sane Growth. The Greater Miami Chamber of Commerce and other interests that were eager to have the jetport built near Miami no longer enjoyed their previous influence over the commission. Later, when Metro's intentions toward the jetport were in doubt, Mayor Orr would observe: "I resent the type of pressure these [business] people here tried to apply to me. It's hard for people who have been running the community for some time to understand that they don't run it any more."[32] The preliminary environmental impact statement issued by the Port Authority in October 1972 itself reflected the changing political climate. "South Florida is now in the midst of an agonizing reappraisal of its destiny," the statement said. "Is there a limit to the population consistent with the 'good life'? If so, what is it or has it been reached? . . . Is continued growth the guarantor or destroyer of economic and environmental health?" The statement emphasized that all that was now proposed for construction was a training airport to replace the one in the Big Cypress, with acquisition of the 50-square-mile site intended merely to allow the Port Authority the option of building a major new commercial jetport later in the century.

In a surprise decision in January 1973, the Metro commission voted four to three to reject the north Dade site. A coalition of civic organizations in north Dade had strongly protested selection of the site because of concern over potential noise pollution and possible air crashes in populated areas. This opposition, coupled with the doubts entertained by Mayor Orr and other commissioners as to whether the proposed commercial jetport would be needed, seemed to account for the commission's action. Also,

30. Minutes of the FCD board meeting of September 8, 1972, p. 8.

31. Quoted in Jan Leslie Cook, "Land Use Guides Urged at Jetport," *Miami Herald*, September 9, 1972.

32. Quoted in Sam Jacobs, "Metro Again Seeks a Decision on the Jetport," *Miami Herald*, February 5, 1973.

Orr believed that by focusing narrowly on the Miami vicinity in its search for a site, the review team had shown that it wore "blinders."[33] The commission was, however, under pressure to reconsider its decision. In Washington, the Everglades Coalition had written to President Nixon protesting that Metro had reneged on its obligations under the Jetport Act. The coalition urged that the training facility in the Big Cypress be closed. Also, the Miami business interests, the airlines, the Airline Pilots Association, and the *Miami Herald* were criticizing the commission's decision.

A few weeks after its rejection of the site, the commission relented and directed County Manager R. Ray Goode to conduct a new search for a site, without excluding from consideration the one in north Dade. At the same time, the Port Authority was made a department of the county government and its director, Richard Judy, previously answerable only to the Metro commission, was placed under the county manager's authority. Aviation user fees would not, however, be commingled with general county revenues but would continue to be spent exclusively for airport improvements and services. Although the new site selection study was supposed to be undertaken in a true regional perspective, there is every indication that this search was as parochial in its orientation as the previous one. The clearest evidence of this is the county manager's failure to pursue seriously the possibility of using Site 11 in the lower Everglades Agricultural Area, which the review team had prematurely dismissed. That this possibility was indeed wide open became clear in late May 1973. The Palm Beach County Board of Commissioners had increasingly been subjected to complaints about noise from aircraft flying in and out of Palm Beach International Airport, a facility on the edge of West Palm Beach. Faced with this problem, the commission now seemed won over to the idea of a regional airport being built in the far southwest corner of the county, that is to say, on Site 11. It voted to ask the Florida Department of Transportation and the Federal Aviation Administration to consider this site covering 46 square miles of state-owned land. J. M. Frazier, FAA coordinator for southeast Florida, found the commissioners' proposal "intriguing." "It would result in less opposition from the populace from the noise point of view, and it would tend to [put] the supplemental airport in the ultimate center of population growth, which we now figure to be somewhere north of Fort Lauderdale."[34] The idea of a site in the middle of south Florida

33. Quoted in Don Bedwell, "Jetport Best Outside Dade, Orr Contends," *Miami Herald,* January 31, 1973.

34. Quoted in Frank Greve, "Palm Beach Offers Regional Jetport Site," *Miami Herald,* May 30, 1973. Metro consultants, as noted earlier, have put the future population center just north of the Dade-Broward county line. What Frazier was alluding to was the fact that there is far more developable land to the north of that line than there is to the south of it. If the land around Lake Okeechobee is included in this comparison the difference is, of course, vast. See the map (figure 1–6) indicating Florida's areas of high and low tolerance for development.

still found little if any acceptance among Dade business interests, however. At a conference called by Goode on the jetport question, Ralph Renick, a spokesman for the Greater Miami Chamber of Commerce, put the matter this way: "If you landed at a jetport 60 miles from here [the distance between the Palm Beach County site and the City of Miami is about 50 miles], where would you go? The beaches north of here are nicer than the ones here."[35]

A CONDITIONAL ACCEPTANCE. Toward the end of July 1973, the county manager recommended that Metro accept the north Dade site.[36] He proposed, however, that the pilot training runway be built 4 miles farther west inside Conservation Area 3B than had been planned. In this way, the noise footprint would be contained largely within Area 3B and no residential neighborhood would be disturbed. Also, according to Goode's proposal, the future commercial jetport, if eventually built, would have fewer runways than the six that had been envisioned. Rather than serve as the regional jetport for south Florida, the new facility would merely be one of a constellation of airports within the region serving similar functions. Goode did not attempt to reconcile this with earlier projections that the number of passengers using a new regional jetport could reach 115 million a year by the year 2000. One responsible individual who has been intimately involved in the site selection process from the beginning has confided in me the suspicion that Goode's new concept was designed solely to make the north Dade site acceptable to the Metro commissioners and the public.

However this may be, the Metro commission promptly accepted the county manager's proposal, although it later stipulated that no new commercial jetport shall be built until Miami International Airport's capacity has been expanded to the "limits of economic and environmental feasibility."[37] (MIA's ultimate capacity has been estimated at from 25- to 30-million passengers a year, as compared to the 12 million using this facility in 1972.) To reassure those concerned at the prospect of a new commercial jetport's generating a surge of growth on the low-lying lands of northwest Dade, Goode had observed that such growth would be subject to Metro's regulation. Subsequently, he declared a moratorium on zoning changes in the area adjacent to the jetport site to allow time to decide how this part of the county should be treated in Dade's revised land use master plan.

35. Quoted in Sam Jacobs, "Jetport: To Be or Not To Be?" *Miami Herald*, May 5, 1973.
36. R. Ray Goode, *South Florida Regional Airport Site Selection Location Study*, the *County Manager's Report*, July 21, 1973.
37. Board of Commissioners of Dade County, resolution of September 18, 1973, establishing policies relating to the south Florida regional jetport.

THE CASE FOR REOPENING
THE SEARCH

As I write, in the early spring of 1974, the U.S. Department of Transportation is waiting to receive a formal request from Dade County for the money necessary to acquire the site and build a one-runway pilot training facility. That request must be accompanied by a draft environmental impact statement that is currently being revised, partly to reflect new plans to reduce the site from 50 square miles to perhaps 40 square miles or less, a size more comparable to that of the Big Cypress site. Ultimately, the Department of Transportation may submit to Congress a fund request which, according to past estimates, might run as high as $55 million to $60 million, with about $40 to $45 million earmarked for land purchases.

Congress may very well regard this as a disproportionately large sum, especially inasmuch as the new training facility would be replacing one that cost (land acquisition included) only about $13 million. In addition, the plan to intrude deep into Conservation Area 3B may be vulnerable to court attack under the Transportation Act's Section 4(f) provision that intrusions into parks, wildlife refuges, and similar areas can be justified only in the absence of a prudent and feasible alternative.

To entertain the possibility of abandoning the north Dade site at this late hour would be painful for many, particularly in view of the money and time spent on the site selection and the political and professional commitments made. Yet, for a number of reasons, it seems clearly in order to reopen the question of whether a jetport—a true regional jetport—should be built, and, if so, where. Of overriding importance is the fact that the regional jetport issue has to this day not been thoroughly or properly considered in terms of state and regional growth policy, nor in terms of either energy policy or a policy looking toward a comprehensive, well integrated system of public transportation for south Florida. Such policies have, of course, been lacking, and they continue to be. A step toward the formulation of state policies on energy and growth was taken in 1973 when Governor Askew called major conferences on these subjects; further progress in this direction was in prospect at the 1974 session of the legislature.

Even in the absence of clearly articulated growth and energy policies, certain considerations that must be weighed with respect to a regional jetport are obvious. If one first asks whether a new regional jetport should be built at all, the answer turns partly on whether there can be further beneficial growth in south Florida and whether growth of the kind a major airport would generate is desirable. Although many will disagree, I believe the answer to both these questions is yes. Large tracts of developable land still exist within the region, and there are large numbers of workers who could earn half again as much as they do now if the commercial aviation work force underwent a major expansion. Furthermore, there is every reason to exploit the fact that, as the southernmost extremity of the continental United States, south Florida is both an appealing place for tourists and a natural hub for domestic and international aviation. In the latter regard, it is worth noting that projections made in the site selection study indicate that better than half of the expected increase in passenger traffic in south Florida would occur without any increase in the region's population.

If a continuing expansion of air travel is to be encouraged for long-haul passenger movement in and out of south Florida, one must then ask how the new airport facilities relate to desirable patterns of regional growth and to other systems of public transportation. As previously suggested, an airport project that would generate strong new pressures for suburban growth in north Dade and the lower Gold Coast seems clearly undesirable, all the more so if the integrity of the regional system of water conservation areas would be breached. On the other hand, to put such a project south of Lake Okeechobee, above the conservation areas and almost in the center of south Florida might prove desirable from several standpoints. The opportunity to create a new, economically self-sustaining growth center in a part of south Florida that is more development-tolerant than most is one advantage. Another is that problems of air traffic conflicts or aircraft noise (as an urban nuisance) would be avoided. In addition, an airport on the Palm Beach County site or one a bit farther west in Hendry county might fit well into an overall regional transportation system. With nearly all long-distance flights in and out of south Florida using this one regional airport, the airlines might make optimum use of the big wide-bodied jets, with few empty seats and good frequency of service. Other airports in the region, including a new one that may be built in southwest Florida between Naples and Fort Myers, would handle general aviation and short-haul commercial service such as flights between south Florida and Jacksonville or Tallahassee.

Eventually, the new regional airport might be served by a high-speed rail system that would be part of a mass rapid transit system for peninsular Florida—a system for which, even now, serious planning is beginning. The Florida Department of Transportation has already contracted for studies of high-speed rail systems for the cross-Florida corridor from Daytona Beach to the Tampa Bay area via Orlando, and for the Gold Coast corridor between West Palm Beach and Miami. The Gold Coast system—which would operate at speeds up to 100 miles per hour—would tie into the Dade Area Rapid Transit System that Metro will build. The possibilities for eventually linking up a south Florida regional airport with such a mass transit system for south Florida and central Florida were noted in connection with the previously mentioned TRW study.

One cannot assuredly say that the foregoing concept of a large integrated regional system for air and ground travel would be the best for south Florida, although it does closely resemble what Port Authority and FAA officials were talking about a few years ago. What can be confidently argued is that this concept (or variations of it) deserves thorough analysis by an agency such as the Division of State Planning or the Florida Department of Transportation that should be better able than Dade Metro to take all state and regional interests into account. In the last part of this book I shall suggest several possible ways to reach a final, politically responsible choice among alternatives in a matter such as this one. It is a sobering commentary that the past failure to have all affected interests represented in the jetport site selection process has contributed to the undertaking of studies—in one case to a $1.2 million study—that have not asked the right questions and that have led to the choice of a site that may yet prove indefensible.

8

Saving the Big Cypress

The jetport controversy had shown dramatically that protection for the mosaic of wetlands and watersheds in south Florida was incomplete and that the largest unprotected piece was the Big Cypress. Establishment of the Central and Southern Florida Flood Control District and the Everglades National Park had brought most of the Everglades under public control and better (if not always enlightened) management, but the controlling interests in Collier and Monroe counties had had nearly all of the Big Cypress excluded from both the park and the FCD system of conservation areas. Now, even with the jetport project forestalled, other new threats to this unique wilderness watershed and ecosystem were plainly visible. For instance, in May of 1971 the Florida Cabinet had found it necessary to authorize the attorney general to seek to enjoin a private drainage project that threatened to disrupt the diffuse flow of surface water to state lands below Gum Slough in the southeastern Big Cypress. (In this unprecedented suit, which is still undecided at this writing in the spring of 1974, it is asserted that a "downstream" landowner has riparian rights even to such ill-defined sheet flow.) Also, landowners were building new private roads and air strips in the Big Cypress, and the once somnolent hamlet of Ochopee on the Tamiami Trail was coming alive, with motels and a 1,050-unit mobile home park being built, land sales offices opening, and a large limestone quarrying operation getting underway.

Under the Jetport Pact, the federal government was committed to undertake environmental studies and to recommend land uses consistent with preserving the Everglades National Park, all estuarine resources related to the Big Cypress, and the shallow aquifer of southwest Florida. What clearly was needed was a comprehensive policy and plan for the Big Cypress and for the overall mosaic of major south Florida wetlands. As matters developed between early 1970 and the spring of 1974 substantial progress was made in protecting the Big Cypress. Nevertheless, no coherent plan had yet emerged, and the measures that were taken would not protect all of the important resources still in jeopardy. Briefly, these were the major developments:

• Congress was moving to establish a 570,000-acre Big Cypress National Preserve that would include most of the watershed's eastern half and nearly all of that part of the Big Cypress tributary to the Everglades National Park (see figure 8–1). With the cost of the land acquisition estimated at $156 million in federal and state funds, the Big Cypress preserve would require a cash outlay larger than any ever previously approved for the purchase of a single federal park or recreation area.[1]

• The Florida Legislature, at Governor Askew's request, passed the Big Cypress Conservation Act of 1973 to have part of the Big Cypress designated as an "area of critical state concern" as well as to authorize a $40 million state contribution to the establishment of the national preserve. The Big Cypress thus became an important testing ground, for this represented the first application of the concept of establishing special protective regimes for "critical areas"—a concept central to the Florida Environmental Land and Water Management Act of 1972.

• Several other actions taken by the governor, the legislature, or the cabinet could have a major bearing on the protection of the Big Cypress. First, under the Water Resources Act of 1972, the Big Cypress was finally to be brought within the jurisdiction of the Flood Control District. Ultimately, any new drainage project in the Big Cypress would be subject to review by the FCD. Second, greatly increased interest in oil exploration in the Big Cypress had led the cabinet to require that all applications to drill in this watershed be reviewed by an advisory committee on which independent environmental interests would be represented.[2] Road building and

1. The largest authorized to date was the $92 million for the Redwoods National Park. The Redwoods Park legislation also provided for a payment in kind to timber companies of national forest lands worth almost $52 million, bringing the total acquisition cost to $144 million, or $12 million less than the estimated cost of acquiring the Big Cypress.

2. To consist of five members, the advisory committee would include: the chief of the state Bureau of Geology, the director of the Florida Petroleum Council (an industry group), a representative from an organized conservation group, and a botanist and a hydrologist, these latter two to be selected by unanimous agreement of the first three.

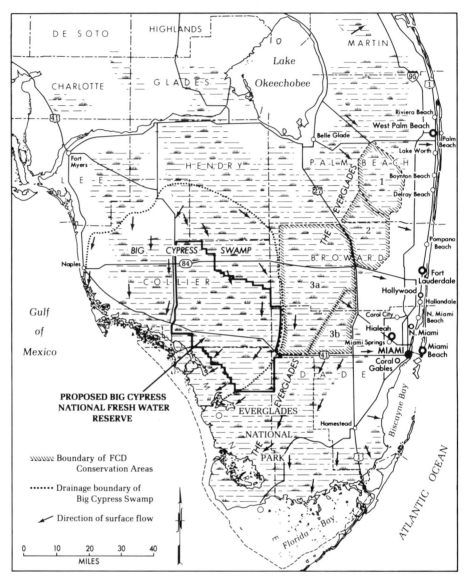

8.1 The proposed Big Cypress National Preserve

other activities involved in the exploration for and recovery of oil would be subject to special conditions and restrictions. Finally, Governor Askew decided to have the south Florida segment of Interstate Highway 75 replace the existing Everglades Parkway or "Alligator Alley" across the Big Cypress and the Everglades. Fearing that such a routing would mean further loss of wetlands and more development in the Big Cypress, some environmentalists had urged the governor to choose a route farther north, outside the Big Cypress watershed. But Askew felt, with reason, that the Alligator Alley routing offered some major environmental advantages.

230 SOUTH FLORIDA: THE PROBLEMS OF GROWTH

• Collier County, which embraces most of the Big Cypress, was now, at long last, showing greater willingness to control development and protect what remained of its natural environment. Long the compliant instrument of development interests, the county government was finally beginning to come to grips with those interests.

Before discussing further these various actions and policies directed at controlling growth and land use in the Big Cypress, I shall set forth, by way of background, some salient items from the generally discouraging record of development and governmental performance in Collier County since Barron Collier's death in 1939.

COLLIER COUNTY: PAST
DEVELOPMENT TRENDS AND
LOCAL GOVERNMENT

THE COUNTY'S SPLIT PERSONALITY—THE DEVELOPERS AND THE SNOW BIRDS. The development of the city of Naples has proceeded in a very different and ultimately antagonistic way from the development of the rest of Collier County. In the county there has been the effort by the Collier interests and other large landowners to sell or otherwise profit from vast holdings of low-lying coastal and interior wetlands. In the Big Cypress this has, in part, meant logging, ranching, and some farming—all activities more or less compatible with maintaining this watershed as a renewable resource, depending on how they are carried out. Unfortunately, it has also led to the sale of hundreds of thousands of acres to land sales and development companies which, in numerous instances, have victimized naive buyers of land parcels and have in some cases done much harm to the environment. From this alone it is clear that, overall, the record of land stewardship on the part of the Colliers and some of the county's other large landowners has been poor. This is true despite the fact that they have made several substantial gifts of land for the Everglades National Park, the Collier-Seminole State Park, and the National Audubon Society's Corkscrew Sanctuary.[3] Until recent years the big land-owning interests, particularly the Collier interests, have been a dominant influence in the Collier County government. Lip service has been paid to county planning and zoning since the mid-1950s (countywide zoning was first established in Collier in 1954), but, as will later be made clear, much of the work done thus far has been a sham or an absurdity.

Simultaneously with the exploitative activity in the county has come

3. As noted in Chapter 4, the Collier family gave 32,640 acres of coastal lands around the town of Everglades for the park. In addition, the Colliers gave 5,760 acres for the Collier-Seminole State Park, and, together with the Lee Tidewater Cypress Company, helped make possible the establishment of the Audubon Society's Corkscrew Sanctuary.

the development of Naples as a winter resort for rich "snow birds" from the North. Back in the 1930s when Naples was a village of no more than 500 people, it was discovered by a few wealthy families and thereafter grew in popularity as a quiet wintering place for the well-to-do. The heavyhanded ostentation and contrived excitement that now characterizes Miami Beach has never found a place at Naples, although during the 1960s and early 1970s developers usually got their way with the city council in seeking permits for condominiums along Gulf Shore Boulevard and for commercial strip development along the Tamiami Trail. "The people who come here just want to get away from the pressures of the modern day," Lester Norris, a former board chairman of Texaco, who has had a home on Keewaydin Island near Naples since World War II, observed to me. "They are all very respectable. It doesn't make any difference how much money you have. You wouldn't know one millionaire from the next." These wealthy newcomers to Naples were for the most part political conservatives philosophically opposed to government interference in the exercise of property rights, but they were also people who now had a personal stake in protecting their new-found winter haven from promiscuous development that would despoil it.

In 1964 Lester Norris and others formed the Collier County Conservancy in a successful effort to raise money to buy several thousand acres of mangrove flats and islands around Rookery Bay, an attractive estuarine area south of Naples that appeared to be on the threshold of development. Ultimately, however, the protection of Rookery Bay (now a National Audubon Society sanctuary) would depend on preventing pollution and other abuses in the bay's hinterland and watershed in the southwestern corner of the Big Cypress. Thus, the conservancy was to be drawn into a commitment to comprehensive planning and land use controls. Its first two executive directors, Joel Kuperberg and his successor, Edward T. LaRoe, both biologists of fortitude and ability, would strongly advocate such measures. Although its influence on county government was at best marginal during the 1960s and early 1970s, the conservancy symbolized what eventually would emerge as a powerful and possibly dominant factor in county politics—the desire of most residents of the Naples urban area to control growth and keep Naples from becoming "another Miami."

GULF AMERICAN AND THE RAPE OF THE LAND. The Colliers emerged from the Depression with their huge inventory of land still intact, but with relatively little in the way of liquid assets. After the death of two of Barron Collier's three sons in the early 1950s, the family sold some of its land in order to pay estate taxes. The largest single sale was one of some 300,000 acres to the Gerry brothers of New York. Over the next fifteen years or so the Collier interests would dispose of all but about 400,000 of the 900,000 acres they once owned in Collier County.

During that same period, the Gulf American Land Corporation, found⸀
by brothers Leonard and Julius Rosen, was mounting what was to becoᴜ.
one of the largest land sales businesses ever undertaken. Altogether, the
land purchases made in Florida by Gulf American and its successor, GAC
Properties, Inc. (in 1969 Gulf American merged with the General Acceptance Corporation),[4] would total some 371,000 acres, or 580 square miles.
The Rosens' first project was in Lee County at Cape Coral, some 30
miles north of Naples, but by 1960 they were also active in Collier County.
They bought large acreages from the Colliers and certain other interests,
especially the Gerry brothers and the Lee Tidewater Cypress Company.
Before the end of the 1960s, Gulf American's acquisitions in Collier County
totaled 182,000 acres, or more than 284 square miles, nearly all in the Big
Cypress (see figure 8–2). Some of Gulf American's early purchases were
made at not much more than $100 an acre, if that. Yet, once subdivided
into parcels of 1¼ to 5 acres, the parcels would be resold on installment
at prices many, many times that amount. The company would, for
instance, first offer a 1¼-acre lot at $2,545, then later raise the price still
higher and thus create the illusion of a rising market. In truth, every
additional swamp lot sold made such property increasingly a glut on the
resale market. Indeed, the resale market for most of the tens of thousands
of small parcels of land sold in the Big Cypress by Gulf American and
other land sales companies has been pathetically weak, if such a market
can be said to exist at all.

The largest of Gulf American's promotions in Collier County, and one
that today remains of critical importance to the future of the western Big
Cypress, is "Golden Gate Estates." This enormous subdivision of 113,000
acres is located deep in the Big Cypress, the greater part of it 15 miles or
more from Naples. Land in Golden Gates Estates was sold on installment
(with monthly payments over as long as twelve and a half years) in parcels
of 1¼, 2½, or 5 acres that could some day—or so the land salesmen
claimed—be resubdivided by the buyer and resold at a profit. Gulf American offered the land neither as finished "homesites" in a well-planned new
community nor as unsurveyed, inaccessible swampland, as in the "raw
land" subdivisions marketed by the multitude of small land sales companies active in the eastern Big Cypress. Instead, Golden Gate Estates was

4. In 1970 the GAC Corporation of Miami, a conglomerate with interests in land
development, finance, mortgage banking, insurance, and other fields, led all other
Florida companies both in sales and in assets. Since then, GAC, partly because of
reverses suffered by its land sales and development subsidiaries, has fallen into serious
financial and legal difficulties. The company is heavily in debt, is the defendant in several
law suits (including one by the Attorney General of California arising out of GAC's
land sales operations in Arizona), is being investigated by the U.S. Department of Housing and Urban Development, and is under order by the Federal Trade Commission to
make financial restitution and other concessions to many land purchasers. The company's
problems are set forth in some detail in the proxy statement sent to shareholders on
November 9, 1973.

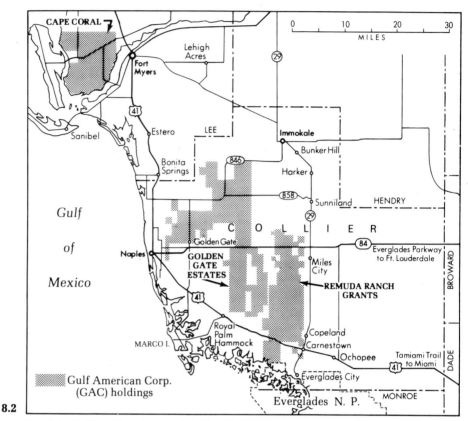

8.2

Land in Collier County acquired by Gulf American Corporation

represented as land "semiimproved" by the construction of a grid of flood control canals and roads.

In January 1972 Judge James L. King of the U.S. District Court in Miami returned a judgment that tells much about Gulf American's promotional tactics and strategy. He ordered Gulf American's successor, GAC Properties, to repay $23,000 to John and Ernestine Vertes, a Philadelphia couple who had signed contracts in 1963 and 1964 for four parcels (three of them in Golden Gate Estates) having a fair market value of about $6,250 (at most) today. In his written opinion, Judge King described the land sales dinners to which the Vertes had been invited by Gulf American some ten years ago:

> When the meeting began the sales manager would make a welcoming speech and dinner would be served. During dinner the salesman at each table would engage in conversations designed to elicit information to determine which persons were the most likely prospects and to establish "an atmosphere of confidence." At one dinner, [the Vertes] were asked to fill out a questionnaire to determine their buying power.

After dinner, [Gulf American] screened a movie featuring prominent sports celebrities and showing building and recreational activities in Florida. The movies were interrupted for a slide presentation showing general statistics of Florida's growth. Included were quotations from prominent historical figures concerning the advisability of owning land and its almost constant appreciation in value. After the movies and slides the manager would turn the prospects over to the salesmen who would start with the most likely prospect. The salesmen were instructed to, and did, emphasize the prospect of increased value of the land to be sold, and the probability of profit on resale. . . . When a prospect indicated an interest in a particular lot the salesman would jump up and shout to the manager, "Put a hold on [the lot under consideration]." The manager would acknowledge a "hold" for five or ten minutes. At the end of that time, he would shout to the salesman to inquire whether he could remove the "hold" and the salesman would renew pressure on the prospect to sign. When a person signed a contract to buy a lot, the sale was publicly announced and at one meeting a button was put on the purchaser's coat. The purpose of all these showmanship techniques was to create an "atmosphere of urgency."[5]

The judge concluded that the Vertes—he was a crane operator and she was a telephone company employee—were people of limited business experience who had been misled by a sophisticated sales organization into believing that the swamp land in which they were investing lay in the "path of progress."

As pointed out in an earlier chapter, Florida land sales scandals go back at least to the turn of the century and have been the subject of recurrent journalistic exposés and legislative investigations. The misrepresentations of Gulf American were cited in the congressional hearings of the mid-1960s that led to the passage of the Interstate Land Sales Full Disclosure Act of 1968, a statute which, while stopping some abuses, has not done much overall to stop unscrupulous practices.[6]

5. Final Judgement and Memorandum Opinion in John A. Vertes and Ernestine W. Vertes v. GAC Properties, Inc. No. 70-416-Civ U.S. District Court, S.D. Florida, Miami Division, January 26, 1972.

6. The act requires that prospective buyers of land be given a "Property Report" containing such pertinent information as whether the land is encumbered by mortgages and whether it is accessible and suitable for development. These reports, though meant to keep the buyer from being misled, can themselves be misleading. For instance, the report issued by GAC Properties, Inc., in 1971 for three units in Golden Gate Estates said that "telephone services will be made available by the franchised utility." A couple who built a home in Golden Gate Estates in 1969 learned from the United Telephone Company of Florida that telephone service would indeed be available to them—at a connection charge of $2,880. Unable to pay so high a fee, they had to forego a telephone, which turned out to be no mere inconvenience in 1971 when, for a sixty-day period, forest fires were raging all around them.

In March 1974, GAC, formally consenting to an order of the Federal Trade Commission, agreed to make partial restitution—totalling perhaps as much as $17 million—to some purchasers who, after signing contracts to buy parcels in Golden Gate Estates and certain other Florida and Arizona subdivisions, later defaulted after making payments over a long period. The order also provides that, besides making water and sewer improvements or offering lot exchanges wherever necessary to ensure past buyers of usable homesites, the company must stop various misrepresentations, such as offering lots as good speculative investments.[7]

Yet, as the Vertes case illustrates, many of those who have bought land in the Big Cypress have simply been small speculators who have had the misfortune to become the victims of other speculators bigger and more worldly than themselves. Much of the public attention given to the plight of such victims might have been more usefully directed at the damage done by some of the land sales companies to the land itself.

Extraordinary damage to land and water resources has been caused by the Golden Gate Estates project. This subdivision stretches 25 miles from north to south across the Big Cypress in a long and generally narrow rectangular configuration, although toward its north end it also extends some 13 miles from east to west. With no more than a few dozen families living there ten years after the sale of the first parcels, the project is a vast, ready-made ghost town. The ghosts are served by 171 miles of canals and 807 miles of roads. Since Golden Gate Estates was promoted largely as investment acreage, it would have made sense, if such promotions were to be allowed at all, for the county and state to have insisted that the land· itself remain undisturbed pending definite proposals for its use and development. Instead, Gulf American was allowed—indeed, apparently encouraged—by the county to file plats and legally commit itself to install the grid of roads and canals according to a definite schedule, which appears to have been observed more or less faithfully. The draglines and bulldozers, together with a giant "treecrusher" machine capable of flattening a forest right into the mud, began work in 1962 and this work was still in progress in the spring of 1974, although by now the greater part had been completed. Many knowledgeable people in Collier County and in Tallahassee have known that construction of the roads and canals was altering the western Big Cypress irreparably, and for no defensible or even ascertainable purpose. Anyone flying over this region and seeing the grid of white limerock roads extending far into the distance could only marvel

7. State regulation is also beginning to catch up with the problem of protecting the land buyer from unscrupulous sales practices. A law enacted in 1973 established important new conditions that have to be met before a subdivision can be registered for sale. Local subdivision regulations pertaining to such things as the construction of streets and the installation of water lines must be satisfied. Also, the subdivider must have in hand all state permits related to dredging and filling and pollution control—permits without which usable lots could never be delivered.

at what was afoot. Once the work began, it was as though some great mindless machine had been set in motion and was now beyond all power of human intervention.

The network of canals by GAC in Golden Gate Estates has impaired freshwater resources, disturbed estuarine regimes, and contributed to highly destructive forest fires. The U.S. Geological Survey has found that the water table has fallen 2–4 feet over a significant part of the western Big Cypress.[8] Further, according to some unverified reports, it has dropped as much as 15 feet in certain areas near the Corkscrew Sanctuary and the farm town of Immokalee. Two major canals discharge fresh water from Golden Gate Estates into the Gulf of Mexico. In 1970 the USGS reported that one of them, the Golden Gate Canal, had been discharging 12½ times the volume of water then used by the city of Naples.[9] In 1973 a draft report prepared by a team of investigators with the U.S. Environmental Protection Agency said that during 1970–72 the volume of fresh water lost through GAC's Fahka Union Canal (which enters the Gulf just to the west of the Everglades National Park) was equivalent to the total water needs of a population of nearly 2 million, computed at 100 gallons per person per day. Yet USGS hydrologists say that, if present trends with respect to population growth and water consumption continue, Collier County will face severe water shortages by the year 2000 unless all its ground water resources are fully used.[10]

Some of the water now passing to the Gulf via the GAC canal system would filter into the estuarine zone even without the canals, but it would come through a myriad of small rivers, creeks, and shallow depressions over a period of eight or nine months. While this extended "hydroperiod" enhances the productivity of the estuarine zone, productivity is reduced by great surges of fresh water from canals. For instance, the fact that Fahka Union Bay is less rich in marine life than the adjoining Fahkahatchee Bay is attributed partly to the massive discharges from the Fahka Union Canal. Furthermore, in the case of estuaries such as Naples Bay that have been polluted, the pollution is aggravated by incoming surges of fresh water. Stratification results, with the heavier, saltwater layer at the bottom not mixing with the lighter, better oxygenated freshwater layer on top.

According to state foresters, the Golden Gate Estates canal system is a cause of the devastation wrought in the western Big Cypress by wild-

8. The system's effect on the aquifer is readily apparent from the map of the Shallow Aquifer of Southwest Florida (Map Series No. 53) published in 1972 by the U.S. Geological Survey. This map, prepared by Howard Klein of the USGS, shows ground water level contours markedly lowered in the vicinity of the canal systems during the 1971 drought.

9. H. Klein, W. J. Schneider, B. F. McPherson, and T. J. Buchanan, *Some Hydrologic and Biologic Aspects of the Big Cypress Swamp Drainage Area, Southern Florida*, Open File Report 70003, U.S. Geological Survey, Tallahassee, Florida, May 1970, pp. 72 and 82.

10. Letter of June 7, 1972, to the author from Thomas J. Buchanan, subdistrict chief, Water Resources Division, U.S. Geological Survey, Miami.

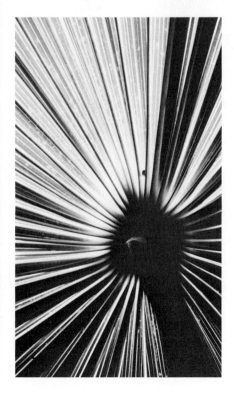

At top, cypress dome with saw grass in foreground; *at left*, palmetto with snail in Big Cypress pinelands; *above*, spider lily in the Big Cypress; *facing page*, strangler fig trees.

fires. Cypress ponds that once remained wet throughout the dry season and served as fire breaks now become tinder boxes. During the drought of 1971, fires swept fully a fourth of Collier County, including large areas within the Fahkahatchee Strand, which abuts Golden Gate Estates on the east. Yet, even in March of 1973, during a normal dry season, a major fire broke out in the Fahkahatchee near a Golden Gate Estates canal and raged fiercely. According to Ken Blackner, a district forester, the canal had caused an "artificial drought."[11]

If construction of the GAC canal system has been bad from a resource conservation standpoint, it has been little better from the standpoint of preparing part of the Big Cypress for urbanization. Indeed, the canals and the accompanying grid of roads will hamper all future efforts at enlightened development. According to what Robert Wheeler, the Collier County sanitarian, has told me, the road embankments act as dikes during the rainy season and retard runoff. Although placement of more culverts in the embankments would reduce the diking effect, the gradient of the canals is so slight that drainage is slow in any event. During the wettest part of the year the water table remains at or near the surface. For this and other reasons, conventional septic tanks will not work in most of Golden Gate Estates—a subdivision so vast that to serve a major part of it with sewers is not economically feasible today and may not be feasible a generation hence.

Also, the trouble and expense of maintaining the many miles of roads and canals in Golden Gate Estates represents a major problem for the county, which already has assumed responsibility for the larger part of the system. The roads deteriorate rapidly but they receive so little use that to maintain them really is pointless, especially when the cost has been put at more than $314,000 a year. As for the canals, they become choked with hyacinths and other nuisance vegetation if not tended to. If the road and canal system is to be maintained, it will probably be by virtue of imposing a special tax on tens of thousands of absentee lot owners.

CONFLICTING INTERESTS AND GOVERNMENTAL INCOMPETENCE. The government of Collier County has, until recent years, been shot through with potential conflicts of interest, although these can be viewed charitably as part of the legacy from the days when the county was literally owned by Barron Collier. Consider, for instance, the case of Harmon Turner, the county's top nonelective official since 1946. Turner, who served as county engineer until 1966 when he became county manager (a position he still holds), is known as a personable and honorable man. But it is hard to credit him with the objectivity and broad professionalism that one looks for in the executive head of a modern county government. He first arrived in Collier

11. Ken Blackner, quoted in Associated Press article "Canals Increase Hazard of Wildlife, Forester Claims," *Miami Herald*, March 8, 1973.

County as a graduate civil engineer in 1934, eleven years after the county was created, and he soon became a part of the Barron Collier organization. After his appointment as county engineer in 1946, Turner remained a salaried employee of the Collier organization with the county paying him a dollar a year and billing the Colliers for such work as he performed. This unusual arrangement continued until 1960, when Turner was finally employed by the county on a regular basis.

Later in the 1960s, Stanley W. Hole, once an engineer on the staff of Gulf American and afterwards an occasional consultant for GAC, became chairman of the county's water management advisory board. Of all the potential conflict-of-interest problems that could be cited, however, none was more glaring than that involving Norman Herren, who for many years has been the top manager for the Collier interests. By the early 1960s, Herren was a member of the county planning board and several years after that he became chairman of the Coastal Area Planning Commission, the planning board's successor agency and the body responsible for advising the Board of Commissioners about planning and development matters in most of the county.

So here was Turner, who had been an employee of the Colliers since the mid-1930s, responsible for matters such as the review of the highly questionable drainage plan for Golden Gate Estates, a project in which the Colliers retained a mortgage interest for some years after their land sales to Gulf American. And there was Hole, a GAC consultant and one-time Gulf American employee, responsible for advising the county commissioners as to the effects of such drainage. And, as for Herren, there he was, a leading member of the planning body that advises the county on a variety of matters that could affect Collier interests in the Big Cypress and elsewhere. At the same time, as the Colliers' manager, he was close to such dealings as the Colliers' joint venture with the Mackle brothers to develop Marco Island, a project involving dredging and filling on a scale even Carl Fisher could not have dreamed of. Herren was still chairman of the planning commission when I first interviewed him in 1971. He rejected the idea that there could be a conflict of interest. "Any time something comes up that involves one of our companies, I excuse myself," he explained. The awkwardness of his position was evident, however, for the Colliers still owned a fourth of the land in the county. Potential conflicts of interest can exist even though the personal integrity of the individuals involved, as in the case of those mentioned here, has not been questioned.

The county's governing body, the Board of County Commissioners, has until recently been largely in the hands of realtors and local politicians of the pork-chop school. In the early stages of the Golden Gate Estates project any county employee who questioned this undertaking found an unfriendly climate at the courthouse. In late 1963, William Clarke, the director of sanitation, was fired by the county commission. Wheeler, the county's present sanitarian, told me that he believes Clarke was dismissed partly for raising serious doubts as to whether septic tanks would work at Golden Gate Estates. In 1967, four years after Clarke's departure, Dr. Clyde Brothers, a retired Air Force officer then serving as county health officer, was also forced to resign. In this case, too, Wheeler is convinced that the dismissal could be attributed at least partly to the fact that Dr. Brothers held that in this project septic tanks would generally be unworkable.

The commissioners were no more ready for a conscientious professional planner than they were for a conscientious sanitarian or health officer. During 1965 the Collier County Conservancy actually paid the salary of a young planner whom the commissioners had been prevailed upon to hire. He not surprisingly came to be regarded by developers as the "conservancy's man," and the commissioners refused to allocate the money necessary to keep him after that first year. "I represented a shift from do as you damn please in land development to land use control arrangements," William R. Vines, the dismissed planner who is today a prominent planning consultant in Naples, explained to me. Vines differed with the commissioners on a number of issues, and took particular exception to the high density and commercial zoning that the commissioners had approved for part of Golden Gate Estates.

Later, however, partly as the result of the jetport controversy and south Florida's traumatic drought of 1971, the Collier County government came under increasing pressure to acquire greater competence in planning and control of land use. For one thing, strong federal and state intervention could now be expected, with the "feds" moving to protect the Everglades National Park's watershed in the Big Cypress and the state demanding new land use controls generally.

THE BIG CYPRESS
NATIONAL PRESERVE

In 1971, even as the search for a new site for the jetport was going on, an Everglades Jetport Advisory Board created by Secretary of the Interior Rogers C. B. Morton was developing proposals for protection of the eastern Big Cypress. In the spring of 1971 the board submitted to the secretary a report outlining alternative courses of action, and in November of that year President Nixon announced that legislation would be submitted to Congress for the creation of what ultimately was called the proposed 570,000-acre Big Cypress National Preserve.[12] Purchase of ease-

12. The name proposed by the advisory board was the Big Cypress National Fresh Water Preserve. Seeking to appeal to the utilitarian instincts of the citizenry (and especially of that part of the citizenry that is deaf to other arguments), environmentalists commonly stress the water conservation issue in their efforts to justify the preservation of interior wetlands.

ments was a possibility not altogether excluded, but Secretary Morton indicated that virtually the entire acreage would be bought in fee simple.

The decision to buy this large area, at what obviously would be a high price, was made only after considerable hesitation. Earlier in the century, the federal government had begun conserving water as well as timber resources in various parts of the nation by establishing the system of national forests. Land for the national forests was obtained either by withdrawals from the federal public domain or by purchase of generally remote and mountainous land available at low prices. But the Big Cypress, although itself once part of the federal and then the state public domain, was now mostly private land that would be appraised at a fair market value seldom if ever less than $200 an acre and sometimes more than twice that. The Jetport Advisory Board and its chairman, George Hartzog, director of the National Park Service, had concluded that to protect the Big Cypress by purchase of the land would be so costly that, even if the administration agreed on such a course, Congress might well not. The federal Land and Water Conservation Fund was already overextended from previous commitments for purchase of park and recreation lands. Also, in south Florida there were already 1.4 million acres under federal ownership in the Everglades National Park, and the 96,000-acre Biscayne National Monument was even then being established at a cost of $25 million. Furthermore, the board members knew that the Everglades National Park was by no means the only park threatened by development just beyond its boundaries and that to protect all such parks through public purchase of buffer zones or tributary watersheds would clearly be impossible. A new and cheaper protective method had to be found, and, as the board viewed the matter, if this new beginning had to be made somewhere, why not in the Big Cypress?

COMPENSABLE REGULATION. The approach that the board recommended was largely one of federal "compensable regulation."[13] Under the regulations recommended, no drainage or construction of any kind would be permitted within the area set aside for special protection unless first approved as in keeping with a regional master plan adopted by the Secretary of the Interior. Any landowners believing themselves deprived of valuable development rights by the regulations would file a claim for compensation with the U.S. Court of Claims; the claims honored would, the board estimated, total no more than $10 million, a small fraction of the cost of buying the land. How this surprisingly low estimate was arrived at was

13. Everglades-Jetport Advisory Board, *The Big Cypress Watershed*, a report to the Secretary of the Interior, April 19, 1971. The compensable regulation proposal is described on pp. 36–39. The advisory board's report was prepared almost a year prior to the enactment of the Florida Environmental Land and Water Management Act of 1972. Therefore, to have looked primarily to state land use control measures for protection of the Big Cypress would have been simply an act of faith.

not explained, but it is true enough that the supposed "development rights" to much of the land in the Big Cypress are, as a practical matter, illusory. With the eastern Big Cypress divided into probably more than 30,000 individual parcels—the greatest number unsurveyed, inaccessible lots of a few acres or less—most of the owners simply cannot either develop their land, resell it, or even find it. Since these owners are scattered over the United States, Europe, and Latin America, there is even a question as to how many would file a compensation claim if the government undertook to regulate use of their land.

THE DEMANDS FOR PUBLIC PURCHASE. That the compensable-regulation approach was unproven was enough to make use of it in the Big Cypress unacceptable to conservation leaders such as Joe Browder (who by now had left Miami to head the Washington office of Friends of the Earth),[14] Arthur Marshall, Alice Wainwright of Tropical Audubon, and officers of Conservation '70s. In fact, Browder worked hard at convincing administration officials that public acquisition offered the only sure way to save the Big Cypress, protect the park, prevent development of a new area of urbanization and water demand, and allow President Nixon to maintain a reputation as protector of the south Florida environment. In a letter to the President's environmental aide, Browder—not bothering to be subtle about his political scorekeeping—observed:

> None of the Administration's other good environmental actions have had the same degree of favorable political impact as the President's decision to move the Everglades jetport. But it is possible that this political asset would be turned into a liability, if the Administration were to try to claim credit for saving the Everglades while sitting back and letting the oil industry and real estate speculators destroy the place.[15]

Browder told Robert Cahn, a member of the Council on Environmental Quality, that compensable regulation would be discredited as a land management tool through an unwise attempt to apply it in the Big Cypress, where he said the water problem and the great multiplicity of ownerships would make it unworkable. Furthermore, he suggested that such an attempt could involve the Nixon Administration in an embarrassing controversy over "un-American land-grabbing tactics." There was indeed potential for such a controversy. The solicitor's office at the Department of the Interior had regarded compensable regulation as clearly constitutional, but, on this score, Senator Lawton Chiles of Florida was expressing "grave reserva-

14. In early 1972 Browder became executive vice-president of the Environmental Policy Center, a Washington-based environmental lobbying organization.
15. Letter of May 10, 1971, from Joe Browder to John C. Whitaker, environmental aide to President Nixon.

tions."[16] And, predictably, the Collier County officials together with some of the Big Cypress landowners, were speaking of compensable regulation as "confiscatory." They were not, to understate the matter, welcoming federal intervention, but, if the federal government was to control the use of their land, they wanted it bought outright. In view of all this, Governor Askew and members of the Florida congressional delegation had every reason to encourage the federal government to buy the eastern Big Cypress. Expensive as this might be, no question of state financial priorities then seemed to be involved, and, if the federal government could be persuaded to preserve the area by acquiring it, why favor an unproved method such as compensable regulation?

ACTION AT THE WHITE HOUSE AND IN CONGRESS. Presidential politics appears to have had something to do with the administration's final decision to establish the Big Cypress preserve, or at least with its timing. Senator Henry M. Jackson, chairman of the Interior Committee and an announced candidate for the Democratic presidential nomination, had joined as a sponsor of a Big Cypress acquisition bill introduced by Senator Chiles, and Jackson was to hold field hearings on the measure in Miami at the end of November 1971. Just a week before those hearings, the administration proposal for the preserve was announced at a White House press conference. Secretary Morton, presiding, introduced five special guests, praising them for having contributed to the administration's decision or to the events that led to it. They were the cochairmen of the Everglades Coalition, Elvis Stahr of National Audubon and Anthony Smith of the National Parks Association; National Audubon's Washington representative, Cynthia Wilson; Luna Leopold of the U.S. Geological Survey; and Joe Browder. The Big Cypress proposal had, of course, received a strong push from some officials strategically placed within the administration, including John Whitaker at the White House and Nathaniel Reed at Interior. Reed had only recently left Tallahassee to become Assistant Secretary for Fish, Wildlife, and Parks. It was he who later proposed that Julie Nixon Eisenhower visit the Big Cypress in January 1972—a visit that was intended to let Florida voters know of the President's interest in the Big Cypress, and, incidentally, to reinforce the President's commitment.

By late 1972, several days of hearings on the Big Cypress preserve bill had been held by the parks subcommittees of the House and Senate Interior committees. Senator Alan Bible of Nevada, chairman of the Senate subcommittee, had received the bill skeptically and chose to defer action on it. He was troubled especially by the unprecedentedly high cost of the Big Cypress acquisition, but he also had to ponder the complexity of the south Florida water issue, the protests of some landowners unwilling to

16. Letter of June 3, 1971, from Senator Lawton Chiles to Rogers C. B. Morton, Secretary of the Interior.

give up their property, and the fact that the administration proposal did not yet have the support of the Collier County Board of Commissioners. County Manager Turner, representing the Collier commissioners, was suggesting that federal acquisition of just that part of the Big Cypress south of the Tamiami Trail might be enough to protect the park, and that, in any case, nothing should be done pending completion of the three-year south Florida environmental study, which the Department of the Interior had underway. Spokesmen for the Collier interests, which owned maybe 70,000 acres in the proposed purchase area,[17] had been expressing similar attitudes.

THE STATE CONTRIBUTES $40 MILLION. Nevertheless, ultimate passage of the Big Cypress legislation seemed all but assured after an exceptional gesture of support in the spring of 1973 by the State of Florida. The legislature, at Governor Askew's urging, authorized the state to contribute $40 million toward the purchase of the Big Cypress preserve, thus allowing the federal government to reduce its commitment from $156 million to $116 million. Even the Collier commissioners had now given the Big Cypress preserve bill its endorsement. The House Interior Committee, chaired by Representative James A. Haley of Florida, reported the Big Cypress bill in September 1973 and the next month it was passed by the House, 376 to 2. Furthermore, Senator Bible was now more amenable to the bill, and in 1974 the Senate completed action on it and sent the measure to the White House for the President's signature.

Thus, by the early fall of 1973 the eastern half of the Big Cypress appeared safe. But what was to become of the western half, including that important part already ravaged by Gulf American? Responsibility for protecting and restoring the western Big Cypress would fall to the state of Florida and Collier County.

THE BIG CYPRESS
CRITICAL AREA

After the passage of the Florida Environmental Land and Water Management Act in 1972, it was widely assumed that one of the first "areas of critical state concern" to be established would be in the Big Cypress. Nowhere else was the need more urgent for the kind of special protective regulatory regime contemplated under that act. In the winter and spring

---

17. Testifying before the House Interior Subcommittee on Parks and Recreation in Fort Myers on February 15, 1972, Norman Herren, manager of the Collier Development Corporation, estimated that the Collier interests owned between 65,000 and 70,000 acres in the proposed reserve with more than half this acreage located north of the Tamiami Trail.

of 1973, Governor Askew made three major decisions pertaining to the Big Cypress. First, Interstate 75 was not to be routed to the north of the Big Cypress, as environmental groups had recommended; instead, it would follow the alignment of Alligator Alley and replace that existing toll road. Second, the $40-million state contribution to the acquisition of the federal preserve was proposed. And, third, the legislation authorizing this contribution was to provide also for a Big Cypress critical area—that is, the area would not be established administratively under the 1972 law, but would be created by special act.

The three decisions were intimately related. There had been predictions that to route I-75 through the Big Cypress, along Alligator Alley, would cause land values in the proposed federal preserve to escalate by $15 million and would lessen the chances of having Congress authorize the purchase of that area.[18] Askew felt that, by limiting interchanges on the Big Cypress segment of I-75 to but one (at the Seminole Indian Reservation), such an escalation could be discouraged. But still further assurance against runaway land prices, from whatever cause, might be had by beginning the land acquisition early and by placing the proposed federal purchase area under critical area status and regulation. Another important objective to be served by establishing the critical area would be to protect the Fahkahatchee Strand. The Fahkahatchee, lying just west of the national preserve area and State Road 29, is the largest of the major subdrainages within the Big Cypress. Rising in the northern part of the Big Cypress, the Fahkahatchee, in most places several miles in width, runs 25 miles to the south, ending just above the Tamiami Trail, below which begin the salt marshes and mangrove flats. The Fahkahatchee was—and, despite much abuse, remains—a complex ecosystem containing nearly all the varieties of terrain, vegetation, and animal life that were common to the Big Cypress under primeval conditions. Besides forests of cypress and pine, there are stands of graceful royal palm and tropical hammocks of gumbo limbo, cocoplum, tamarind, ficus, and strangler fig. Beneath the forest canopy are large-leaved fire flags, ferns, and a variety of air plants—spanish moss, orchids, and a plant that grows in clusters of pale green blades. Heron and egret fish carefully in the Fahkahatchee's shallow ponds, and wood ibis, redtailed hawk, and swallowtail kite soar overhead. Even a few Florida panther (or cougar) and black bear, as well as numerous whitetail deer still survive in the Fahkahatchee.

Governor Askew had every reason to want the Fahkahatchee Strand placed in critical area status, especially in light of the area's recent history. This great freshwater slough was purchased cheaply by Gulf American

18. UPI article " 'Alley' Route Labeled Peril to Cypress Deal," *Miami Herald*, December 6, 1972, quoted Johnny Jones, director of the Florida Wildlife Federation, as saying that such escalation would "wipe us out in Congress." Jones cited Nathaniel Reed, assistant secretary for fish, wildlife and parks, as the source of the $15 million estimate.

in 1966 from the J. C. Turner Lumber Company. In its boldest scheme yet, Gulf American then subdivided the land into 2½- and 5-acre parcels for sale as unimproved recreational and investment property. This grandiose "Remuda Ranch Grants" promotion found a ready market. Buyers, who would pay $1,000 per acre for their parcels, got a piece of unsurveyed, inaccessible swampland, some "club memberships" (in marina, stable, skeet range, and other facilities built in a small complex on Tamiami Trail), the right to hunt and fish in the Fahkahatchee, and the familiar assurance that their land lay in the path of progress. The General Acceptance Corporation, after the merger between GAC and Gulf American in 1969, stopped the unconscionable Remuda Ranch promotion. In 1972, the company, to satisfy state claims for illegal dredging and filling by Gulf American on sovereignty lands in Lee County, deeded to the I.I. Board 9,500 acres of salt marsh and mangroves below the Fahkahatchee Strand; then, in 1974, it entered into an agreement to sell about 24,500 acres to the state for $4.4 million. Nevertheless, the pattern of land ownership in the strand remains a mess, with much of the area still broken up into small parcels owned by persons who bought from Gulf American.

Besides making special land use controls possible in the proposed federal purchase area and such contiguous areas as the Fahkahatchee, the proposed Big Cypress Conservation Act of 1973—drafted under the direction of the governor and Senator Robert Graham of Dade County—was designed to get around certain shortcomings of the Environmental Land and Water Management Act of 1972. Whereas that earlier law had arbitrarily provided that not more than 5 percent of all land in Florida could be designated as critical, the proposed special act stated that the Big Cypress critical area would not count against that limitation. The special act would also allow the state to exercise power of eminent domain in purchasing the land. And, finally, it would permit the Division of State Planning to begin work immediately on the land use regulations for the critical area, thus allowing the cabinet to approve them at the same time it acted on the area boundaries that the division would likewise propose. A weakness in the 1972 law was that a critical area might remain unprotected for six months or longer after its designation by the cabinet, pending the preparation of special regulations for the area by the local government. A provision for interim controls had been proposed by the sponsors of that earlier law but had been rejected.

In June of 1973, when the legislature passed the special Big Cypress Act, many of the legislators apparently believed that that act's critical area provision was intended chiefly to give early protection to the land within the proposed national preserve and to some undefined but presumably modest buffer zones. The act's stated purpose, however, was, besides the protection of the preserve area pending public acquisition, to protect such "contiguous" lands and water areas as are "ecologically linked" with the

Everglades National Park, the Ten Thousand Islands, and the Shallow Aquifer of southwest Florida.

THE BASIC POLICY QUESTIONS. In fact, the new act raised at least implicitly, several basic questions of policy that had been left unresolved by the 1972 land and water management law:
• Was the critical area concept really to be applied on a scale sufficient to protect even the largest environmentally sensitive lands in Florida?
• Would critical areas established under the act include some areas already ravaged by unwise development and now greatly in need of remedial action? Or was a much abused area such as the 177-square-mile Golden Gate Estates simply to be written off as lost?
• What would be the primary means of protecting lands within the critical area? Would many, or even most, of these lands—or at least such development rights as are associated with them—be purchased by the state? Could this not be inferred from the fact that the legislature, in enacting the 1972 law, had insisted that no critical area be established until Florida voters approved a bond issue for environmentally endangered lands? Or was the state to rely primarily on noncompensable regulation whenever the landowner could enjoy some remaining benefit from use of his property? This question was crucial, for noncompensable regulation would have to be the state's primary recourse if it was to protect all lands in the state worthy of critical area status.

The Division of State Planning interpreted its mandate broadly, and the critical area boundaries and regulations recommended in its report of late August 1973 stirred up immediate controversy. The division recommended that three-fourths of the entire watershed, or some 1.2 million acres, be designated as critical (see figure 8–3). Taking in 650,000 acres besides the land in the proposed national preserve, the critical area embraced virtually all of Collier County except the Naples urban area, and even some undeveloped portions of that area were included—notably, the land around the Audubon sanctuary at Rookery Bay.

For regulatory purposes, four subareas were delineated within the critical area:

Area I. Lands where, in seven out of ten years, water is on or at the soil surface year round. These included the mangrove swamps and islands, the coastal marshes, and the freshwater cypress strands and sloughs.

Area II. The prairie and hammock lands adjoining the marshes and swamps, or lands subject to flooding for generally more than two months of the year and sometimes for all or the better part of the year.

Area III. The pine flatwoods and the ridges and knolls of the upland palmetto-pine regions, such lands being subject to flooding for usually less than two months of the year.

Area IV. Such towns and other areas undergoing urban development

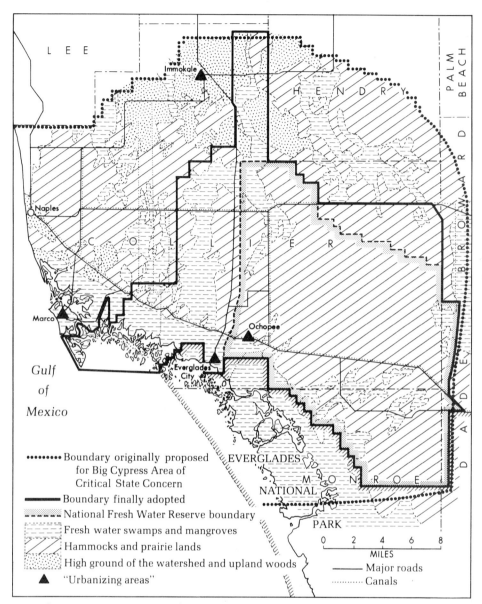

8.3 The Big Cypress critical area as first proposed and subsequent reduced boundaries

as Immokalee, Ochopee, and Marco Island. Naples was the only community not included in this category.

Set forth in the regulations were some general objectives followed by specific dos and don'ts for developers, with the regulations that were to apply to wetlands and other floodprone areas being especially restrictive and demanding. The basic objective was to maintain in the Big Cypress and related estuarine areas the indigenous hydrologic and ecologic systems. In the sloughs and coastal wetlands, only 5 percent of any given site could be disturbed and only half of that could be paved over or otherwise covered with impermeable surfaces. For instance, if the owner of 100 acres of coastal marsh hoped to erect a high-rise condominium there, he could build on from 2½ to 5 of those acres, provided his plans met other requirements, such as those for efficient sewage disposal. For the higher lands (Areas II and III), the regulations were less restrictive, but, even there, not more than 10 or 20 percent of any site could be "disturbed" and only 5 or 10 percent covered with impermeable surfaces. Although some drainage could be allowed, discharges would be expected to simulate natural surface flows and no discharges to tidewater were to be permitted. Even in the existing urbanizing areas (Area IV), the regulations would be significant; for instance, no mangroves could be disturbed, no new drainage facilities discharging to tidewater could be built, and no new construction would be allowed that did not meet standards prescribed under the national flood insurance program. The proposed boundaries and regulations were indeed far reaching, but, in light of the fact that most of the Big Cypress is not naturally habitable, a strong case for them could be made.

"HOW WOULD YOU LIKE TO LIVE IN A POLICE STATE?" Many landowners regarded the proposed regulations as an abomination. The public hearing held by the Division of State Planning in Everglades City a few days after the proposals were announced was, according to one observer, "boisterous and angry."[19] An estimated 500 persons were present, and some snickered and jeered as a state planner sought to explain the regulations. Some were there hoping somehow to block establishment of the national preserve. Owning land within the proposed preserve, they were unwilling to sell it even though the government could be expected to pay the fair market price, if not better. Many others present, however, were people with land outside the preserve boundaries who, given the proposed critical area regulations, saw themselves as about to be shorn of possibly valuable development rights—without prospect of compensation. One angry landowner demanded rhetorically, "How would you like to live in a police state? We will be [living in one] with these proposed regulations. They would depreciate land values, tell you how you can use your land, or rather how you can't use it, and they're not going to give us one red cent."

Farmers, cattlemen, realtors, builders, and developers in Collier County, and even many well beyond the county, were upset about the

---

19. Andy Rosenblatt, "Big Cypress Controls Protested," *Miami Herald*, September 6, 1973.

critical area proposal, either as viewed in its own right or as a precedent. The reaction of the agricultural interests was particularly noteworthy. Their farming and ranching operations would not be affected, because, by law, agricultural activities were explicitly excluded from coverage. In making the compromises felt to be necessary to pass the Land and Water Management Act, the sponsors of this measure had agreed, in effect, that, while the alteration of a given area in the name of urban development might be looked at closely and perhaps forbidden, the alteration of the same area in the name of agriculture would be treated as though necessarily benign. This discrimination is so patently arbitrary that farm interests have reason to think that some future legislature will remove it. A further reason, however, for their opposition to the Big Cypress critical area proposal is that many Florida ranchers and farm operators who have substantial landholdings are speculators at heart.[20] There is no need to surmise why the big developers were opposed to the critical area proposal. Completed or ongoing projects such as the Golden Gate Estates promotion would apparently be exempted from regulation by the "grandfather" provision written into the 1972 law. But new projects, such as the "Remuda East" development then contemplated by GAC for a tract along the Tamiami Trail near the Fahkahatchee Strand would be affected severely, if not made altogether impossible.

Three of the five Collier County commissioners were opposed to the proposed critical area boundaries and regulations, although the commission had actually been coming around to favor meaningful land use controls. The fact that the county was denied an opportunity to develop the regulations itself was deeply resented by some commissioners. However, for officials such as county manager Turner, who had been philosophically opposed even to *compensable* regulation when that approach was being considered as an alternative to federal acquisition of the eastern Big Cypress, noncompensable regulation would have been wholly unpalatable regardless of who had the initial responsibility for drafting the regulations.

RETREAT FROM THE FIRST PLAN. Besides the substantial local opposition to the critical area proposal, many state legislators and even the governor and his staff felt that it went beyond the legislature's intent. And, in Washington, Joe Browder, anxiously observing opposition to the proposal build up, was concerned lest it lead the state to repudiate its commitment to establishment of the national preserve. The proposal was clearly un-

20. Certainly this is the view of W. K. McPherson, recently retired professor of agricultural economics at the University of Florida. In an interview with the author in early 1971, McPherson observed: "The major interest of the landowner today is in the increase in value of a fixed amount of land in a society characterized by economic and population growth. Agriculture and forestry become secondary, tenant industries."

tenable, and the Division of State Planning beat a retreat by redrafting both the critical area boundaries and regulations before submitting them to the cabinet for adoption.

As the boundaries were redrawn, the amount of land to be contained within the critical area was reduced drastically (see figure 8–3). Now, only 285,000 acres outside the national preserve—in contrast to the 650,000 acres first proposed—were to be included. For the most part, the revised boundaries took in only Area I lands (mangrove islands and flats, salt marshes, and freshwater sloughs) and only part of those. Included were the Fahkahatchee Strand and the Okloacoochee Slough, together with the Ten Thousand Islands and their adjacent mangrove and salt marsh areas south of the Tamiami Trail, plus a strip of intermixed cypress, pine, and prairie lands a few miles deep between the trail and the lower end of the Golden Gate Estates. A sizeable area in the eastern Big Cypress between Alligator Alley and the national preserve area was also included as part of the proposed critical area to provide a protective buffer for the preserve. The critical area boundaries still embraced two areas that GAC Properties had hoped to develop, one the Remuda East tract along the Tamiami Trail, the other a tract along State Road 29 at the eastern edge of the Fahkahatchee Strand.

Places excluded from the critical area boundaries included nearly all of Golden Gate Estates; the extensive pine-palmetto lands and cypress heads between Golden Gate Estates and the Naples urban area; and the mangrove and salt marsh areas adjoining the Marco Island and Rookery Bay areas to the east and north. The exclusion of the areas adjoining or tributary to the Rookery Bay Sanctuary was especially notable because of the studies made under the auspices of the Conservation Foundation, the Collier County Conservancy, and the county government itself. The studies had looked to the preservation of Rookery Bay through enlightened land use practices around the sanctuary. Also notable was the exclusion of about half the 100-square-mile area east of State Road 29 and north of Alligator Alley that soon would have to serve as the Naples urban area's principal well field.

Now that the critical area was to be confined largely to coastal wetlands and major freshwater sloughs, the initial plan to prepare a distinct set of regulations for each of four subareas was abandoned and only one set was proposed. Although not quite as stringent as the regulations first proposed for sloughs and coastal wetlands, they were nevertheless restrictive and demanding. For instance, generally not more than 10 percent of any site could be altered—as opposed to the 5 percent proposed initially—and not more than half of that could be covered with impermeable surfaces. As in the original regulations, no finger canals and no new drainage canals discharging fresh water to tidewater would be allowed.

The retreat from the sweeping and ambitious first proposal to the more modest though still significant second one perhaps could not be easily justified environmentally, but it was understandable politically. Indeed, criticism of the critical area proposal did not abate with the issuance of the new plan; if anything, it intensified. State Representative Lorenzo Walker of Collier County, a realtor and veteran legislator, drafted a bill for consideration at the 1974 legislature that would exclude everything from the critical area boundaries except the land designated for the national preserve. The Walker bill, together with a companion bill introduced by a state senator, was reportedly cosponsored by more than half the members of each chamber of the legislature. Most of the legislators appeared to regard the Big Cypress critical area proposal as a product of overzealous bureaucrats.

THE CABINET ACTS. Notwithstanding the opposition in the legislature to the Big Cypress critical area proposal, the Florida Cabinet adopted the proposal by a vote of six to one. Here was an illuminating study in contrasts: a body of officials elected by a statewide constituency and faced with a new election in 1974 had, with but one dissent, approved a new plan of land use regulation at the same time that plan was being severely attacked by representatives and senators elected by local and regional constituencies. The question of restraining and restricting growth and development in the interest of environmental quality was one of high statewide visibility, and, as the first proposal for a critical area to come before the cabinet, the protective scheme for the Big Cypress was of symbolic importance. Although there had been speculation that several members of the cabinet might oppose the proposal (or seek to modify it drastically), Commissioner of Agriculture Doyle Conner was the only one who actually did so. Development interests often seem able to work their will more effectively the smaller the constituency, and quite a few legislators are large landowners or developers themselves. Some legislators, especially those from areas not well served by any major Florida newspaper, represent constituencies still largely ignorant of the issue of land use controls. But Representative Walker's constituents are now alert to that issue, and most do not agree with him. In a straw vote taken in Collier County in February 1974, the outcome was about four to one in favor of the establishment of the Big Cypress critical area. Walker sought to minimize the straw ballot's significance by pointing out that most of the voters who participated were residents of Naples; but, even among the noncity voters who took part, almost two-thirds favored the critical area. One revealing aspect of the straw ballot was that, while a large majority clearly favored greater protection of natural areas through regulation, the idea of the county's issuing bonds and levying a special tax for public purchase of beach access and environmentally endangered lands was overwhelmingly rejected.

END OF THE COLLIER FIEFDOM

The fact that the Collier county government was given no responsible role in preparing the land use regulations for the Big Cypress critical area was perhaps unfortunate. Indeed, it might even have been desirable to allow the Board of Commissioners the initiative—though certainly not the last word—in the drawing up of boundaries for that very large part of the critical area that was to be in Collier County. During 1972 and 1973, the county was advancing rapidly both in political maturity and in the competence needed to cope with questions of land use policy and control. Now, as I write in the spring of 1974, the county still has far to go, but it may be ready to meet challenges that would once simply have pointed up its inadequacies.

THE DEVELOPERS LOSE THEIR POLITICAL DOMINANCE. During 1972, the development interests began to lose their political dominance both in Naples and in the county at large. The first indications of a major change in local politics came in a municipal election early in the year. All five of the candidates endorsed by a new group called the Committee to Support Naples Values were elected to the City Council despite the opposition of the Collier-owned *Naples Daily News*. One of the successful candidates and a prime mover in the formation of the new committee was Arnold E. Lamm, a retired executive formerly active in the coal mining industry and a resident of Naples since 1969.[21] By 1972, Lamm had become intensely interested in the problem of controlling growth in Naples and Collier County—and well he might, for, after experiencing population increases averaging 14 percent a year during the 1960s, the county was now showing an annual growth rate of 28 percent. As Lamm has told me, he was becoming convinced that growth should be governed by two principles: (1) it should not outpace the development of such essential public services as roads and facilities for waste collection and treatment, and (2) it should, by and large, pay for itself—for instance, Naples might levy an "impact fee" on new users of municipal water inasmuch as a new and more distant well field would soon have to be developed. (The city now has in fact imposed such a special fee.)

Lamm and the other councilmen of his persuasion succeeded in having the population densities allowed under the Naples zoning plan rolled back by half or more. The city council deadlocked on a motion to endorse the Big Cypress critical area proposal (some councilmen felt that this was no

---

21. Incidentally, even as Arnold Lamm tries to cope with problems of growth and land use as a municipal official in south Florida, a son in Colorado, State Representative Richard Lamm, is running for governor of that fast-growing mountain state. Moreover, he is running as an outspoken advocate of bringing growth and land use under better public control.

proper business of the city's), but it later was unanimous in expressing concern at the failure of the critical area plan to include all of Naples' future well field. Candidates backed by the Committee to Support Naples Values swept the municipal elections again in February 1974, with the result that the advocates of "managed growth" now constituted a clear council majority. Further zoning rollbacks and other measures such as new height limitations for buildings were expected.

Prior to the county election in the fall of 1972, the Committee to Support Naples Values tried to extend its influence to county government by forming another group, the Voters League of Collier County, Inc. Personalities and not issues dominated this election, however, and, perhaps for this reason, only one of the league's three candidates was successful. But the opposition paid it the high compliment of imitation by forming a counter group called Citizens for Orderly Growth. (Despite its name, this latter group is considered strongly prodevelopment.) Moreover, the Board of Commissioners pleased managed-growth advocates by adopting a population ceiling of 200,000 (including 25,000 in Naples) for the year 2000. Although this ceiling contemplates a population several times larger than the 1970 population of 41,000, it nevertheless implies some unprecedented restraints and a major reduction in the current rate of growth. Managed growth had been furthered when Governor Askew, in early 1973, appointed Ruth Van Doren, a strong believer in land use controls, to the seat of a commissioner now become ill, who had for years regarded indiscriminate development complacently and permissively.

THE MODERNIZATION OF COUNTY GOVERNMENT. Perhaps the Board of Commissioners' most significant achievement to date has been to establish county planning and zoning staffs of some depth and competence. By late 1973, the county had fourteen professionals and technicians in its planning and zoning departments, and it was still recruiting. The newly named director of planning, zoning, and building was Neno J. Spagna, who had come to Collier from Manatee County (south of Tampa), where he had led in formulating that county's new Optimum Population and Urban Growth Policy (OPUG). This policy rests on the concept of having urban growth—and the public facilities necessary to support that growth— expand outward in a gradual and measured way from the existing urban area.[22] In November 1973 the Collier Board of Commissioners, acting on Spagna's advice, declared a freeze on zoning throughout the county's unincorporated areas. It was to last six months, pending completion of a new general land use master plan and the adoption of an OPUG-type policy. Had such a policy been in effect in 1960, when the Rosens first

22. *OPUG: A Growth Policy for Manatee County, Fla.*, brochure printed by the Manatee County Planning Department, May 1973.

began eyeing the Big Cypress, the disastrous Golden Gate Estates project would not have been allowed.

The foregoing changes in politics and government in Collier County and Naples mark the disappearances of the last vestiges of the county's former status as a Collier family fiefdom. Representatives of the Collier interests themselves are now behaving more discreetly. Norman Herren, manager of the Collier interests, has resigned from the planning commission, and his deputy, George Huntoon, has given up his seat on the county's environmental advisory committee, both pleading the press of other business.

THE SEARCH FOR NEW LAND
MANAGEMENT MECHANISMS

WATER MANAGEMENT DISTRICT 6. Any Urban Growth Area delineated under the kind of policies Collier County is now considering will necessarily include all or part of what is known as Water Management District 6 (WMD 6), a 63-square-mile area immediately south and southeast of Naples. Maybe a third of WMD 6 consists of mangrove and salt marsh wetlands, including the Rookery Bay Sanctuary, while the rest is made up of land in the Big Cypress watershed. Scarcely any of the district's estuarine areas have been developed, and only about a fourth of its lands in the Big Cypress have been urbanized or cleared for agriculture. WMD 6 fell within the boundaries first proposed for the Big Cypress critical area, but, as I have said, most of the western Big Cypress was later excluded from that area for reasons that were essentially political.

Since the Collier County Water District Conservation Act was passed in 1961, the Board of County Commissioners has had authority to establish one or more water management districts, impose a special tax on landowners within these areas, and adopt water control plans and see that they are carried out. The first two districts established have served largely to bring about land drainage and, as in the case of the district that embraces Golden Gate Estates, to provide a mechanism for maintaining drainage works with taxes to be raised from the people who supposedly benefit from those works. Yet water control is so essential to development in most of the county that, by allowing the county board to decide what water control facilities will be built and where, the 1961 act gives the board a potentially strong tool that can be used to require an environmentally acceptable plan for all major projects. WMD 6 was created in 1971 by the board expressly with a view to helping landowners develop the areas adjacent to the Rookery Bay Sanctuary as residential property of high value while at the same time recognizing the need for protecting environmental resources. The Collier County Conservancy, which had raised the money to buy lands within the sanctuary, was itself one of the prime movers in the formation of WMD 6, for it believed that the district plan could be a model in harmonizing development with the preservation of natural values. The completed plan was submitted to the county board in February of 1974, and the question of whether the conservancy's hopes for it were justified presumably would be answered before the end of the year. What that question boiled down to was whether the county would regard WMD 6 as, in effect, a critical area and insist that development there be limited accordingly.

All land within WMD 6 would fall into one or another of three basic zoning categories: a preservation zone, covering tidal lands and freshwater sloughs where no development would be allowed; a development zone, taking in the higher land (having such vegetation as pine and scrub oak) and appropriate for development at up to medium densities; and a conservation zone, an intermediate category for land such as "high marsh" areas immediately adjacent to lands prone to regular tidal flooding where the only development permitted would be at very low densities and subject to special construction requirements. Although appropriate environmentally, this kind of zoning raises a problem of fairness and equity in the treatment of landowners, as is also true of the critical area regulations referred to earlier. At this writing, how this problem will ultimately be met has not been determined, but the possible courses of action are relatively few. If the money were available, the county or state could buy fee title or conservation easements to all land where development is either to be prohibited altogether or limited drastically. This is what many who opposed the critical area plan said should be done. But to follow such a policy wherever preservation and conservation zoning are in order in Florida would probably cost several billions of dollars, far more than could conceivably be devoted to such a purpose.

Every really promising approach to the problem of compensating or rewarding the landowner whose property is zoned for preservation or conservation involves use of the Planned Unit Development (PUD) concept, and the transfer or pooling of development rights. For instance, in a PUD embracing several hundred acres of mixed terrain, the county could reward the developer for leaving the sloughs and cypress heads undisturbed by allowing him to build several clusters of moderate to high density housing on the low ridges, sandy knolls, or other more development-tolerant land. But, while the PUD concept is applied easily enough in the case of a large tract of mixed terrain owned by a single party, its use is more difficult where the land is owned by several or perhaps many parties. In such a situation, the solution may have to be sought through the sale or pooling of development rights.

The Center for Urban Studies at the University of Miami, in a study to develop land management concepts for WMD 6, has recommended that the owners of land zoned for conservation have the option either of

Fire in pinelands adjacent to the Big Cypress

Patricia Caulfield

developing that land at the low density of one dwelling unit for 5 acres or of selling their developments rights.[23] The incentive to sell would be powerful because under the recommended concept, the right which the owner of such land would transfer (to someone owning developable land) would not be for the construction of one unit per 5 acres but three units for every 1 acre. For such a scheme of transferable development rights to be tried in Collier County or elsewhere in the state, enabling legislation would have to be passed in Tallahassee.[24] If there is a major flaw in this

23. Albert R. Veri, Arthur R. Marshall, Susan U. Wilson, and James H. Hartwell, *Rookery Bay Land Use Studies*, Study No. 2, "The Resource Buffer Plan: A Conceptual Land Use Study" (Washington, D.C.: The Conservation Foundation, 1973), p. 5. John Clark, of the Conservation Foundation staff, recommended such an approach in a paper circulated among those participating in the study just cited.

24. A bill to authorize the subdividing of local political jurisdictions into development districts and the allocation of transferable development rights was introduced in the Maryland Legislature in 1973 by Senator W. J. Goodman of Prince Georges County. This measure, (Senate Bill 254) has not been enacted. Although the development rights concept seems to enjoy increasing currency, it has not yet received a practical test.

approach it is that the assignment of the same rights to all land within a particular zoning classification could be arbitrary because the land would not be of uniform development potential.

An alternative approach, with development rights pooled rather than transferred, would involve the establishment of PUD districts vested with the power to have all development rights to land within their borders brought under common ownership and control. The land owners whose rights have been taken would receive negotiable shares in the PUD, with the distribution of shares to be based on the amount of land each party owned and its relative value as determined by a panel of assessors. If the county should prohibit the development of more than a fixed percentage of any tract of land zoned for conservation, many landowners might quickly see the advantage in forming PUD districts after the legislature authorized such entities. Once a majority of the landowners within a particular area voted to establish a district, the others would have to go along unless they could convince the county board that implementation of the proposed plan would be unworkable or contrary to the public interest or that the distribution of shares was unfair.

Before anyone protests that this PUD district concept is not in keeping with Florida tradition, let him be reminded of the Florida law of 1913 (chapter 298, Florida Statutes) authorizing the establishment of drainage districts. Under that law, where any contiguous body of land is subject to flooding, a majority of the owners or the owner of the majority of the land can petition a state circuit court for the formation of a drainage district according to a specified engineering plan. Such districts can condemn land, levy a tax, and contract for water control works. The legislature has already shown that the drainage district concept lends itself to remarkable extension and enlargement. To facilitate the establishment of Disney World, the legislature in 1967 created the Reedy Creek Improvement District, an entity that allows the Disney interests to enjoy special immunities and sweeping governmental powers.

In WMD 6 and in other environmentally sensitive areas, the board of commissioners clearly has an opportunity to try innovative concepts. Indeed, the transfer or pooling of development rights could find application in many places in Florida where the preservation of environmental values and the upholding of property rights come into conflict.

A COMPREHENSIVE POLICY FOR THE BIG CYPRESS

To sum up, since 1970 the efforts of the federal, state, and county governments to protect the Big Cypress have, taken altogether, been tending toward what in the *aggregate* would be a policy placing much of this important watershed under special protection or regulation. Most of the eastern part of the Big Cypress may soon be protected as a national pre-serve. Several major areas contiguous to the preserve, including the Fahka-hatchee Strand, will be under the stringent protective land use regulation to be applied in Florida's first critical area. Interstate 75 will be built across the Big Cypress, but in a manner that should actually improve water flow and reduce development pressures below those generated by the existing Alligator Alley. The county government, for its part, is moving toward a growth policy that may discourage early development in most of the west-ern Big Cypress. Also, in formulating plans for WMD 6, it is groping for an environmentally and politically acceptable way of restricting development sharply while at the same time not ignoring property rights. Yet, while what already has been done represents important progress, no compre-hensive and coherent land use policy for the Big Cypress now exists. Further, until there is a conscious effort by state and local officials to pull all the threads together, there will never be such a policy.

What should go into a comprehensive policy? I suggest the following:
• *A general land use master plan for the entire Big Cypress Watershed, all 1.5 million acres, should be prepared as a joint state, federal, and local effort.* This plan would, as in the case of the one being prepared for Dade County, represent an overall regional strategy of conservation and develop-ment. State participation in the planning would, of course, be led by the Division of State Planning. The U.S. Department of the Interior would continue to lead federal involvement in the Big Cypress, and, at the local level, Collier County would have the dominant role.

All of the Big Cypress would be zoned. The three basic zoning cate-gories discussed in connection with WMD 6—preservation, conservation, and development—would be delineated, together with an agricultural zone in any areas where farming promises to be an important and continuing activity. (Agriculture would no longer be allowed to escape special regula-tion, as it now does under the exemption in the 1972 land use law.) Preser-vation zoning would be confined to large, self-contained areas such as the Fahkahatchee Strand and the Ten Thousand Islands, which ultimately should be brought under public ownership. Conservation zoning would be applied in most of the Big Cypress outside the national preserve, and regulations similar to those for the Big Cypress critical area would be imposed. State law should provide for such zoning and regulation and for a requirement that all new development occurring within a conservation zone be planned unit development. The formation of PUD districts should be authorized, possibly together with authorization of some legal mecha-nism for the sale of development rights where this alternative approach seems attractive. Also, there should no longer be a "grandfather" clause allowing preexisting developments such as Golden Gate Estates to escape regulation. The developer's vested interests would not be ignored, but these would be subordinated to the public's overriding interest in maintaining properly functioning hydrologic and ecologic systems. The absurd zoning that now exists in Golden Gate Estates would be wiped out. Given the inability of the vast and scattered multitude of owners of parcels in this subdivision ever to act in concert, the state itself perhaps should take the initiative in forming PUD districts there by condemning all land within a district, with the owners of parcels to be compensated not in cash but through receipt of shares in the PUDs. Such action would be more than fair to the owners of those parcels, mostly gullible small-fry speculators who foolishly bought land that under present conditions of ownership may never become homesites in an attractive community. (GAC is committed under the FTC consent order to help build a community at Golden Gate Estates by such means as allowing parcels that are not habitable to be exchanged for parcels that are. The efficacy of this plan is, however, open to doubt.)

• *Whatever new transportation, waste control, and water control facilities that are built in the Big Cypress would have to be in keeping with the objectives of the master plan.* Unlike the practices of times past, no new airport, road or highway interchange, trunk sewer, or canal would be built without careful consideration of its secondary as well as primary effects on the environment and on regional growth and development.

• *Areas zoned for preservation would all gradually be bought by the state.* The prices paid for these areas should be fair to the taxpayer as well as to the landowner and should not reflect speculative values. The state is in control, and land within preservation areas simply should not be bought until it becomes available at prices that the taxpayer can reasonably bear.

• *A program of remedial engineering should be undertaken to correct past mistakes that have needlessly disrupted Big Cypress hydrologic and ecologic systems.* The plan proposed by consultants to the Florida Department of Transportation for Interstate 75 is an excellent case in point. Alligator Alley, which I-75 would replace, is said to impede the southward flow of surface water down through the Everglades and the Big Cypress. Under the consultants' proposal,[25] I-75 would not be flanked by continuous borrow canals of the kind seen along Alligator Alley.[26] Instead, there would be a specially designed water dispersion system featuring a series of elongated, discontinuous pools through which surface flows would pass from one side of the highway to the other.

Urgently needed is a project to remedy the damage done by the Golden Gate Estates canal system. GAC Properties has itself taken a small step

25. Set forth in *Environmental/Section 4(f) Statement, Interstate 75* (from Fort Myers to Andytown), prepared for the Florida Department of Transportation by H. W. Lochner, Inc., Consultant Engineers, of Chicago, Illinois, 1972.

26. A roadside borrow canal is one that has been created by the excavation of fill material used to build up the roadbed above flood levels. All roads in the Big Cypress and the Everglades are paralleled by such canals.

in this direction by installing two self-adjusting weirs capable of maintaining constant water levels upstream from the structure. An objective study might lead to a plan to fill in some of the canals, and, especially, to plug up the Fahka Union Canal before it reaches tidewater. One idea considered by the EPA team that recently investigated conditions in the Big Cypress would be to replace the existing canal system that is discharging surface waters directly to the Gulf of Mexico with a system to redistribute part of the surface flows from developing areas to wild areas such as the Fahkahatchee Strand. Under this concept, the Alligator Alley and Tamiami Trail borrow canals might be used as "distributor canals" from which water could be discharged wherever it would be beneficial.

THE STATE AS A SENIOR PARTNER. In this program of land use controls suggested for the Big Cypress the senior partner would be the state of Florida (except in the national preserve, where federal authority would be controlling). The state would establish broadly defined basic policies for conservation and development, with the county government left to decide, subject to some state review, the details of the land use master plan and the outcome of particular development proposals. Even today the Florida Cabinet has authority to intervene in a variety of land use matters in the Big Cypress, and that authority should now be made more comprehensive. The legislature may already have gone farther in this direction than many of its members realize. The Water Resources Act of 1972 could prove to be a potent statute that gives the Central and Southern Florida Flood Control District—and, ultimately, the governor and the cabinet—substantial, if indirect, powers of review over plans such as those for WMD 6. In any event, state review of local land use decisions is clearly overdue, and, while this holds even for decisions made by a county such as Dade that is relatively mature politically, it is especially true of those made in a county such as Collier, only recently delivered from the developers.

9 The barge canal: The uses of power

The Florida peninsula and keys jut southward some four hundred miles from the main landmass of the United States, and the idea of cutting a canal across the peninsula's relatively narrow northern waist is not, on its face, implausible. At that point, from the Gulf of Mexico to easily navigable waters leading to the Atlantic is, as the crow flies, about 70 miles; further-more, land elevations are in some places almost at sea level and nowhere are they more than a few hundred feet above it. But the north Florida penin-sula is not one of those few places in the world, such as the Isthmus of Panama or the Isthmus of Suez, where, from a glance at the map, one can say a canal clearly must be built.

Nevertheless, for many influential Florida citizens and politicians the idea of building a canal across this part of Florida has long been compelling. Twice between 1935 and 1971 a cross Florida canal project (see figure 9–1) was begun, then halted. It was stopped the first time partly for fear that the

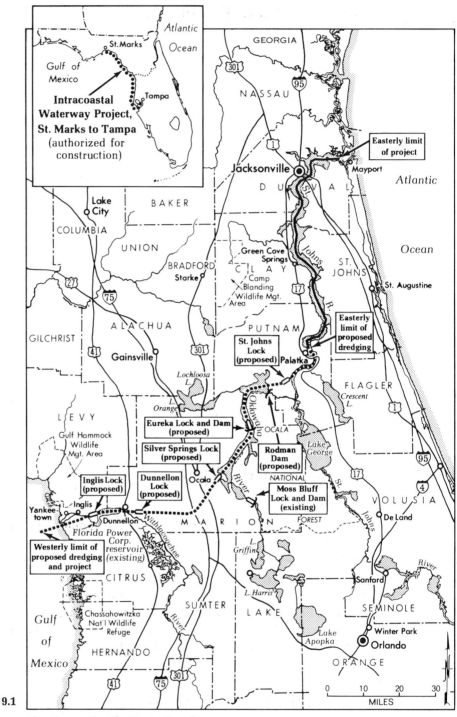

Intracoastal Waterway Project, St. Marks to Tampa (authorized for construction)

Easterly limit of project

Easterly limit of proposed dredging

St. Johns Lock (proposed)

Eureka Lock and Dam (proposed)

Silver Springs Lock (proposed)

Rodman Dam (proposed)

Inglis Lock (proposed)

Dunnellon Lock (proposed)

Moss Bluff Lock and Dam (existing)

Westerly limit of proposed dredging and project

Florida Power Corp. reservoir (existing)

9.1 The Cross Florida Barge Canal

Floridan Aquifer would be badly contaminated and partly for fiscal reasons; the second time, it was stopped almost entirely out of environmental considerations, especially the desirability of preserving the Oklawaha River Valley as measured against the questionable economic benefits promised by the canal. Indeed, the story of the cross Florida canal is mostly one of policy makers and institutions often ignorant of environmental values, responsive chiefly to local development interests, and innocent of land and water management strategies that take account of the special natural attributes of north central Florida.

My account in an earlier chapter of the south Florida jetport controversy pointed up the conflicts over conservation and development that arise—and the dubious solutions likely to be found—when a local agency has the dominant voice in deciding whether a major regional facility is needed and where it should go. Here, the controversy over the barge canal shows how easily—in the absence of fair, rational procedures, political sensitivity, and foresight—land and water management can go awry even with state and federal leadership, whether motivated by goals of development or conservation.

THE OKLAWAHA RIVER AND ITS REGION

The Oklawaha River, about which the struggle over the barge canal has largely been waged, rises in Florida's Central Highlands as the major outlet for the Oklawaha chain of lakes, of which Lake Apopka is the largest and most famous (see figure 9–2). A surprisingly strong-flowing, sand-bottomed river, the Oklawaha begins as the outlet of Lake Griffin and runs north and eastward for some 75 miles before entering the St. Johns. Most of the upper twenty miles of the Oklawaha, from Lake Griffin almost to State Road 40, was destroyed as a natural stream prior to the turn of the century by farmers who channelized it to try to keep the river from overflowing onto their rich muck lands. Later, the river was partially regulated by means of a small dam at Moss Bluff. Beginning in the 1880s lumbermen invaded the middle and lower reaches of the river swamp, in most places about a mile wide, and removed nearly all the virgin cypress of commercial value. A luxuriant second growth of cypress and mixed hardwoods came quickly, however, and the Oklawaha retained the wild, junglelike character imparted by the half-enclosing canopy of green, the palms that lean out over the dark tannin-stained waters, the oaks and cypress draped with Spanish moss, and the dozing 'gators and evening flights of white ibis going to roost. The Oklawaha's only major tributary, and virtually its only source of water during droughts is the seven-mile-long run formed by Silver Springs, a beautiful spring and one of the world's largest, usually flowing at about 22 million gallons per hour. Overnight steamboat trips for tourists, from Palatka up

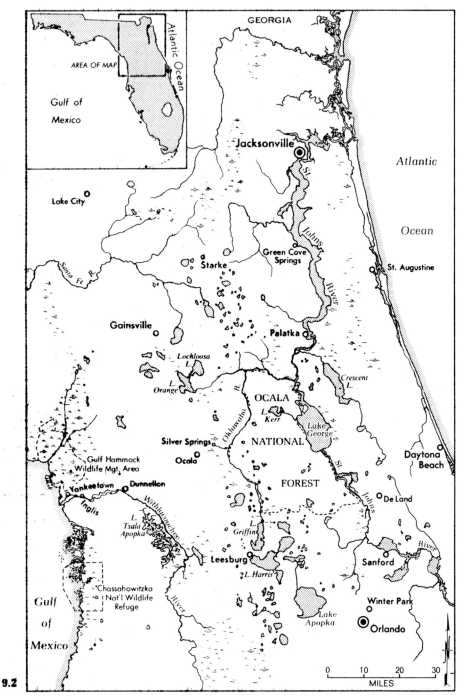

The Oklawaha River and its region

the Oklawaha to Silver Springs, began after the Civil War and continued until the early 1920s. Accounts of these trips recall how, at night, as the small paddle wheelers negotiated the twists and turns of the river, the looming walls of the river forest would be "lighted fantastically by fatwood fires burning in iron baskets slung out from the forecastle."[1] Some famous people of the time—Ulysses S. Grant, Harriet Beecher Stowe, William Cullen Bryant, and Lafcadio Hearn among them—took this extraordinary voyage through what the poet Sidney Lanier was moved to call the "sweetest water-lane in the world."[2] In recent times, the Oklawaha has lost some of the solitude of a wilderness stream because it is so popular with motorboaters that, on a Saturday or Sunday, numerous high-speed craft roar up and down the river.

The Oklawaha River and swamp forest represent an important and distinctive feature of a large, still predominantly rural region noted for the variety and attractiveness of its landscape. A major feature associated with the Oklawaha chain of headwaters lakes to the south of the river are this area's citrus groves: at many points the groves extend as far as one can see in undulating waves of green. To the northwest of the Oklawaha is a hilly region dotted with lakes and sinkholes, while to the northeast is the Saint Johns and the flat coastal plain. Then, to the east and south of the river, lies the Big Scrub of Ocala National Forest, a region described in *The Yearling* and other novels of Marjorie Kinnan Rawlings. Predominantly a country of low hills and spindly sand pines and scrub oak, the Big Scrub today retains its old air of strangeness and isolation despite heavy use by deer hunters, campers, lumbermen, and even by Navy pilots who use part of the Ocala as a bombing range.

To the west of the Oklawaha, beyond Silver Springs, is largely a country of rolling pasture land, thoroughbred horse farms and small towns. The city of Ocala (pop. 25,600 in 1970), about six miles from the Oklawaha, is the only sizeable community near the river and is much larger than any other community in the Oklawaha basin. But, just beyond this basin, within a 100-mile radius of the Oklawaha and Ocala National Forest, are cities such as Jacksonville, Orlando, Tampa, and St. Petersburg. Many of their residents need and desire the kind of high quality outdoor recreation in a natural setting that the Oklawaha and the Ocala forest can provide. This, then, is the region that the canal project would affect critically by eliminating the wild Oklawaha valley and extinguishing one of Florida's few remaining large natural ecosystems.

1. Gordon E. Bigelow, "History of Man in the Oklawaha Valley," in *Environmental Impact of the Cross Florida Barge Canal* (Florida Defenders of the Environment, 1970), pp. 47–49.
2. Ibid.

THE ABORTIVE SHIP CANAL,
1826–1936

SELECTING A ROUTE. The first of several government surveys of the feasibility of building a canal across north Florida was authorized by Congress in 1826, during the presidency of John Quincy Adams. Since then, twenty-eight possible routes for the canal have been considered, but the one through the Oklawaha Valley has offered a major advantage in that less excavation would be required than on alternate routes. The first actual attempt at constructing such a canal was to follow the survey, authorized by the Rivers and Harbors Act of 1927, of the feasibility of a Gulf-Atlantic Ship Canal. In the spring of 1934 an interdepartmental board appointed by President Franklin D. Roosevelt designated the route believed to be the most practicable, and, as matters turned out, this route would be used for both the sea-level ship canal project of the 1930s and the high-level barge canal project of the 1960s. It goes generally as follows (see inset, figure 9–1): from the mouth of the Saint Johns River to Jacksonville and Palatka, then some 8 miles through a lowland region to the Oklawaha River; up the Oklawaha Valley for about 30 miles to a point south of Silver Springs, then an overland cut again for about 35 miles westward through a saddle in the Central Highlands ridge south of Ocala; then, after following the lower reaches of the Withlacoochee River for a short distance, another overland cut for 8 miles west to the Gulf of Mexico, entering the Gulf only a few miles south of the village of Yankeetown. At no point would the ground elevation exceed 110 feet above sea level and, for about half of the 87-mile crossing from the Gulf to the upper Saint Johns, ground elevations would be below 30 feet.

THE CANAL AS A NOSTRUM OF THE NEW DEAL. Even while the new survey was being prepared in the early 1930s some important initiatives on behalf of a Gulf-Atlantic Canal were mounted from the port city of Jacksonville, then the largest city in Florida and the place where the major thrust of cross-state canal proposals always has been generated. A Jacksonville engineer named Henry H. Buckman was a prime mover and persistent promoter of the ship canal and of the later barge canal from the 1920s until his death in 1968. In 1932, Buckman and the mayor of Jacksonville went to New Orleans and established a National Gulf-Atlantic Ship Canal Association. Thus, early on, the strategy was to make construction of the canal the goal of port interests and shippers on both the Atlantic and Gulf coasts and up the Mississippi Valley.

The onset of the Depression might have been expected to discourage Buckman and other canal promoters, but instead they found in this economic calamity an opportunity to offer the canal as a symbol of the New Deal's aim of building needed public works and putting the jobless back to work. The Gulf-Atlantic Ship Canal Association made application to New Deal

Silver Springs in 1886

agencies for construction loans and grants. It also prevailed upon the Florida Legislature of 1933 to establish at Jacksonville a Florida Ship Canal Authority empowered to acquire a canal right-of-way and to construct and own and operate the facility. Later, the legislature would, in addition, create a special tax district embracing the six counties through which the canal would pass. After a referendum, this latter entity would issue $1.5 million in bonds for right-of-way purchases and impose a tax on property owners. The theory used to justify this tax was that the canal would benefit the counties along the canal right-of-way more than it would the rest of Florida. Establishment of the Canal Authority and the tax district had long-term political consequences. Citizens in the tax district would be continually reminded by many of their elected officials that they had a vested interest in the canal project. The Canal Authority, for its part, served as a kind of permanent, state-supported canal lobby built into the state government itself. Indeed, the canal project would, over the years, undergo many vicissitudes but even in the most discouraging times the Canal Authority would endure as a hardy seed capable of sending forth green shoots of hope at the first good rain.

Construction of the Gulf-Atlantic Ship Canal began in 1935 and was stopped the next year. Although Congress had not authorized this project, President Franklin D. Roosevelt, acting under the Emergency Relief Act, allocated some $5.4 million for it to the Corps of Engineers. At home at Hyde Park, FDR started the work with his usual flair by pressing a telegraph key mounted on a gold nugget and thus, as the Jacksonville *Journal* put it, "blasting his name into Florida history."[3] How splendidly the canal promoters' strategy of offering a relief project as well as a proposed navigation facility had worked was evident when, shortly after the groundbreaking, the President's action was endorsed in a letter signed by seventy-two United States senators, thirty-six governors, and the heads of the major national waterway associations.

UNBEARABLE SHORTCOMINGS. Yet there were problems about the canal project. Railroads in Florida opposed the canal, and the Corps of Engineers had not, for its part, shown the project to be needed. Indeed, a Department of Commerce survey of potential shippers had produced discouraging results. Still worse, the Geological Survey was warning that the canal would damage the Floridan Aquifer. A 30-foot-deep channel would have to be dug at sea level through some 35 miles of water-bearing Ocala limestone, in some places cutting into the aquifer to a depth of 85 feet. The prospect was for massive saltwater intrusion in some areas along the canal and for a drastic loss of fresh water in others. The flow of both Silver Springs and Rainbow Springs probably would have been cut off.[4] Although the Corps of Engineers held that the project would have only minor effects on the hydrologic regimen, many people were not reassured; they feared that the water supplies for central and southern Florida were endangered. This was the beginning of a persistent split between north Florida and the rest of the state in regard to the canal. Some canal proponents are said to have joked about "cutting off south Florida and letting it drift to Cuba."

The combined weight of the ship canal's economic shortcomings and its possibly disastrous effect on water resources was more than the project could bear. Moreover, the very fact that so large a project had been started

3. Quoted in J. Richard Sewell, "Cross Florida Barge Canal, 1927–1968," *Florida Historical Quarterly*, Vol. 46, No. 4 (April 1968), pp. 369–383.

4. Glen L. Faulkner, "Geohydrologic Aspects of the Cross Florida Barge Canal," American Society of Civil Engineers, Irrigation and Drainage Division, Selected Papers, Social and Ecological Aspects of Irrigation and Drainage Specialty Conference, November 4–6, 1972, pp. 307–325.

without specific congressional authorization made it a political target. Senator Arthur H. Vandenberg of Michigan, a contender for the Republican presidential nomination in 1936, called for an investigation. In any case, after the initial allocation of relief funds, President Roosevelt left it to Congress to appropriate the money necessary to finish the canal, which Congress refused to do. By mid-1936 all funds were exhausted and work on the canal stopped. This was a severe disappointment for many Floridans living near the canal's path, and especially for those in the Ocala area where the construction of "Camp Roosevelt" for WPA workers assigned to the project had generated a boom. Some 19,000 acres of right-of-way had been or were on the point of being acquired by the Ship Canal Authority and excavation had begun along more than 5 miles of it, with nearly 13 million cubic yards of material already moved. The most visible monuments to the project were several concrete piers for a highway bridge, left standing like huge tombstones.

BEGINNINGS OF THE BARGE CANAL

AN ANSWER TO THE SUBMARINE MENACE. The canal project was not dead, however, merely dormant. Florida's two senators—one was Claude Pepper,[5] an enthusiastic New Dealer—and some of its representatives persisted in trying to revive the project. Their efforts finally began to show results after the United States entered World War II. Just as the Ship Canal had been offered as a response to the Depression, the Cross Florida Barge Canal was to be an answer to the German submarines that were sinking American shipping along the Florida coast. The Corps of Engineers report of June 1942 recommended construction of a 12-foot-deep, high-level canal with a series of locks. Petroleum and other war materials would be carried safely across Florida by barge instead of through U-boat infested waters around the peninsula. Moreover, the Chief of Engineers declared that the barge canal would leave ground water conditions essentially unchanged. Along its highest (or "summit") reach, south of Ocala, the barge canal would cut into the Floridan Aquifer to depths of up to 27 feet,[6] compared to depths up to three times that in the case of the sea-level ship canal. Economically, the project, estimated to cost $44 million, promised to be a loser, with annual charges exceeding benefits by a ratio of greater than five to one. But the national defense rather than economics was Congress's overriding concern in authorizing the canal as part of a legislative package made up of several waterway and pipeline projects.

---

5. Pepper was defeated for reelection to the Senate in 1950, but in 1962 he ran successfully for the House of Representatives, where he still serves.

6. Glen L. Faulkner, *Geohydrology of the Cross-Florida Barge Canal Area with Special Reference to the Ocala Vicinity*, Open File Report, U.S. Geological Survey, Tallahassee, Florida, 1970, p. 5.

In the Senate, Arthur Vandenberg and other senators questioned the value of the canal for any purpose and tried to remove the project from the package. They failed, but by only a bare margin. Vice-President Henry Wallace, evidencing the Roosevelt Administration's continuing support of the cross Florida canal idea, broke a tie vote. In the House, a Miami congressman tried to kill the canal proposal but he too was unsuccessful.

LANGUISHING IN THE CORPS' UNFUNDED BACKLOG. No money was appropriated for the canal, however, because the project would require scarce labor and materials and probably could not in any event be finished before the end of the war. So for twenty years, from 1942 until 1962, the barge canal took its place in the Corps of Engineers' large backlog of authorized but unfunded projects. But efforts to revive the project persisted, and with surprising effect.

In central and southern Florida during the late 1940s and 1950s one continued to find skepticism about the canal; critics of the proposed project pointed out that Florida already had a cross state canal—the Okeechobee Waterway between Stuart and Fort Myers—which was little used. But, in the main, most Floridians either were indifferent about or ignorant of the canal issue. In this situation, the active proponents of the canal in Jacksonville and other communities along the canal route had the field to themselves. Besides their base in the Canal Authority, they had the support of the Jacksonville Chamber of Commerce, the state legislators for the six counties in the special tax district, legislators for north Florida coastal counties generally, and the Florida State Federated Labor Council. With these forces behind the project, the proponents could count on strong support from the Florida Cabinet, the legislature and its dominant Pork Chop Gang, and Florida's congressional delegation, particularly the congressmen from north Florida. Among the latter, especially important were Representative Charles E. Bennett of Jacksonville and Representative Robert F. Sikes of Crestview in the Florida panhandle. Sikes was (and is) a shrewd and resourceful member of the House Committee on Appropriations, and, inasmuch as the project already had been authorized, he, especially, was the man to watch. As later events would eventually bear out, however, support for the canal was broader than it was deep. Its main source was the Jacksonville business community. It should be well noted that Jacksonville is Florida's major financial and industrial center and that its business leaders have enjoyed substantial political influence. Their dream was that the barge canal would open for the port of Jacksonville a vast mid-continental hinterland. In their scenario domestic water-transported cargoes—petroleum products, pulpwood, chemicals, fertilizers, and so on—would increasingly pass through Jacksonville, as would larger volumes of cargo from or enroute to foreign ports. Cargoes from abroad would reach Jacksonville by deep-draft vessels, then be transferred to barges for reshipment via the canal to destinations on the Gulf Coast and in the Mississippi Valley. Similarly, there would be a flow of exports, including grain, coming to Jacksonville from these coastal and hinterland regions for trans-shipment abroad.

In 1951, with the Korean War being fought, President Truman, at the urging of Congressman Bennett, informed the Department of Defense that in his view "this canal is essential to the welfare of the country"[7] but the department replied that military benefits from the project would be "so limited they should not be used as a basis for decision."[8] The canal proponents were thus at an impasse unless the project could be justified upon a restudy of its economics. A small appropriation for such a restudy was finally obtained and by 1958 the Corps of Engineers was claiming that, if built, the canal would produce an annual return of 5 percent on the investment (1.05 to 1). Marginal though this promised benefit admittedly was, the barge canal now reappeared on the corps' list of "active" projects.

JFK DELIVERS ON A CAMPAIGN PROMISE. The critical break came during the presidential campaign of 1960 when John F. Kennedy, as part of an unsuccessful effort to carry Florida, assured canal proponents of his support for the project. Later, as president, Kennedy would more than fulfill his campaign promise. A supplemental appropriations bill submitted to Congress by President Kennedy in 1962 contained money for final planning and design of the canal. A struggle in Congress followed, in which the canal proponents succeeded in obtaining the appropriation despite the opposition of the House Appropriations Committee and its chairman, Representative Clarence Cannon of Missouri, who as a strong fiscal conservative habitually viewed with skepticism such costly projects as the barge canal. Before this struggle was joined, the Corps of Engineers reported two new economic analyses of the project, one prepared by the Jacksonville District Engineer, the other by the Office of the Chief of Engineers. Both used a discount rate[9] of 2⅝ percent—up slightly from the rate used in the earlier study but still unrealistically low in the opinion of many resource economists. In the new studies it was assumed that new construction practices, together with some changes in project plans, would allow the project to be built for less than the $164.6 million that the corps had estimated in 1958. The Chief of Engineers put the total at $157.9 million. His office also counted two new project benefits,

7. Sewell, op. cit.

8. William M. Partington, "History of the Cross Florida Canal," Florida Defenders of the Environment, op. cit.

9. In water resource economics the term "discount rate" has a special meaning. In this context, a discount rate is applied to express a project's future benefits in terms of present values. This is necessary because the dollar to be received some years hence in deferred benefits is worth less than the dollar received today which, if reinvested, may begin right away to yield a further return. If a dollar in benefits to be received fifty years from now is "discounted" at 3 percent, that dollar is worth only 23 cents today; if discounted at 10 percent, it is worth slightly less than 1 cent.

flood control (in a region having a vast mile-wide river swamp), and enhancement of land values. As for the latter, this took account of the fact that some of the private land abutting the project would look out over the reservoirs—onto vistas dominated in some places by ghostly, partly submerged forests of dead trees. The Chief of Engineers' office recomputed the benefit-cost ratio at 1.17 to 1, promising a 17 percent return. (Later, when recreation benefits were first claimed for the project, the corps would again revise the benefit-cost ratio upward—this time to 1.4 to 1.) Nevertheless, the corps' new benefit-cost figures left many people still unconvinced. To raise the discount rate to anything even approaching the "opportunity cost" of private capital borrowed at long term would have been enough to make the canal a sure loser. Moreover, while costs in such a project are real and usually rising, the benefits are mostly speculative, which generally means that any project with a benefit-cost ratio of less than 2 to 1 should be regarded as possibly marginal or worse.[10] In any case, canal proponents had no chance of making dour old Clarence Cannon see merit in their project.

By mid-October 1962, the Senate had included funds for the project in its public works appropriation bill but the House had not. Representative

10. This is a rule of thumb applied to projects such as the barge canal by Robert E. Jordan III, now an attorney in private practice in Washington, but formerly special assistant (for civil functions) to the Secretary of the Army. In an interview with the author Jordan acknowledged that some Corps of Engineers navigation projects have actually returned substantially higher benefits than those reflected in the project's "B-C" ratio. Yet, he said, the explanation here is that in years past the corps often stopped looking for benefits once enough had been found to give a project an acceptable ratio. Thus, according to Jordan, where a project with a B-C ratio of, say, 2 to 1 has turned out to have a ratio of 4 to 1, there is the strong possibility that the higher ratio would have been established in the first place had the corps study been more thorough. Jordan believes, however, that in the economic analyses being made today, the corps is scratching for all the benefits it can find.

Lonely relics of the 1935 barge canal project that was halted within a year of its commencement. *Facing page, left,* aerial view of the Oklawaha River in the foreground and part of the Cross Florida Barge Canal; *right,* a completed segment of the Cross Florida Barge Canal.

William Partington

Photos by Patricia Caulfield

Robert Sikes, a senior member of Cannon's committee, offered an amendment in the best pork-barrel tradition: besides money for the barge canal, it would provide funds for projects in Texas, Oregon, Washington, and Illinois. The canal proponents were putting all they had into this vote. At their urging, President Kennedy had asked Speaker John W. McCormack and Majority Leader Carl Albert to support the amendment actively. The venerable chairman of the Armed Services Committee, Carl Vinson, had earlier obliged Congressman Bennett (a member of Vinson's committee) by stating that the canal was "very essential [to] our national defense." As the Sikes amendment was about to carry, Clarence Cannon was moved to observe: "No bigger bunch of pirates ever sailed the Spanish Main. All the money that Captain Kidd and Long John Silver stole is infinitesimal compared to this raid on the federal treasury."[11] Thereafter, however, the canal project was to fare well enough in Congress.

Work on the canal began with a chicken barbecue and groundbreaking near Palatka in February 1964 and President Lyndon B. Johnson was there to set off the first dynamite charge. Johnson gave his remarks a pronounced biblical ring. "God was good to this country," the President said, "but in His wisdom, the Creator left some things for men to do themselves. . . . The challenge of a modern society is to make the resources of nature useful and beneficial to the community. This is the passkey to economic growth, to sensible and valid prosperity." By the end of the decade, environmentalists would challenge the point of view LBJ expressed and would argue that in many cases the way to get the most out of nature is to leave her alone.

In any event, the groundbreaking put Floridians on notice that the canal project was indeed again alive and well, although several more years would pass before major work would begin along the Oklawaha River. The project's environmental implications extended beyond the regions directly affected by the canal itself. For instance, construction of the barge canal would help revive interest in another old unbuilt waterway project—the Intracoastal Waterway's so-called Missing Link between Tampa and the tiny Gulf port town of St. Marks in the Florida panhandle. A sheltered coastal passage could serve the same ordinary river barges that would use the cross Florida canal, such barges being cheaper to build and operate than the big barges capable of crossing the open Gulf. Yet if this 234-mile-long waterway (first authorized by Congress in 1937) were built largely through the coastal marshes—as the Corps of Engineers had proposed—another of Florida's few relatively undisturbed large regional ecosystems (see figure 1–8) might be lost.

THE CAMPAIGN TO SAVE THE OKLAWAHA

The campaign to save the Oklawaha began in Gainesville, a city some 25 miles from the Oklawaha, mostly among people associated with the University of Florida. In fact it is fair to say that, without this university, there probably would have been no campaign at all, or at least not an effective one. The university, with its old buildings, live oaks, palms, and small ponds or sink holes, has the distinctive flavor of north central Florida. Although not one of America's great institutions, this university, along with Florida State University in Tallahassee, is preeminent in Florida, both in the extent of its intellectual resources and in the position and influence of its alumni. By national standards, the school itself is conservatively run, yet, in the

11. Quoted by Edward A. Fernald, in his unpublished study *An Optimum Land Use Model for a Delimited Area Contiguous to the Cross Florida Barge Canal*, prepared for the Canal Authority of the State of Florida, 1967, p. 55.

Florida context, its faculty is relatively liberal and includes some social activists.

One highly respected faculty member at the university is Archie F. Carr, graduate research professor of zoology and leading authority on the life history of marine turtles. Although long concerned about the steady degradation of the Florida environment, Carr himself has usually stayed busy at his campus laboratory and his field station in the Caribbean. However, his wife, Marjorie, a professional naturalist in her own right, was one of the two prime movers in the campaign to save the Oklawaha. Her long familiarity with the river goes back to the time when, as a student, she worked as a biological research station technician. An open, friendly person, Carr is committed, energetic, and, she would concede, politically naive enough to lead an unpromising cause.

At a board meeting of Gainesville's Alachua Audubon Society in the late fall of 1962, Carr and David S. Anthony, a biochemist and associate professor in the university's Institute of Food and Agricultural Sciences, discussed the canal project, which was then in the news because of the recent appropriation by Congress. Their subsequent inquiry to a Florida congressman about how the Oklawaha River would be affected was referred to the Corps of Engineers. It brought a bland reply. "The obfuscation was so consistent we came to believe that it was deliberate," Anthony told me. As the result of further inquiries, however, a clear picture emerged: of the some 50 miles of the Oklawaha that still remained a free-flowing wilderness stream the corps planned to eliminate about 40 miles of it by building two large, shallow reservoirs through which the channel for barges would be cut. Furthermore, not only would most of the natural river be lost but also some 27,000 acres of the adjacent swamp forest would be destroyed. This hydric hammock and swamp forest was important both in itself and as a part of the larger regional ecosystem that included the Ocala National Forest. For instance, it was a roosting place for birds such as the white ibis, an escape cover for the heavily hunted deer in the Big Scrub, and an important part of the habitat of the wide-ranging Florida panther (an endangered species), which frequents both upland and lowland areas. The upshot was that Marjorie Carr and David Anthony, using Alachua Audubon as their base, set about to persuade the Corps of Engineers to change its plans and spare the Oklawaha.

The "Save the Oklawaha" effort had two early objectives: one was to arouse Florida conservationists and Floridians generally against the plan to route the canal through the river valley; the other was to get the Corps of Engineers to hold a public hearing on the question of an alternative routing. No real hearing about the canal had been conducted in Florida since 1940. During the first few years of their campaign to save the river, Carr, Anthony, and other Alachua Audubon leaders such as Jack Ohanian, a physicist at the university, wrote hundreds of letters to conservation leaders, newspaper editors, Corps of Engineer officers, state officials, members of Congress—indeed to anyone who might be able to help or give useful information. At this time, there was no intention on the part of the Save the Oklawaha group to stop the canal project altogether. "We conservationists don't give a hoot about the canal, either way," Carr told an interviewer in 1966. "We are just pro-Oklawaha."[12]

UP AGAINST A FORMIDABLE APPARATUS. From the time the campaign to save the Oklawaha began in late 1962 until almost the end of the decade it would seem truly hopeless. Marjorie Carr and her small band of Alachua Audubon people were up against a formidable federal-state institutional apparatus as well as the political and business establishments of Jacksonville and the canal right-of-way counties together with their supporters in the legislature and Congress. These institutions were:

• *The Corps of Engineers and the office of its Jacksonville District Engineer.* Although the 1942 authorization act did not prescribe a specific route for the canal, the district engineer's office was committed to the Oklawaha Valley route. And, in the early and middle 1960s, the corps' prestige and authority as an experienced water resources agency was such that its judgments on the routing of a canal, which many would regard as a largely technical matter, were not easily challenged. Also, there was the fact that many of the corps' most important policies and practices, such as its way of establishing benefit-cost analyses, were expressly mandated by Congress.

• *The Canal Authority.* This agency, successor to the Ship Canal Authority, was established under a 1961 statute and was now directed by a retired Corps of Engineers colonel. Based not in Tallahassee but in Jacksonville and governed by its own board of gubernatorial appointees, the authority was free to do largely as it chose, at least within those budget constraints that the governor, cabinet, and legislature saw fit to impose. In 1969, the Canal Authority would be placed in the new Department of Natural Resources, but it would be a loosely attached appendage.

• *The Florida Board of Conservation* (later to become the Department of Natural Resources). Randolph Hodges, a former state senator from the Gulf coast village of Cedar Key and a strong supporter of the canal project, was director of this agency from 1961 until early 1974. Upon assuming this position, Hodges, together with his board (the governor and the cabinet), initiated an important new policy: instead of allowing the various localities and water resource agencies, such as the Central and Southern Florida Flood Control District, to make their own individual—and competitive—requests to Congress for public works funds, a comprehensive water resources budget would be developed each year by Hodges and his staff and reviewed

12. Andrew Sparks, "One Woman's Fight to Save a River," the Atlanta *Constitution and Journal* magazine, August 14, 1966.

for cabinet approval. In principle, this was a rational policy and procedure, but, in practice, the effect was to put a premium on maintaining a united front in the face of the U.S. Bureau of the Budget and Congress and to leave priorities obscured. For instance, it would be difficult to argue that building the barge canal was as important as expanding water storage capacity in south Florida; yet $52 million in federal funds were spent on the canal while work on raising the Lake Okeechobee levee was allowed to lag. In 1967, Hodges hired as head of the unit responsible for water resources development Colonel J. V. Sollohub, the former Jacksonville District Engineer who recommended the canal project for construction in 1962. By the end of the 1960s Hodges would have four other former Corps of Engineers officers on his staff (one being the manager of the Canal Authority), giving rise to sardonic comment around Tallahassee that he was running a retirement village for corps colonels. For Hodges the key to tenure in his job was not so much to please the governor as it was to please the cabinet well enough on any given mix of issues to keep a majority of the members always behind him. Thus, in a real sense, "Senator" Hodges, as he was still known in Tallahassee, performed in a political as well as an administrative role.

• *The Cabinet.* Development-oriented by long tradition, this body was committed to the barge canal project both by philosophy and by virtue of the backgrounds of some of its most influential members. During the early and mid-1960s two successive governors, who served of course as cabinet chairmen, were from localities along the canal route: Farris Bryant of Ocala, during the years 1961–64; followed by the former mayor-commissioner of Jacksonville, Haydon Burns, governor during 1965–66 (serving a special two-year transitional term). Secretary of State Tom Adams, also a cabinet member, was not only a former state senator from Clay County, on the canal route, but was chairman of the board (and later president) of the Mississippi Valley Association, one of the major waterway development groups.

THE CABINET WON'T LISTEN. David Anthony recalls how, in October 1965, a few years after the Save the Oklawaha campaign began, his group tried to be heard at a meeting of the Canal Authority in Ocala. "They would not hear us at all. When Mrs. Kenneth Morrison [wife of the director of the Mountain Lake Sanctuary at Lake Wales] tried to speak for Audubon, the attorney for the authority tried to outshout her." Nevertheless, by early 1966 the Save the Oklawaha group was getting attention in the Florida press and its cause was no longer possible to ignore. Governor Burns agreed that all who wanted to speak on the canal issue would be heard at the cabinet's annual water resources development conference, which in effect is a hearing on the makeup of the entire water resources development program for which federal funds will be sought. The January 1966 hearing is the one that I re-

ferred to in Chapter 2 as the event that marked the beginning of concerted action by Florida conservation leaders and led ultimately to the
establishment of Conservation '70s as a potent Tallahassee lobby. Carr,
Anthony, and others at Alachua Audubon urged conservationists throughout Florida to attend this meeting. The response was remarkable. People
came from as far away as the keys, and an entire busload showed up from
southeast Florida. Altogether, more than 400 persons crowded into the
chamber of the Florida House of Representatives where the hearing was
held, and most were there to support the Save the Oklawaha campaign.
Some sixty persons managed to get to speak in support of the campaign,
either as individuals or representing garden clubs, state and local Audubon
and Izaak Walton League organizations, and other conservation groups. The
only cabinet member who had bothered to be present to hear their appeal
for a rerouting of the canal was Secretary of State Adams. Furthermore, the
pro forma nature of the hearing as viewed by the Corps of Engineers had
been revealed when the corps announced, not long before the hearing, that
bids on the contract for building the first of two dams on the Oklawaha
would soon be opened.

In a statement presented for Alachua and Florida Audubon, David
Anthony observed that, by sheer good luck, the attractive features of the
Oklawaha basin and its surrounding lands, which naturalist William Bartram
had marveled at two centuries earlier, still remained: the clear-flowing
springs, the numerous lakes, the Big Scrub, and the Oklawaha and its vast
swamp forest. Now, however, the Oklawaha was threatened by a canal
routing adopted by the Corps of Engineers some twenty-five years earlier
and since retained without evaluation by any state or federal agency concerned with use of wilderness resources. Interior's Bureau of Sport Fisheries and Wildlife and the Florida Game and Fresh Water Fish Commission
had been consulted about the details of the project but not about the canal
alignment, Anthony noted. He pointed out that in 1963 a joint study team
of the departments of Agriculture and Interior had identified the Oklawaha
as one of several score streams in the United States worthy of preserving
as wild and scenic rivers. "We want to know [the study team's] estimate of
the monetary value of the Oklawaha as a wild river," Anthony said. The
recreation benefits later claimed by the Corps of Engineers for the two
reservoirs planned for the Oklawaha valley would constitute about a fourth
of all project benefits and would be critical to maintaining a favorable benefit-cost ratio. Yet implied in Anthony's argument was the point that, as a
wild river, the Oklawaha was a relatively rare asset, whereas the value of
two new reservoirs would be limited in view of the fact that in north central
Florida lakes are anything but rare. Indeed, within a radius of 85 miles from
the reservoir sites there are 875 lakes above small pond size and these include numerous large and publicly accessible lakes such as Lake George,
Lake Orange, Lake Lockloosa, Lake Weir, and the six Oklawaha basin

headwaters lakes (see figure 9–2). Within 30 miles of the reservoir sites, there are some 200,000 acres of water surface.

Some months earlier, the staff of the U.S. Senate's Committee on Public Works had, at the request of the Save the Oklawaha group and Senator George Smathers, asked the Corps of Engineers to consider an alternate route for the canal which would largely avoid the Oklawaha valley by crossing the Ocala National Forest. The corps had done so from a review of available maps, and, just prior to the cabinet hearing, a copy of its report was given to the cabinet and Secretary of State Adams but not to the Save the Oklawaha people. The report, a brief, five-page document, said that, if the canal were rerouted, that part of the Oklawaha below Silver Springs run would virtually dry up during severe droughts. It overlooked the possibility that a pumping station could be installed to maintain the flow of the river under drought conditions. The report also concluded that the rerouting would ruin the project's economic feasibility by increasing costs and reducing benefits. As Colonel Avery S. Fullerton, Jacksonville District Engineer from 1970 to 1972, acknowledged to me, relatively little effort had gone into this study. Yet, without doubt, the report was correct in its strongly implied conclusion that to consider rerouting the canal now would be to risk losing the project altogether. At the hearing, Secretary of State Adams embittered the Save the Oklawaha supporters by what they regarded as his hostile, harassing questions. His performance was captured in a half-hour movie on the canal that would be played for years afterwards to arouse people against the project. About a month after the hearing the cabinet voted unanimously to reconfirm its support for routing the canal through the Oklawaha valley.

PART OF THE OKLAWAHA IS LOST. The first phase of the Save the Oklawaha campaign was over, and it appeared for a time that it was the last. Maybe a third of the canal project was completed during the years 1966 through 1969, and counties at the east and west ends of the canal were moving to establish barge ports. The Rodman Dam was built in the lower Oklawaha valley and, behind it, a huge 306-ton Crawler Crusher smashed some 6,445 acres of swamp forest in the mud and thus prepared the reservoir for filling. The dam was closed in September 1968 and by mid-1969 about 20 miles of the lower Oklawaha had been flooded by the waters of the so-called Rodman Pool. South of this pool work was underway on the Eureka Lock and Dam, and, once the Eureka Pool was cleared and the dam closed, the wild Oklawaha, or all but the lower 10 miles of it, would be gone. Altogether, three of the canal system's five locks were finished by mid-1969, and the excavation of the canal at its east and west ends (except in the Saint Johns River) was also completed. What primarily remained to be done, besides clearing and filling the Eureka Reservoir, was to dredge the channels in the reservoirs and to build the canal's 35-mile-long "summit" reach, which was to be costly and time-consuming because of the higher terrain.

THE PROJECT IS IN TROUBLE

Signs of trouble for the canal project began appearing in 1968 and '69. The Vietnam War had led to sharply reduced canal appropriations, and project sponsors were deploring the fact that, at the current rate of funding, the project would not be finished until the end of the century. Furthermore, after legislative reapportionment became effective in 1967, there was a growing potential for conflict in Tallahassee over the project: there were fewer legislators on hand from north Florida to promote the canal and more from south Florida to ponder it with concern. In addition, there was growing evidence to substantiate predictions by Save the Oklawaha people that the tree-shaded, free-flowing river would become a sunlit, weed-choked nutrient trap if impounded as a reservoir. During two and a half months in 1969 some 3,000 acres of Rodman Pool became covered with a luxuriant and explosive growth of water hyacinths. To destroy them with chemical spray as the corps had to do only meant an increased rate of accumulation of rotting organic material in the reservoir and faster recycling of weed-trapped nutrients. Also, smashing the river forest with the Crawler-Crusher had been an error in public relations as well as a dubious tactic in resource management. The forest was crushed into the mud because to have cut and removed the trees would have taken more money than sale of the timber would have brought. On the other hand, with logs continually popping to the surface, the reservoir was unsightly and a threat to boatsmen. Articles and photographs in Florida newspapers about the "tree crusher," the mats of water hyacinths, and the loss of the river were putting the Corps of Engineers and the canal project in an embarrassing light at the very time ecology was becoming a household word. In late 1968, these developments were reviewed in a special edition of the Florida Audubon Society's *Conservation Digest*, and the digest's editor, William M. Partington, concluded that the Oklawaha might be saved after all. Partington was right, and he was himself to be a leader of the effort to kill the canal project.

THE FLORIDA DEFENDERS OF THE ENVIRONMENT. The revival of the Save the Oklawaha campaign in 1969 was, in part, directly related to the rapid growth during the late 1960s of what was coming to be known as "environmental law." A number of attorneys and law school professors were working in this relatively undeveloped field of legal action, but, if there was any one individual chiefly responsible for dramatizing it, this was Victor J. Yannacone, Jr., a ubiquitous young Long Island attorney whose motto was "sue the bastards." The Environmental Defense Fund (EDF), established in 1967 with Yannacone as one of the prime movers, was not the first organization established to undertake suits in the interests of conservation. But EDF nevertheless represented a major innovation—an organization with a significant scientific capability dedicated to using the courts for environmental protection. Charles F. Wurster, Jr., a biologist at the University of New York at Stony Brook and cofounder of EDF, developed a large scientists advisory committee for EDF, which provided information—and often witnesses—for court challenges on use of hard pesticides and other environmental issues. Furthermore, EDF suits were often initiated and supported financially by university scientists. In early 1969 an article appeared in Sports Illustrated about EDF and the ebulliently aggressive Yannacone.[13] Lee Ogden, an industrial design consultant in Gainesville and a member of Alachua Audubon, read it with excitement. If EDF could bring suit against agencies threatening ecosystems by use of DDT, why couldn't it sue to stop the Corps of Engineers from destroying the Oklawaha ecosystem? Reaching Yannacone by phone, Ogden told him he must come to Florida and challenge the corps. Yannacone was enthusiastic at the idea, but he made it clear that local sponsors of the suit would have to raise the money to support the action.

As matters turned out, EDF would later get enough support from foundations and a fast growing list of contributors (up to 47,000 by 1974) to meet the cost of the barge canal suit and other cases, but this was not then foreseeable. In an act of faith, Ogden promised that the money would be found, somehow. The Florida Defenders of the Environment was to be the vehicle for accomplishing this. As noted in an earlier chapter, the Florida Defenders or "FDE," a switch on "EDF," was formed in mid-July 1969 at the same time Conservation '70s was established, with a number of the same people becoming members or trustees of both. Wurster of the Environmental Defense Fund was present when FDE was organized and the example set by EDF with its scientists advisory committee was reflected in the makeup of the board: of the twenty-nine FDE trustees twenty would be Ph.D.s, mostly biologists but with a geologist, an economist, and a political scientist also included. A third of the trustees were from the University of Florida, but there were some from the University of Miami and other institutions. A few conservation group leaders were among the trustees; Marjorie Carr of course was one, and another was William Partington of Florida Audubon, who was to become president of FDE and give it all of his time for over a year and a half.

Forming an entirely new group to oppose the canal offered several advantages. One was that FDE could focus exclusively on the canal fight. Another was that, by creating FDE, canal opponents neatly sidestepped the troublesome fact that the leadership of established conservation groups was divided on the canal issue. Even among the officers of Florida Audubon

13. Gilbert Rogin, "All He Wants to Save Is the World," Sports Illustrated, February 3, 1969.

there were some who favored the canal project. As for C-70s, some of its members, such as State Representative Gus Craig of St. Augustine and State Senator J. H. Williams of Ocala, had been leading proponents of the canal. Also, neither of Governor Kirk's environmental advisers, Nathaniel Reed and Lyman Rogers, could become identified with FDE without embarrassing the governor, who at the time felt he had to favor completion of the project. This new group, unlike the Save the Oklawaha group, was bent on not merely saving the river, but also stopping the canal project. Reinforcing this attitude was the influence of Paul E. Roberts, a young University of Florida economist who regarded the project as economically indefensible; of Ariel Lugo, a botanist and systems analyst who foresaw tragic environmental consequences if the project went forward; and of Martin D. Mifflin, a geologist much concerned about the project's possible effect on the Floridan Aquifer. Also, there was on the part of some FDE trustees a strong sense of grievance against the Corps of Engineers and the Florida Cabinet, an attitude traceable to the 1966 cabinet hearing on the canal and the hostile reception that conservationists felt they got there.

The Florida Defenders of the Environment was to provide a striking example of how a small, university-based group with modest financial resources but a lot of volunteer help sometimes can influence judicial and other governmental decisions, both directly and by altering the political climate surrounding an issue. FDE was to do this by establishing credibility with the press, government study teams and advisory groups, and some strategically placed legislators. Certainly, some of FDE's findings and views would be debatable, but they were persuasive for many competent environmentalists not party to the anticanal campaign as well as for a wide public. During the first three years of its existence, from mid-1969 to mid-1972, FDE would raise about $65,000, most of which was obtained in small contributions through mailings directed at members of Florida conservation organizations and other sympathetic groups. Nearly all this money was to be available for maintaining a small staff and headquarters inasmuch as the $50- to $60,000 burden of carrying on the suit against the Corps of Engineers during this period was to be borne by the Environmental Defense Fund. For an office, FDE rented a tiny room for $40 a month in a shabby downtown Gainesville office building. Partington worked for FDE partly out of his Florida Audubon office at Maitland and partly at the Gainesville office, where numerous volunteers and a succession of meagerly paid young office assistants also worked. This modest team equipped only with a typewriter, a telephone, and a Xerox machine, was taking on the Corps of Engineers and the Canal Authority in what might have seemed an unequal match. But FDE was to receive the help of some of the best scientific and professional talent in Florida, and the work thus obtained would appear all the more credible because no consultant's fees were involved. On the matter of credibility, David Anthony believes that FDE built up trust with visiting writers and reporters by giving them unrestricted access to its extensive files, containing news clippings going back to the early 1960s and hundreds of scientific papers, Corps of Engineers reports, letters, and other documents. Such visitors came in considerable numbers, especially in late 1969 and 1970 as the environment became an increasingly popular topic with the public and the press. The Canal Authority would, in desperation, take on a public relations consultant at $1,600 a month, distribute "Cross Florida Canal Booster" bumper stickers, and, on one occasion, spend $1,500 taking outdoor writers to Rodman Pool for fishing and sight-seeing.

EDF SUES, FDE WRITES AN IMPACT STATEMENT. The EDF suit against the Corps of Engineers was filed by Victor Yannacone in September 1969 in the U.S. District Court for the District of Columbia. The court was asked to stop construction of the project pending a determination of the canal's "total social cost and real social benefits." However, in thus challenging a congressionally authorized project, Yannacone (who would shortly be parting company with EDF and leaving the canal case to other EDF attorneys) was attempting to do something that the Florida lawyers consulted by the Save the Oklawaha group had said could not be done. Indeed, it was only the passage, late in the year, of the National Environmental Policy Act of 1969 (NEPA) that caused prospects for the outcome of this lawsuit to brighten. NEPA would figure importantly in the controversy over the canal by requiring environmental impact statements on such projects and by providing for the establishment of the President's Council on Environmental Quality, which would give FDE a chance to influence policy directly at the White House.

In the fall of 1969, several months before NEPA became law, FDE began working on its own environmental impact study of the canal's potential impact on the Oklawaha valley and the Floridan Aquifer. The idea of making such a study was discussed by the FDE leaders in the late summer of 1969 but was not sharpened and refined until after the impact report on the Big Cypress jetport had appeared in September. In fact, the coauthor of that report, Arthur Marshall, was invited by Partington to come to Gainesville and participate in an FDE meeting at which preparation of the report on the canal was encouraged. With Partington and Marjorie Carr pushing and cajoling the others participating in the effort, such a document was finally prepared under the imprimatur of a board of editors of twenty-six members, a majority of them FDE trustees. In this 117-page document, entitled *Environmental Impact of the Cross Florida Barge Canal with Special Emphasis on the Oklawaha Regional Ecosystem*, FDE recommended that the canal project be stopped immediately and that the Rodman Pool be drained in order to permit regrowth of the swamp forest. This recommendation was arrived at after a description of the Oklawaha region, a brief account of the region's history and the origins of the canal project, a critique of the Corps of Engineers' benefit-cost analysis, and a detailed discussion of the project's impact on the Oklawaha basin environment. Although its principal thrust was that north central Florida's only remaining large natural ecosystem was being destroyed for a navigation project of doubtful economic value, the report also warned that, along part of the canal's summit reach, water would flow from the canal into the aquifer and discharge at Silver Springs, representing about 8 percent of the springs' total flow. There was thus at least the possibility of the canal's polluting and discoloring the marvelously clear waters that make these springs one of central Florida's major tourist attractions. The report was completed and made public in March 1970 at a hearing of the Committee on Natural Resources of the Florida Senate, and it contributed to that committee's recommendation that the corps restudy the canal project.

The findings of the FDE report were consistent with, and in part supported by, those in two earlier reports, also critical of the canal project but of more limited scope. In 1967, the Corps of Engineers itself had received, at its request, a report from the Federal Water Pollution Control Administration but chose not to make it public. Then, in November 1969, a report on the canal requested by a Florida legislative committee was released by the Florida Game and Fresh Water Fish Commission. Graphics contained in this document and reproduced in the FDE report illustrated strikingly (see figure 9–3) the drastic ecological upset that construction of the canal would cause in the Oklawaha valley. The Game and Fish Commission, it should be noted, was only nominally a part of the new Florida Department of Natural Resources created under the Governmental Reorganization Act. Neither the cabinet nor Randolph Hodges, director of the department, was able to assert authority over the commission because of that agency's independent status under the Florida Constitution, a status first conferred in 1942 but since reaffirmed. As it was, the Game and Fish Commission staff, largely free of inhibiting bureaucratic controls, had acted boldly in an intensely controversial situation and had produced a forthright document.

By the time the FDE report was made public in March 1970, major developments in the campaign against the canal project were occurring in both Florida and Washington. In most of Florida, the project was now probably more of a political liability than an asset for any legislative or gubernatorial candidate supporting it. Governor Kirk, in a letter written in May to Secretary of the Interior Hickel, said "The current controversy over the canal is like a cancer gnawing at the citizens of my state."[14]

WASHINGTON: THE BUREAUCRATIC INTERPLAY. In Washington, besides the case pending in federal court, the canal project was coming to the attention of the White House, the President's new Council on Environmental

14. Letter from Kirk to Hickel, May 14, 1970.

1. Oklawaha River flood plain with natural average water level

2. Oklawaha River flood plain with natural high water level —nature's biological waste treatment complex at work.

Nutrients seeping into flood plain floor utilized by vegetation

3. Oklawaha River with reservoirs drowning the waste treatment complex, exposing it to conditions of eutrophication.

4. Oklawaha River flood plain —Rodman and Eureka Pools (near future)

5. Oklawaha River Flood Plain —Rodman and Eureka Pools (ultimately)

9.3

Ecologic changes to result from flooding the Oklawaha River

Source: Addendum Report, Florida Game and Fresh Water Fish Commission, March 1970.

Quality, (CEQ), and the officials of two federal departments, Army and Interior. The complex interplay I shall touch on here points up how abstract most issues become at high levels in the federal establishment, how much chance and personality play in what (if anything) is done about them, and how the deliberations of officials at this level are hidden from public view. Apart from the officials at the White House itself, no one in Washington was to play so important a role in the canal controversy as the officials at the CEQ. What brought this agency into the matter was a letter to President Nixon by environmental scientists urging that he declare a moratorium on construction of the canal and have environmental studies made. At the suggestion of Kenneth Morrison of the Mountain Lake Sanctuary at Lake Wales and a trustee of Conservation '70s, David Anthony and other FDE people had prepared such a letter in late January and mailed copies to 175 scientists in Florida and elsewhere. Within ten days, signed copies of the letter had been returned by 150 of the scientists and others would be returned later to bring the total to 162. The signers included many of the best-known environmentalists in the United States: among them were Barry Commoner, René Dubos, G. Evelyn Hutchinson, Eugene P. Odum, and three past presidents of the Ecological Society of America, Frank W. Blair, John E. Cantalon, and Lamont C. Cole. Many of the signers had no firsthand knowledge of the Oklawaha basin or the canal project and were taking their Florida colleagues' assessment of the canal issue on faith—a fact which would give rise to bitter, contemptuous comment among canal supporters after the project was stopped.

The scientists' letter, mailed to the President on February 6, was well timed. The President was just then appointing the members of CEQ, and one of the first matters referred to the new council was this letter. Both Russell Train, chairman of CEQ, and John Whitaker, the White House aide on environmental matters, made inquiries to the Department of the Army about the canal project. These were referred to Robert E. Jordan III, the secretary's special assistant for civil functions, and he, in turn, delegated the task of preparing a memorandum on the canal to an assistant, Charles Ford. By coincidence, Ford was a native Floridian and had known the Oklawaha from boyhood, having fished and camped on the river with his father. Moreover, since he had been chief of the hydraulic design section of the Corps of Engineers Jacksonville District during the early-to-mid-1960s, the canal project was one with which he was also intimately familiar. "I'd never thought it was a good project," Ford told me. "I always had to lean over backwards to give it its due." Ford let Jordan know this, but Jordan trusted his aide's objectivity. By late April, the report had been prepared, reviewed by Jordan, and submitted to Whitaker and CEQ. The essence of the report was this: construction of the canal should continue, but along an alternate route that would spare the still undisturbed part of the Oklawaha valley. About this same time, Colonel Avery S. Fullerton, the corps' Jacksonville

District Engineer presented the idea of an alternate routing to Partington, who viewed it dubiously. He did not believe that FDE members or other canal opponents would accept this compromise. In his view, the proposal ignored the fact that the project, even though somewhat modified, might nevertheless threaten both the river swamp ecosystem and the Floridan Aquifer. Also, Partington felt that termination of the project could be justified purely on economic grounds.

In Ford's opinion, however, abandonment of the project was clearly not warranted given the $52-million federal investment already made in it. Ford gave no credence to some of the allegations that had been made, such as the charge that Rodman Pool was doomed to rapid eutrophication or that the aquifer was endangered. Yet his report to Jordan suggested that, in deciding what should be done, CEQ should not look to federal resource agencies but to independent experts "whose vision is not blurred by bureaucratic myopia." This suggestion was also put to Partington by Colonel Fullerton, who suggested that the study be made by the National Academy of Sciences. Partington countered that FDE itself constituted a ready-made group of independent experts.

The recommendation for an independent study was not followed up by CEQ. Russell Train and his two colleagues on the council, Gordon MacDonald and Robert Cahn, already were persuaded that the canal project should be stopped. Prior to Earth Day, the CEQ staff had prepared, at the council's direction, a list of water projects to be recommended for cancellation or restudy. This list, which MacDonald reviewed for the council and personally endorsed, gave cancellation of the barge canal as its top priority. Alvin L. Alm, then CEQ's staff director for program development, and one of his associates, William K. Reilly (now president of the Conservation Foundation in Washington), discussed the list at a meeting with John C. Whitaker, the presidential aide responsible for environmental affairs, and Edwin L. Harper, a member of the White House Domestic Council staff. According to one of those present at this meeting, Whitaker was favorable to the idea of terminating the canal project except for one troublesome consideration. Harold Carswell, one of two Nixon nominees for the Supreme Court whom the U.S. Senate had refused to confirm, was now running for the Senate and was afraid that a White House order killing the canal would also kill his chances in the upcoming Florida Republican primary election. The upshot was that no further thought was given to terminating the project until the late fall, after both primary and general elections were over.

Secretary of the Interior Hickel and his department had stepped into the canal controversy even before CEQ as the indirect result, it appeared, of a *Reader's Digest* article entitled "Rape on the Oklawaha." James Nathan Miller, author of this article in the magazine's January 1970 issue, had followed closely the emergence of FDE and was even present at the July 1969 meeting in Orlando at which the group was organized. Miller described the canal project as a "promoter's dream," a "boondoggle" being justified by benefit-cost analysis flimflammery, and an assault on a "magnificent primordial river" where the stillness may be broken by the "slurp of an alligator slithering off a log." The *Reader's Digest* has few intellectual pretensions, but the fact that its American subscribers number more than 18 million gives it an influence greater than that of many publications that have a high brow and a low circulation. Miller's article inspired hundreds of letters protesting the canal project and many of them were addressed to Secretary Hickel, who long since had succeeded in changing his public image from that of one who wanted to pave the world to that of the conservationists' champion. These letters were referred to the Bureau of Sport Fisheries and Wildlife's river basin studies division, which reviews Corps of Engineers projects in connection with Interior's responsibilities under the Fish and Wildlife Coordination Act. Arthur W. Dickson, the branch chief who drafts replies to such letters, had seen the canal a year or so before this, while traveling with Art Marshall, then still a top Florida employee of the bureau. They had stopped at the Highway 19 bridge over the west end of the canal and walked down to the spoil embankment. The only green living thing in sight was a tiny cactus, which Dickson uprooted and took back to Washington as a souvenir. Now, with outraged letters about the canal piling up on his desk, Dickson and his agency had to respond. Before the end of January 1970, the river basin studies division had, on its own initiative, asked its Atlanta regional office for a review and appraisal of the barge canal project. The report by the Atlanta office, ready by the end of March, was essentially a brief summary of some of the existing information about the canal project's environmental impact and it quoted extensively from both the FDE and the Florida Game and Fish Commission reports, among others. The Bureau of Sport Fisheries and Wildlife moved swiftly to ask Secretary Hickel to initiate the further investigations which the report indicated were needed. Accordingly, on June 5, 1970, in a letter to Secretary of the Army Stanley Resor, Hickel requested a fifteen-month moratorium on further construction of the canal project pending an environmental study by Interior. Hickel also asked the director of the interagency Water Resources Council to have his staff review the canal project's economics.

By normal bureaucratic standards, Secretary Hickel was behaving in a meddlesome manner. In the case of the Big Cypress jetport, Hickel intervened in a project supported by the Department of Transportation in order to protect Everglades National Park; but there was nothing in the Oklawaha valley under his jurisdiction and nothing that Interior had even proposed to acquire. Yet here he was trying to hold up a Corps of Engineers project on which many millions had already been spent. Without waiting for a reply from the Secretary of the Army or bothering to consult CEQ or the White House, Hickel announced publicly that the moratorium had been requested. Further, he indicated that the special environmental study would soon be underway. Yet, in June of 1970, Hickel was in a poor way to expect the White House backing needed if, in this new dispute, he was to score the kind of success he had won in the jetport controversy. His well publicized letter advising President Nixon that the President was alienating American youth with his prosecution of the Vietnam War had somehow "leaked" to the press. Some observers already were predicting, accurately, that after the fall elections Hickel would be dismissed from the cabinet. Also, the secretary's proposal for a moratorium and study was as coldly received in Congress as it was at the White House. In a letter to Hickel, Spessard Holland, a senior member of the Senate Committee on Appropriations, declared himself opposed to the moratorium and to the release of any funds for the study. The House and Senate subcommittees on public works appropriations stated that no further study was needed. An amendment offered on the Senate floor by George S. McGovern to withhold further construction funds pending an ecological and economic study was easily defeated.

THE CORPS PROPOSES AN ALTERNATE ROUTE. Yet, while there would be no moratorium declared and no funds allocated for a special Interior study of the canal project, Hickel's proposal would bring a response from the Department of the Army and the Corps of Engineers. After the enactment of NEPA and the inquiries made by CEQ and John Whitaker, the White House aide, the corps' South Atlantic Division and Jacksonville District had—in keeping with Charles Ford's thinking—begun developing a plan to "save" the 20-mile-long stretch of the Oklawaha above the Rodman Pool. This was not, however, to be accomplished by rerouting the canal out of the Oklawaha valley as the corps had perfunctorily considered doing in 1965. Instead, it would be done by confining both the canal channel and the Eureka Reservoir to the western edge of the Oklawaha flood plain by enclosing them behind a levee (see figure 9–4). The existing Rodman Pool would remain part of the canal system. The corps wanted to follow management practices (such as periodically raising and lowering the pool by a few feet) by which the reservoir might be kept in good condition for recreational use. According to the corps' estimates, the cost of the overall project would be increased by about $5 million, and the benefit-cost ratio would remain favorable at about 1.3 to 1, or about 0.1 less than the ratio for the original plan. Moreover, according to the new plan, enough water would be available, even during droughts, to provide for the lockage needs of the canal system and maintain a flow in the river at least equivalent to the minimum of record. Pending a decision on its proposal, the corps would initiate no new work for the Eureka segment of the canal but would continue work elsewhere.

At the Secretary of the Army's office, Robert Jordan saw in the new plan an acceptable way to save an economically dubious project, which he wished never had been started but which was now so far along that he felt

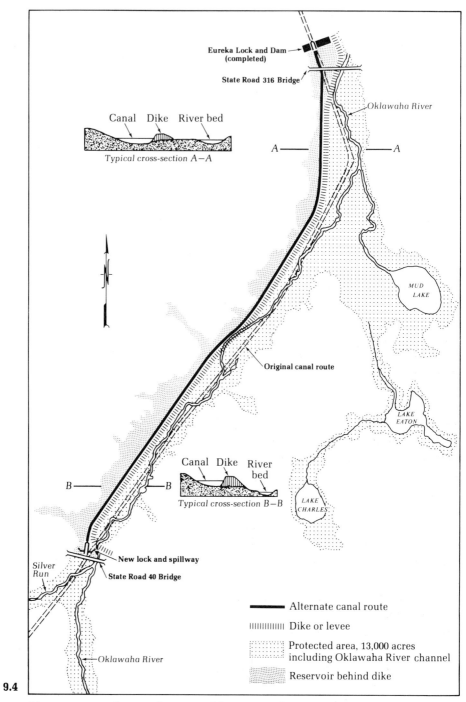

9.4 Alternate route for canal proposed by Corps of Engineers

it should not be stopped. In July, Jordan disclosed the plan to Assistant Secretary of the Interior Leslie Glasgow (for fish, wildlife, and parks) and James T. McBroom, special assistant to the director of the Bureau of Sport Fisheries and Wildlife. Both Glasgow and McBroom felt that, given the circumstances, the plan represented a substantial effort by the corps and the Department of the Army to develop a compromise solution. But when Glasgow brought the new proposal to his attention, Secretary Hickel was not interested. "He asked me, 'Would you rather compromise or cancel the project?' " Glasgow told me. "I said that, if I had a choice, I'd rather cancel it." The assistant secretary brought up the subject of the compromise plan again about two weeks later, but Hickel's attitude had not changed and Glasgow got the clear impression that the secretary had information—or at least a strong intuition—that the canal project really would be abandoned. Jordan's office called more than once about arranging a briefing for the secretary, but Glasgow, somewhat embarrassed, put Jordan off with vague replies about lack of time in Hickel's schedule. The Jacksonville District Engineer, Colonel Fullerton, and his staff felt that the alternative plan should be made public, but the Chief of Engineers' office in Washington believed that it should not. "One reason we did not disclose the plan was that there had been so much high-level interest [in the canal issue], all the way up to the White House," explained Colonel James B. Newman, who was then executive director of civil works, "We did not want to reduce flexibility at that level."

No recommendation in regard to the canal project was submitted to President Nixon by CEQ and the White House staff until December, but the canal issue came to the President's attention in a telling way while he was on a fall campaign trip in Florida. Campaigning on behalf of Governor Kirk and other Republican candidates, the President noticed, at one stop, placards urging "Stop the Barge Canal!" Nixon then turned to Kirk and said, "Governor, there is opposition to your canal," or words to that effect. Whereupon Kirk, who assured me of the truth of the story, waggishly replied: "No, Mr. President, not my canal, your canal." Canal opponents found this widely publicized incident amusing, but more than a little frustrating too, for it suggested that none of the thousands of letters conservationists had written the President about the canal had gotten through.

THE CEQ SAYS "TERMINATE THE PROJECT." After the fall election, the canal issue was brought to a head by a memorandum prepared for the President by CEQ. The three council members favored simply killing the project rather than trying merely to save part of the Oklawaha valley through a realignment of the canal route. CEQ was not yet a year old and was still defining its own procedures as well as those which other agencies should follow to comply with NEPA. Therefore, there were neither precedents nor guidelines to help CEQ decide how to advise the President to proceed. Yet the council members faced an important choice, although that choice seems not to have been clearly perceived at the time. One obvious possibility was for the council, after study of the canal issue, simply to recommend to the President that he terminate the project.

Alternatively, consistent with the letter and spirit of NEPA, the council could have recommended that the President initially not do more than declare a moratorium on project construction pending preparation of a detailed environmental impact statement. The project had, in effect, established a new environmental status quo, as in the creation of the Rodman Pool and the big 6-to-8-mile-long overland cuts at the east and west ends of the project right-of-way. With termination of the project, there would inevitably be proposals to drain Rodman, and to plug or fill in the unfinished portions of the canal—and, in any event, these facilities would be affected in the real sense that their intended purpose would be lost. Furthermore, $14 million in state and local funds had already been invested in land acquisition for the project. Prudence alone would have seemed to dictate that, before taking any definitive action, the White House consult with state officials on the basis of a well-prepared impact statement showing what alternatives were available. Moreover, given the fact that the Corps of Engineers had proposed a plan purportedly adequate to save most of what was still left of the Oklawaha, there was now a particular need to try to determine how excavation of the canal's summit reach below Ocala would affect the Floridan Aquifer and Silver Springs—a question about which there was much professional disagreement. To such an open, even-handed approach to the canal issue there would have been but one drawback: at the first mention of the project's possible termination, the outcry from canal proponents and their friends in Congress would have been so great that the President might have chosen to do nothing or to compromise a matter that perhaps should not be compromised. But while the foregoing describes real alternatives that CEQ had open to it, the council never entertained the idea of calling for an environmental impact study and for comment from Florida officials as part of the basis for decision. What CEQ actually did, through Russell Train, its chairman, was to call for termination of the project, without further consideration or delay.

THE PRESIDENT'S DECISION AND THE COURT ORDER. A president will often, as in this case, decide questions of some moment without talking to anyone, acting solely on the strength of staff papers. President Nixon ordered the canal project terminated on the basis of two documents, a memorandum by Russell Train and a brief "decision paper" prepared for him by John Whitaker, his environmental aide. The latter document, which has remained confidential, laid out the President's options. Principally, these were to terminate the project or to adopt the plan for the canal realignment through the Oklawaha valley, which Robert Jordan had set forth more definitively in a November memorandum to Whitaker (Appendix Exhibit A). A copy of Train's memorandum (Appendix Exhibit B) would ultimately fall into the hands of a canal booster and become public. In this paper, dated December 1, 1970, and addressed to Whitaker, Train said, in sum, that the canal project was environmentally damaging, economically marginal, and politically unpopular and that it should be terminated even though its "sunk cost" would finally be from $71 to 77 million. He acknowledged no substantial lessening of the project's environmental impact under the plan for a partial realignment, and stated that "potential pollution from the project may be transferred to the Floridan Aquifer, setting off a destructive chain reaction affecting the water supply for many users." Furthermore, he observed—gratuitously, he would later insist—that "there are probably more political advantages than disadvantages in stopping the project, compared to a partial realignment." He added:

> I have been told that if the project were voted on as a referendum by the people of Florida, it would be defeated. Essentially, only a small minority of people in the Tampa and Jacksonville areas have a real interest in it. As you know, Governor Kirk backed away from the project in the last election and the governor-elect opposed it. . . . I concluded that the benefits nationally of dropping the project would greatly outweigh the benefits of continuing it. I further believe that a by-pass over only 20 miles of the project would be considered "tokenism" by conservationists and many others.

Train's long dedication to conservation causes, as president of the Conservation Foundation and then as a government official, is itself reason enough to discount the criticism—of which there would later be much from canal supporters—that the CEQ recommendation derived chiefly from political considerations. The council's seriousness of purpose could also be assumed from the credentials of its other two members: Cahn, a former journalist whose reporting on environmental issues had won him a Pulitzer Prize, and MacDonald, a distinguished geophysicist who had been elected to the National Academy of Sciences at the age of only thirty-four. Also, CEQ staff people, notably Lee Talbot, an ecologist formerly with the Smithsonian Institution, had devoted substantial time to evaluating the canal project. Major land and water resource management decisions are in fact always politically significant, and it would have been surprising if the Train memorandum had not noted that popular support for the canal project was waning. And, as one former CEQ staff member observes, at all White House meetings in which the canal had been discussed, Whitaker had made clear that the political consequences of any action taken should be weighed.

Some individuals of long experience in the federal bureaucracy believe that the President's decision on the canal project was preceded by more and better staff work than that supporting many other presidential decisions of equal importance. Nevertheless, the information that went to the President and the work that had gone into developing it fell short of the procedural and analytical standards set by NEPA. In particular, although granted that memorandums for the President must be brief, Train's memorandum was indeed "extremely superficial" (as Robert Jordan has said), and contrary in intent both to NEPA's emphasis on open consideration of alternatives and to CEQ's and the President's own emerging concept that the state governments should assert a key role in land use policy. In this latter regard, terminating the canal project obviously represented a significant change in land use plans and one that would require careful follow-through by the state of Florida as well as the federal government. Nevertheless, however CEQ's advice to the President may be judged, without the council's intervention in the canal controversy, work on the project probably would have continued with no reprieve for the Oklawaha valley. Except for Secretary Hickel, a maverick whose influence was on the wane, no high federal officials other than Train and his colleagues at CEQ were putting pressure on the Department of the Army in 1970 to face up to the project's environmental impact.

The President's decision was announced in a White House press release (Appendix Exhibit C) on January 19, 1971. "The Council on Environmental Quality has recommended to me that the project be halted, and I have accepted its advice," the President said. The canal, he added, would destroy "a uniquely beautiful, semitropical stream." The release stated that the canal project was conceived and designed at a time when "federal concern in such matters was almost completely on maximizing economic return." In calculating that return, the President added, "the destruction of natural, ecological values was not counted as a cost, nor was a credit allowed for actions preserving the environment."

On January 15, 1971, four days before the President's termination order was announced, Judge Barrington D. Parker of the U.S. District Court for the District of Columbia, temporarily enjoined further work on the project in its summit reach and in the undisturbed part of the Oklawaha valley. His ruling cited the fact that no environmental impact statement had been prepared on the project, as required by NEPA. In granting the injunction, Judge Parker gave "great probative weight" to documents such as the Bureau of Sport Fisheries and Wildlife report which had been heavily influenced by the FDE impact study.

It is instructive to note the interplay between the court ruling and the White House action. Whitaker has told me categorically that the ruling did not influence the Presidential decision—and, indeed, that the

"decision paper" had come back from the Oval Office several days prior
to that ruling. What the ruling clearly did do was to cause the White House
to announce the decision hurriedly and with less care than was called for.
The ruling came on a Friday. Over the weekend, William Reilly of the CEQ
staff was summoned to prepare a press release announcing the project
termination order. His first draft contained a reference to a threat to the
aquifer. But this assertion was challenged by Robert Jordan of the Department of the Army, and the White House asked Reilly to justify it. Reilly
called CEQ member Gordon MacDonald for guidance, and, as Reilly recalls,
MacDonald said that, if the reference to contamination of the aquifer had
been questioned and was causing a problem, then leave it out.

In subsequent litigation arising from the President's order, the administration would take the position that no environmental impact statement in
support of that order was required. But MacDonald and Cahn (both of
whom left CEQ in the fall of 1972) have indicated that they believed the
contrary was true. They told me that, had the court ruling not come when
it did, an impact statement probably would have been prepared before the
President's order was announced. If there had in fact been any such
possibility, it was apparently undercut by a White House desire not to let
the court steal the President's thunder.

The court order, which probably would have resulted only in a delay
of the project and possibly in some modification of it, was of course
eclipsed by the President's termination order, an action without precedent.
Presidents have terminated military projects (such as the B-70 bomber
development) even in the face of strong congressional resistance, but no
one in the Chief of Engineers office can recall a president's ever before
having ordered an ongoing public works project permanently stopped. As
for the legality of President Nixon's termination order, it rested on the
belief that an appropriation of funds by Congress is ordinarily permissive
rather than directive, and that whether the money is actually spent is up
to the President. The manner of the President's action in this case was
extraordinarily ironic: over the years canal supporters had benefited from
some undemocratic, high-handed, and devious or arbitrary actions by
presidents and other politicians to further the project. Now, the project,
though already partly completed, was being stopped by a presidential
order arrived at wholly in private, without public hearings, without consultation with Florida congressmen or the Florida Cabinet, and, one could
contend, without compliance with NEPA.

There is much truth in Russell Train's view, as expressed to me, that
the important thing about the termination of the canal project was "not
the way it was done but that it was done at all." The very fact, he says,
"that the President of the United States bit this kind of a bullet on a
major public works project already so far underway was of fantastic

Above, the Oklawaha River; *below,* 306-ton crawler crusher at work in the Rodman Reservoir; *at right,* floating logs and water hyacinths in Rodman Pool.

significance." The President was challenging the established practices and attitudes of the Corps of Engineers, the public works committees in Congress, and of state agencies such as the Florida Cabinet and Department of Natural Resources. More specifically, whether the President fully realized it or not, he was challenging their make-believe economics, their single-minded concern for economic development and token regard for esthetic values and biological diversity, and their habit of catering to narrow economic interests. Nevertheless, how the project was stopped was to have a bearing on how readily, or even whether, the government was to have the support of the State of Florida, the Congress, and the federal courts in putting the project beyond all hope of revival. As the opinion that would be rendered by a federal judge in early 1974 would make all too clear, the canal project is by no means yet certifiably dead. Indeed, the Nixon termination order was held to have been unlawful. I shall return to this opinion in a moment, but I first want to discuss some rather obvious implications of the termination order, which the White House seems not to have taken into account.

Patricia Caulfield

To have stopped the project after an investment of more than $70 million would make little sense unless the state of Florida could be persuaded to join the administration in restoring and protecting the Oklawaha valley. In May of 1972, some sixteen months after the termination order, CEQ and the Department of the Army did, in fact, finally recommend that all of the lower and middle Oklawaha be formally designated as a "study river" for possible inclusion in the National Wild and Scenic River System; that steps be made toward having Ocala National Forest expanded to include a much larger part of the Oklawaha swamp forest; and that the Rodman reservoir be lowered to save about 1,000 acres of trees—this to be an interim step before draining Rodman entirely and allowing the Oklawaha to return to its natural channel. But no such proposals could be carried out without congressional approval, which probably would be forthcoming only if Florida officials were reconciled to the termination of the canal project.

REACTION TO THE PRESIDENT'S ORDER

Political reaction in Florida to the termination order was more complex and, on the whole, less favorable than Russell Train had forecast. On the one hand, there were indeed manifestations of strong public support for the President's action. Leaders of the FDE and other conservation groups were jubilant, of course. The newspapers that applauded the decision included the St. Petersburg *Times* and the *Miami Herald*, both influential and highly respected. As an indication of how politicians were judging the winds of public opinion, neither of Florida's U.S. senators joined the congressmen from north Florida in protesting the termination order as such. Yet the extent of public disapproval of the peremptory and summary nature of the President's action was by no means insignificant. Long-time promoters of the canal project naturally tried to make the most of the way the project was stopped. Leaders such as Congressman Bennett and the heads of the Canal Authority and the Florida Waterways Association set about, in a fury, to discredit the termination order. They argued that the President's action was unconstitutional and purely "political," and that, somehow, the canal project had become a symbolic target in a nation suddenly aggrieved at "pollution." They demanded to be shown the documentation on which the President acted and were scornful when, some three weeks after the termination order, a summary of the considerations that went into the CEQ recommendation was finally made public.

THE CABINET WITHHOLDS SUPPORT. More serious from the Nixon Administration's standpoint, however, was the fact that the termination order found little support in the Florida Cabinet, where support might have been expected. As it happened, former Secretary of State Tom Adams—the FDE people's *bête noire*—was Reubin Askew's running mate in the 1970 election and Adams was now lieutenant governor. Nevertheless, Askew's campaign position had been clear and specific: the canal project should not be allowed to destroy the still undisturbed part of the Oklawaha valley, and the Council on Environmental Quality should study the possible threat to the aquifer before any excavation occurred in the summit reach. Moreover, besides Askew, its chairman, the cabinet had three other newly elected members, all Miamians apparently without strong political ties to north Florida where support for the canal project was greatest. They too had said during the campaign that the project should be delayed or stopped if necessary to prevent major environmental damage. Thus, there seemed potentially to be a majority of the cabinet in favor of stopping the project, even if there were no change in the attitude of the three who had been in the cabinet in 1966 when the Save the Oklawaha group's appeal was given short shrift. Yet only one of the seven cabinet members supported the President's action—the exception being Attorney General Robert L. Shevin, a former state senator from Miami. This was not to be explained as simply an indication of official unresponsiveness to environmental values. In all probability, had Askew, as Florida's popular new governor, supported the termination order, a majority of the cabinet would have followed suit.

Askew chose neither to protest nor to endorse the order after trying to elicit from CEQ a more convincing justification for the termination but failing to get it. Several weeks after the order was announced, Askew called Lee Talbot, the CEQ senior scientist who had been studying the canal issue, and asked for further information as to why CEQ believed the canal would degrade the aquifer. The geologist responsible for the FDE report's pessimistic conclusions in this regard depended for his basic data on the work of a U.S. Geological Survey hydrologist whose views as to the canal's effects were optimistic. This scientist, Glen L. Faulkner, in preparing his *Geohydrology of the Cross Florida Barge Canal Area (with Special Reference to the Ocala Vicinity)*, which was released in January 1970, had made the most recent and thorough field study on the subject available. Faulkner said that the "design of the canal and the plan of operation are consonant with the hydrologic regime" and that pollution of the ground water could be averted, although he did acknowledge that, if surface waters were polluted, dissolved contaminants could pass into the aquifer. In the FDE study, Faulkner's conclusions were viewed as unsupported by the body of the report and FDE people suspected that these conclusions had been influenced by the Corps of Engineers, which paid for this three-year study and reviewed the report in draft.

By his inquiry to CEQ, Governor Askew hoped somehow to resolve these contradictory assessments. "I explained to the governor that the [Faulkner Report] provided the data [supporting the CEQ view] but that its conclusions were ambiguously worded," Lee Talbot told me. Talbot then called the USGS headquarters and asked for a statement of conclusions more consistent with Faulkner's data. Before night, that statement was in hand. It had been prepared by an assistant director of the survey, checked with the survey's Florida office and with Faulkner, and then reviewed and signed by the director of the USGS, who at the time was William T. Pecora, later to become Under Secretary of the Interior. "The statement by Pecora's office was a matter of going through my report and simply listing the impacts the canal could have," Faulkner later commented to me without, however, deserting his own optimistic interpretation of the data. "It's difficult to get the true meaning of a fact if you just state it," he told me.

In an interview with a *Miami Herald* reporter on February 25, Governor Askew observed: "At this point, it would appear to me that a lot of [the information] we are receiving is justification after the decision already has been made rather than information on which the decision was based."[15] In the governor's opinion, the President's decision terminating the project was "essentially political."[16] Askew had not yet seen the new USGS statement, but upon receiving it a few days later he regarded it as by no means persuasive.

State policy in regard to the canal issue was to drift in confusion for a year and a half. In the absence of a new statement of position by the cabinet, the procanal people in the Department of Natural Resources, especially in the Canal Authority, would tend to follow their own inclinations, just as though state policy on the canal question were unchanged. And technically they were right, because the 1966 resolution affirming cabinet support for the project had not been rescinded. The most significant development to occur in this policy vacuum was the suit that the Canal Authority, acting on its own initiative and without cabinet approval, brought against the Department of the Army. The Canal Authority argued, persuasively as it turned out, that the President's termination of a congressionally authorized and funded project was unconstitutional and that his order was based on a CEQ recommendation that flouted NEPA. The authority claimed that, quite aside from any thought of reviving the canal project, the suit was necessary to protect future claims against the federal government for recovery of state and local funds for project purposes. Attorney General Shevin dismissed this argument as specious, but his

15. William R. Amlong, "Accept Canal Death, Askew Urges State," *Miami Herald*, February 26, 1971.
16. Ibid.

motion to have the cabinet deny funds to the Canal Authority for this legal action failed to get a second. Shevin felt that, with Askew's help, he would have prevailed. "The governor hasn't assisted my position at all," he said. "The cabinet is just skirting the issue."[17] The cabinet did, however, reject a Canal Authority proposal that Congress be asked to appropriate funds to continue project construction. And, at Shevin's suggestion, it struck from the authority's budget a $1,600-a-month item for what the attorney general called public relations "puffery."

THE PROJECT IS IN "LIMBO." In Congress the attitude toward the President's termination order was, among most who cared, predictably sour. Representative C. W. Bill Young, a freshman Republican congressman from St. Petersburg who seems to have been among the few people to know of the President's decision before it was announced, became spokesman for the White House and made statements on the House floor and in committee defending the termination as entirely justified and long overdue. Congressmen from north Florida and several members of the Subcommittee on Public Works Appropriations took quite a different view of the matter. The chairman of the subcommittee, Representative Joe L. Evins of Tennessee, regarded the termination of the canal project as politically motivated and a flouting of the will of Congress. Yet, even though displeased by the President's action, Representative Evins told me that the canal project is in "limbo" until Florida's governor and its congressional delegation unite in an effort to revive it.

In 1972 congressmen Bennett and Sikes, acting on behalf of canal proponents in Jacksonville, did persuade the Evins subcommittee to include in the public works appropriations bill an item which the administration wanted no part of: $150,000 for the Corps of Engineers to prepare an environmental impact study on the canal project. Here was a complete turnabout from two years earlier when the subcommittee had dismissed as wholly unnecessary Secretary Hickel's proposal for a study of the project's economics and environmental impact. Moreover, just as the Save the Oklawaha group had once sought a study of an alternate route for the canal, the canal proponents were now emphasizing that, in the new Corps of Engineers study, consideration should be given to the rejected corps plan to reroute the canal and save most of the Oklawaha valley above Eureka. The money for the restudy, which was to be directed at the project's economic justification as well as its environmental impact, remained in the appropriation bill as finally passed by Congress. The Florida senators did not promote this measure but maintained a benign neutrality.

17. Ben Funk (Associated Press) "Florida's Big Ditch: Is It Temporarily Out of Order— or Permanently Closed?" Jacksonville *Times-Union* and *Journal*, April 18, 1971.

This congressional action, together with several other events in 1972, left the question of dismantling the canal project and restoring the Oklawaha valley far from settled. The Canal Authority clearly would be pressing to have the federal court require the administration to make the study as Congress had provided. On the other hand, CEQ and the White House hoped to satisfy the requirements of NEPA by having the National Forest Service prepare an environmental impact statement on the proposals to establish an Oklawaha national river, expand the Ocala National Forest boundaries, and lower Rodman reservoir. In that statement, already available in draft by the summer of 1972, completion of the canal according to the last corps plan was touched upon only briefly, then dismissed as an alternative to the restoration and protection of the entire lower and middle Oklawaha and river swamp.

At about this same time, the Florida Cabinet overcame its past indecision and adopted a position of sorts on the canal. With Governor Askew's and Attorney General Shevin's leadership, the cabinet rescinded its 1966 resolution favoring completion of the canal through the Oklawaha valley. It also suspended further support of the canal project as a whole pending an evaluation of (i) an environmental impact statement prepared in keeping with NEPA and (ii) a new benefit-cost analysis made with a realistic discount rate and realistic projections of construction costs and recreational benefits.

JUDGE HOLDS TERMINATION IS UNLAWFUL. In late July of 1973 the protracted litigation over the barge canal, by now consisting of a mare's nest of issues raised by five different sets of plaintiffs representing both canal proponents and opponents, finally came to trial on the merits in the U.S. District Court in Jacksonville. Six months later, on January 31, 1974, Judge Harvey M. Johnsen, the senior judge of the Eighth Circuit Court of Appeals specially assigned to the case, delivered a lucid forty-page opinion, which included the major finding that the President's termination order was unlawful. He said in part:

> I am unable to regard the President as having any general executive power to terminate whatever legislatively authorized public works projects he chooses, even though he may believe that it would be in the public interest to have some particular project or projects put to an end. Nor am I able to rationalize any basis, on constitutional principle, or within democratic political philosophy, or from our national experience, that could in my opinion even arguably be contended to make the existence of such a general executive power desirable. Too much opportunity and possibility of purely political action and favor, or of other official arbitrariness, exists for the concept to be reconcil-

able with or at all tolerable under the protective design of our political system.[18]

Judge Johnsen held that it was up to Congress to decide the canal project's ultimate fate. He had hoped that a judicial solution might be found, but in vain. "The situation," he said, "is going to have to be allowed to grind its way along . . . until Congress sees fit to provide the final answer." The court found that the environmental impact statement prepared by the Forest Service was not sufficient to meet the requirements of NEPA and that the impact study mandated by Congress should be undertaken forthwith and completed expeditiously. The administration's impoundment of the $150,000 appropriated for the study was held to be unlawful. Disposing of one of the key technical issues raised in the litigation, Judge Johnsen found that, contrary to arguments advanced by EDF, the Chief of Engineers' conclusion that the canal project would have "no effect on the ground water . . ." did not, certainly in the legal sense, constitute an abuse of administrative discretion. (As for the Rodman Pool, the court at first permanently enjoined the lowering of this reservoir pending some new authorization by Congress as to the future of Rodman or the canal project as a whole. The injunction was later rescinded, but, at the end of May 1974, it remained unsettled whether a new drawdown would be carried out or not.)

Judge Johnsen's ruling was not appealed by either the government or by EDF. Richard Nixon, threatened with impeachment for various abuses of discretion and authority, was no longer the man on a white charger envisioned by some canal opponents back in January 1971, when he ordered the project terminated. Furthermore, although the Canal Authority prevailed in the litigation, the canal project remains in "limbo," as Representative Evins put it, and it may in fact eventually be deauthorized. Before passage, any deauthorization bill (such as the one introduced in 1973 by Representative L. A. Bafalis, a congressman from south Florida) will no doubt have to travel a long, tortuous path and survive many ambushes. On the other hand, the task faced by those who would like to revive the canal project seems far more difficult than that of those who would deauthorize it. They will have to make a convincing affirmative showing that the project is worth completing in view of the financial and environmental costs. As the entire history of the canal project bears out, that will not be easy to do, especially given the more searching standards of economic and environmental analysis now demanded. Whatever is decided about the canal, Governor Askew indicated to me in an interview shortly after Judge Johnsen's ruling that he definitely will not

18. Harvey M. Johnsen, Opinion and Judgment, The Canal Authority of the State of Florida, et al., v. Howard W. Callaway, Secretary of the Army, and related cases, U.S. District Court, Middle District of Florida, Jacksonville Division, January 31, 1974, p. 14 of the opinion (Docket No. 71-92-Civ-J).

support any revival of the project plan for it to go through the Oklawaha valley.

AN OVERLOOKED OPPORTUNITY

Given the benefit of hindsight, it seems clear that the President and his advisers, in seeking to terminate peremptorily an arguably "bad project," overlooked an opportunity to bring the project to an end in a manner that could have proved both politically acceptable and productive in terms of better use of the Oklawaha valley.

I am persuaded that the President's first step should have been to declare a moratorium on further construction pending thorough environmental and economic studies, and pending comment by Florida's governor and cabinet as to the best of the available alternative courses of action. And, here, it would have been well to establish the principle that benefit-cost analyses done by the Corps of Engineers (and by other public works agencies) are subject to review by specially assigned panels of economists, drawn from both inside and outside the government. Responsibility for the coordination of the overall economic and environmental studies could have been left to the Secretary of the Army's office or to an interdepartmental committee, but with some oversight and participation by CEQ.

After comment on the studies had been elicited from the Florida Cabinet and from other public and private organizations and groups, CEQ could have distilled the recommendations from these sources for submission to the White House along with its own recommendation. At this point, the President would have made his decision whether to withdraw White House support for the project permanently or to continue such support with certain strings attached, such as the condition that Congress provide the legislation and funds necessary to preserve part of the Oklawaha valley. If the decision was to withhold support, the President's first move could have been to announce that no further construction funds for it would be requested of Congress. Given the intensely controversial nature of the project, such action on the President's part very likely would have led Congress to stop funding it.

The campaigns by the Save the Oklawaha group and the Florida Defenders of the Environment have pointed up dramatically the growing sophistication, resourcefulness, and influence—exercised through the courts and by political action—of people who want to redirect or stop development where necessary to save what is left of Florida's natural environment. The success scored by FDE can be taken as another indication that an equilibrium of sorts is being reached with regard to the respective abilities of developers and conservationists in Florida to influence public opinion.

Yet, even though in terms of public attitudes the influence of conservationists and developers may be coming into desirable balance, this will not be reflected in official state policies and actions until Florida's top executive body, the cabinet, truly functions as a politically responsive body. As presently constituted, the cabinet may never become truly responsive. The cabinet might not have delayed a year and a half to take a position on the canal issue if CEQ and the White House had acted less peremptorily, but it is to be blamed for having behaved in a passive manner scarcely appropriate to a body that is supposed to set policy for development of Florida's water resources.

Moreover, short shrift was given to a proposal made in June 1971 by Conservation '70s for the cabinet to have the University of Florida coordinate a regional planning program for the Oklawaha basin—a program to be staffed by architects, planners, and scientists serving as unpaid volunteers. The Florida Association of the American Institute of Architects, the Florida Defenders of the Environment, the Florida Conservation Foundation, and a number of individual scientists were behind this unprecedented offer by highly qualified professionals to volunteer their time for a model planning effort. In such an effort, important concepts going beyond anything the federal agencies had in mind could have been developed or reviewed. For instance, in 1972 an FDE trustee proposed the establishment of a Bartram Memorial Trail for hikers, cyclists, and horseback riders, a major segment of it to follow the 50-mile-long canal right-of-way between the lower Withlachoochee River and the Oklawaha.[19]

In sum, the cabinet's role in the barge canal controversy offers further evidence of the cabinet system's inadequacies. If Florida is to cope effectively with problems of land and water management there is need for a reform of the state's executive branch of government comparable in importance to the one that has occurred in recent years in the legislature. Fundamental governmental changes seem in order with respect to the makeup of the Department of Natural Resources, the relationship of that department and other agencies to the governor and cabinet, and the abolishment of the cabinet as it presently exists and its replacement by a new and different kind of elected body, but one by no means wholly alien to the Florida tradition. These matters I come to next.

APPENDIX EXHIBIT A

Honorable John C. Whitaker   11 Nov. 70
Deputy Assistant to the President

John:

Since last writing you on 10 September about the Cross-Florida Barge Canal, the Corps of Engineers has been studying quietly several alternatives

---

19. The proposal for the Bartram Memorial Trail was made on July 27, 1972, by Lee Ogden, a trustee of FDE, who, however, in this case was acting independently.

to continue construction of the canal as presently planned and approved. As you know, we have done no additional work in the reach of the Oklawaha River between Silver Springs Run and Eureka Dam.

The objective of the Corps' recent studies is to find a practical way to save a large portion of the Oklawaha River and its environs and still allow the Barge Canal to be completed. We now believe that there are no engineering impediments to relocating the Canal along an alignment parallel to, but northwest of, the present alignment (map attached). Along with the realignment we would adjust and modify the present plan to preserve as much as possible of the natural environment and mitigate the impact of the changed environment to the extent practicable. This will include re-planning the recreation facilities, significantly reducing the land area required for the project, providing facilities to reduce the chances of barge accidents and minimize the damage in the event of accident, and extensive landscaping to maintain a natural appearance. This plan would preserve all or nearly all of the natural Oklawaha River channel south of Eureka Lock and Dam (over 20 miles) and extensive areas around Lake Charles, Lake Eaton, Mud Lake, and possibly the entire Dead River Swamp area.

A rough estimate of the added cost of this alternative over the cost of the present project is 5 to 7 million dollars depending on the extent of the modifications finally selected. With changes within these limits the project would still be justified economically. The attached Fact Sheet explains the general provisions of the realigned channel.

Also, presented in the Fact Sheet is an indication of the costs to the nation of abandoning the project, as well as the costs of various moratoria for further study. I am sure that you remember the strong opposition of the Public Works Appropriations Committees to further study and the floor action in the Senate defeating an amendment to withhold expenditures for this project until June 1, 1971 to allow an ecological and economic review.

I suggest that you consider carefully the alternative of a six-to-twelve month moratorium on work within the Eureka Pool area. This would allow time for detailed planning of a realigned channel, and—more important—would provide time for a multi-agency joint study of all environmental aspects of the 20-mile preserved reach of the Oklawaha River. Perhaps this would lead to the best practical solution to the entire problem of the Cross-Florida Barge Canal making the best use of the changed environment.

Sincerely,
(Signed) Robert E. Jordan, III
Incl.   Special Assistant to the Secretary
as   of the Army (Civil Functions)

Dec. 1, 1970

EXECUTIVE OFFICE OF THE PRESIDENT
Council on Environmental Quality
722 Jackson Place, N. W.
Washington, D. C. 20006

MEMORANDUM FOR MR. WHITAKER

SUBJECT: Cross Florida Barge Canal

I recommend termination of the Cross Florida Barge Canal, rather than the partial realignment proposed by Army, for the following reasons:

1. This project could seriously affect the environment in Florida by degrading water quality, altering the water supply in central Florida, vitally affecting the fish and wildlife of the area, and combining what are now separate ecological systems. Potential pollution from the project may be transferred to the Florida aquifer, setting off a destructive chain reaction affecting the water supply for many users. Many unique ecological features would be destroyed. This would pose a serious threat to the survival of rare alligators, panthers and wild turkeys through the alteration of their habitat. The Canal could add to the spread of pests from the Gulf to the Atlantic Coast where they would spread virtually unobstructed throughout the East Coast Waterways.

2. The project itself is marginal from an economic point of view and hence very undesirable in the face of the potential and actual environmental problems it presents.

3. The estimated sunk cost of this $179 million project is from $71 to $77 million. If the project were abandoned, annual benefits of $1.2 million would still accrue. The budget savings this year and in subsequent years for this marginal project is a strong reason in itself for stopping it.

4. I believe there are probably more political advantages than disadvantages in stopping the project, compared to a partial realignment. I have been told if the project were voted on as a referendum by the people of Florida, it would be defeated. Essentially, only a small minority of people in the Tampa and Jacksonville areas have a real interest in it. As you know, Governor Kirk backed away from the project in the last election and the Governor-elect opposed it. Although this certainly is not a detailed analysis of the political situation, I conclude that the benefits nationally of dropping the project would greatly outweigh the benefits of continuing it. I further believe that a bypass over only 20 miles of the project would be considered "tokenism" by conservationists and many others.

Because of these reasons, I believe that termination of the project would bring maximum political benefits, would prevent potentially significant environmental problems and would save a great deal of Federal money for a marginal project.

Attached is a draft Presidential statement on cessation of the project.

(sgd) Russell E. Train
Attachment   Chairman

APPENDIX EXHIBIT C

FOR IMMEDIATE RELEASE   JANUARY 19, 1971

OFFICE OF THE WHITE HOUSE PRESS SECRETARY

THE WHITE HOUSE

STATEMENT BY THE PRESIDENT

I am today ordering a halt to further construction of the Cross Florida Barge Canal to prevent potentially serious environmental damages.

The purpose of the Canal was to reduce transportation costs for barge shipping. It was conceived and designed at a time when the focus of Federal concern in such matters was still almost completely on maximizing economic return. In calculating that return, the destruction of natural, ecological values was not counted as a cost, nor was a credit allowed for actions preserving the environment.

A natural treasure is involved in the case of the Barge Canal—the Oklawaha River—a uniquely beautiful, semi-tropical stream, one of a very few of its kind in the United States, which would be destroyed by construction of the Canal.

The Council on Environmental Quality has recommended to me that the project be halted, and I have accepted its advice. The Council has pointed out to me that the project could endanger the unique wildlife of the area and destroy this region of unusual and unique natural beauty.

The total cost of the project if it were completed would be about $180 million. About $50 million has already been committed to construction. I am asking the Secretary of the Army to work with the Council on Environmental Quality in developing recommendations for the future of the area.

The step I have taken today will prevent a past mistake from causing permanent damage. But more important, we must assure that in the future we take not only full but also timely account of the environmental impact of such projects—so that instead of merely halting the damage, we prevent it.

PART IV * **Conclusion**

10
Finding the way

The development of state policy for managing Florida's land and water resources under immense pressures of growth and development had reached a critical threshold by 1974. In enacting the land and water laws of 1972 the legislature in effect moved a step nearer acceptance of the proposition that, to protect and enhance the quality of life in Florida, new development must stay within state approved policies and guidelines as to its location, type, areal extent, and the density of population to be accommodated. Yet those new laws represented only a beginning on which subsequent legislatures could build. In the spring of 1974, the legislature took up two proposals which, once adopted, will represent another important step in the evolution of an overall state policy for the control of land use and growth.

One of these was the Local Government Comprehensive Planning Bill of 1974, a measure prepared by the Environmental Land Management Study Committee (a group set up under one of the 1972 statutes), and strongly supported by Governor Askew, House Speaker Terrell Sessums, and a number of other prominent legislators. This measure, calling for the preparation of an enforceable comprehensive land use master plan for each county and municipality, was viewed as a vital complement to the special regulation of developments of regional impact (DRIs) and selected critical areas, required under the 1972 laws. The other proposal was a growth policy resolution which, while it would not itself carry the force of law, would put the legislature on record as favoring imposition of local impact fees to make "growth pay for growth" (as the current jargon among planners expresses it) and observance of the principle that growth should not be allowed to outpace or exceed the "carrying capacity" of natural and man-made systems. As introduced, the resolution stated that carrying capacities should be determined by a uniform method of measurement to be applied statewide.[1] The resolution, either directly or by implication, called for the state government to assume a number of important new responsibilities. It would have the state seek, among other goals of growth policy, conservation of energy; better distribution within the state of residential settlement, industry, and tourism; preservation of prime farm land; and the modernization of local government to equip it to assume most of the responsibility for the control of growth and development met to a large extent locally.

Controversy has attended both the growth policy resolution and the comprehensive planning bill, and, as I write in the late spring of 1974, their adoption in any very meaningful form is in doubt. Yet, with an average of about 6,000 persons still immigrating to Florida each week, the state's problems of runaway growth and poor land management are becoming more severe by the day. If present trends continue, the legislature will eventually have no choice but to establish policies and mechanisms for controlling growth and development that may seem drastic by present lights. The question is, will the necessary reforms come in time, or come too late to prevent many avoidable mistakes and further loss or degradation of important natural systems and precious living amenities.

1. Central to the carrying capacity concept as it is usually thought of by Florida environmentalists is the belief that it is unwise to depend on costly technology for tasks, such as advanced waste treatment, which can be better performed by natural systems if the latter are not upset or overextended. An influential advocate of this point of view is Howard T. Odum of the University of Florida, who has argued thus:

> As growth of urban areas has become concentrated, much of our energies and research and development work has been going into developing energy-costing technology to protect the environment from wastes, whereas most wastes are themselves rich energy sources for which there are, in most cases, ecosystems capable of using and recycling [them] as a partner of the city without drain on the scarce fossil fuels. Soils take up carbon monoxides, forests absorb nutrients, swamps accept and regulate floodwaters. . . . [T]here is rarely excuse for tertiary treatment because there is no excuse for such dense packing of growth that the natural buffer lands cannot be a good cheap recycling partner. Man as a partner of nature must use nature well and this does not mean crowd it out and pave it over; nor does it mean developing industries that compete with nature for the waters and wastes that would be an energy contributor for the survival of both.

This quotation is from an article by Odum in *AMBIO*, an English language journal published by the Royal Swedish Academy of Sciences, vol. 2, no. 6 (1973).

In my view, the need to bring growth and development under close public regulation should not, however, be viewed by Floridians in a grudging spirit, or as something only the force of circumstances could bring them to accept. The prospect of achieving a significant measure of public control over the process of growth and development is one that can be embraced positively. Admittedly, comprehensive land use planning and regulation will have the effect, directly or indirectly, of placing new limits and constraints on the decisions, actions, and life-styles of all who buy, sell, or use land, which is to say everybody. Yet such planning and regulation will be no more coercive in its effect upon the average citizen than the random and piecemeal land use decisions that are made in response to market forces, the desires of particular local interests, and the bureaucratic predilections of state highway departments, water management agencies, and the like. The overall result of such random decision making itself constitutes a plan, inchoate and unsatisfactory though that plan may be.

If growth and development can be made to conform to the policies and decisions of responsible elected officials, the individual citizen and voter will surely benefit. In fact, the citizen may come to enjoy more meaningful political influence than ever before, especially if innovative methods are developed for him or his community representatives to take part in the planning process or even to vote on alternative futures for his city, county, or region. The average citizen does not build oil refineries, 40-story condominiums, or huge new retirement communities, and his freedoms are not much affected by public regulation of those who do. Indeed, through his participation in local planning processes the citizen has a chance to influence the behavior of the out-of-state investors—such as the insurance firms, banking houses, and national companies and conglomerates so active in land speculation and development in Dade County—who could undertake projects that might change the entire character of his community, for better or worse.

In a larger context, if effective democratic processes at the state and local level—particularly for the regulation of growth and development—could be established in Florida and other states, this would counteract to some degree the greater centralization of government at the federal level. Perceptive observers such as Robert L. Heilbroner predict that future efforts to cope with increasing scarcities of food, fuel, and other materials in a world experiencing exponential population growth will accelerate such centralization,[2] which has been in any event a feature of American life for the last forty years. Given this unwelcome but probably inescapable prospect, it would seem wise to have as much of the burden of government as possible carried below the federal level. It should not, for example, be necessary for the President of the United States, or unseen White

2. Robert L. Heilbroner, *Inquiry Into the Human Prospect* (New York: W. W. Norton, 1974).

House aides, to be deciding whether a jetport or a barge canal is to be built in Florida, and, if so, where it should go. Nor should conservationists in Dade County have to appeal to the Secretary of the Interior to save South Biscayne Bay from an electric utility that would use it as a heat dump. Some federal involvement in decision making is, of course, necessary where large sums of federal money or federal interests are involved. But the personal intervention of officials at the highest Washington levels in matters pertaining to regional development within a state can only signify serious shortcomings in the democratic process.

The establishment of policies and a process fully responsive to Florida's critical need to control growth and development will, I am convinced, require changes in law and governmental structure even more far-reaching than those the governor and legislature have already attempted. What these changes may be, I come to in a moment, but first let me try to sum up the extraordinarily complex regulatory system that now exists. If the reader will bear with me, here are the major elements:

• The planning and zoning programs of Florida's counties and municipalities, or at least of those where meaningful programs exist. According to Florida's Environmental Land Management Study Committee, 60 percent or more of the land area within the state is yet to come under any comprehensive planning program.[3] If and when the some 450 units of local government each develops its own comprehensive plan, Florida will probably be covered with a crazy-quilt of plans giving rise to many problems of incompatibility.

• A three-tiered state comprehensive planning program that represents a collaborative effort by the governor's office, the Department of Administration (an agency under the governor and beyond direct cabinet influence), ten regional planning councils, and the city and county governments. Although designated for their mission by the Department of Administration, the regional planning councils are actually creatures of the local governments, primarily the county governments.

• A three-tiered water resource management system consisting of: the Department of Natural Resources or DNR, a cabinet agency; five regional water management districts, governed by boards appointed by the governor but also answerable to the DNR and the cabinet; and some 175 or more local districts. Although some of the local districts are under county government, most are districts established through special act or court petition as small, independent governmental entities run by boards made up of landowners. (Hundreds of other special districts have been established by land developers to provide water and sewer facilities and other services related to land development.)

• A state Department of Pollution Control, directed by a board of guberna-

3. Environmental Land Management Study Committee, *Final Report to the Governor and the Legislature*, December 1973, p. 21.

torial appointees. The department enforces air and water quality standards through a system of emission and effluent permits which is administered either directly by the department itself or by local pollution control agencies that it has certified. It also reviews and approves local sewer and waste treatment systems.

• A two-tiered system in which the cabinet and the local governments, county and municipal, have authority over bulkhead lines, dredge-and-fill permits, ocean and Gulf beach setback lines, and, since 1972 when the land and water laws of that year were enacted, also over "critical areas" and DRIs. Where DRIs are concerned, there is also a third tier—the regional planning councils and their staffs, which submit impact analysis reports to the local governments and to the Department of Administration's Division of State Planning.

Granted, there can be no simple solutions to the problems of growth and land and water management, and no simple administrative arrangements for dealing with them. Yet the above described "system," if it can be called that, is clearly of such mind-boggling complexity as to be scarcely capable of producing satisfactory results overall.

A PROPOSED SOLUTION

Although recognizing the value of much of what the governor and legislature have already done toward establishing land and water management policies, I shall nevertheless set forth my own prescriptions. Finding the solution will, I am persuaded, require:

• A state policy, with supporting standards and guidelines, establishing a program of comprehensive planning and zoning and a clear set of goals for conservation and development.

• Reforms and innovations in the structure of government at the state and local levels to facilitate the adoption and observance of plans—and of budgets conforming to the plans—that properly reflect the aforementioned goals. Also, existing tax policies should be modified in keeping with the goals and structural changes that have been adopted.

• Steps to give citizens a meaningful part in regional and state planning and to increase their influence through better information, more honesty in government (i.e., less conflict of interest), more participation in the shaping and review of alternatives, and better access to the courts.

The above points may be referred to in a loose, shorthand manner as *policy, structure,* and *politics.*

POLICY

The legislature should spell out clearly a policy for growth and land use in Florida. It should go beyond bland statements that merely call for an "orderly accommodation" of growth or for the best possible balance between conservation and development. The legislature might begin with three propositions. First, that Florida, as the only subtropical region of the continental United States, is in many ways unique in its natural and esthetic endowment. Second, that it is to the benefit of all Floridians to cultivate a strong sense of place and a sense of responsibility for keeping development in harmony with natural and esthetic values—call this a "land ethic" or what you will. Third, that while Florida (taken as a whole) has the land and other resources necessary to accommodate continued growth and development, much of the land in the state has only slight tolerance for development and some has none at all; further, that certain parts of Florida do indeed seem to be outgrowing their resources and present ability to accommodate more people. The legislature would assert that the state, acting chiefly but by no means solely through local government, shall control development in an attempt to have optimum use made of available land and water resources. It would emphasize that citizens are to be deeply involved in the preparation, review, and sometimes the final selection (through referendums) of alternative plans. The policy should, I submit, have these four basic objectives:

(i) To try to answer, under the rubric of a "growth policy" for Florida, these three questions: What are reasonable and legally defensible limitations on growth? What kind of growth should be encouraged? And where will growth be most desirable?

(ii) To establish a comprehensive set of "Florida Standards" that would extend the existing concept of environmental quality standards beyond the protection of air and water quality to the conservation of natural systems and the enhancement of living amenities. These standards would apply throughout Florida, wherever development is allowed.

(iii) To have all land in Florida placed into one or another of these four basic classifications: *Preservation* zones, where little or no development would be allowed; *conservation* zones, where development would be limited and confined to enclaves carefully designed for compatibility with natural ecological and hydrologic systems; *agricultural* zones, where development would again be limited and stringently regulated; and *development* zones, where most urban and suburban growth and development would occur. Land zoned for preservation would, with rare exceptions, remain in that classification permanently. Land zoned for conservation, agriculture, or development could be transferred from one classification to another, though never routinely or without a clear showing that transfers are in the public interest.

(iv) To plan the placement of those public facilities that are necessary to development—that is, the roads, interceptor sewers, power transmission lines, and water control works—in such a way as to reinforce growth policies and zoning. These will be the *infrastructure plans*.

FIRST POLICY: DIRECTING GROWTH. Once established, a growth policy for Florida would influence, often decisively, the outcome of a variety of specific land use decisions facing state and local officials. An appropriate policy would necessarily take into account such considerations as the "intolerance" (as defined in Chapter 1 on page 15) of some areas for development; the relative importance of various kinds of economic activity to overall prosperity, plus their effect on environmental quality; the existing distribution of population and the imbalances found as between, say, the population of southeast Florida and that of the panhandle; and, of course, the question of what Floridians want their state to be.

Where growth and development might best occur is a question treated extensively in the first part of this book, where I delineate various areas in terms of their tolerance or intolerance for development. Very briefly, the coastal ridge areas of south Florida and that region's few sandy inland plateaus, together with the "highlands" of central Florida, north Florida, and the panhandle, can be regarded as development-tolerant—bearing in mind the caveat that, in the citrus and lake country of the Central Highlands, protection of aquifer recharge, water quality, and scenic amenity will require strict limits on growth. A further point to be emphasized is that, thus far, only one fully acceptable means for disposal of large volumes of sewage effluent has been found: the ocean outfall, with the effluent (after secondary treatment) being discharged well offshore and carried away by ocean currents. For this reason, large urban concentrations can be accommodated more easily along the coasts of peninsula Florida than in inland areas. With this in mind, one could argue that a project such as Disney World, which could have been a success in any number of different locations, might have been better situated in a thinly populated coastal county such as Flagler (north of Daytona Beach) than in the metropolitan Orlando area, which needs no major new growth stimulus. On the other hand, Disney World, attractively landscaped and built to include some of the most advanced environmental protection systems, would pose no threat to the quality of life in central Florida if the detrimental land speculation and development which its presence is helping to encourage were prevented by appropriate public policies.

With respect to whether certain kinds of growth are desirable or not, some judgments are easily made. Florida is clearly not the place for polluting industries of any kind, and any company that wants to build an oil refinery, a chemical plant, or similar facility should bear the burden of showing that it will not pollute. Any permit for the construction of a plant that could conceivably give rise to a damaging pollution incident should perhaps be conditioned upon the posting of a high bond to indemnify the state in case such an incident does in fact occur. Had the phosphate companies been subject to such a requirement, the Peace River would probably not have been devastated four times during the past 14 years by the escape of clay slimes. The exigencies of a developing national fuel shortage will dictate some oil drilling off the Florida coast, but, again, any permits for drilling within the state's territorial limits should be conditioned on promise of substantial indemnity to the state in case of spills.

The growth of nonpolluting light manufacturing activities will continue to be regarded as desirable in most of Florida, especially if most of the labor is to be recruited locally. Manufacturing jobs pay better than most tourist-oriented jobs and offer further opportunity for the upwardly mobile. As for the expansion of agriculture in south Florida, the disadvantages of this will often outweigh the advantages, particularly if drainage of wetlands is involved. For instance, although elaborate water control methods make it possible to grow citrus on the flatwoods lands of south Florida, where frost is infrequent, there are major drawbacks to this kind of agricultural development—namely, a loss of wetlands and wildlife habitat, a lowered water table over a considerable area, increased consumption of water, and more competition for growers in the Central Highlands who must in any event worry about overproduction. However, consumption of water in south Florida by agriculture probably will not increase, and may actually decrease if farming in the Everglades Agricultural Area declines as the result of soil subsidence, as predicted.

Perhaps the most controversial question to arise with respect to growth policy will be that of striking an appropriate balance between tourism and the "retirement industry." Many Floridians intuitively believe that the state should encourage tourism but discourage the continued influx of retirees, especially into the Gold Coast region. This intuition, I would submit, is essentially well founded if an exception is made for the numerous thinly populated counties of north Florida and the panhandle where the establishment of retiree communities could be beneficial. The tourist and retirement industries are actually in conflict in some places. In Miami Beach no new modern hotels have been built in recent years; yet the old hotel district of south Miami Beach has been allowed to become a kind of ghetto for many retired Jewish people living on meager pensions. From the standpoint of both economic payoff and the number of people benefitted, tourism would generally seem to deserve priority over the retirement industry. However, the idea of using land use controls to limit the influx of retirees and to impede immigration generally, is one that many thoughtful people find troubling. Why, they ask, should the people now living in south Florida— many of them only recently arrived—have the right to say no to those who wish to come? The best answer, I believe, is that few people really benefit much when environmental quality is sacrificed to excessive growth, or to growth that occurs at the wrong place or the wrong time. Also, is it not better to keep all of Florida attractive for the some 25 million visitors the state receives annually than to accept increasing environmental degradation along the Gold Coast as retirees and other migrants continue to arrive faster than essential public services can be provided? Furthermore, no one is talking about erecting a fence at the state line to keep out newcomers. All that is being seriously discussed is the need to guide settlement within the state in a way beneficial to all, newcomers and established residents alike. A new retirement community in the panhandle or north Florida will not have as many warm winter days as one in Dade County, but it will be pleasant enough, with golfing weather extending essentially year round. In many respects, it will be more pleasant, for the residents of such a community will not suffer the problems of growth found in Dade. It should be pointed out, moreover, that "exclusionary zoning"—the practice of excluding lower-income people by devices such as establishing very large minimum lot sizes or high square-footage requirements for floor space —need not be allowed to pass under the guise of land use controls essential to prevent environmental abuse. If zoning practices in some areas do so discriminate, the state and local governments have the option—although admittedly it may be an option politically difficult to exercise—of requiring developers either to reserve a certain percentage of new housing units for low-to-moderate income people or to contribute to the financing of such housing.

Growth policy issues of the kind raised by the south Florida regional jetport project are less open and shut than many environmentalists believe. Let us assume that future policies call for a redirection and slowing down of growth along the Gold Coast, with construction of housing there aimed chiefly at the retiree market to be sharply curbed. Under such circumstances, there might be a need to encourage certain other economic activities that generate jobs and income but are compatible with a lower rate of population growth. Further development of tourism, light manufacturing, and commercial aviation could perhaps serve this need. Building a regional jetport somewhere in south Florida, though not necessarily in Dade County, could contribute significantly to that development. Finally, I would observe that a growth policy for south Florida should play to the region's natural advantages, and one of those advantages is its gateway location in the Americas and its position as a natural hub for international air traffic.

As for the question, "How much growth?", hard and fast growth ceilings for an entire local jurisdiction—such as the one adopted in 1972 by Boca Raton—may be unwise and legally indefensible. Usually it should be enough to observe a policy of allowing only such development as can be accommodated without loss of environmental quality.

SECOND POLICY: THE FLORIDA STANDARDS. The establishment of comprehensive environmental protection and amenity standards to apply to development throughout the state will be essential to effective land use control. Why? Because they can be made responsive to the following critical realities of land use policy and regulation:

(i) Comprehensive planning and zoning tend to be long-drawn-out and rather abstract. Pending preparation of a comprehensive plan, standards can themselves help serve to prevent abuses of land and water resources. Also, after the plan has been adopted, standards should help ensure the protection and enhancement of environmental quality in those numerous areas where development is allowed and encouraged.

(ii) Development is, by virtue of the market economy, a dynamic and continuing process that occurs unevenly, in large and small increments. Or, in other words, while development can be restricted with respect to kind, size, and place, it surely cannot be systematically programmed according to a preconceived plan. But, given the enforcement of appropriate standards, even the piecemeal development of an area can occur in a rational and desirable manner.

(iii) The local and state officials who make land use decisions are fallible men and women exercising wide powers of discretion. Standards will not only guide official decisions but could also give citizens acting as "private attorneys general"—a concept I shall come to later—better means of challenging in court any private or official actions that flout the public's interest in a high quality of life.

What precisely would the Florida Standards consist of? First, they would include existing standards of air and water quality. Those standards have always had major implications for land use, a fact which many Americans perceived for the first time in 1973 when the U.S. Environmental Protection Agency began calling for restrictions on the use of automobiles in those urban centers afflicted with severe air pollution. Some of the implications of water quality standards for land use in Dade County were discussed in an earlier chapter. But the Florida Standards would be related not to just a few indices of environmental quality, but to many. They would, for instance, ensure public access to ocean and Gulf beaches and to all publicly owned lakes—the standard for beach access might ordinarily require landowners to make available public rights-of-way at regular intervals, say of one-half mile. The standards would also reinforce those provisions of existing law intended to protect coastal wetlands. Buyers of lots in new water-oriented communities would know not to expect to keep their boats in finger canals adjoining their property. Instead, all would use a common marina and a single small boat channel connecting to open water, thus minimizing disturbance to the estuarine ecosystem. Under the standards, the only facilities that might be permitted to encroach upon ecologically valuable marine bottoms would be those few that actually require a waterfront location for their normal functioning, as in the case of a marina.

The standards would aim at making every new community, whatever the income level of its residents, a place of esthetic appeal—indeed, given Florida's lush subtropical climate, every community could literally become a garden through imaginative landscaping and planting. The preservation of natural features such as sloughs and cypressheads would be strongly encouraged if not made mandatory. Such abominations as strip development along urban highways would be forbidden. In the case of both new commercial and residential construction, the Florida Standards would encourage planned unit development, and, in appropriate situations, use of the PUD-district and "development shares" concepts earlier discussed with respect to the Big Cypress. The Florida Standards would not remain static, but would evolve as new concepts and technologies open up possibilities for a better adjustment between man and his environment. For example, solar energy units capable of heating homes in winter and cooling them in summer may soon be available at prices competitive with the cost of installing and using electric or oil-fired units. If so, the Florida Standards could be amended to encourage, if not require, builders to equip new homes to tap this inexhaustible energy source and not place additional demand on nonrenewable sources. (Even today, in Greater Miami more than 60,000 homes have solar water heaters, most of them installed in the 1930s and 1940s before all-electric living came into vogue.)[4]

For all their potential, however, the Florida Standards are best regarded as an important complement to comprehensive planning and zoning and not as a substitute for them. Planning and zoning are needed to give direction to growth and development and provide a basis for infrastructure plans.

THIRD POLICY: ZONING. The zoning that I have in mind would differ greatly from the conventional kind practiced in many Florida counties. In the past, private interests have generally been allowed the initiative in deciding what land in Florida is to be developed, even if recently many developers have had their plans frustrated by local officials who are feeling the heat from citizens demanding moratoriums on new construction. What is needed is a zoning policy that firmly guides the developer away from areas where development will not be in the public interest to other areas where it will be.

Lands to be placed in *preservation* zones would include, for example, undeveloped flood plains and wetlands of high ecologic, hydrologic, and esthetic value, these to include many of the "high marsh" areas along the coast (areas subject only to periodic tidal flooding and hence not presently protected as regular tidal or submerged lands) and some of the more important interior wetlands. Many preservation areas would, of course, be publicly acquired for inclusion in either the state or federal system of parks and wildlife refuges. Public acquisition seems indicated in the case of lands whose owners can be allowed virtually no use of their property,

4. Florida Energy Committee, *Report to the Governor and Florida Legislature*, March 1, 1974, p. 18.

as, for instance, if in order to protect the biota, traditional uses such as ranching, hunting, or use of swamp buggies are banned. On the other hand, if traditional uses are to be allowed, preservation through noncompensable regulation should be an option open to the state, although the best course for the long term probably would be for the state or federal government to buy the land once it becomes available at a reasonable price.

Conservation zones would be established for environmentally sensitive areas where limited development is to be allowed. Again, as suggested in the chapter on the Big Cypress, PUD districts could be authorized by law and allowed to undertake such development, even in the face of problems of multiple property ownerships. Conservation and preservation zoning, together with the establishment of additional parks and preserves, should protect most of the important remaining natural ecosystems in Florida.

The preservation of much of Florida's farmland should, in my view, be provided for through *agricultural* zoning, but such zoning should take into account the complex relationships between land committed to agriculture and land devoted to other purposes. The unfavorable environmental effects associated with certain forms of Florida agriculture have constituted a major public burden. Most significant have been the bad effects of wetlands drainage, which have included soil subsidence, saltwater intrusion, muck fires, loss of wildlife and natural ecosystems, high consumptive demand for water, and the water pollution caused by agricultural runoff. On the other hand, there are some highly beneficial environmental effects associated with agriculture, not to mention the fact that Florida agricultural products have a market value of $1.3 billion a year and represent, in part, a subtropical resource found nowhere else in the United States. Agricultural zoning might be broken down into several subclassifications (A-1, A-2, and so on). The highest classification would denote several things: that the land is capable of producing a high value crop; that the environmental effects associated with farming it are, on the whole, beneficial; and, perhaps also, that the land is strategically placed in an interurban region where a critical need for open space exists. Conversely, the lowest classification would denote that the land is of mediocre productivity; that the environmental effects of the farm operations are, on balance, unfavorable; and that the land is not well situated with respect to interurban open space requirements. Citrus groves in the Central Highlands would usually fall in the highest agricultural classification—this in light of their productivity, scenic beauty, and value for aquifer recharge. Groves in the flatwoods of south Florida would have a lower classification, as they are less scenic and have a negative environmental impact. Yet, by issuance of special permits, even land in the highest agricultural classifications could be opened to limited development, with land owners again making use of the concept of the PUD district. In fact, the amenities of the Central Highlands grove country are such as to make a mix of urban and agricultural uses eminently desirable. The transfer of large blocks of agricultural land (as opposed to smaller tracts intended for development enclaves) to development or conservation zoning normally would be allowed only for land in the lower agricultural classifications. Uncultivated land in the Everglades Agricultural Area might, for instance, initially be given a low agricultural classification, with part of it possibly to be reclassified for development (as for use as a regional jetport site) and part to be diked off, reflooded, and reclassified for conservation. Transfers of land from conservation to agricultural zoning would, of course, be especially appropriate where the land in question is naturally suited for the production of farm products for which there is rising demand.

· *Development* zoning would, at its broadest, cover all existing cities, and suburbs and land designated for new towns, industrial parks, transportation or utility rights of way, and, more generally, land that local and state authorities have not placed in any other zoning category. In the main, this would be land that is easily developable (with little or no drainage or filling required) and not in intensive agricultural use. What I already have written about growth policy and the Florida Standards speaks to some of the strategies and regulatory concepts under which urban development can proceed. In a moment, I shall discuss the important questions of how control of land development should be structured administratively and how citizens can influence the decisions reached.

FOURTH POLICY: INFRASTRUCTURE. The construction of facilities such as roads, airports, interceptor sewers, and the like has of course generally followed development in Florida, and has not preceded or accompanied it according to a deliberate plan. Yet one of the most powerful levers available to local and state officials for controlling land use lies in their authority to decide when and where essential public facilities will be built. The infrastructure plans and the zoning that will determine patterns of future growth and development should be prepared in close concert. The infrastructure plan would include at least three distinct functional plans: one for transportation, another for waste management, and the third for water management. Although each of these might continue to be prepared and executed separately, all should reflect objectives and priorities established for the overall regional plan.

The infrastructure plan can be made still more persuasive in its effect on developers if tied to a "point system" of the kind the town of Ramapo, New York, has been using since 1972. In Ramapo, a building permit for a residential development is issued only if the project meets enough basic requirements to qualify for a certain minimum number of "development points." Issuance of the permit is assured if the project can hook onto established sewer, storm drain, and arterial street systems and will be near a fire station, school site, and public park. If, however, the project is seriously deficient in two or more of these particulars, the permit will be denied. The Ramapo system reflects a special concern to encourage relatively compact development and thus minimize the capital investment to be needed for urban services.

STRUCTURE

If Florida's growth and development is to be guided in a positive and politically responsible manner, a comprehensive structure for planning and decision making must be established, with ultimate power residing in Tallahassee but with local government, and especially county government, playing the principal implementing role.

REFORM OF LOCAL GOVERNMENT. At the bottom of the structure, most urban counties perhaps should have the kind of two-tiered local government contemplated in the Metropolitan Dade County charter and now apparently approaching fruition under Dade's new political leadership. An alternative, however, would be a countywide consolidated government on the Jacksonville-Duval County model. In either case, I would propose that the county government be responsible for establishing an enforceable general land use master plan and at least minimum zoning regulations for the entire county. All decisions by independent municipalities or specialized agencies (such as water management districts) having a substantial impact on land use would be subject to review by the county governing body.

Several points should be made in justification of the foregoing proposal. The first is that the county is generally a jurisdictional unit quite large enough to serve for most (though certainly not all) regional planning purposes. Of Florida's sixty-seven counties, five (Palm Beach, Dade, Collier, Polk, and Monroe) contain some 2,000 square miles or more, making them comparable in size to the state of Delaware; another nineteen contain about 1,000 square miles or more, an area about the size of the state of Rhode Island. Only five counties contain substantially less than 500 square miles, and there is no compelling reason why boundary adjustments cannot be made among the counties, with some of them to be consolidated if that should seem desirable.

Just as nearly all Florida counties themselves constitute sizeable regions, they also constitute traditional and well-established political jurisdictions, which are not so large that their governing bodies are remote from the citizens. If strengthened administratively and politically under state policies designed to accomplish those ends, the county governments can be made to coordinate effectively all local planning and decision making in matters pertaining to growth policy and land use. That such coordination is essential is evident: the 383 municipal governments in Florida—of which nearly 100 are found in the Gold Coast counties—cannot be allowed much longer to exercise exclusive jurisdiction over most matters of land use regulation within their boundaries.

I prefer the Metropolitan Dade County model over the Jacksonville-Duval consolidated county-municipal government model because I share the common belief that governmental responsibilities should be met at the lowest levels of government where they can be dealt with competently. In that spirit, the two-tier Dade metro model offers the clear advantage of allowing many questions of planning and zoning to be decided at the municipal level. Furthermore, under the metro charter, the municipalities have a right to apply more demanding or restrictive zoning regulations than the county itself might prescribe. This last safeguard would be particularly important to many people living in counties such as Collier where county officials generally have been less concerned about protecing the quality of life than have the municipal officials. In fact, voters in the city of Naples a few years ago voted down a proposed county charter because they feared the county commission would gain control over the city's affairs. Indeed, a strong case can be made for encouraging the establishment of new municipalities in situations where the residents of a particular area want more restrictive land use regulations. Even as I write, the residents of Sanibel Island, in Lee County, are taking steps to gain control over the rampant growth and development that lenient county regulations have encouraged. At their bidding, the legislature has just provided for the incorporation of Sanibel as a city, subject to a local referendum.

Although I prefer the Dade Metro model, the Jacksonville-Duval consolidated government may be a model that is more practical and politically realistic for a number of counties which, like Duval, contain but one municipality of consequence. Such counties as Alachua (Gainesville), Marion (Ocala), and Leon (Tallahassee) fit that description. Whichever model is to be preferred, the state government will have to take a hand in seeing that the restructuring of local government actually takes place, for usually nothing is more controversial than proposals to bring about such reform. The legislature must either direct that the necessary changes be made or provide strong incentives.

The comprehensive local land use plans that I envision would be similar to what was contemplated in the comprehensive planning bill introduced in the 1974 legislature, with one major exception. Each county government would be responsible for assembling and approving an overall plan for the entire county, including those areas within municipal boundaries. (Under the bill considered by the legislature, the counties and cities would be on an equal footing in the preparation of plans.) The state, for its part, would play the dual role of exercising general oversight with respect to the counties' comprehensive plans and meeting its special statutory responsibilities with respect to matters such as DRIs, areas of critical state concern, and the review and approval of coastal bulkhead lines and beach setback lines.

REFORM IN TALLAHASSEE. The major governmental reforms that swept over Tallahassee in the late 1960s made the cabinet system only somewhat less objectionable than it had been before. A top reform priority now, I believe, should be to abolish that system for once and always. The governor should be given the power to appoint all department heads except possibly the head of the Department of Legal Affairs, which perhaps should continue to be under an independently elected attorney general. The advantages of getting rid of the cabinet system would be many, and I shall refer to some of them in a moment.

Floridians have had an understandable attachment to the cabinet system, however, perhaps chiefly because of its relative openness and because many people prefer to entrust especially important issues to a group of independently elected officials than to any one official, even though that official might be the governor. These are indeed virtues not to be lightly given up, especially when they are associated with a body that has been a part of Florida tradition for nearly ninety years. For this reason, if for no other, there is an argument to be made for establishing a new body of elected officials to cope with the intensely political issues of growth policy and land and water management. This body might be called the Florida Conservation and Development Commission, or simply the Florida Commission. I would suggest that it be made up of the governor, who would be its chairman, and six other members to be independently elected at large for four-year staggered terms.

The commission's duties would be:

(i) To make up and approve the "Florida Plan," which would be the annual plan setting forth the broad planning and policy framework for the state's physical development. In preparing the plan, the commission would pull together into a coherent whole the policies and plans of the various departments of state government, such as those of the departments of transportation, community affairs, pollution control, agriculture, and natural resources. It would also review and integrate the comprehensive land use master plans and infrastructure plans received from the sixty-seven counties, resolving conflicts among those plans and making sure that each plan conforms to state policy. Each year's Florida Plan would be tied closely to the state budget, and, like the budget itself, would be subject to the review and approval of the legislature.

(ii) To adopt and keep up to date the Florida Standards, doing so within general policies established by the legislature.

(iii) To assume the statutory duties of the cabinet with respect to matters such as bulkhead lines, dredge-and-fill permits, beach setback lines, areas of critical concern, developments of regional impact, and the state water resources plan. The commission's burdens could be lightened somewhat through the use of administrative hearing officers. (The cabinet itself is now using hearing officers before acting on appeals from the decisions of local government in DRI cases, and, as Governor Askew has told me, the cabinet's future work load will probably be such as to make reliance on such officers routine.)

Ordinarily, the commission would decide questions by majority vote, the governor's role counting the same as those of the other members. But the governor perhaps should be given the prerogative of vetoing any commission decision that fails to receive the support of at least five of the other six commission members. Giving the governor this limited power of veto could discourage commission members from dividing up into prodevelopment and antidevelopment blocks. Each commission member would serve full-time, receive the same salary as a department head, and have a small personal staff. The present state Department of Administration, with its planning and budget divisions, would provide the staff support for the commission. The staff director would be appointed by the governor, with the commission's concurrence.

The present cabinet system should be abolished if only because it flouts principles of political accountability. Voters cannot properly hold the governor accountable for the performance of all the executive departments because some of the most important departments are headed either by officials who are independently elected or, as in the case of the Department of Natural Resources (DNR), by an official named by the cabinet as a whole. Randolph Hodges did not retire as director of the DNR until early 1974, long after Governor Askew wanted him to go. He had had the support of a majority of the cabinet and was thus able to disregard Askew's wishes in the matter. His successor, Harmon Shields, known around Tallahassee as a good ole boy distinguished for his excellent political connections, was chosen on a four to three cabinet vote, with the governor again in the minority.

As I pointed out in the chapter on pork chop rule, there is also a serious problem of political accountability with respect to the election of the six cabinet members. In the election for commissioner of education or state comptroller, it makes no sense for the voter to have to worry about how the candidates feel about the Cross Florida Barge Canal or the loss of mangroves to dredging and filling. The cabinet system may be coming into particularly bad odor now because of the indictment of one of its former members for bribery and the investigation of two incumbent members for possible malfeasance. The time is perhaps ripe to try to sweep the thing away.

The Florida Commission could be made up of appointive instead of elected officials, but such a body almost certainly would be too weak politically to decide effectively the many controversial issues on its agenda.

The tendency would be for those developers and local officials who happened to be outraged by some decisions to go over its head to the governor and the legislature and try to get those decisions reversed. This has happened repeatedly in the case of the pollution control board, an appointive body. As an elective body, the Florida Commission would be in a far stronger position to defend its actions. Furthermore, public understanding of issues of growth policy and land and water management could be much enhanced by the debate preceding the biennial election of members to several commission seats. (In years of gubernatorial elections a majority of the seven seats would be at stake.) Environmental groups, chambers of commerce, land development companies, farm groups, and other interests all would be promoting candidates. The development-oriented candidates would have an advantage in raising campaign funds, but, if the past is any guide, the conservation-oriented candidates would receive much attention and support from the major Florida newspapers.

SOME EXECUTIVE REARRANGEMENT. To make the structural reforms complete, abolition of the existing cabinet system and establishment of the Florida Commission should perhaps be accompanied by some rearrangement of the executive departments. The temptation to tidy things up by establishing a super-department of environmental protection and natural resources should be resisted, however. For in such departments, conflicts between agencies with different missions tend to be "internalized" and decided without receiving the attention of elected officials. Some gains in bureaucratic efficiency may be possible from establishing a super-department, but this advantage is likely to be more than offset by the suppression of open competition between agency viewpoints. Shortly after the Cross Florida Barge Canal project was stopped by President Nixon, W. A. McCree, Jr., president of the Florida Waterways Association and former chairman of the Canal Authority, appeared before the cabinet and deplored the "bickering and name calling" going on among spokesmen for the Pollution Control Department, the Department of Natural Resources, and the Florida Game and Fresh Water Fish Commission. But what McCree regarded as bickering, others had found to be an illuminating clash of viewpoints on an important question of water resources development.

"One-Stop" Permit System. To provide for a "one-stop" state permit system in Tallahassee for all development projects requiring state permits would be, I believe, a highly desirable reform. The present two-stop system that applies to dredge-and-fill projects causes the developer needless frustration and does not make much sense from the standpoint of the environmentalist either. The developer loses both time and money making his case first before the I.I. Board or cabinet in applying for a dredge-and-fill permit, then again before the Florida Pollution Control Board in seeking the "cer-

tification" that is required under the Clean Water Act of 1972 before the Corps of Engineers can issue a permit. Environmental groups opposed to a particular project are given, in effect, a second chance to block the project if they fail to persuade the cabinet to their point of view. Yet there is no logical justification for the cabinet itself not thoroughly considering a project's potential impact on water quality, especially inasmuch as that impact will be inseparable from the project's other physical and biological effects.[5] For this reason, if for none other, the pollution control board's certification authority should, I believe, be transferred to the Florida Commission I have proposed. The one-stop permitting authority now vested in the board with respect to the siting of electricity generating plants probably also should be given to the commission. This would be in keeping with the concept of vesting ultimate authority for the most important matters of land and water management in one highly visible elected body.

Integrity in Environmental Surveys. Special measures should be taken to protect and ensure the integrity of those agencies and units responsible for making environmental surveys and assessing the probable impact of development projects. For instance, the Department of Natural Resources' Bureau of Geology and Office of Survey and Management (responsible for the biological surveys required for dredge-and-fill projects) might be placed in a new Office of Environmental Survey. This office could remain part of the Department of Natural Resources (DNR) for most administrative purposes, but its director should be appointed by the governor and have direct access both to him and the Florida Commission. Public confidence in the office could also be enhanced by having the governor appoint a panel of distinguished scientists to advise it.

The need to protect scientific and technical assessment from the suspicion or reality of political influence can be readily illustrated from the recent past. Conservationists were distrustful in 1970 when Robert O. Vernon, who was then chief of the Bureau of Geology, declared that construction of the barge canal would not harm the Floridan Aquifer. Although quite

5. The long-drawn-out controversy over the Deltona Corporation's Marco Island and Marco Shores developments is a case in point. The cabinet has made deals with Deltona in which approval of extensive dredge-and-fill operations has been exchanged for the gift of certain company-owned lands (title is in some dispute) to the state. These agreements were reached in good faith and represent a commendable effort by the I.I. Board staff to use the permit requirement to obtain from Deltona substantial concessions in the public interest. Nevertheless, they would allow large-scale degradation of the estuarine environment. In the spring of 1974, the pollution control board finally granted certification for three remaining dredge-and-fill projects on Marco Island, but still had not certified an especially controversial Marco Shores project that abuts the National Audubon Society's Rookery Bay Sanctuary. In a legal sense, the cabinet is presumed to have already disposed of the land use issues arising under the permit application, and the pollution control board and its staff are now supposed to consider only the effects the project would have on water quality. Yet, in biological terms, the land use and water quality considerations are really inseparable and should be dealt with as such.

possibly unjustified, such distrust was understandable—Vernon's immediate superior in the DNR was the retired Corps of Engineers colonel who had recommended that the canal be built. In another case, the biologist heading the Office of Survey and Management resigned in 1972 because of differences with Hodges, the DNR director. Hodges had reduced his responsibilities and placed the supervision of his budget under another retired Corps of Engineers colonel.

THE ROLE OF REGIONAL PLANNING COUNCILS. Regional planning councils comprised of local government representatives have not, in either Florida or other states, generally distinguished themselves by their influence on land management or the growth process. But this may be in part because such bodies have too seldom been put in a position where their reports and recommendations could prove a decisive influence. Under Florida's Environmental Land Management Act of 1972, however, regional planning councils now have the role of preparing impact analysis reports on large-scale developments or DRIs. These reports, of course, become publicly available and are an important source of information about the merits of pending projects. For example, as noted in the chapter on Dade County, the staff report filed by the South Florida Regional Planning Council (SFRPC) on the proposed new community of Doral Park pointed out how this project could be expected to increase traffic congestion, possibly cause pollution of ground water, and, while offering little or no housing within the means of present county residents of low to moderate income, accommodate affluent new migrants from out of state.

By law, if a planning council disagrees with the decision reached by the city or county governing body with respect to a DRI, the council can appeal to the cabinet. Its reports and recommendations must, therefore, be taken seriously by both developers and the local governments. While it is true that the councils are largely creatures of the local government, they may nevertheless behave objectively and in a true regional perspective. Especially is this true in those parts of Florida where the influence of developers is now counterbalanced by the influence of people who would restrain growth. In fact, the incumbent chairman of the SFRPC is Harvey Ruvin, leader of the successful campaign in 1971–72 for Dade County's building moratorium ordinance. Rigorous and objective performance by the regional councils can be encouraged by having them receive formal reports from the regional water management agencies on all DRIs and other important planning and development questions. The SFRPC is in fact receiving such reports from the Flood Control District, an agency now quite plainspoken about the hazards of excessive or misplaced development. With its governing board made up of gubernatorial appointees, the FCD is most definitely not local government's creature.

In sum, the governor and legislature appear to have acted quite wisely in giving the regional planning councils an enhanced role and some state financial support. If any suggestion is in order, it is that it might be well if some planning council members could be appointed by the governor, especially in the case of councils serving regions where there is not yet much public concern about uncontrolled growth and its effect on the quality of life.

POLITICS

The political feasibility of any program for the regulation of growth and development will, quite obviously, depend on whether it is understood and supported by a majority of the citizens affected. Accordingly, there is a need for truly meaningful, not merely pro forma, citizen participation in land use planning at the county level.

CITIZEN PARTICIPATION IN PLANNING. The county plans will be of such importance that innovative methods to bring about public participation in their development will be needed. For each county, and for some large areas within a county, the basic question for planners and decision makers will be: What is the best mix of developmental, agricultural, conservation, and preservation zoning? Although state policy will provide much guidance, questions of emphasis and of how to resolve potential conflicts will remain.

County governments could point up these questions by having citizens help formulate and review two or more alternative plans, with one plan perhaps emphasizing conservation goals, while another emphasizes development. The county board, in cooperation with the Florida Commission, could schedule planning conferences and invite all interested individuals and groups to offer statements and plans as to the best pattern of conservation and development for the area in question. Conferees would presumably include representatives of municipalities, state and federal agencies, conservation groups, chambers of commerce, associations of architects and builders, labor unions, farm groups, inner-city minorities, and so on. A conference pertaining solely to an area within one county could be presided over by that county's elected board chairman or mayor; one pertaining to an area lying in more than one county, or to some question of regional or statewide concern, might be chaired by a representative of the regional planning council or the Division of State Planning. The conference could run several days and be reconvened as often as necessary. The end product would be a report broadly setting forth, for the area under consideration, an array of alternative plans or "futures." (Where the formulation of alternatives is hindered by a lack of technical information—as might occur in considering alternate routes for, say, a mass transit system—the conferees could nevertheless identify and illuminate some of the relevant policy issues.) At this point, the appropriate planning staff, whether of the county government or the regional planning council, could be instructed to set forth the various plans more precisely and in whatever detail necessary for public understanding. All of the plans considered, however much they might differ in emphasis as between conservation and development, would be expected to satisfy the minimum requirements of state policy. Finally, the governing body of the county or counties concerned would choose the plan to be put into effect. Alternatively, the voters could be allowed to make their own choice of plans in a referendum.

The Florida Commission, with the help of the legislature, would see to it that every county government has the capability to prepare such alternative plans. Otherwise, county land use planning is likely to be dominated by elites or special interests of one kind or another. The Collier County Conservancy in Naples, which has initiated and joined with the county government in financing a land use study for the area around Rookery Bay (a prime estuarine area south of Naples), is a good example of a private group that can make a strong contribution to county land use planning. However, given its membership roster made up mostly of wealthy retirees, the conservancy cannot pretend to speak for a broad public, even though I believe its goals to be generally in the public interest. The Mangrove Chapter of the Izaak Walton League in Miami also has sponsored useful studies, including one suggesting a concept of limited development for south Dade County; but, again, one could argue that the league is no more representative of the people of Dade County than is the Greater Miami Chamber of Commerce. The best course is to put these and other groups on a more or less equal footing and encourage them all to take part in a plan-formulating process that is led by elected officials and paid for with tax money.

If the integrity of the county plans is to be protected, all zoning should be consistent with those plans and no change of zoning should be permitted without a corresponding plan amendment. To prevent such amendments from being made routinely, they could be allowed only by a two-thirds vote of the county governing board.

TAX REFORM. The political acceptability of any effective program of land use planning and regulations may be compromised if some property owners are allowed large profits as a result of zoning and infrastructure decisions while others are denied the most profitable use of their land. Although this problem exists even under conventional land use regulations, the problem will be more acute under a system where zoning changes and variances are relatively few and where roads and other facilities are planned more to guide development than to respond to it. Perhaps the best way of coping with this problem is to enact laws allowing the state to levy a special capital gains tax on profits realized from the sale of unimproved land. The state of Vermont may have shown the way in this matter with its 1973 tax law designed to discourage short-term speculation. This statute provides for a capital gains tax on land sales, which varies from 60 percent on profits from land that has been sold within one year of its purchase down to 5 percent on land held for a number of years. An antiwindfall law of this kind should tend to cool the speculative fever that will inevitably continue in regard to those lands zoned for agriculture that are near urban areas where some rezoning for development may be inevitable. Like the special capital gains tax, a fair and rigorously administered property tax would also do much to eliminate inequities associated with land values created through zoning and infrastructure decisions.

State leadership in matters of growth policy and land use controls is likely to be better received if the state contributes more to the financing of local government. Accordingly, it seems in order for the state to impose such additional taxes—possibly including a personal income tax—as are needed to help the county and municipal governments meet their basic needs. Such aid would help compensate local governments for any losses in tax receipts resulting from zoning rollbacks and other land use policy decisions bringing about lower taxable values. Also, if a substantially greater part of the funds for the support of local government comes from the state, local governments should be less tempted to accept new development promising tax benefits at the price of a decline in the quality of life.

PRIVATE ATTORNEYS GENERAL. All bureaucracies, at whatever level of government, seem eventually either to lapse into a comfortable, unflappable routine or to become otherwise unresponsive to legitimate demands made upon them by citizens. Part of the problem is that the people running them often have reason to fear that, should they demand strict observance of the laws and regulations for which their agency is responsible, they will anger influential legislators or others who can cause serious trouble. Evidence of such administrative paralysis can be seen in the leniency with which pollution control laws sometimes have been enforced in Florida and other states. Citizens concerned about proper enforcement of laws pertaining to growth policy and land and water management may ultimately have to go to court. They may well lack the means to do so, however, and, under the rules which American courts generally follow, a successful plaintiff cannot recover his attorney's fees from the defendant. This is true even though the defendant may be a wealthy corporation or a government agency. The legislature could offer relief here by providing for recovery where the plaintiff either prevails on the merits or is found by the court to have otherwise performed a valuable public service. Already, there have been a number of federal court rulings in public interest law cases calling for fee recovery, doing so on the theory that the plaintiffs have been acting in the role of private attorneys general.[6]

6. "Attorneys' Fees: The Growing Number of Awards to Public Interest Plaintiffs," *Environmental Law Reporter* (February 1974), 4 ELI 10021.

Because of its government-in-the-sunshine law, Florida already has done more than most other states to abate corrupt practices, including those that have abounded in the regulation of land use. It could do still better, however. Problems of conflict of interest persist in many counties and undercut the integrity of the local planning and zoning process. These problems could be much reduced if the legislature were to enact a stronger conflict of interest law, perhaps one modeled on the Dade County ordinance of 1972. Such a statute would prohibit not only every state and local official, employee, and advisory board member, but also every member of his immediate family from conducting business with the state or county and from profiting in any way from his government position. Any official or employee violating this law could be removed from office, fined, and jailed. Still more important from the standpoint of protecting the integrity of government would be better enforcement of the existing state law regulating campaign financing, a reform which may in fact now be accomplished as the result of a state election commission recently established by act of the legislature. The 1974 legislature also has had under consideration a bill, given high priority by the governor, that calls for disclosure of all significant sources of the income received by public officials.

A MAJOR TESTING GROUND

Because of the urgency of its problem of accelerated growth, Florida is clearly a major testing ground for the development of growth policy and a better process of land and water management. What are Florida's prospects of succeeding in bringing growth and development under effective and enlightened public regulation? The answer, which must be equivocal, involves a paradox. The continuing heavy influx of new people into Florida will, in one sense, make success less likely because it allows no respite. Plans for instituting controls tend to be overridden by events. On the other hand, the very massiveness of the growth pressures keeps people aroused and determined to find a way to protect their quality of life. Further, there is the ironical fact that the very newcomers who add to the severity of the growth problem help make that problem politically more amenable to strong remedies. They generally are not beholden to local business or political interests, and their self-interest lies chiefly in preserving and enhancing the living amenities that attracted them to Florida.

Many Floridians, especially in the rural counties, continue to think they have an absolute right to do as they please with their property. Such attitudes appear to be gradually fading, however, as it becomes increasingly evident that the old unrestrained individualism of frontier Florida cannot be sustained under present-day conditions. The 1973 report of the Task Force on Land Use and Urban Growth chaired by Laurance S. Rockefeller predicts that, in forthcoming decades, Americans will abandon the traditional assumption that ownership of land necessarily carries development rights.[7] Court precedents bearing on this point differ widely, and it was the task force's opinion that state and local law-making bodies should proceed boldly in adopting land use control measures. The stringent land use regulations imposed by the cabinet in the Big Cypress critical area are at least a tentative thrust in that direction.

Also, those Floridians who argue that prosperity is not dependent on population growth find increasing support for their opinion among demographers, economists, and other specialists. Indeed, the 1972 report of the Commission on Population Growth and the American Future affirmed such a view. And it is frequently pointed out by concerned Floridians that, with uncontrolled population growth contributing to pollution and other problems, Florida will become less attractive to tourists at the same time that more and more of them are discovering the attractions of competing resorts in the Bahamas and the West Indies. Furthermore, increasing numbers of Floridians are realizing that, while the state and local governments can do nothing about population growth trends nationally, they can reduce or at least direct and redistribute such growth in Florida by land use controls. This idea, I suspect, will prove to be an increasingly powerful one in public debate about the "growth problem." It could eventually become as appealing to the leaders of the thinly populated counties in north Florida and the panhandle who want more people, as it is to those leaders on the Gold Coast who think that the population growth in their area must be restrained.

RESPECT FOR THE LAND

Underlying major changes in the behavior of people and their political institutions are usually a few powerful ideas. In the case of what has been called "the quiet revolution in land use control,"[8] popularization of the principal insight of ecology—that we occupy a finite biosphere of interdependent life support systems—is such an idea. Less grand but more intimate than that, however, is the idea of a "land ethic." Although necessarily vague in application, the land ethic is not lacking in meaning and substance. The oft-quoted words of Aldo Leopold, written shortly before his death in 1948, are appropriate here:

> Conservation is getting nowhere because it is incompatible with our Abrahamic concept of land. We abuse land because we regard it as a commodity belonging to us. When we see land as a community to which we belong, we may begin to use it with love and respect. There is no

7. *The Use of Land: A Citizens Policy Guide to Urban Growth*, a task force report sponsored by the Rockefeller Brothers Fund (New York: Thomas Y. Crowell Company, 1973), pp. 143 and 173.

8. Fred Bosselman and David Callies, *The Quiet Revolution in Land Use Control*, report prepared for the Council on Environmental Quality, 1972.

other way for land to survive the impact of mechanized man, nor for us to reap from it the esthetic harvest it is capable, under science, of contributing to culture.

That land is a community is the basic concept of ecology but that land is to be loved and respected is an extension of ethics. . . .[9]

In *So Human an Animal*,[10] René Dubos, the distinguished microbiologist and environmentalist, illuminates the land ethic in its profoundest dimension. Meticulously and with a fine eloquence, Dubos argues that man cannot escape a genetic inheritance acquired over the course of a long history during which he evolved as part of the natural world. In the Dubos view, modern man has, both consciously and unconsciously, tried foolishly to set himself above nature, as though his understanding of his own human needs and potential were not dependent upon a sympathetic awareness of nature and upon a sense of his own identity as a part of it.

The land ethic clearly has major implications for regulation of land use and for environmental management generally. In matters of land use policy, the tendency of even the more enlightened policy makers in Florida and other states has been to think in terms of "balancing" conservation and development. The land ethic refers to something more subtle, to a harmony between nature and the works of man. In delightful spots such as Eola Park in downtown Orlando, with its beautiful (albeit polluted) lake and huge spreading live oaks, one can sense how badly Floridians have deprived themselves by not trying to make more of a garden of the urban environment. The land ethic may also lead one to prefer the natural over the contrived. If all of Florida's wild rivers were sacrificed to commercialization and development, one might nevertheless get by with a Disney World "Jungle River" and its mechanical crocodiles. But such substitutes will not be enough for people who want Florida to be made whole again, in keeping with an ethical sense of man's relationship to the land. For nowhere better than in Florida's remaining wild places—and, despite all abuses, some splendid places remain—can one regain perspective and a sense of the wonder and mystery of life.

The opportunity for Floridians to have Florida remain a place of exceptional natural interest and esthetic appeal is the greater because nature, though it can tolerate only so much abuse, is remarkably resilient and forgiving. The fact that man and the natural world can coexist in an almost intimate way, given a bit of care, was brought home to me by an experience my family and I had a few summers ago during a stay at Delray Beach, midway along the Gold Coast. Although condominiums, motels, and other structures now line most of the 60 miles of ocean front from Palm Beach

9. Aldo Leopold, *A Sand County Almanac* (New York: Oxford University Press, 1966), p. X of Foreword.
10. Rene Dubos, *So Human an Animal* (New York: Charles Scribner's Sons, 1968).

south to Miami Beach, there are some stretches where the developers have shown enough restraint not to encroach directly upon the beach and to leave the dunes and the sea grapes largely undisturbed. Although the dunes have been replaced by a seawall along downtown Delray's eroding beach, no such encroachment had occurred farther south where we stayed. Each night our beach afforded us a chance to witness the reenactment of a scene that has been part of the rhythm of the seasons since the mists of pre-history. It was nesting time for the loggerhead turtles and these two-to-three hundred pound reptiles were emerging from the foaming surf to crawl awkwardly onto the beach, leaving deep prints in the soft sand resembling the tracks left by a caterpillar tractor. The loggerhead would lay her eggs in a hole neatly augured with her rear flippers; she would then fill in the nest, wallow about over it to conceal its location, and crawl heavily back into the surf whence she would not return for another two years. I am told that unless harrassed, turtles nesting along an inhabited beach such as ours at Delray may produce more young than if they nested along a wild beach, where raccoons are numerous and adept at discovering new nests. Observing these great sea turtles on the beach, in the most rapidly growing region in America, gave me a deeper insight into the possibilities for Florida if the people who live there cultivate a sense of place and a sense of respect for the land.

Epilogue

Implementation of the Florida Environmental Land and Water Management Act of 1972 did not begin until the last half of 1973, when the writing of this book was in its final stages. For this reason, I have been unable to attempt a thorough evaluation of the act and how it is being carried out (procedures prescribed in the act are diagrammed in figures 5–2 and 5–3). Indeed, the experience to date—as I write, it is October 1, 1974—is much too limited to allow such an evaluation. I will, however, briefly note a few salient facts and apparent trends from the first year's experience with this new law.

Areas of Critical State Concern. As noted in Chapter 8, the conferring of "critical area" status on part of the Big Cypress was not done under the Land and Water Management Act of 1972 but under a special 1973 act concerned only with the Big Cypress. Nevertheless, it is pertinent here to note that the efforts led this year by State Representative Lorenzo Walker of Collier County to have the legislature drastically reduce the boundaries of the Big Cypress area have come to nothing. If the legislature had done Walker's bidding by overriding the cabinet in this matter, a disturbing precedent would have been established for the whole critical area program.

Thus far, only one critical area has been established under the Land and Water Management Act itself—the Green Swamp critical area created by the cabinet, on a four to three vote, in July 1974. This new Green Swamp area, valued especially for water conservation and aquifer recharge, embraces 322,960 acres in two central Florida counties, Lake and Polk. Under the law, those counties would have six months from the time of the establishment of the area to adopt regulations—to conform to principles laid down by the cabinet—governing all development there.

The next critical areas established are expected to be in the Florida Keys and along the Apalachicola River. If a critical area embracing the keys is created, this will be a significant precedent because, for the first time, land use within most if not virtually all of a county's *inhabited area* will have become subject to state oversight. The keys are in Monroe County, and, while only Key West is heavily developed, all of the keys connected by U.S. 1 have seen development in varying degrees.

Developments of Regional Impact (DRIs). The Division of State Planning's Bureau of Land and Water Management issued in September 1974 a summary report for the first year's experience in regulating DRIs. One can conclude from the statistics contained in this document that, whatever the DRI program may be doing to improve the quality of large-scale development, little is being done either to reduce the amount of such development or to redirect much of it away from such already heavily developed areas as the Gold Coast and Tampa Bay regions.

Some 140 DRI applications were received by the local governments during the first year. Almost three-fourths of them were for residential developments. These residential DRIs would contain 632,287 dwelling units, which at 2.5 persons per unit would be enough to accommodate 1,580,000 people—or the equivalent of one-fifth of Florida's population of about 8 million (as estimated by the University of Florida's Bureau of Economic and Business Research, the population increased by more than 1 million between the 1970 census and mid-1973). Only 57 residential DRIs had been acted upon by local governments before the end of the period covered by the bureau's report; of those, only three were denied and they were among the smaller projects proposed. The 54 that were approved—in some cases outright, but usually with conditions—would contain 367,623 units, or enough for more than 1 million persons.

Out of 81 local decisions on DRIs of all kinds during the first year, only nine were appealed to the cabinet and eight of those involved residential DRIs (the ninth involved a proposed oil refinery in the Tampa Bay region). The regional planning councils, made up of local officials, initiated seven of the appeals and developers initiated two. The Division of State Planning (DSP), the only other party enjoying right of appeal (private groups have no such right), joined in one appeal by a regional council but initiated none on its own—a generally passive performance to which I shall return in a moment. The governor and cabinet have just unanimously disapproved the first DRI to come before it on appeal—a residential project in Lake County called "Three Rivers." Reversal of the Lake County Board of Commissioners' approval of the project had been recommended by the East Central Florida Regional Planning Council (which initiated the appeal), the DSP, the cabinet's own hearing examiner, and Seminole County, which the 5,300-acre project would adjoin. Opposition to the project, which Seminole County has led, turned on uncertainties about potable water supplies, sewage treatment, the disposal of storm runoff, the accommodation of the traffic to be generated, and possible incursions on flood plains.

Better than a third of all the dwelling units approved by local governments under the DRI program during the first year are to be built in the three Gold Coast counties—Dade, Broward, and Palm Beach. Together, these counties had some 130,500 units approved, enough to accommodate more than another third of a million people (Broward alone had more than 93,000 units). This means that the greatest growth, as measured in residential DRIs, is occurring in the very region where Governor Askew and many other thoughtful Floridians have wanted to see growth slowed down. Moreover, by far the largest number of new units would be built west of the coastal ridge, on land once a part of the Everglades and still valuable for recharging the Biscayne Aquifer. And one must bear in mind that probably half or more of all residential development is occurring in projects too small to come under the DRI program—in any of the three Gold Coast counties a project is not a DRI unless it has at least 3,000 units.

Clearly, the DRI program will not contribute importantly to controlling or directing growth until Florida has a comprehensive land use and growth policy. If the state had unequivocally laid down a policy to limit development west of the coastal ridge in south Florida, the DSP would surely have appealed certain of the affirmative DRI decisions by Dade Metro and other local governments along the Gold Coast. For its part, the South Florida Regional Planning Council has initiated six appeals against southeast Florida DRIs since the DRI program began, including three during the first year. In several instances, negotiations have resulted, with the council ultimately withdrawing the appeal in return for changes making the project more acceptable. But the council, a creature of local government, does not have either the political strength or the money that would be necessary for it to carry through numerous appeals against developers and the local governments that approve their projects.

The 1974 legislature. Before concluding its 1974 session, the legislature finally adopted a growth policy resolution, although in a much shorter form than the one first proposed. But the legislature adjourned without enacting the several measures regarded as vital to the policy's implementation, namely: The proposed Comprehensive Planning Act, whereby each county and municipal government would have to prepare *and enforce* a land use master plan; the impact-fee bill to have those who benefit directly from development to pay their equitable share of all new services that it requires; and, finally, the "carrying capacity" standards bill that would have uniform standards established for determining any given area's natural and man-made capacity to support new growth. A related measure that failed to win enactment would have given special protection to wetlands.

Yet, however slow its progress in building upon the start made in 1972 toward controlling growth and development, Florida is still far ahead of most other states in this area of policy. Indeed, the land use bill that the U.S. House of Representatives rejected in June 1974 would have all states adopt programs based on the same concepts—control of critical areas and critical uses—that Florida is now putting to a practical test.

Index

Adams, Tom, 281, 282, 283, 303
Aerojet Corporation, C-111 canal, 149, 181
Agriculture, 24–25, 27, 62, 73
  Avocado farming, 182
  Citrus farming, 16, 19, 25, 27
    decline, 35–36, 38
  Corporate farming, 96
  Dade County, 155–156, 182
  Environmental effects, 24, 26, 324
  Expansion, projected, 30, 92, 121
    disadvantages, 320
  Land reclamation, 92, 94, 96–97
  Pollution, runoff, 8, 24, 26, 38–39, 123
  Sugar, 27, 36, 97, 105
  Water demands, 27, 92, 117–118, 121
  Winter vegetables, 25, 27, 105, 182
  Zoning, 318, 324–325
  See also Everglades Agricultural Area
Air conditioning, 144
Airline Pilots Association, 223
Alachua Audubon Society, 279, 280, 282
Albert, Carl, 277

Albright, Horace, 109
Alligators, 2, 86, 87, 120
  Alligator holes, 86, 88, 120, man-made, 86
Allison, R. V., 89
Alm, Alvin L., 291
Amelia River, pollution, 46
American Cyanamid, 38
American Law Institute, Model Land
    Development Code, 130–131
Amusement parks, 38, see also Disney
    World
Anthony, David S., 279, 281, 282, 286, 290
Apalachicola National Forest, 108
Apalachicola River, 16
Apopka, Lake, 267
  Eutrophication, 27, 38
Aquifers, 16
  Recharge areas, 16, 21, 23, 27, 36, 39, 178,
    182
  Shallow aquifers, 16, 21, 237, 239
  See also Biscayne Aquifer; Floridan
    Aquifer

Army Corps of Engineers, 45, 195, 278, 308
  Cross Florida Barge Canal, 273, 275–276,
    279, 280, 281, 282, 283, 284, 288, 293,
    295, 296, 301, 303, 305, 309–310
  Disregard for biological factors, 50, 95
  Dredge-and-fill permits, 50, 75, 160
  Flood Control District, 89, 91, 92, 94, 95,
    101, 106, 118
  Gulf-Atlantic Ship Canal, 272
  Suits against, 181, 285, 286–287
  Water resources report, 121–122
Arnold, Norman, 217
Arvida Corporation, 136
Askew, Reubin, 7, 55, 125, 132, 137, 221, 225,
    229, 230, 246, 247, 248, 256, 303, 304,
    305, 307, 313, 329
Atlantic coastal ridge, 141, 143, 182
  Development tolerance, 22, 23, 141, 179,
    319
Atlantic Coastline Railway, 4, 73, 79
Atomic Energy Commission, 163
Aviation industry, economic impact, 188

Babcock, Richard F., 131
Bacon, Robert, 214
Bafalis, L. A., 307
Baker v. Carr, 47
Ball, Ed, 45
Bankhead-Jones Farm Tenant Act of 1937,
    108
Barrier islands, 2
Bartram, William, 3
Bartram Memorial Trail, 309
Bass fishing, Everglades, 95
Beaches, 2, 22, 34, 140
  Erosion, 8, 34
  Minimum construction setback lines, 54,
    317, 328
  Public access, 322
Belle Glade, 73, 89
Bennett, Charles E., 274, 275, 277, 302, 305
Bible, Alan, 245
Big Cypress Conservation Act of 1973, 229,
    248
Big Cypress National Preserve, 229,
    242–246
Big Cypress Swamp, 20–21, 42, 57, 58, 110,
    112, 115, 187, 228–231, 239
  Critical area, 246–255, 340–341
  Development tolerance, 21
  Highways, 79–80, 230, 247, 261, 262
  Importance, 20–21
  Indians, 81
  Land grants, 78
  Land sales and development, 29, see also
    Golden Gate Estates
  Oil field, 39, 112
  Proposed jetport site, 50, 190–194, 196,
    206, 212, environmental impact,
    202–204
  Tributary, 23
  Water, sheet flow, 118, 202
  Water Management District 6, 257–258,
    260, 261

Big Scrub, Ocala National Forest, 267
Bill, Harthon L., 122
Birds, 3, 21, 88, 120, 128–129, 247
  Plume hunters, 57
Biscayne Aquifer, 16, 179
  Recharge areas, 20, 92, 178, 220
  Saltwater intrusion, 88, 92, 94
  Water management, 119, 141
Biscayne Bay, 140, 159, 179
  Dredge-and-fill, 74–76, 177
  Park status, 184
  Siltation, 71
  See also South Biscayne Bay
Biscayne National Monument, 139, 141,
    160–162, 167, 168, 243
Blair, Frank W., 290
Bloxham, William D., 64
Boca Ciega Bay, 46
Boca Raton, growth ceiling, 321
Bolles, Richard J., 69–71
Bosselman, Fred P., 130
Boulder zone, sewage disposal, 179
Boyd, Alan, 194
Braman, James D., 205, 207
Brothers, Dr. Clyde, 242
Broward, Napoleon Bonaparte, 67, 68, 69
Broward County, 89, 190, 191, 217–218
Browder, Joe, 162, 195, 196, 197, 198, 206,
    212, 244, 245, 252
Buckeye Cellulose Corporation, pollution
    by, 46
Buckman, Henry H., 270
Building moratoriums, 172–174, 175, 185,
    323
Bulkhead Act of 1957, 54
Bulkhead lines, 155, 161, 168–169, 172, 317,
    328
Bureau of Reclamation, Everglades projects
    in West, compared to, 96
Burns, Haydon, 43, 47, 281
Bryant, Farris, 281

Cahn, Robert, 291, 297, 299
Caldwell, Millard F., 113
Callison, Charles H., 197
Caloosahatchee River, canals, 64, 91, 100
Caloosahatchee Waterway, 71
Cambridge Research Survey, growth
    control poll, 10
Canal Authority, 271–272, 280, 281, 287, 302,
    304–305, 306, 307
Canals, 26, 64, 83, 88, 89, 91, 100, 103, 147,
    166, 263
  Barrow canals, 94, 95, 262, 263
  C-38, 103
  C-111, 149, 181
  Cross-Florida, 91, 274, see also Cross
    Florida Barge Canal
  Drainage, 17, 21, 61, 62, 71, 72–73, 85, 94,
    181, 253
  Finger canals, 21, 30–31, 46, 253, 322
  GAC Corporation, 234, 236, 237, 240
  Navigation, 64–65
  Water conservation, 92–93, 94, 104, 122

Cannon, Clarence, 275, 276, 277
Cantalon, John E., 290
Cape Coral, 233
Card Sound, 166, 167
Carr, Archie F., 279, 285
Carr, Marjorie, 279, 280, 282, 287
Carrying capacity, 314
Carswell, Harold, 291
Central Highlands, 1
  Citrus groves, 19, 23, 27, 35–36, 320, 324
  Development tolerance, 23–24, 35, 319
  Growth boom, 5
  Tourism, 34, 35, 38
Chiles, Lawton, 244, 245
Choctawhatchee National Forest, 107, 108
Citizens Conference on State Legislatures, 47
Citizens for Orderly Growth, 256
Civilian Conservation Corps, 46
Clark, Stephen P., 173, 174
Clarke, William, 241–242
Clean Water Act of 1972, 331
Clewiston, 73
Coastal Coordinating Council, 54
Coconut Grove, housing development, 170
Coe, Ernest F., 108–109, 110
Cole, Lamont C., 290
Collier, Barron G., 77–80, 110, 112
  Family, 114, 231, 232, 241, 246
Collier County, 112, 191, 228, 231
  Big Cypress preserve, 191, 228, 245–246, 261, critical area, 249, 251–254, 255
  Formation, 78–79
  Government, 231, 240–242, 256–257
  Growth rate, 255, ceiling, 256
  Jetport issue, 191–192, 202, 203
  Land sales and development, 202, 231, 232–233, see also Golden Gate Estates
  Road bonds, 79
  Water management districts, 257, zoning, 258–260
Collier County Conservancy, 231, 242, 253, 257, 334
Collier County Water District Conservation Act (1961), 257
Collier Development Corporation, 112, 246
Collier Seminole State Park, 231
Collins, John, 74, 75
Collins, LeRoy, 115
"Committee for Sane Growth", 174
Committee to Support Naples Values, 255, 256
Commoner, Barry, 290
Compensable regulation, 243–244
Condominiums, 28, 31, 132, 146, 232, 251, 338
Conner, Doyle, 254
Conservation Foundation, 253
Conservation groups, lobbies, 50, 54, see also names of groups
Conservation '70s, 53, 54, 136, 244, 282, 285, 286, 309
Construction industry, 5, 28, 136, 173

Container Corporation of America, pollution, 46
Coral Gables, 144, 153
Coral Springs, 103
Corkscrew Sanctuary, 231
Corlett, Ed, 158
Craig, Gus, 286
Critical areas, 10, 131, 133, 135–136, 340, 341
  Big Cypress, 246–255, 340–341
Cross Florida Barge Canal, 26, 52, 53, 265–312
  Beginnings, ship canal, 270–273
  Benefit-cost analyses, 273, 275–276, 280, 293
  Construction to date, 275–276, 283
  Environmental impact, 267, 272, 288
  Funding, 271, 272, 274, 275, 284
  Ground-breaking, 278
  Letters and memos, 309–311
  Termination, 296–299, 301–302, 312
Cuban refugees, 145–146
Cutler Ridge generating plant, 163
Cypress trees, 12, 20, 239
Cypress Gardens, 35

Dade Area Rapid Transit (DART), 178, 186, 226
Dade County, 69, 76, 79, 89, 97
  Agriculture, 155–156, 182
  Area, 138
  Aviation industry, 188
  Building moratorium, 172–173, 185
  Climate, 140
  Development tolerance, 141
  Housing shortage, 150
  Industry, 145, 178
  Metropolitan government, 152–154
  Population, 138, growth, 145, 146
  Public parks, 151
  Segregation, 150
  Sewage problems, 147–148, 156, 179
  Strip development, 150
  Transportation, 148, 150
  Zoning, 151–152, 154, 173–175
  See also Jetport; Miami
Dade County Coordinated Planning Council, 152
Dade County Port Authority, 144, see also Jetport
Dail, G. E., Jr., 122, 220
Davis, Darrey, 168
Deer, 94, 121
De Grove, John M., 126–127, 131, 221, 222
Delray Beach, 338, 339
Deltona Corporation, 136, 331
De Sylva, Donald, 158
Development of Regional Impact (DRI), 131, 133, 136, 314, 317, 327, 328, 332, 341–342
Dickson, Arthur W., 292
Disney World, 23, 260, 319
  Impact, 5, 34
Disston, Hamilton, 64

Division of State Planning, 248, 251, 341–342
Doral Park, 185, 332
Drainage. *See* Everglades; Flood Control
  District
Dredge and fill, 21, 22, 58, 141, 177, 184
  Acres lost to, 8
  Miami Beach, 74–76
  Permits, 50, 75, 160, 317, 328, 330–331,
    curtailed, 54
Droughts
  Everglades, periodic, 16-17, saw grass
    fire, *99*
  1943–1945, 84, 85, 93
  1962, 119, 120
  1971, 117, 125, 240
Dubon, S. H., 51
Dubos, René, 290, land ethic, 338
Duck Stamp Act of 1934, 108
DuPont, political influence, 45

East Central Florida Planning Council, 342
Ecosystems
  Estuaries, 8, 20, 21, 46, 51, 141, 237
  Everglades, 86, 88
  South Biscayne Bay, 163, 165
Ehrlichman, John D., 200, 206
Eisenhower, Julie Nixon, 245
Electric power
  Growing demands for, 5–6, projections,
    13
  Power plants, *see* Turkey Point
Elliot Key, 160
Emergency Relief Act, 272
Empire Land Company, 79
Environmental Defense Fund, 284–285, 287
Environmental inventory act, 54
Environmental Land and Water
    Management Act (1972), SB129, 133,
    135, 136–137, 167, 185
Environmental Land Management Act of
    1972, 332
Environmental Land Management Study
    Committee, 313
Eola Park, Orlando, 338
Erosion, beaches, 8, 34
Escambia Bay, pollution, 38
Escambia Chemical Company, 38
Estuaries
  Dependence on inland wetlands, 20
  Effect of dredge and fill, 141
  Fresh water surge, 237
  Importance, 20, 21
  Mangroves, importance, 51
  Threats to, 8, 21, 46
Eureka Lock and Dam, 283, 293
Eutrophication, 8, 24, 26–27, 38, 104, 123
Everglades, town, 80
Everglades, 2, *13*, 16–17
  Development tolerance, 20
  Drainage, *36*, 58, *61*, 83, 144, effect of, 88,
    overdrainage, 85–86
  Droughts, periodic, 16–17
  Ecology, 86, 88

Fires, 125, muck, 17, 84–85, saw grass, *99*
  Highways, 26, *see also* Tamiami Trail
  Importance, 20
  Mapping of, 90
  Rainfall, 122
  Soil subsidence, 85, *87*
  Water management, *see* Flood Control
    District
Everglades Agricultural Area, 36, 73, 83, 94,
    96–99, *105*
  Corporate farming, 96, *105*
  Effect of water run-off, 27
  Irrigation projects, 96
  Muck fires, 85
  Protection, 92–93
Everglades Assets Corporation, 221
Everglades Coalition, 196–197, 198, 223
Everglades Conservation Area 3, *104*, 118,
    120, *121*, 139, 141, 182
  Jetport site, 185, 190, 192, 194, 195,
    218–219, 220, 225
Everglades Drainage District, 68, 71, 84, 89,
    90–91
Everglades Jetport Advisory Board, 242,
    243
Everglades National Park, *18*, *86*, 139, 141,
    231, 243
  Bird rookeries, 120
  Boundaries, 110–111, 112, 114
  Development near, *36*, *37*
  Droughts 1962–1968, 119–120
  Establishment, 82, 107–108, 109–110
  Northwest Extension, 114
  Proposed expansion, 51
  Water needs, 95, 100, 101, 107, 109,
    118–119, 122, guarantee, 123–124
Evins, Joe L., 305, 307
Executive Reorganization Act of 1969, 48

Fahka Union Canal, 237, 263
Fahkahatchee Strand, 240, 247–248, 253,
    261, 263
Fairchild, David, 109
Fascell, Dante, 160–161
Faulkner, Glen L., 303, 304
Federal Airport Act (1946), 193
Federal Aviation Agency, 190, 193, 208, 223
Federal Housing Administration, 145, 156
Federal Trade Commission, 236
Federal Water Pollution Control
    Administration, 288
Felda oil field, 39
Fenholloway River, 46
Ferre, Maurice, 182
Finnell, Gilbert L., Jr., 130, 132, 137
Fires, 125, 240
  Muck fires, 17, 84–85
  Saw grass fire, *99*
Fisher, Carl, 74, 143
Fishing, sport, 34, 95, 140
Flagler, Henry M., 66, 113, 143
Flatwoods, defined, 23
Fletcher, Duncan U., 110

Flood Control Act of 1936, 91
Flood Control District (FCD), 82, 89, 91–107,
    118, 119, 121, 145
  Benefit-cost ratio, 96
  Canals and pumping stations, 92–93, 101,
    103, *104*, 181
  Jetport stand, 193, 195
  Kissimmee channelization, 103–104,
    106–107
  Perimeter levee, 92, 94, 101, 103
  Purpose, 82, 89
  Water conservation areas, 92, 140, *see
    also* Everglades Conservation Area 3
  See also Army Corps of Engineers
Floods, 83, 88
  Frequency, 106
  1947, 89, *98*, 141, 144, 145
Florida
  Area, 1
  Climate, 3, 4
  Counties, 326
  Shoreline, 1, 59
  Topography, 1–2
Florida Agricultural Experiment Station, 90
Florida Association of Homebuilders, 136
Florida Association of the American
    Institute of Architects, 8–9, 51, 127,
    136, 309
Florida Audubon Society, 51
Florida Bay, 109, 110
  Bird rookeries, 57
  Effect of drought on, 120
Florida Board of Conservation, 101, 122, 280
Florida Board of Health, 156
Florida Bureau of Planning, 48, 209
Florida City, 143
Florida Comprehensive Planning Act of
    1972, 133
Florida Conservation Foundation, 309
Florida Department of Administration, 133,
    316, 317
Florida Department of Commerce, 9
Florida Department of Natural Resources,
    133, 161, 193, 195, 280, 301, 304, 309,
    316, 329, 331–332
Florida Department of Pollution Control,
    165, 316
Florida Department of Transportation, 209,
    214, 216, 223, 226, 262
Florida Defenders of the Environment, 8,
    53, 136, 285–288, 308, 309
Florida East Coast Railway, 66, 69, 73, 108,
    113, 143
Florida Everglades Land Company, 70
Florida Federation of Women's Clubs, 108
Florida Fruit Lands Company, 69
Florida Game and Fresh Water Fish
    Commission, 123, 193, 195, 282, 288,
    292
Florida Keys, 109, 113
  Development, 22
  Railroad land grants, 66
Florida Land Sales Board, 47
Florida Pollution Control Board, 52

Florida Power and Light Company, 45, 113
  Power plants, 5–6, 162–163, 165–167
Florida Ship Canal Authority, 271, 272, 273
Florida Standards, 321–323, 328
Florida State Planning Board, 90
Florida Statutes, Chapter 298, 73
Florida Wildlife Federation, 51
Floridan Aquifer, 16, 267
  Recharge areas, 22, 24
  Ship canal threat, 272, 273, 291, 296, 297
  Water level decline, 8
Ford, Charles, 290, 291, 293
Forestry, commercial, 26
Fort Lauderdale, 31, 178
  1947 floods, 89, *98*
Frazier, J. M., 223
Fullerton, Avery S., 283, 290, 291, 295
Funk, Ben, 146, 147

GAC Corporation, 136
GAC Properties, 38, 233, 234, 235, 241, 248,
    253, 262
General Development Corporation, 29, 136
George, Lake, 3, 282
Gerry brothers, 232
Gibbons, Boyd, 198–200
Gibbs, Robert F., 213, 214
Glasgow, Leslie, 295
Gold Coast
  Air traffic, 213, 219
  Condominiums, 31, 132
  Growth, 11, 39, 221, 321
  Jetport issue, 188, 190, 191, 214–217, 226
  Municipal governments, 326
  Retirees, 34, 320–321
  Water supply, saltwater intrusion, 88,
    118, 119
  Water usage, 100–101
  See also Dade County
Goldberger, Marvin L., 207
Golden Gate Canal, 237
Golden Gate Estates, 30, 233–237, 240–242,
    252, 253, 261–262, 263
Goode, R. Ray, 175, 223, 224
Government, Local, 313, 326–327
  Citizen participation, 333–334
  Regional planning councils, 332
  See also Dade County
Government, State, 41–49, 314
  Cabinet, 44–45, 46, 48, 136, 329
  Executive branch, 43–44, reform, 48
  Legislature, 43, 46–49
  Reforms, 46–49, 328–330, 336
"Government in the Sunshine" law, 49, 336
Governor's Natural Resources Committee,
    52–53
Graham, D. Robert, 127, 132, 136, 248
Gray, Oscar, 204, 207
Greater Miami Chamber of Commerce, 159,
    184, 191, 208, 210, 222, 334
Greater Naples Chamber of Commerce, 192
Green, Herschel V., 173
Green Swamp, 22, 24, 29, 135, 341

Griffin, Lake, 267
  Eutrophication, 38
Growth, 4–8, 39, 141–146, 255
  Carrying capacity, 314
  Control, 127, suggested policies, 313–339,
    see also Land Use Control
  Population ceilings, 171, 176, 256, 321
  Problem defined, 9, 10–11, 39–40
Gulf American Land Corporation, 47, 233,
    234–235, 241, 247–248
Gulf-Atlantic Ship Canal, 270–272, 276
Gulf Coast, development tolerance, 22
Gurney, Edward J., 124
Guthrie, Lain, p. 158

Haley, James A., 246
Hall, Chuck, 196
The Hammocks, 185
Hanna, Alfred Jackson and Kathryn Abbey,
    69
Harney, William S., 62–63
Harper, Edwin L., 291
Harris, Marshall, 47
Hartzog, George, 217, 243
Hawaii, Land Use Law, 130
Heald, E. J., 51
Heilbroner, Robert L., 315
Hendry County, 191, 226
Herren, Norman, 241, 246, 257
Hialeah, 144, 145
  1947 floods, 89
Hialeah Gardens, 151
Hickel, Walter J., 166, 197–198, 200, 205, 206,
    208, 288, 291, 292, 293, 295, 298
High speed ground transit systems,
    proposed, 191, 214, 226, see also
    Dade Area Rapid Transit
Highways, 26
  Interstate 75, 230, 247, 261, 262
  State Road 29, 80
  Tamiami Trail, 67, 77–80
  U.S. 1, 22, 141
Hillsboro canal, 71
Hillsborough County, 38
Hillsborough River, 62
Hodges, Randolph, 107, 122, 280, 281, 288,
    329, 332
Hole, Stanley W., 241
Holland, Spessard L., 112, 113, 114, 115, 120,
    124, 293
Homestead, 143, 182, 184
Homestead Air Force Base, 190
Hoover, Herbert, 91
Hoover, Herbert, Jr., 161
Hoover Foundation, 161
Housing developments, 5, 27–28, 36, 37, 145,
    149, 170
  New towns, 28, 30, 31, 127, 162, 167–168
  Retirement living, 28
  Under regulation of, 30
Howard, Needles, Tammer, and Bergendoff,
    189, 210, 211
Huntoon, George, 257

Hurricanes, 179–180
  Frequency, 101
  1926, 83, 165
  1928, 83–84, 91, 104
  1947, 89, 91
Hutchinson, G. Evelyn, 290
Hydroperiod, 20, 237

Immokalee, 23, 250
Immokalee Rise, development tolerance,
    22, 23
Indian Claims Commission, Seminole
    decision, 80
Indian River, 52, 107
Industry, 25–26, 38–39, 46, 145, 178, 319–320
Internal Improvement Board, 63–64, 65, 66,
    110, 114, 248, 331
  Jetport stand, 193
  Railroad land grants, 63–64, 65, 66, 103,
    107
Interstate Land Sales Full Disclosure Act
    of 1968, 235
Intracoastal Waterway, 30–31, 278
Islandia, 155, 156, 159, 160, 161, 162, 191
ITT Corporation, 30, 136
Izaak Walton League, 160
  Mangrove Chapter, 158, 334

J. C. Turner Lumber Company, 248
Jackson, Henry M., 198, 245
Jacksonville, 11, 42, 269, 270
Jacksonville Chamber of Commerce, 274
Jacksonville-Duval County consolidated
    government, 326–327
Jacksonville, Tampa, and Key West
    Railway, 65
Jacksonville Times-Union, 68
Jay oil field, 39
Jennings, William S., 66
Jetport, 50, 162, 187–227, 321
  Aerial view, 199
  Cost, 194, 225
  Groundbreaking, 194
  Impact studies, 198, 200–205, 207
  Need for, 188–189
  Outcome, 224
  Proposed sites, 190–191, 211–224
  Senate hearings, 197, 198
Jetport Pact, 207–210, 229
John Pennekamp Coral Reef State Park,
    167
Johnson, Harvey M., 306–307
Johnson, Lamar, 111
Johnson, Lyndon B., 278
Jones, John C., 51
Jordan, Robert E., III, 290, 291, 293, 296, 299
Judy, Richard, 193, 195, 210, 223
Jupiter Island, 52

Kennedy, John F., 275, 277
Key Biscayne, 28, 140, 146, 172–173, 174

Key Biscayne Property Owners
    Association, 172
Key Largo, 110
King, James L., 234
Kirk, Claude, 48, 50, 52, 55, 161, 165, 194,
    200, 205, 206, 208, 210, 288, 295, 297
Kissimmee, lake, 35
Kissimmee, town, 5
Kissimmee River and basin, 2, 22, 27, 35, 58
    Canals, 64
    Channelization, 22, 103–104, 106–107
    Drainage and flood control, 94, 97
Kuperberg, Joel, 232

Lake County, 35
Lakes
    Eutrophication, 8, 24, 26–27, 38, 104, 123
    Surveying errors, 59
Lamm, Arnold E., 255
L'Amoreaux, Ray, 216
Land
    Classification, 39, 131, 318, see also
        Critical areas
    Development tolerance, 15–24
    Prices, 35, 76, 78, 233
    Reclamation, 73, 92, 94, 96–97
    Speculation, 8, 29, 236, 252
    Zoning, 54, 151–152, 154, 174–175,
        258–259, 261, 316, 323
    See also Drainage; Dredge and fill;
        Public Lands; Submerged land
Land ethic, 318, 337–338
Land Conservation Act of 1972, 133
Land Sales Act of 1963, 47
Land sales companies, 29, 69, 70–71, 202,
    231, 233, 234–235
Land use, 24–26, 40, 102–103, 150–151,
    155–156, 317–326
    Control, 14–15, 39–40, 130–132, 138–139,
        172–175, 262, 315
    Early trends, 42, 46, 58
    Legislation, 10, 53–55, 126, 133–136, 137,
        313–314
    See also Agriculture; Development of
        Regional Impact; Housing
        development; Planned Unit
        Development
Landers, Joseph (Jay), 212
LaRoe, Edward T., 232
The Last Word, condominium, 31
Lee County, 78, 79, 191, 248
Lee Tidewater Cypress Company, 79, 231,
    233
Lehman, Herbert H., 68
Leopold, Aldo, 200, 337–338
Leopold, Luna B., 200–201, 204–205, 245
Levees, 92, 94
    Everglades perimeter, 92, 94, 101, 103, 144
    Lake Okeechobee, 91, 106, 121
    #29, 118
Lignum Vitae Key, 113
Lilies, 12, 239
Live oaks, 170

Lobbies, 44–46, 136
    Conservation groups, 50, 54
Local Government Comprehensive
    Planning Bill of 1974, 313, 314
Loxahatchee Refuge, 107, 108
Loxahatchee Slough, 27
Ludwig, Daniel K., 158, 159, 161, 166
Lugo, Ariel, 286

McBroom, James T., 295
McCormack, John W., 277
McCree, W. A., Jr., 330
McDermott, John, 49
MacDonald, Gordon J. F., 207, 291, 297, 299
McGovern, George S., 293
Mackle brothers, 28–29, 241
Mallory, Stephen R., 3, 63
Manatee County, 38, 256
Manatees, 95
Mangroves, 12, 18, 21
    Importance, 20, 51
Marco Island, development, 30, 241, 250,
    331
Marion County, 52
Marshall, Arthur R., 50, 84, 127, 160, 195,
    196, 201, 216, 221, 222, 244, 287, 292
Masland, Frank, Jr., 197
Mason, C. Russell, 51
Matheson, Hardy, 147, 161
Meander lines, 59
Medley, 151
Megalopolis, 7, 11
Merrick, George, 144
Merritt Island Refuge, 108
Metropolitan Dade County Planning
    Department, 155, 169, 171, 175–176
Miami, City of, 45, 47, 48
    City services, 182
    Early development, 42, 143
    Hurricanes, 89, 165
    Population growth, 10, 42, 140–141
    Rainfall, 89
    Water supply, saltwater intrusion, 88, 125
Miami Beach, 28, 35, 143, 164, 168, 169, 173,
    320
    Development, 74–76
    Zoning ordinance, 151
Miami Canal, 71
Miami-Dade Water and Sewer Authority,
    184
Miami Herald, 49, 107, 109, 113, 115, 152,
    153, 184, 223, 302, 304
Miami International Airport, 140–141, 144,
    178
    Air traffic, 188, 189, 212–213
    Noise pollution, 148
Miami Lakes, 127
Miami News, 49, 153, 160
Miami River, 62, 71, 118, 147, 178
Miami Springs, 89, 144
Miccosuki Indians, 61, 80–81, 194
Mifflin, Martin D., 286
Miller, James Nathan, 291

Miller, Lloyd, 158, 160
Mobile homes, 34, 37
Model Land Company, 108, 113
Monroe County, 114, 191, 202–203, 228
Monsanto Chemical Company, 38
Moore Haven, 73
Morris, Manuel, 195, 196, 198
Morrison, Kenneth, 290
Morton, Rogers C. B., 242, 245
Muck soil, 83, 86, 88, 89–90
  Fires, 17, 84–85
  Subsidence, 85, 87
Murphy Act of 1937, 112
Muskie, Edmund, 124

Naples, 232, 250, 253, 255–256
Naples Bay, 237
Nassau County, 46
National Academy of Sciences, 207
National Audubon Society, 181, 208, 232
National Environmental Policy Act of 1969,
  163, 198, 216, 268, 293, 295, 296, 298
National Gulf-Atlantic Ship Canal
  Association, 270
National Park Service, 112, 114, 122, 123,
  195, 209
National Resources Planning Board, 90
National Wild and Scenic River System,
  302
National Wildlife Refuge System, 107–108
Nelson, Gaylord, 123
"New towns", 28, 30, 127, 162, 167–168
Newman, James B., 295
Newspapers, political influence, 49
Nix, Frank, 101, 119
Nixon, Richard M., 197, 242, 290, 293, 295,
  296, 298, 301, 307, 308
Norris, Lester, 231
North New River canal, 71
Nuclear power plants, 163, 165–167

Ocala, 269
Ocala Banner, 68
Ocala National Forest, 107, 108, 302
  Big Scrub, 269, 279
Ochopee, 228, 250
Odum, Eugene P., 290
Odum, Howard T., 314
Odum, Perry, 136
Odum, W. E., 51
Ogden, Lee, 285
Ohanian, Jack, 279
Oil, 39, 112, 320
Okloacoochee Slough, 23, 253
Okeechobee, Lake, 83
  Caloosahatchee outlet, 64
  Eutrophication, 8, 27, 104, 123
  Flood control, 91, levee, 91, 106, 121
  Silt discharge, 52
  Water levels, 84, 123, control, 100–101
  Water source, 16

Okeechobee Waterway, 274
Oklawaha River and valley, 22, 57, 267, 300
  Aerial view, 276
  Channelization, 267
  Dams, 267, 283
  Lakes, 269, 282–283
Optimum Population and Urban Growth
    Policy, Manatee County, 256
Orange County, 35
  Citrus decline, 36, 38
Orlando, 47, 269
  Eola Park, 338
  Growth, 5, 11, 39
Orlando Sentinel, 137
Orr, John B., Jr., 140, 174–175, 183, 185,
    222–223
Osceola County, 35
Osceola National Forest, 108
Overview Group, jetport report, 207

Padrick, Robert W., 194–195, 196, 210, 222
Pahokee, 73
Paine's Prairie, 22
Palm Beach, 42
Palm Beach County, 69, 76, 191, 205, 214,
    216, 223, 226
  Water consumption, 100
Palm Coast, 30
Palmetto, 239
Paper and pulp industries, 45, 46
Papy, Bernie C., 113
Parker, Barrington D., 298
Partington, William M., 284, 285, 286, 287,
    291
Patten, Arthur H., Jr., 189
Paul, Dan, 208
Peace River, pollution, 8, 38, 319
Pearson, Gilbert, 109
Pecora, William T., 304
Pegues, Rodger W., 195, 196
Pelican Island Refuge, 107
Pennekamp, John, 113
Pennsuco, 151
Pensacola, 11, 38
Pepper, Claude, 273
Perphyton, 13
Pettigrew, Richard, 47
Phipps, Ben, 136
Phosphate mining, 8, 26, 38, 46
Pickard, Jerome, 11
Pierce, Neil R., 45
Pinecrest, 202
Pinelands, 164, 239
  Development tolerance, 23
Pinellas County, 28
Planned Unit Development, 170, 258–260,
    261–262, 323, 324
Plant, Henry B., 66
Poinciana development, 38
Point View, 74
Polk County, 35, 38

Pollution
  Agricultural, 24, 38, 39, 123
  Air, 148
  Control, 53–54, 317–318
  Industrial, 8, 26, 38–39, 46, 159
  Legislation, 53, 54
  Noise, 148, 149
  Sewage, 8, 34–35, 39, 147
  Water, 8, 38–39, 46, 147, 237
Population
  Density, 10
  Distribution, 24, 191
  Growth ceilings, 171, 176, 256, 321
  Immigration, 11
  Percent of elderly, 27–28
  Projected growth, 11, 12, 120
Port Charlotte, 30
President's Council on Environmental
      Quality, 130, 286, 288, 289, 295–296,
      297, 298
Proctor, Samuel, 67
Progresso, 69–70
Public lands
  Federal, 58–59, 62
  State, 58, 59, 62, disposal of, land grants,
      63–64, 65, 66, sale, 64, 69

Raftery, John, 197
Railroads, 42, 60, 272
  Land grants, 63, 64, 65, 66
Rainbow Springs, 272
Ramapo, N. Y., development point system,
      325
Randell, Ted, 54
Randell Act, 54, 168
Rayonier Corporation, 46
Real estate, 5, 31, 35, 109
Recreation areas, 94, 269
Red Flag Charette, 8–9, 51, 135, 136
Redford, Jim, 158, 162, 174
Redford, Polly, 75, 158, 160, 162, 171
Reed, Nathaniel, 50, 52, 53, 54, 107, 161, 165,
      195, 196, 198, 200, 205, 206, 216, 217,
      245, 286
Reedy Creek Improvement District, 260
Reilly, William K., 291, 299
Remuda Ranch Grants, 248, 252
Renick, Ralph, 224
Resor, Stanley, 292
Retirement industry, 27–34, 320–321
Riparian Act of 1855, 74
Riparian Act of 1921, 74
Riparian rights, sheet flow, 228
River swamps and marshes, importance,
      22, 103
Rivers and Harbors Act of 1927, 270
Roberts, Paul E., 286
Robertson, Willis, 110
Rodman Dam, 283
Rodman Pool, 283, 284, 287, 291, 293, 296,
      301, 302, 307
Rogers, Lyman E., 52, 53, 286

Rookery Bay Sanctuary, 232, 249, 253, 257,
      331
Roosevelt, Franklin D., 270, 272, 273
Roosevelt, Theodore, 107
Rosen, Leonard, 47, 233
Royal Palm State Park, 108
Ruvin, Harvey, 172, 173, 174, 186, 222, 332

Safe Progress Association, 158–162
Safreed, William, 183
Saga Development Corporation,
      developments, 149, 162, 167–168,
      169–172
St. Cloud, 5, 104
Saint Johns River, 2, 3, 22, 23, 94, 267, 270
St. Lucie Canal, 71, 100
St. Lucie County, 123
St. Lucie Inlet, 52
St. Mark's Refuge, 107
St. Petersburg, 47, 269
St. Petersburg Times, 49, 302
Salt marshes, 2, 4, 21
Sanibel Island, 327
Sarasota County, 28
Save the Oklawaha campaign, 279–280, 281,
      283, 284, 305, 308
Saw grass, 13, 17, 128, 239
  Fire, 99
Scheffel, Belle, 158
Schweizer, Nils M., 51
Scott, Hal, 51
Seadade deepwater port and refinery, 155,
      156, 157, 158–161
Seadade Industries, proposed development,
      163, 166–167
Seminole Indians, 41, 42, 80–81
Senate Committee on Interior and Insular
      Affairs, 197, 198
Sessums, Terrell, 313
Sewage
  Condominiums, 31
  Deep-well injection, 179
  Florida Keys, 22
  Ocean outfall, 35, 147, 179, 319
  Pine flatlands, 23
  Pollution, 147–148
  Septic tanks, 30, 148, 156
Shallow Aquifer, 237, 249
Shell Key, 113
Shepard, Ben, 214
Shevin, Robert L., 303, 304, 305
Shields, Harmon, 329
Shreve, Jack, 133
Shrimp, 21
  Nurseries, 46
Shultz, Frederick, 47
Sikes, Robert F., 274, 277, 305
Silver Springs, 267, 271
  Canal threat, 272, 288, 296
Simonds, John O., 169
Smathers, George, 283
Smith, Anthony, 245

Smith, Buckingham, 62, 63
Smith, McGregor, 113
Sofen, Edward, 152, 153
Soil Conservation Service, 90, 97
Soil Science Society of Florida, 89
Soil subsidence, 85, *87*
Solar energy, 323
Sollohub, J. V., 281
Soucie, Gary, 195, 196, 206, 212
South Biscayne Bay, 73
    Bulkhead line, 155, 168–169
    Character, 163
    Ecology, 163, 165
    Importance, 160
    Power plants, *see* Turkey Point
South Florida Regional Planning Council,
    203, 217, 332, 342
South Florida Water Management
    Conference, 125, 132
South Miami Beach, 150
South Miami Heights, *149*
Southeastern Florida Joint Resources
    Investigation, 90
Southern Express Company, 66
Southern States Land and Timber
    Company, 68
Sovereignty lands, 59, *see also* Submerged
    lands
Spagna, Neno J., 256
Speir, W. H., 90
Spike rush, *12*
Spring Hill, 30
Stahr, Elvis, 197, 245
Standard Metropolitan Statiscal Areas, 24
Star Island, 76
Stewart, Alan C., 191
Stoneman, Frank B., 109
Strangler fig, *238*
Strip development, 150
Submerged lands, 54, 74
    I. I. Board title, 76
    Sale of, 46
    Surveying errors, 59
    See also Dredge and fill
Suburban Acres, *37*
Sugar Act, 97
Sunniland oil field, 39, 112
Sunny Hills, 30
Suwannee River, 16, 22
Swamp and Overflowed lands.
    See Big Cypress; Everglades
Swamp Lands Act (1850), 60, 108
Swanson, Henry F., 36, 38

Talbot, Lee, 297, 303, 304
Tamiami Trail, *67*, 77–80
Tampa, 45, 48
Tampa Bay, 10, 11, 39, 269
Tampa Tribune, 49
Task Force on Land Use and Urban
    Growth, 1973 report, 336–337
Task Force on Resource Management, 125
Tate's Hell, 22

Taylor County, 46
Taylor Creek Watershed, 27
Taxation, 45–46
    Capital gains tax, 334–335
    Corporate income tax, 55
    Cross-Florida canal, 271
    Drainage tax, 68, 69, 71
    FCD, *ad valoram* tax, 97, 99–100, 102
    Need for reform, 334–335
    Severance tax, 46
Tebeau, Charlton W., 65
Ten Thousand Islands, 16, 21, 30, 57, 109,
    110, 114, 253
Thomas, C. A., 83–84
Thomas, Jerry, 9
Three Rivers, 342
Tohopekaliga, lake, 35
Tourist industry, 5, 34–36, 320
Train, Russell E., 198, 200, 205, 206, 290, 291,
    296, 297, 298
Trammell, Park, 71
Transportation, 148, 150, *see also*
    High-speed transit systems
Trosper, Thurman H., 217
Truman, Harry S, 275
TRW Systems Group, 214
Turkey Point power plant, *149*, 156, 157,
    162–163, 165–167
Turlington, Ralph, 47
Turner, Harmon, 240–241, 246, 252
Typhoid fever outbreak (1973), 148

Udall, Stewart L., 160, 207
U.S. Bureau of Reclamation, 96
U.S. Bureau of Sport Fisheries and
    Wildlife, 50, 106, 282, 292
U.S. Bureau of the Budget, 281
U.S. Department of Agriculture, 70, 90, 282
U.S. Department of the Interior, 109, 115,
    160, 195, 196, 197, 200, 201, 206, 210,
    244, 246
U.S. Department of Transportation, 197,
    200, 201, 204, 206, 207, 214, 225, 292
U.S. Environmental Protection Agency, 237,
    322
U.S. Geological Survey, 90, 100, 201, 237
U.S. Indian Claims Commission, 80
United States Sugar Corporation, 97
U.S. Supreme Court, 47, 80
University of Florida, 51–52, 278–279
University of Miami, 51
Urban Mass Transportation Act of 1964,
    194, 196, 208, 216

Van Doren, Ruth, 256
Van Ness, William J., 198
Vandenberg, Arthur H., 273, 274
Vernon, Robert O., 331–332
Vertes, John and Ernestine, 234
Vertes vs. GAC Properties, Inc., 235
Vines, William R., 242
Vinson, Carl, 277

Volpe, John A., 194, 197, 198, 205, 206, 208
Voters League of Collier County, Inc., 256

Wainwright, Alice, 162, 244
Wakulla River, 45
Walker, Lorenzo, 254, 340
Wallace, Henry, 274
Wallis, W. Turner, 102
Water
  Common enemy, 5, 73
  Disposal of excess, 26, 91–92, 121, 123
  Pollution, 8, 38–39, 46, 147, 237
  Riparian rights, 54, 74, 228
  Sheet flow, 20, 116, 202, 228
  Standing water, 4, 83
  Water tables, 21, 26, 85, 88, 94, 237, 240
  Watershed areas, 16, 27, see also Big
    Cypress Swamp
  See also Floods; Lakes
Water hyacinths, 95, 301
Water Management, 89–90, 133
  Conservation areas, 47, 91, see also
    Everglades Conservation Area 3
  Districts, 316, district 6, 257–258, 260, 261
  See also Flood Control District
Water Resources Act of 1972, 133, 229, 263
Water supply, 16
  Saltwater intrusion, 20, 88, 92, 94, 125,
    249
  Shortages, 7, 117, 122, 125, 237, see also
    Droughts
  Surface storage, 92, 100–101

Use, 24, 27, 117–118, 121, increasing
    demands, 92, 100
  See also Aquifers
Weeks Act of 1911, 108
West Palm Beach Canal, 71
Westcott, J. D., Jr., 62
Wet prairies, 12, 185–186
Wetlands, 16, 22
  Development policy, 249–251, 253
  Development tolerance, 16
  See also Big Cypress; Everglades
Whitaker, John C., 206, 245, 290, 291, 293,
    296–297
White, John, 130
Wilbur, Ray L., 109
Williams, J. H., 286
Willoughby, Hugh L., 4
Wilson, Cynthia, 245
Withlacoochee River, 270
Wurster, Charles F., 285
Wylie, Philip, 158

Yannacone, Victor J., Jr., 284, 287
Young, C. W. Bill, 305

Zoning, 316, 323
  Coastal lands, 54
  Conservation, 258–259, 261
  Dade County, 151–152, 154, 173–175
  Exclusionary, 321

THE JOHNS HOPKINS UNIVERSITY PRESS

*This book was composed in Linotype Melior by
the Monotype Composition Company from a design
by Susan Bishop. It was printed on S. D. Warren's
50-lb. 1854 regular paper and bound in
Kivar 5 material by Universal Lithographers, Inc.*

Library of Congress Cataloging in Publication Data

Carter, Luther J
   The Florida experience.

   1. Regional planning—Florida. 2. Land—Florida.
   3. Coastal resource management—Florida. I. Resources for
the Future. II. Title.
HT393.F5C37   333.7'09759   74-6816
ISBN 0-8018-1646-7

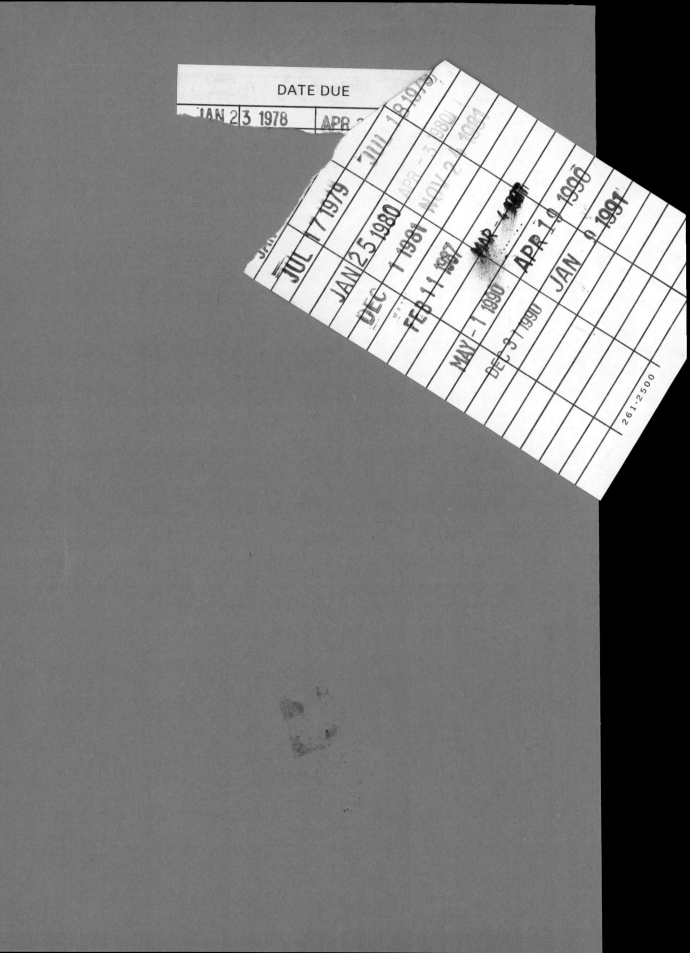